Please Save My Earth

Saki Hiwatari

Please Save My Earth ™

Vol. #5

Shôjo Edition

Story and Art by

Saki Hiwatari

English Adaptation by
Fred Burke

Translator Lillian Olsen
Touch-up & Lettering Bill Schuch
Graphics & Design Judi Roubideaux
Editor P. Duffield
Supervising Editor Ian Robertson
Managing Editor Annette Roman
Editor in Chief Alvin Lu
Production Manager Noboru Watanabe
Sr. Director of Licensing and Acquisitions Rika Inouye
Vice President of Marketing Liza Coppola
Executive Vice President Hyoe Narita
Publisher Seiji Horibuchi

Boku no Chikyuu wo Mamotte by Saki Hiwatari
© Saki Hiwatari 1988

First published in Japan in 1988 by HAKUSENSHA, Inc., Tokyo. English language
translation rights in America arranged with HAKUSENSHA, Inc., Tokyo. The Please Save My
Earth logo is a trademark of VIZ, LLC. New and adapted artwork and text

© 2004 VIZ, LLC

Printed in Canada.
Published by VIZ, LLC.
P.O. Box 77010
San Francisco, CA 94107

Shôjo Edition
10 9 8 7 6 5 4 3 2 1
First printing, June 2004

www.viz.com

Story thus far

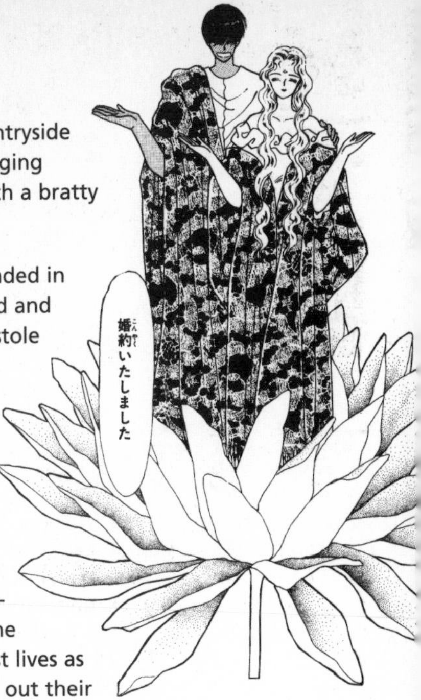
婚約いたしました

Alice has been transplanted from the countryside of Hokkaido to crowded Tokyo. As if changing schools isn't enough, Alice has to cope with a bratty neighbor boy, Rin.

The day Alice was forced to babysit Rin ended in an accidental fall. Fortunately, Rin survived and held no grudge against Alice. Indeed, he stole her first kiss and managed to convince Alice to become his fiancée! The stress caused Alice to pass out and dream of Shion and Mokuren, two of the characters her classmates Jinpachi and Issei mentioned were part of their strange "moon dreams."

Once they find the "moon dream" characters Hiiragi and Shusuran, they discover the terrible truth. The dreams are of their past lives as alien observers of the Earth. A war wiped out their star system, then an incurable disease quickly claimed their lives.

Rin accompanies Alice to one of their meetings, and convinces them he's Shukaido, though he is actually the reborn Shion. Feeling guilty that the fall she caused is responsible for his tragic awakened memories, Alice quits going to the meetings. Add to that Jinpachi's poor reaction to learning of Alice's engagement to Rin, and Alice feels even more alienated from the others.

Unbeknownst to the rest, Rin has met Haruhiko, the true reincarnation of Shukaido, and forced him to remember his past life's vicious betrayal. After nearly drowning himself, Haruhiko also remembers his password, one of the seven that will allow Rin to destroy the Moon Base. Now Rin plans to use Haruhiko to convince the others to share their passwords, but he wants Haruhiko to claim to be Shion...

In the meantime, Tamura's traumatic, supernatural experience with Haruhiko has him researching psychic powers. From Mikuro, an old friend's brother, Tamura learns the powers Haruhiko has displayed may not be human, but his efforts must be put on hold as he accompanies his charge to Kyoto.

Earth Characters

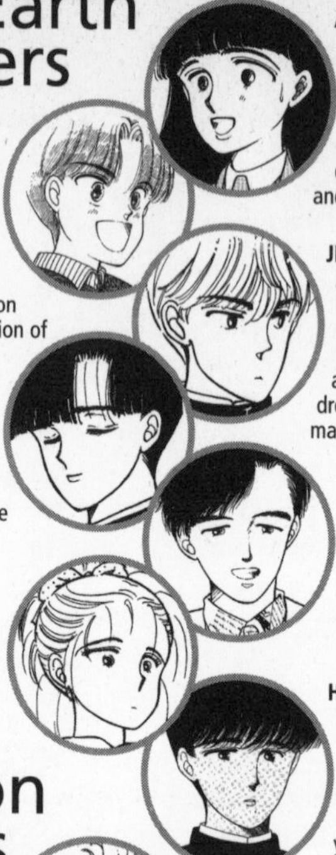

ALICE SAKAGUCHI Transplanted from the countryside of Hokkaido to Tokyo, this shy and sensitive girl can communicate with plants, even those suffering in the pollution of the city. Alice has had only one "moon dream," in which she was Mokuren and insists she is merely Alice.

RIN KOBAYASHI Initially fond of teasing her, bratty Rin's interest in Alice has only grown more serious since his fall–he's even arranged an engagement with her! What no one else knows is that Rin has developed psychic powers and is secretly plotting to destroy the Moon Base. Although he is the reincarnation of Shion, he has told the others he is Shukaido.

JINPACHI OGURA Alice's classmate, Jinpachi is impulsive and gregarious. He's learned that his strange dreams of the moon are shared by Issei, a classmate from junior high. Jinpachi and Issei regularly discuss their dreams, in which Jinpachi is always a man named Gyokuran.

ISSEI NISHIKIORI A sensitive, easy-going charmer, Issei attends the same high school as Jinpachi and Alice. In the "moon dreams," he is always Enju, a woman who's in love with Gyokuran.

DAISUKE DOBASHI Having had "moon dreams" since the age of seven–in which he is Hiiragi–mild-mannered Daisuke met Sakura by accident on a junior high field trip.

SAKURA KOKUSHO Friendly and vivacious, in the "moon dreams," she is Shusuran.

HARUHIKO KASAMA A boy with a heart condition, Haruhiko is Shukaido in his "moon dreams." He was unaware of the others until his third encounter with Rin. His health has held him back two years in school.

Moon Characters

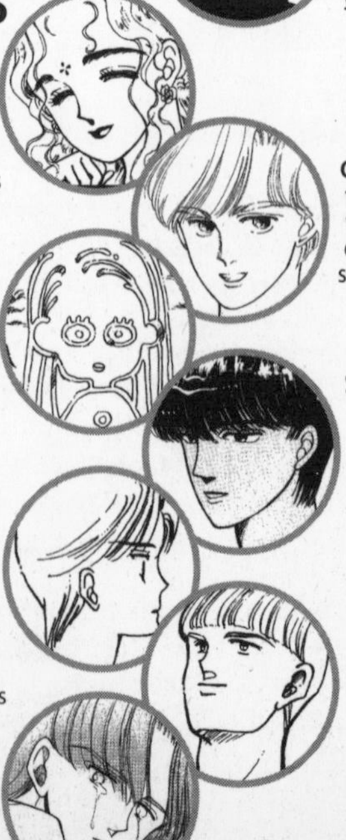

MOKUREN All guys fall in love with kind and beautiful Mokuren, but surprisingly, she is engaged to anti-social Shion. Mokuren is the biologist of the moon team and has ESP.

GYOKURAN The archeologist of the team, Gyokuran is charismatic, has telekinetic powers and is infatuated with Mokuren. He's also insensitive toward Enju's interest in him.

ENJU Gentle, introspective and an empath, Enju is the team's paleontologist. She is quietly in love with Gyokuran and jealous of Mokuren.

SHION Brilliant, sensitive but socially awkward, Shion is the team's engineer. He suffered alone on the moon for nine years after the others died.

SHUSURAN Enju's best friend, Shusuran is the team technician.

HIIRAGI Leader of the team, Hiiragi is a linguist.

SHUKAIDO Shukaido is the team's doctor. He is responsible for giving Shion the vaccine that prolonged his life.

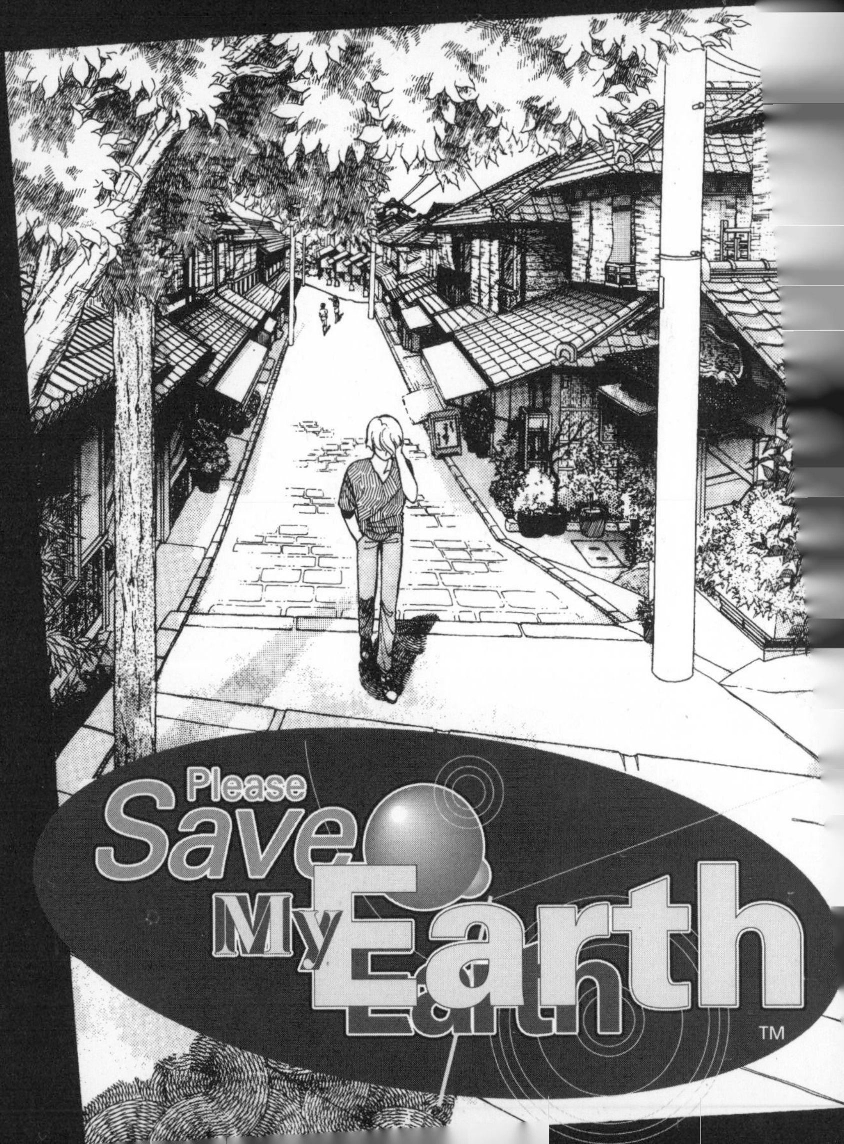
Please
Save
My Earth
TM

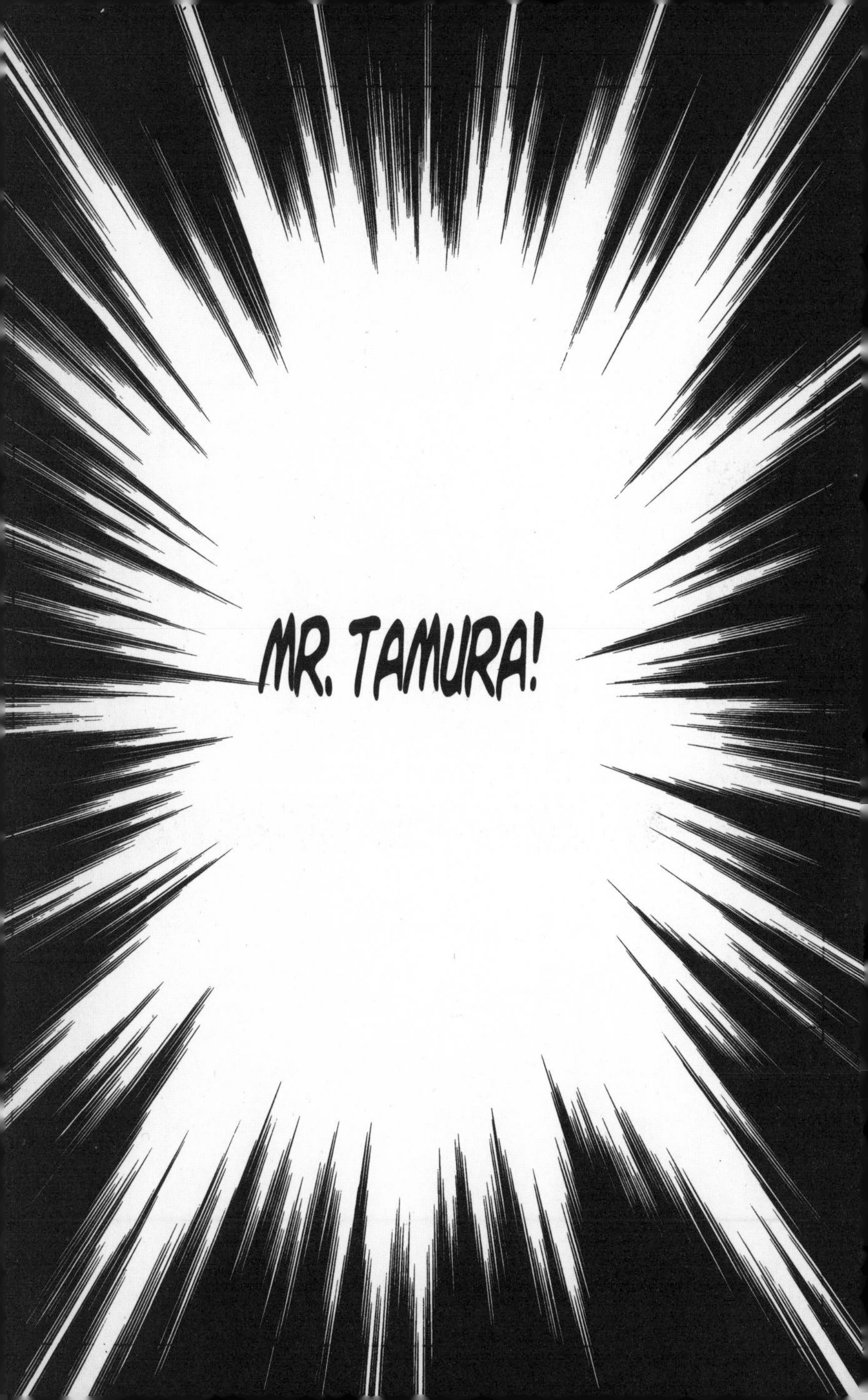
MR. TAMURA!

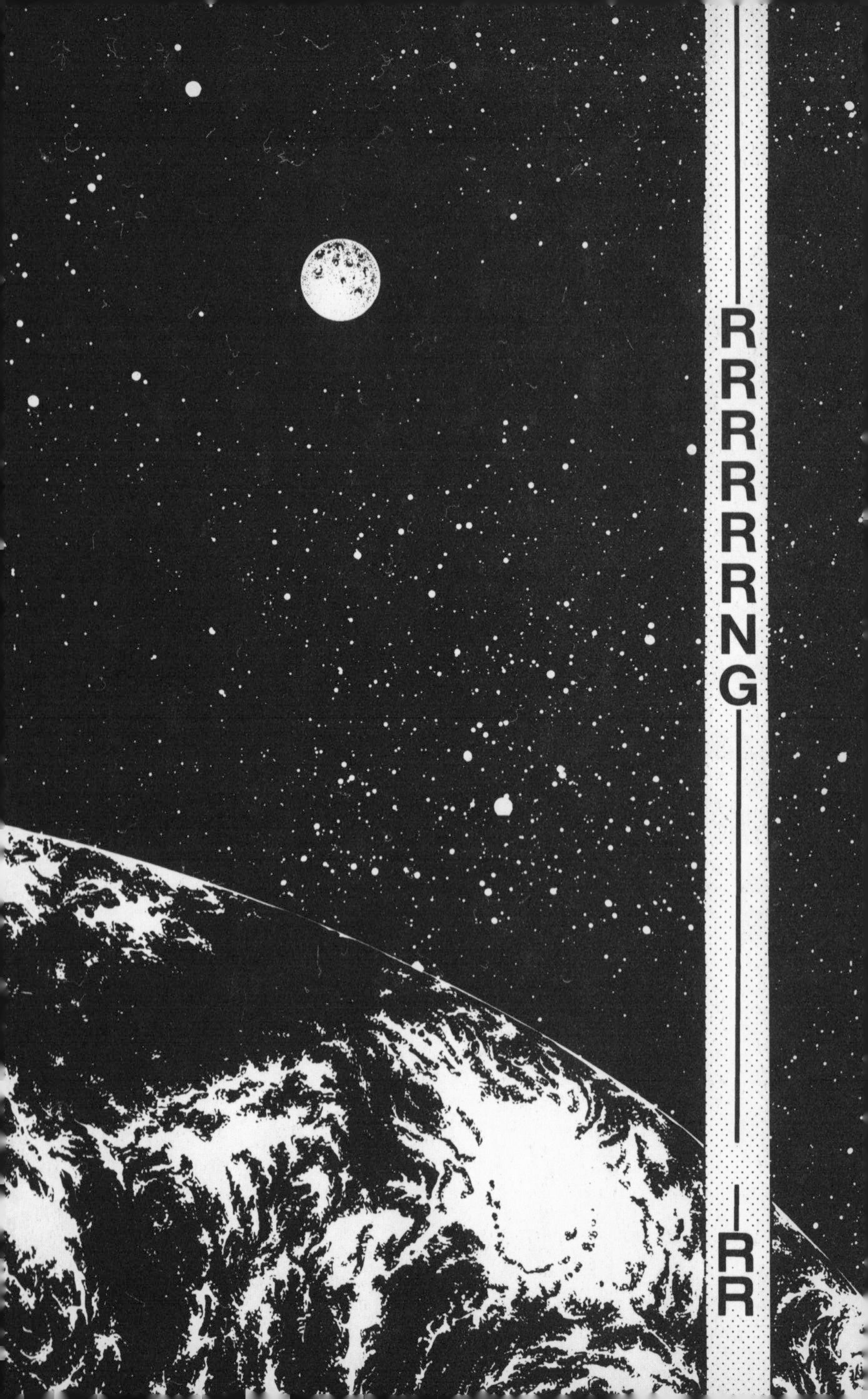
RRRRRRNG
RR

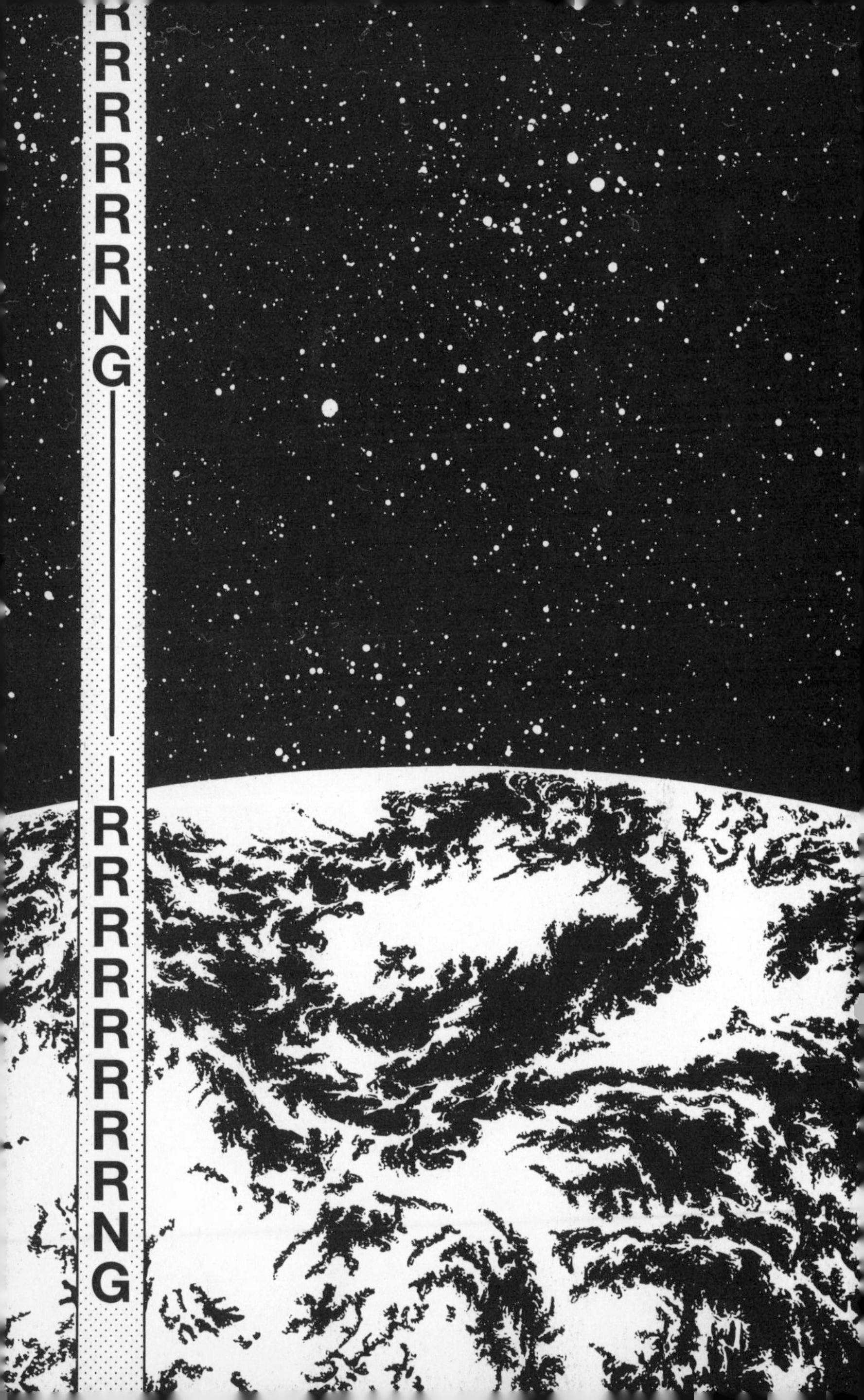
RRRRRRNG—
—RRRRRRRRNG

KLIK!

RRRRRRRR

COSMOS 7

SPECIAL:
THE 月 MOO

HOW TO GAIN COSMO POWER
AN INTERVIEW WITH SEIYA, IKKI,
...GA AND SHUN

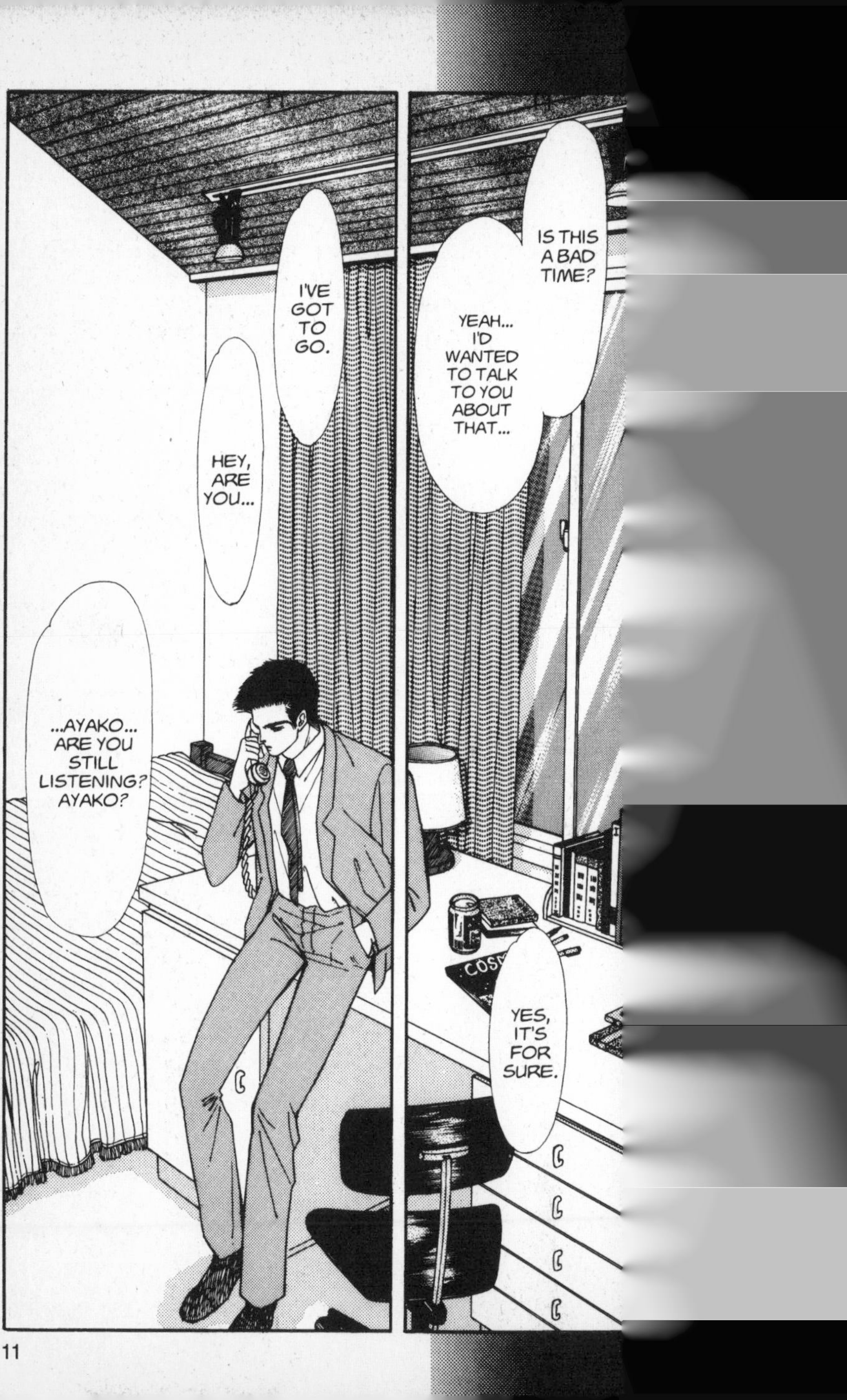
IS THIS A BAD TIME?
YEAH... I'D WANTED TO TALK TO YOU ABOUT THAT...
YES, IT'S FOR SURE.
I'VE GOT TO GO.
HEY, ARE YOU...
...AYAKO... ARE YOU STILL LISTENING? AYAKO?

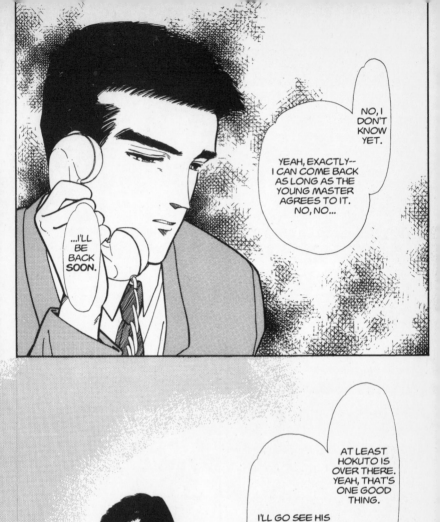

NO, I DON'T KNOW YET.

YEAH, EXACTLY-- I CAN COME BACK AS LONG AS THE YOUNG MASTER AGREES TO IT. NO, NO...

...I'LL BE BACK SOON.

AT LEAST HOKUTO IS OVER THERE. YEAH, THAT'S ONE GOOD THING.

I'LL GO SEE HIS BROTHER RIGHT AWAY--GET MYSELF A NICE LONG CRASH COURSE IN E.S.P.

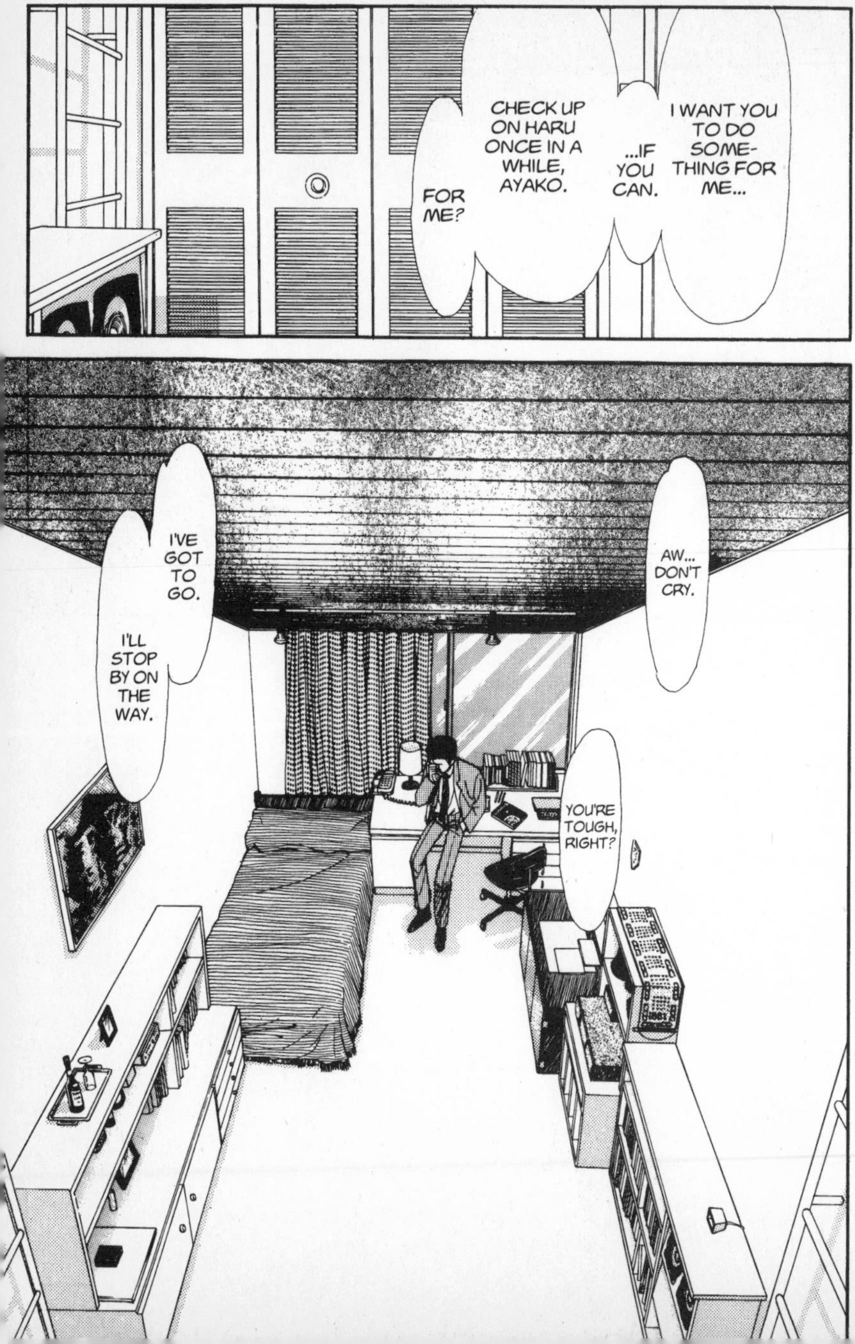
I WANT YOU TO DO SOME-THING FOR ME...
...IF YOU CAN.
CHECK UP ON HARU ONCE IN A WHILE, AYAKO.
FOR ME?
AW... DON'T CRY.
I'VE GOT TO GO.
I'LL STOP BY ON THE WAY.
YOU'RE TOUGH, RIGHT?

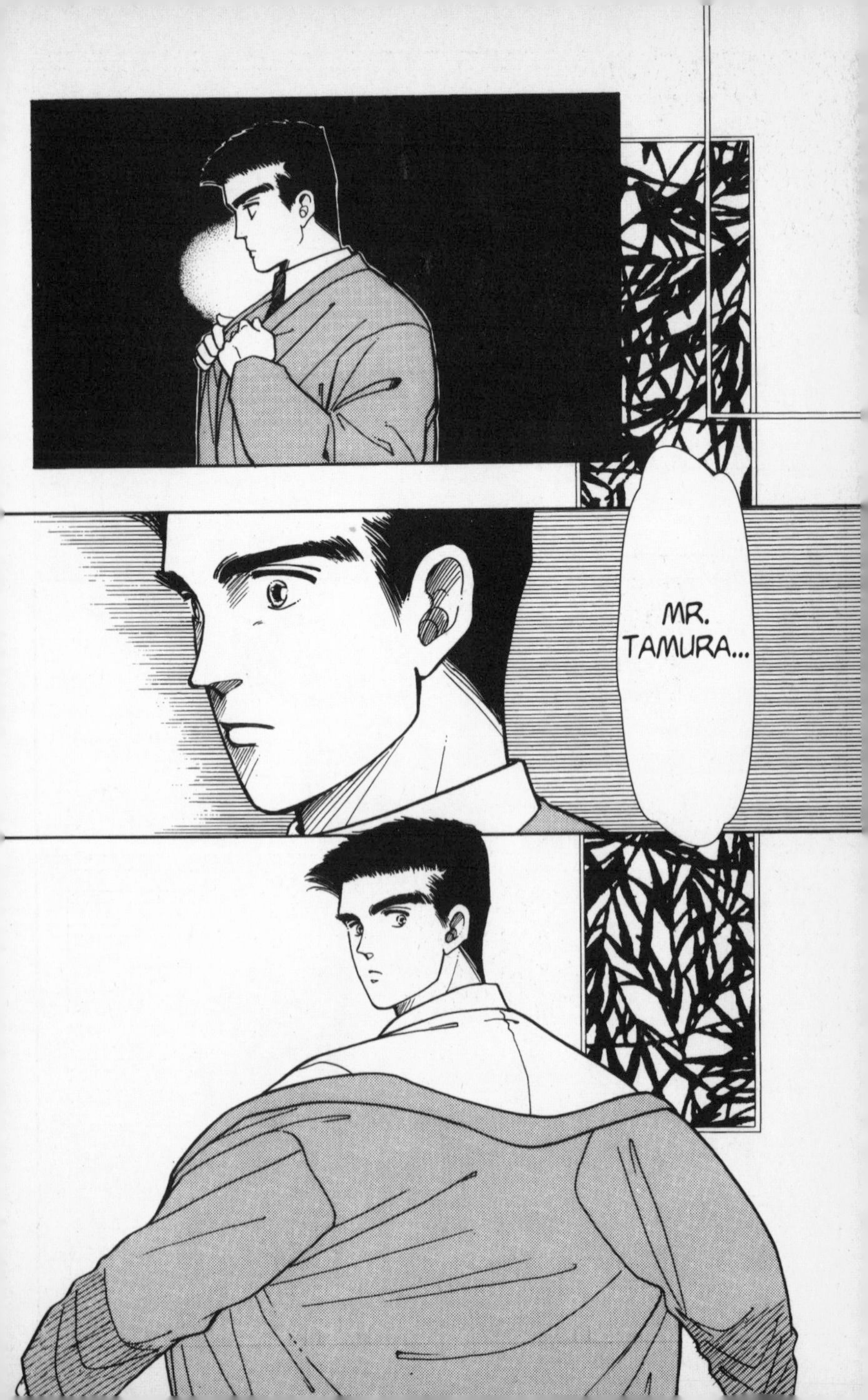
MR. TAMURA...

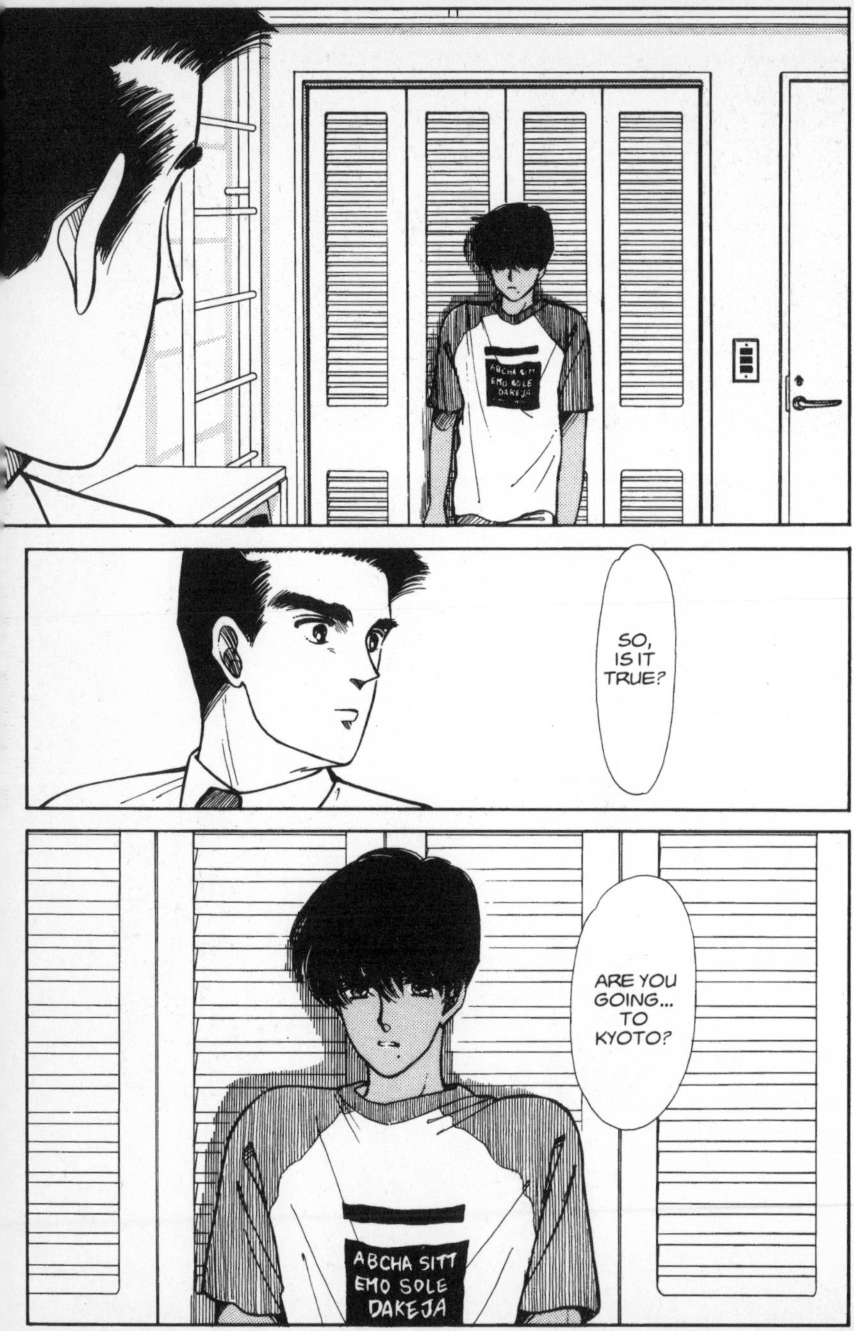
ABCHA SITT
EMO SOLE
DAKEJA
SO, IS IT TRUE?
ARE YOU GOING... TO KYOTO?
ABCHA SITT
EMO SOLE
DAKEJA

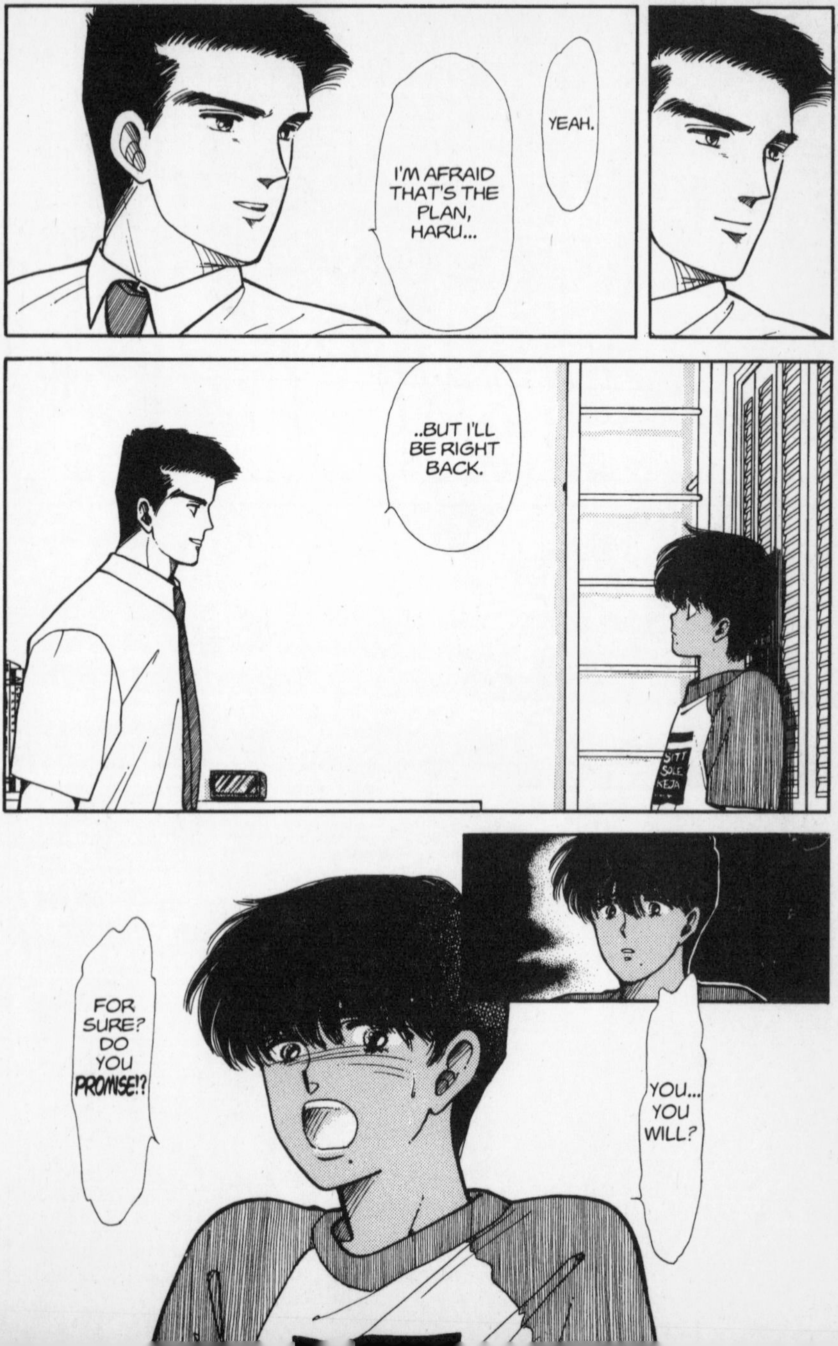
YEAH.
I'M AFRAID THAT'S THE PLAN, HARU...
..BUT I'LL BE RIGHT BACK.
YOU... YOU WILL?
FOR SURE? DO YOU **PROMISE!?**

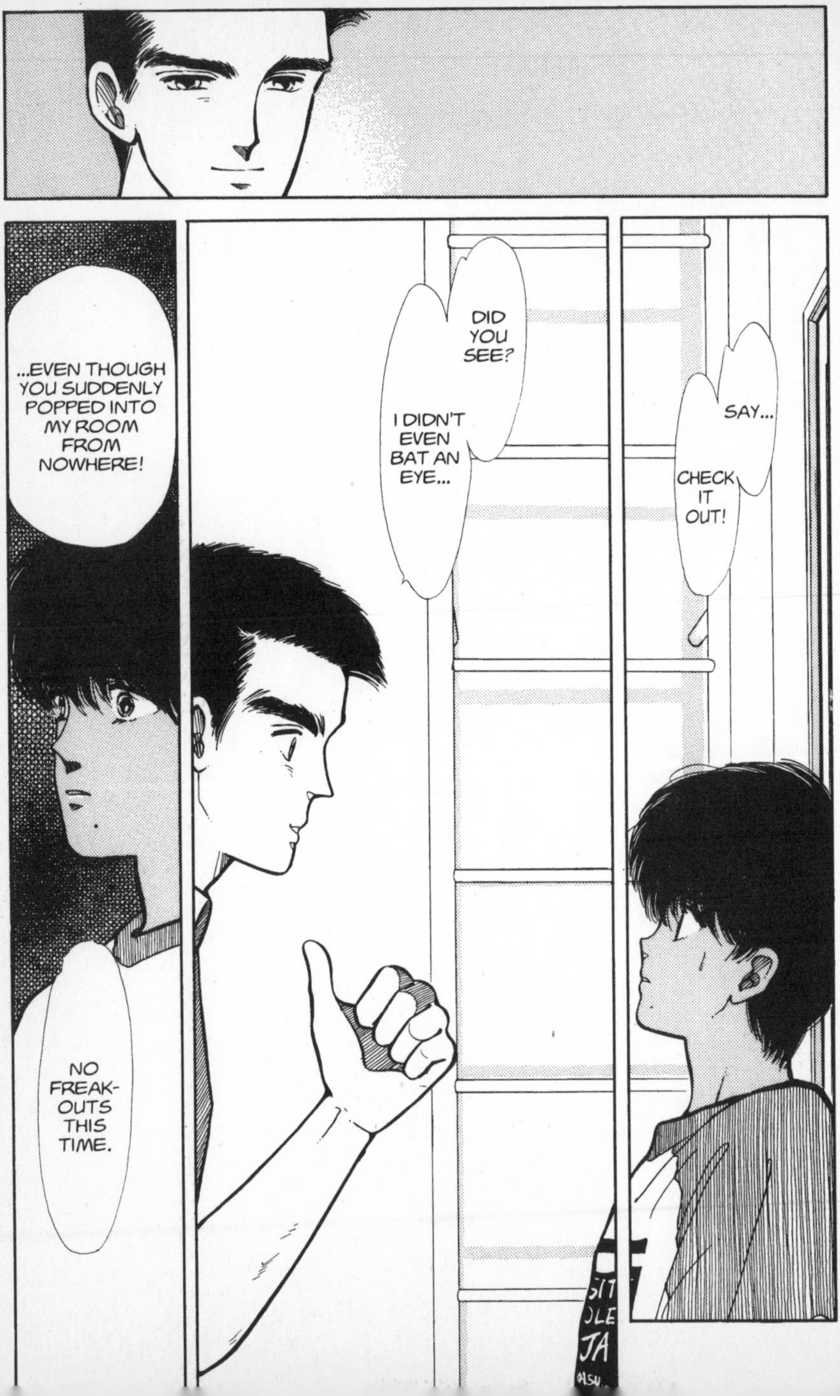
SAY...
CHECK IT OUT!
DID YOU SEE?
I DIDN'T EVEN BAT AN EYE...
...EVEN THOUGH YOU SUDDENLY POPPED INTO MY ROOM FROM NOWHERE!
NO FREAK-OUTS THIS TIME.

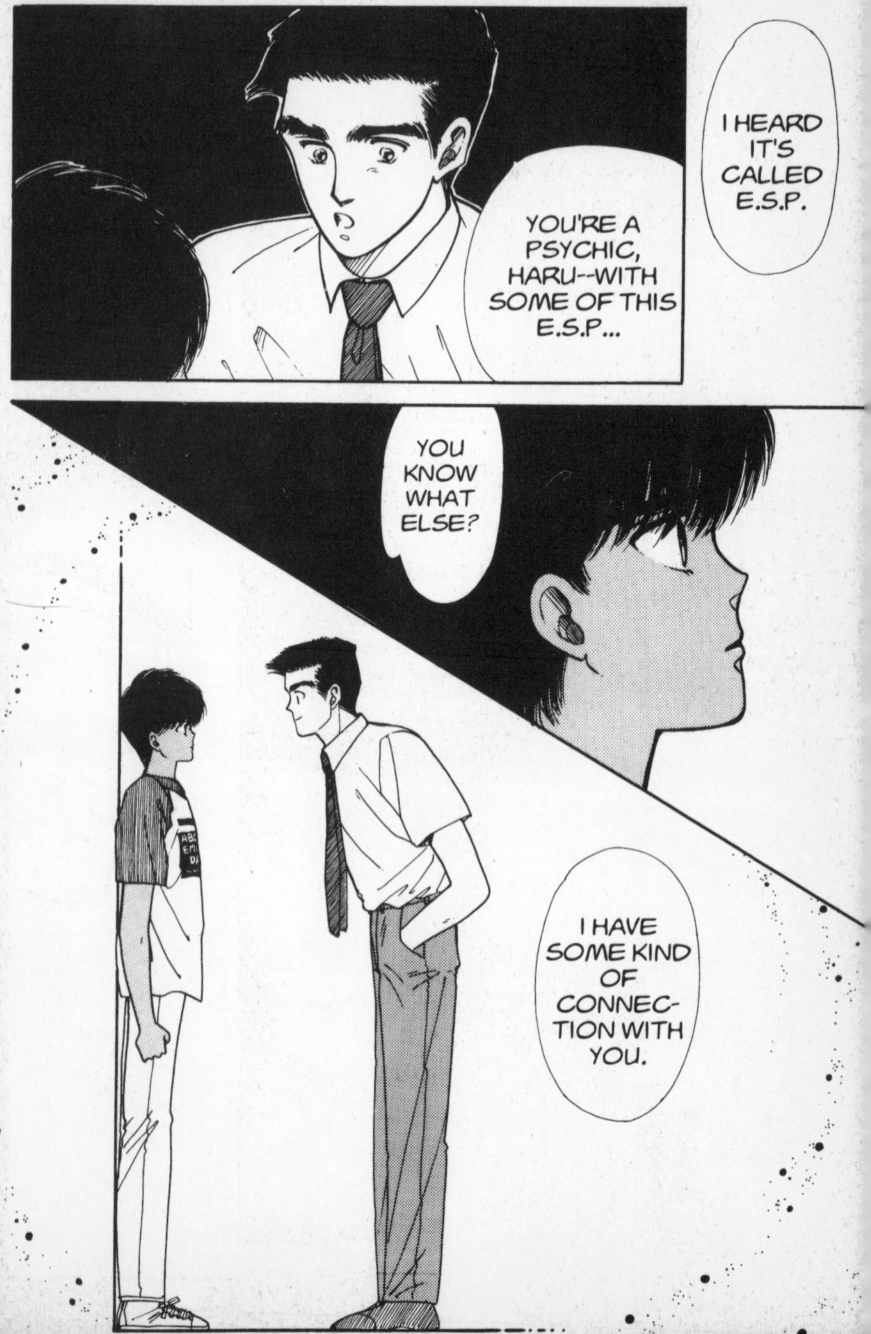
I HEARD IT'S CALLED E.S.P.
YOU'RE A PSYCHIC, HARU--WITH SOME OF THIS E.S.P...
YOU KNOW WHAT ELSE?
I HAVE SOME KIND OF CONNECTION WITH YOU.

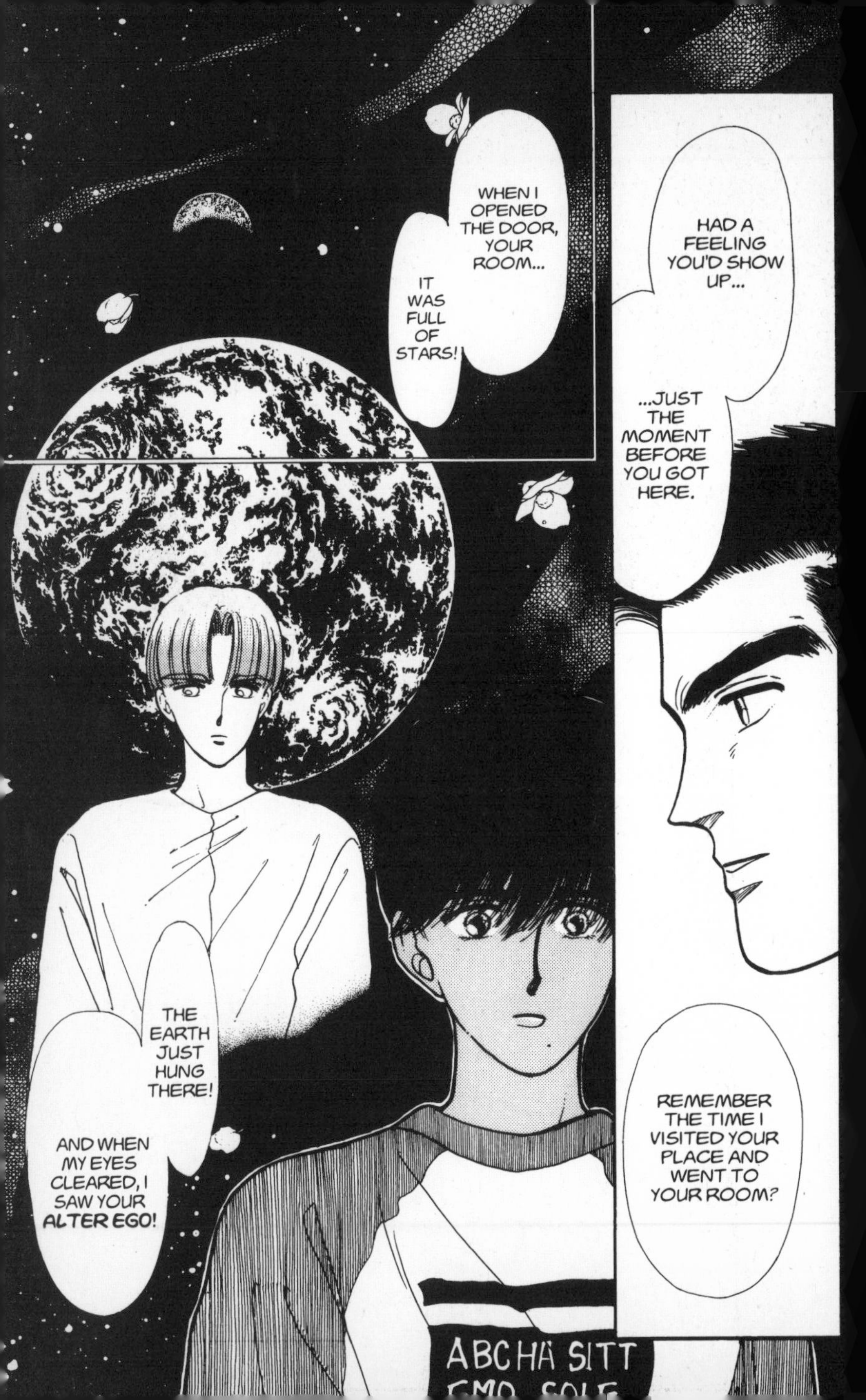
HAD A FEELING YOU'D SHOW UP...
...JUST THE MOMENT BEFORE YOU GOT HERE.
REMEMBER THE TIME I VISITED YOUR PLACE AND WENT TO YOUR ROOM?
WHEN I OPENED THE DOOR, YOUR ROOM...
IT WAS FULL OF STARS!
THE EARTH JUST HUNG THERE!
AND WHEN MY EYES CLEARED, I SAW YOUR **ALTER EGO**!
ABCHA SITT

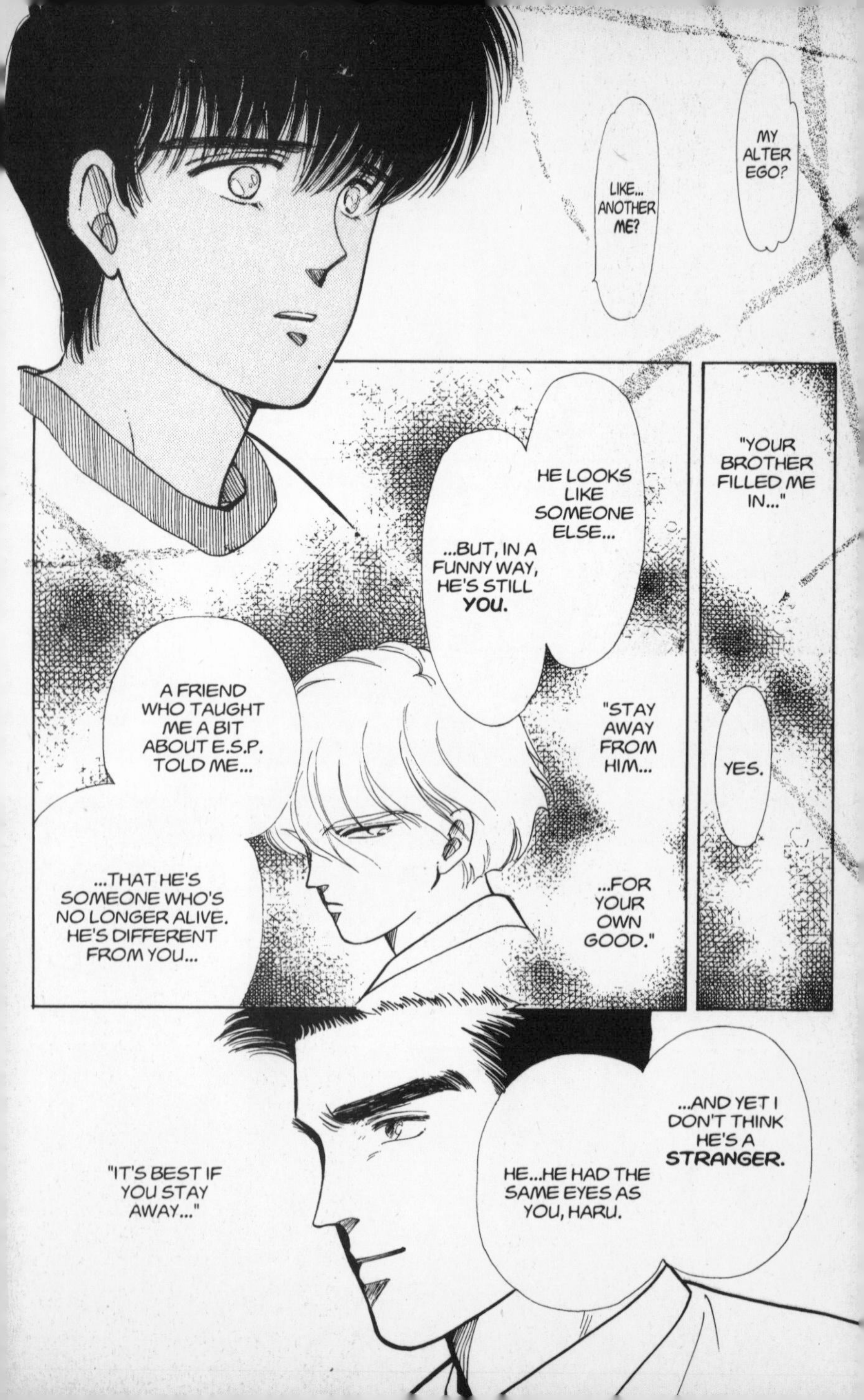
MY ALTER EGO?
LIKE... ANOTHER ME?
"YOUR BROTHER FILLED ME IN..."
YES.
HE LOOKS LIKE SOMEONE ELSE...
...BUT, IN A FUNNY WAY, HE'S STILL **YOU.**
"STAY AWAY FROM HIM...
...FOR YOUR OWN GOOD."
A FRIEND WHO TAUGHT ME A BIT ABOUT E.S.P. TOLD ME...
...THAT HE'S SOMEONE WHO'S NO LONGER ALIVE. HE'S DIFFERENT FROM YOU...
...AND YET I DON'T THINK HE'S A **STRANGER.**
HE...HE HAD THE SAME EYES AS YOU, HARU.
"IT'S BEST IF YOU STAY AWAY..."

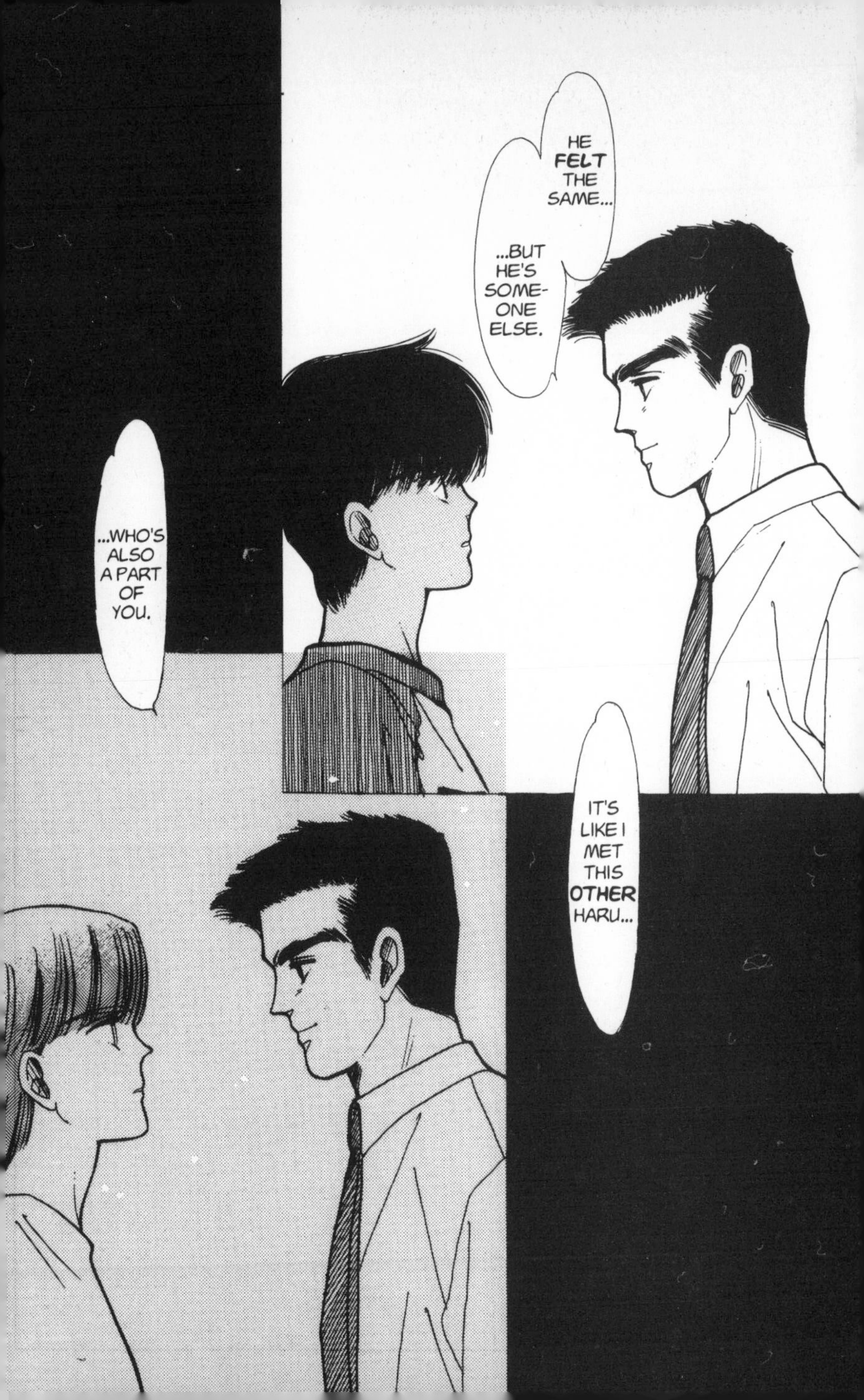
HE **FELT** THE SAME...
...BUT HE'S SOME-ONE ELSE.
IT'S LIKE I MET THIS **OTHER** HARU...
...WHO'S ALSO A PART OF YOU.

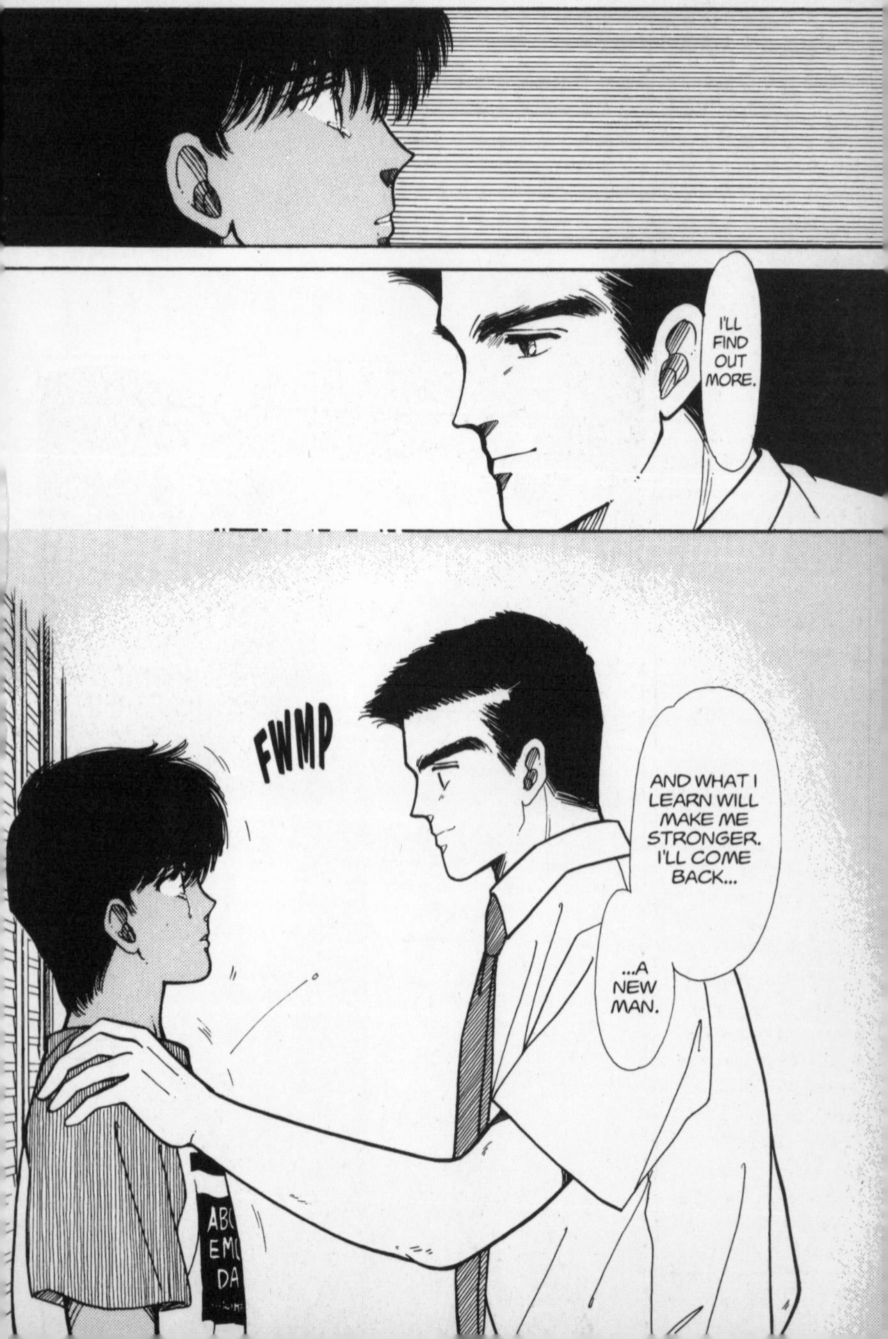
I'LL FIND OUT MORE.
FWMP
AND WHAT I LEARN WILL MAKE ME STRONGER. I'LL COME BACK...
...A NEW MAN.
ABC EMC DA

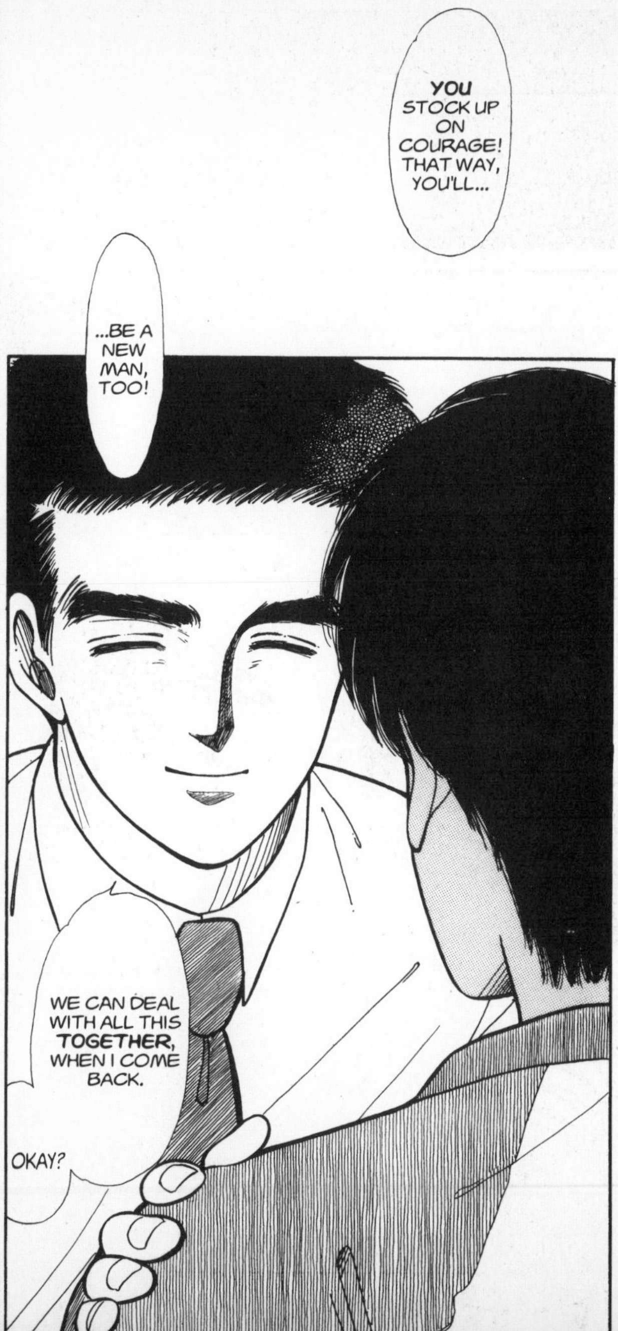
YOU STOCK UP ON COURAGE! THAT WAY, YOU'LL...
...BE A NEW MAN, TOO!
WE CAN DEAL WITH ALL THIS **TOGETHER**, WHEN I COME BACK.
OKAY?

1/4 COLUMN NONSENSE

— PART 1 —

Hi!
Hiwatari here! A lot has happened in the time it took to compile this graphic novel. The biggest thing of all was the sale of the record album. Wow.

I don't know much about the music industry, but I heard it's been selling well, thank goodness. Right now, it's seventh on the LP chart (number 19, overall). That's impressive.

And it's all thanks to those amazing musicians!

The great Taeko Onuki actually let me shake her hand--I'm not worthy! (And I shook hands with her again when I went to her concert yesterday!)

Miss Sakurai was very pleased with the album, and the comments from the readers have also been positive so far. I'm so glad!
It was a lot of extra work, but I'm glad I gave the go-ahead.

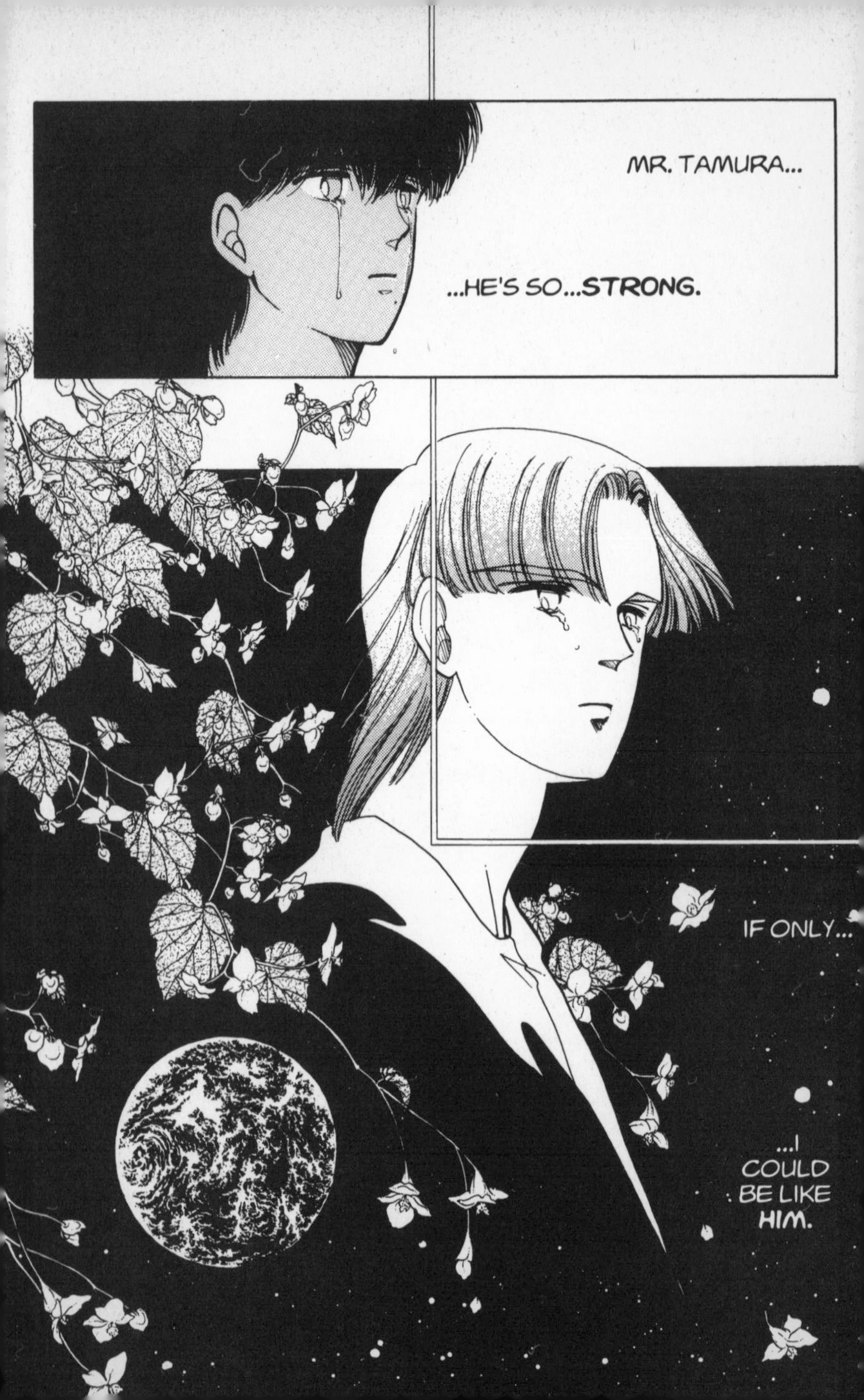
MR. TAMURA...
...HE'S SO...STRONG.
IF ONLY...
...I COULD BE LIKE HIM.

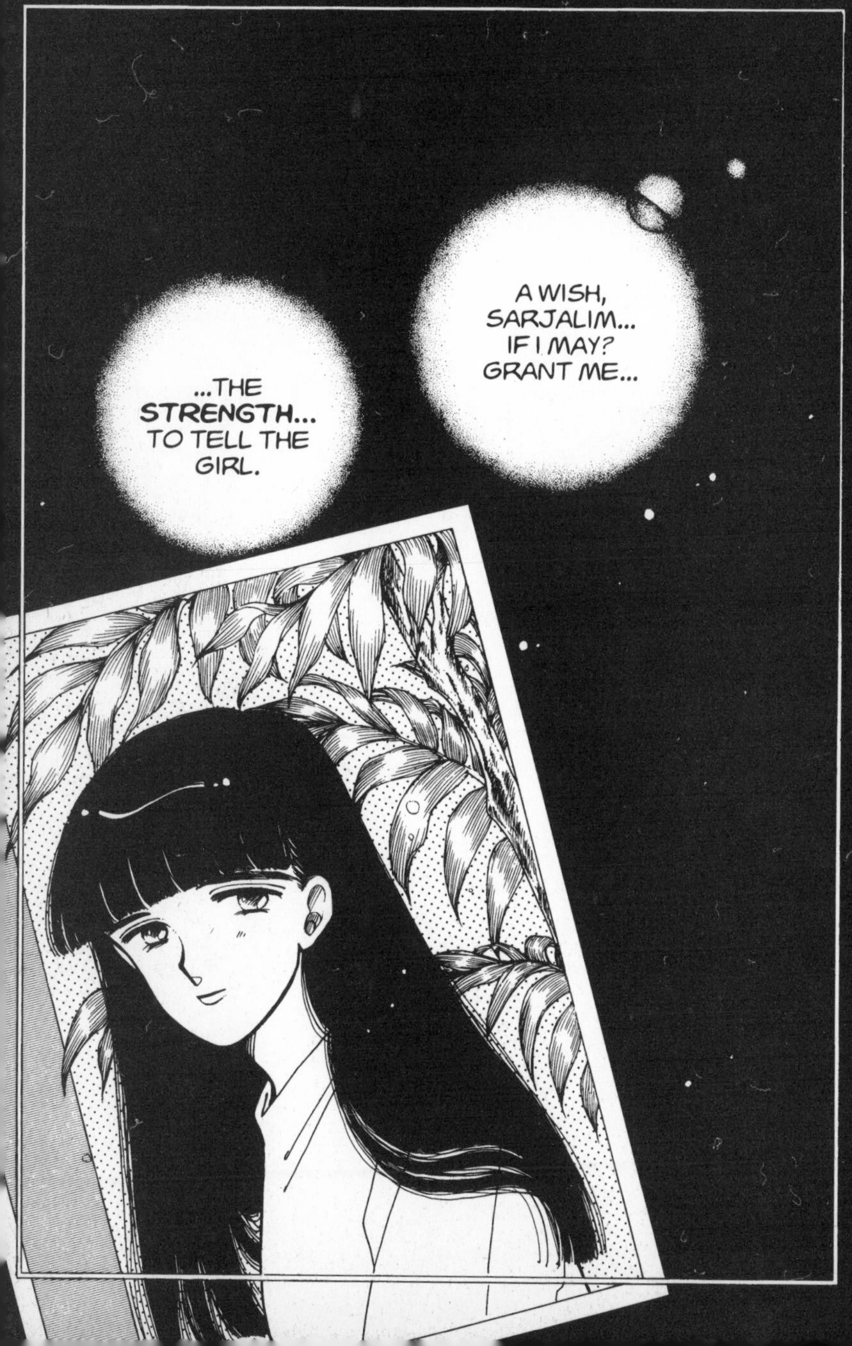
A WISH, SARJALIM... IF I MAY? GRANT ME...
...THE **STRENGTH...** TO TELL THE GIRL.

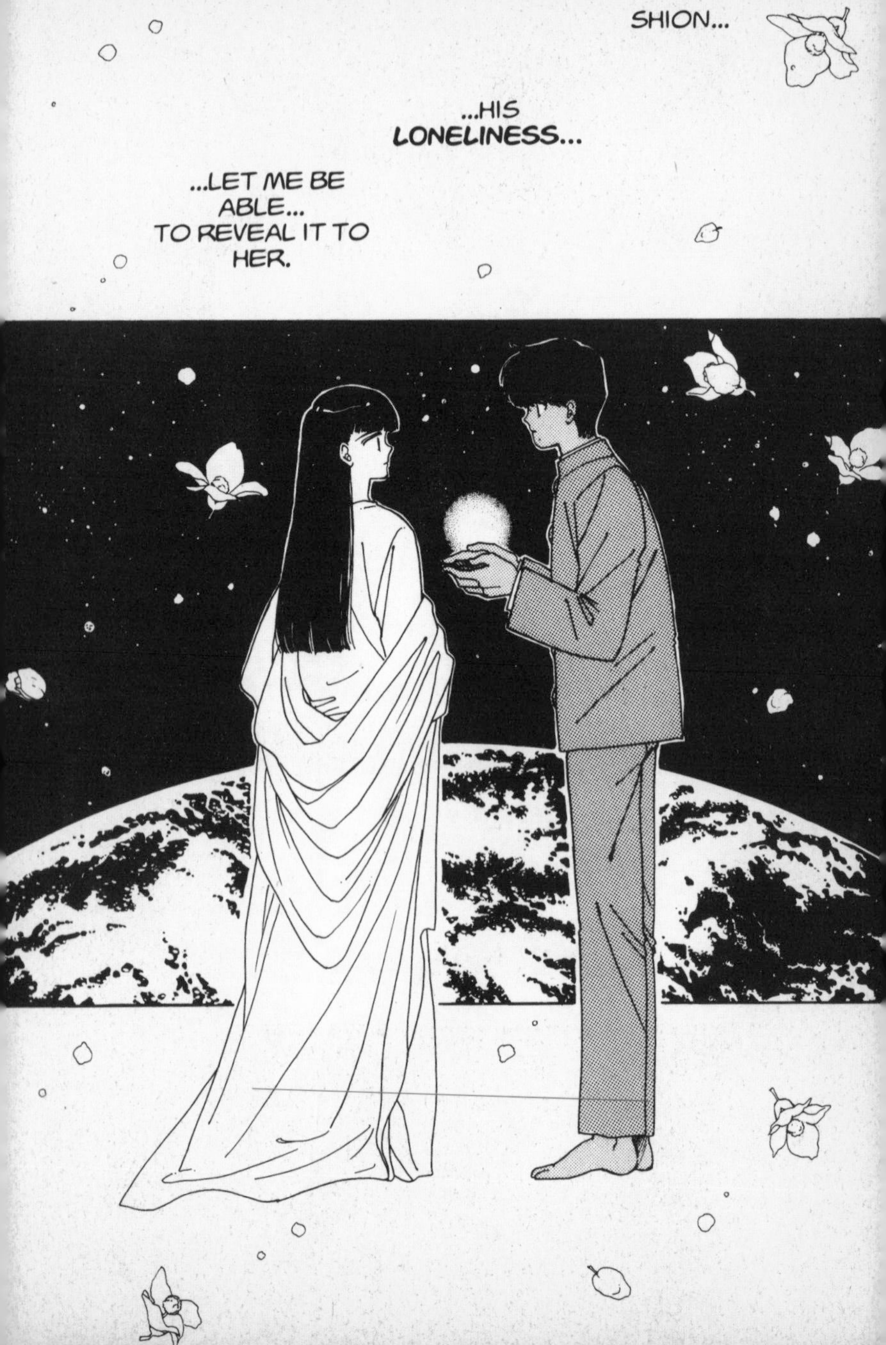
SHION...
...HIS LONELINESS...
...LET ME BE ABLE... TO REVEAL IT TO HER.

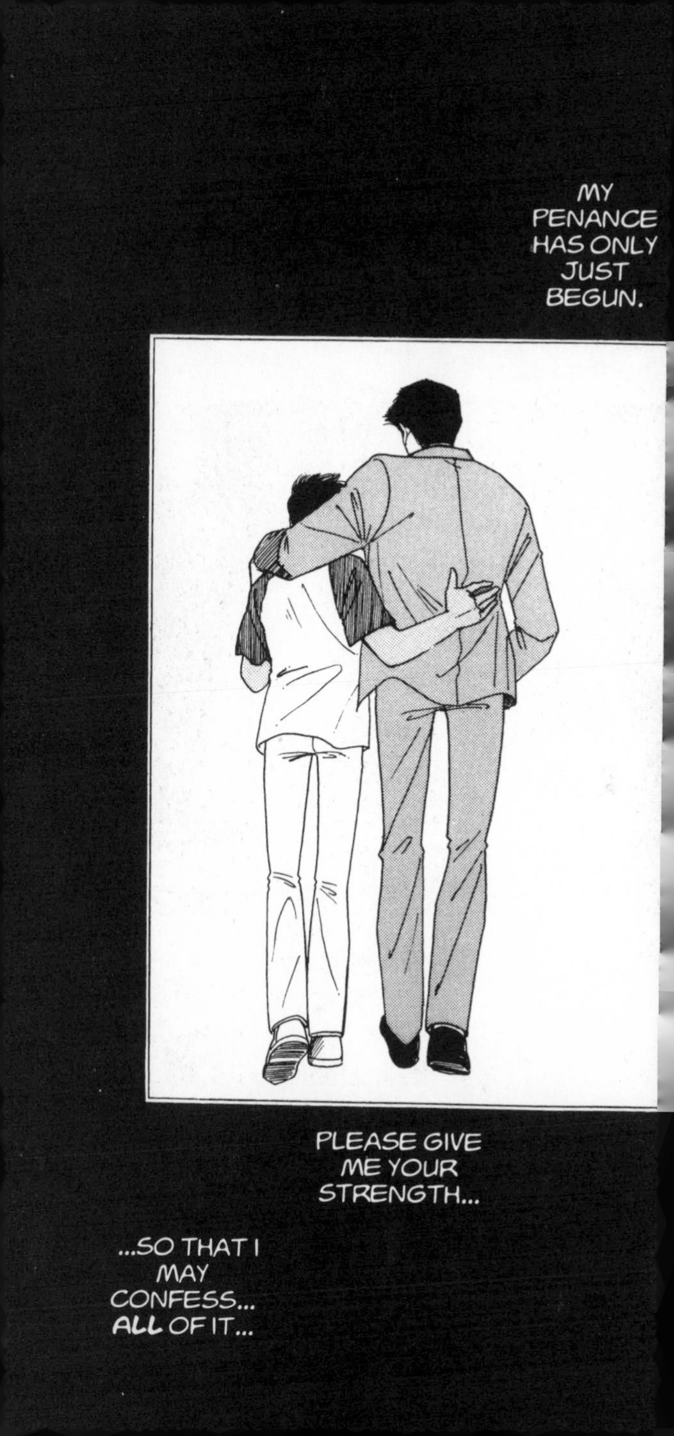
MY PENANCE HAS ONLY JUST BEGUN.
PLEASE GIVE ME YOUR STRENGTH...
...SO THAT I MAY CONFESS... **ALL** OF IT...

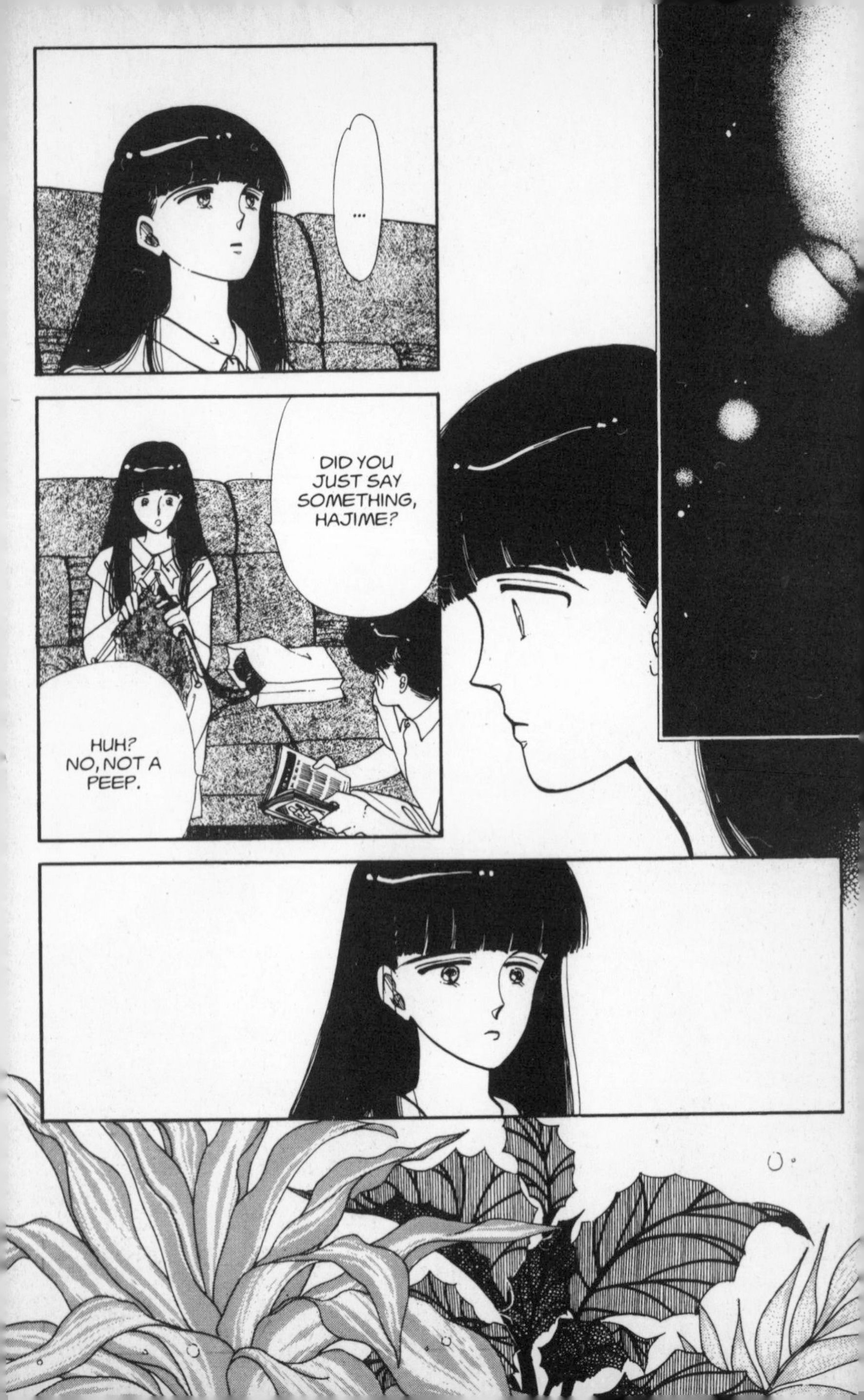
...
DID YOU JUST SAY SOMETHING, HAJIME?
HUH? NO, NOT A PEEP.

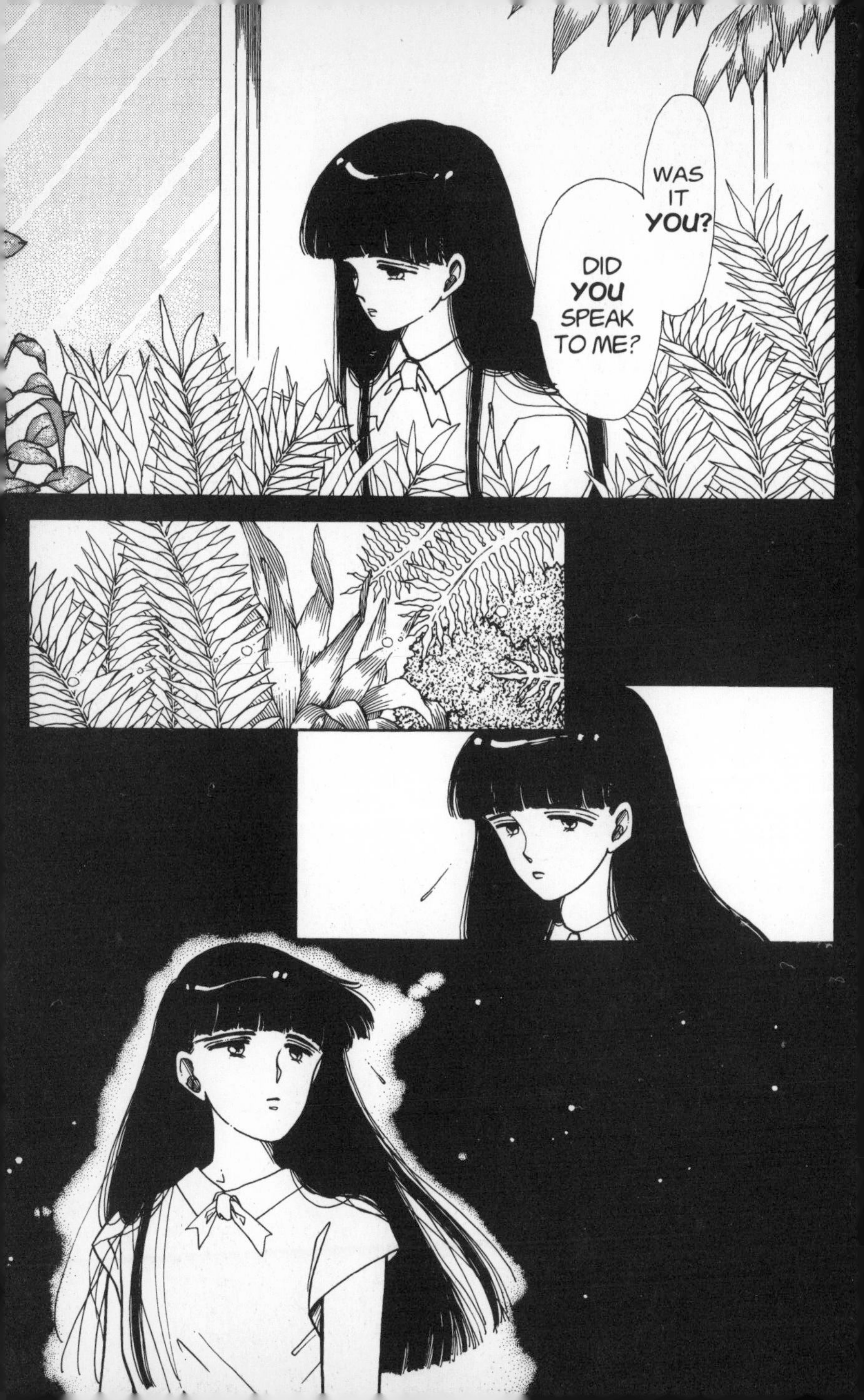
WAS IT YOU?
DID YOU SPEAK TO ME?

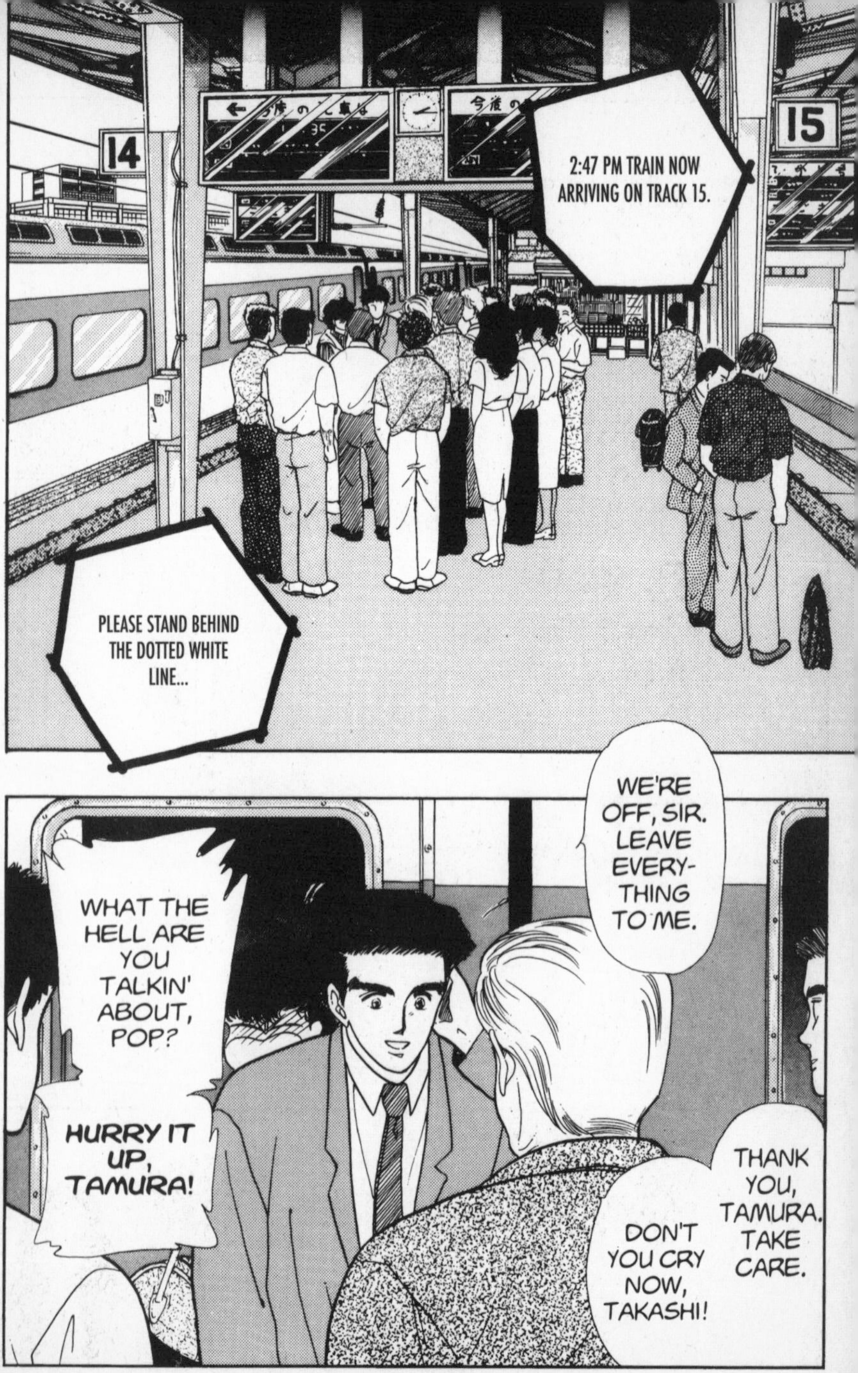
15
14
2:47 PM TRAIN NOW ARRIVING ON TRACK 15.
PLEASE STAND BEHIND THE DOTTED WHITE LINE...
WE'RE OFF, SIR. LEAVE EVERY-THING TO ME.
THANK YOU, TAMURA. TAKE CARE.
DON'T YOU CRY NOW, TAKASHI!
WHAT THE HELL ARE YOU TALKIN' ABOUT, POP?
HURRY IT UP, TAMURA!

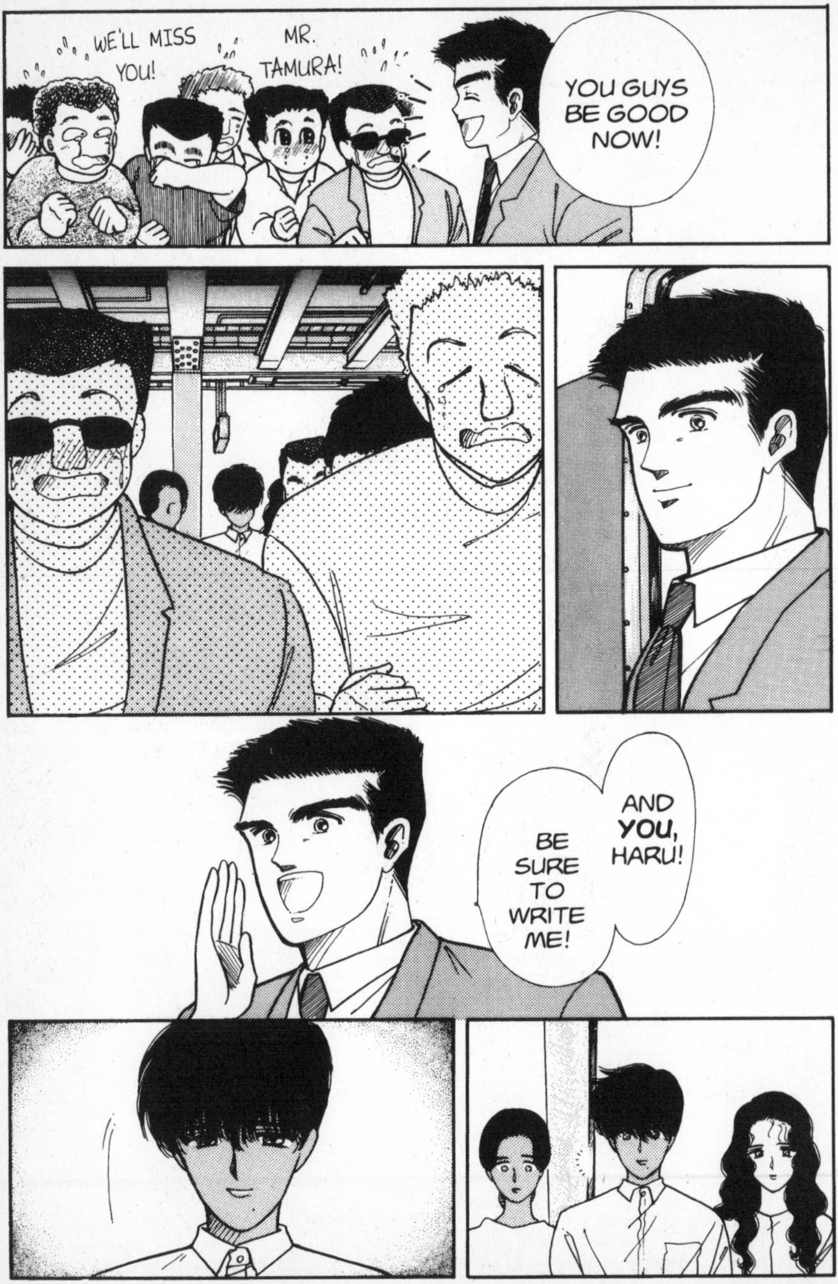
YOU GUYS BE GOOD NOW!
MR. TAMURA!
WE'LL MISS YOU!
AND **YOU**, HARU!
BE SURE TO WRITE ME!

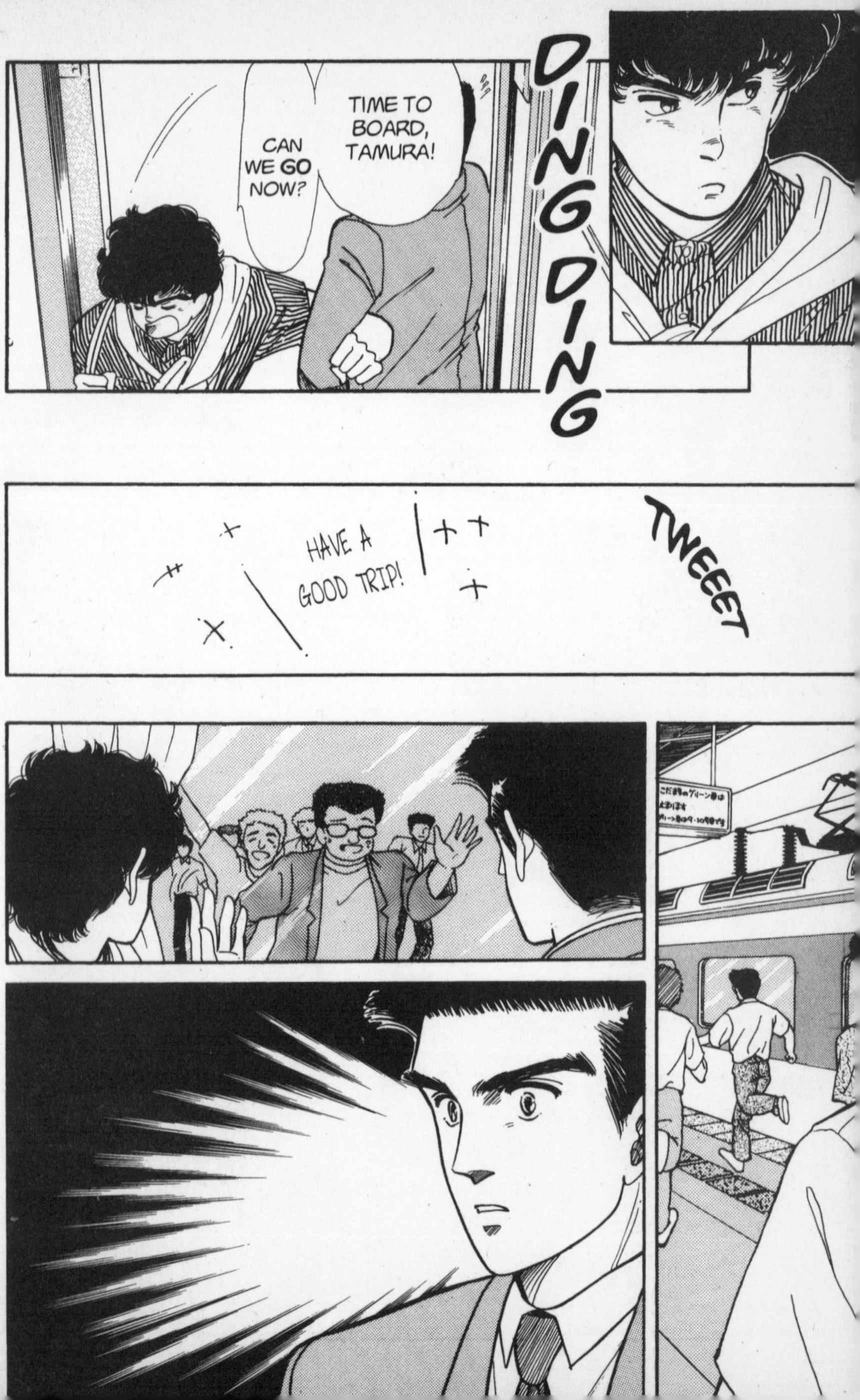
DING DING
TIME TO BOARD, TAMURA!
CAN WE GO NOW?
TWEEET
HAVE A GOOD TRIP!

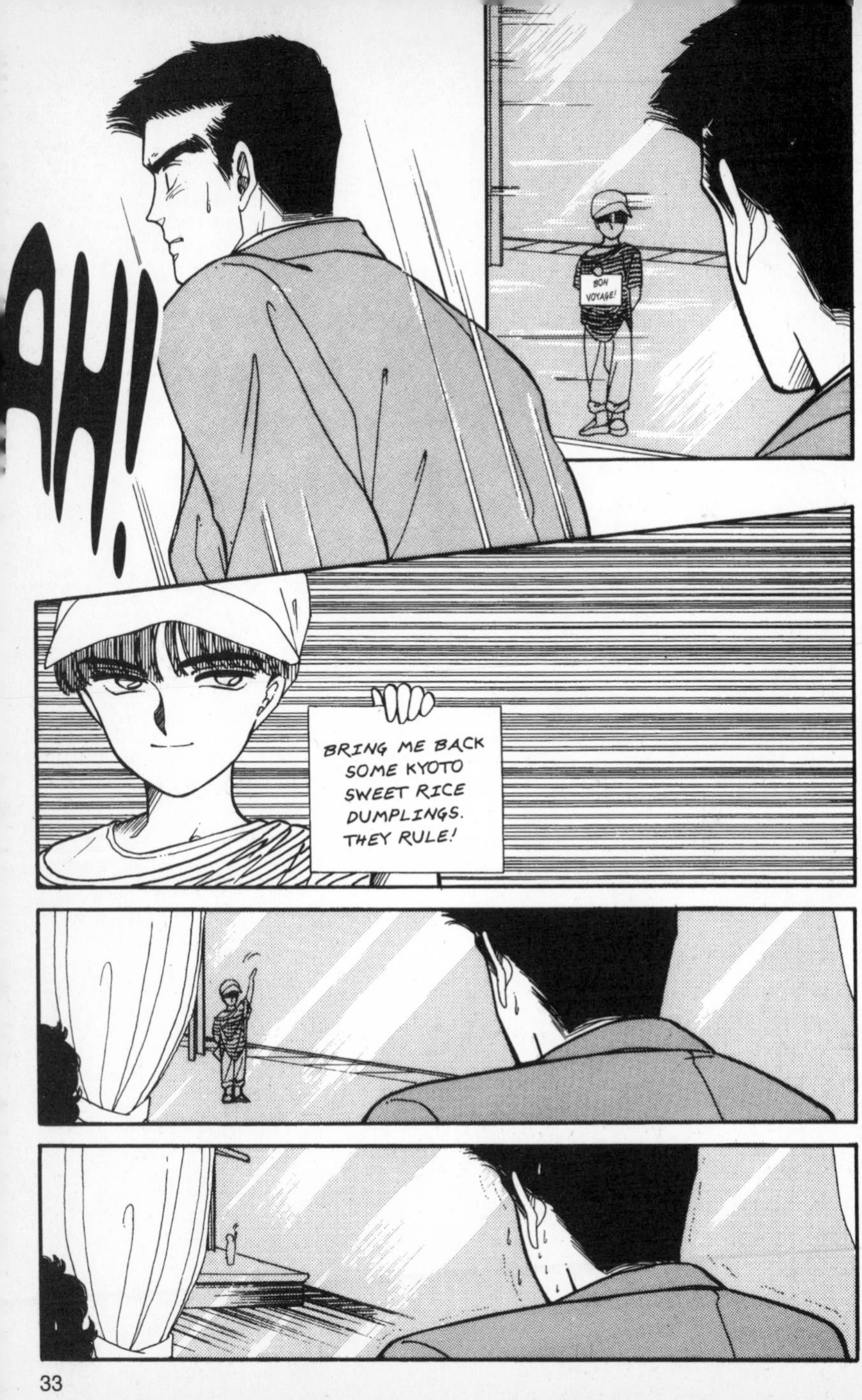
BON VOYAGE!
AH!!
BRING ME BACK SOME KYOTO SWEET RICE DUMPLINGS. THEY RULE!

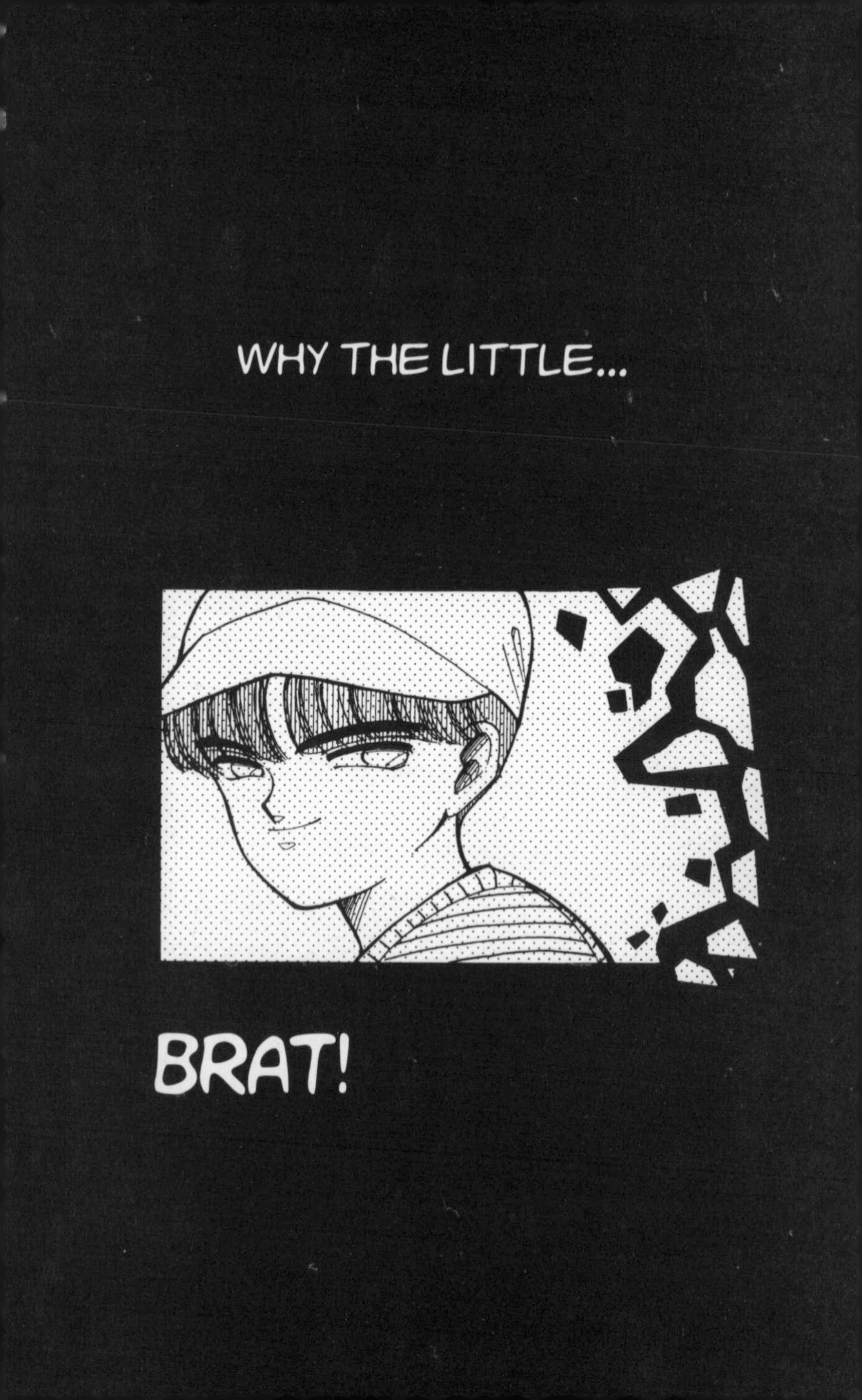
WHY THE LITTLE...
BRAT!

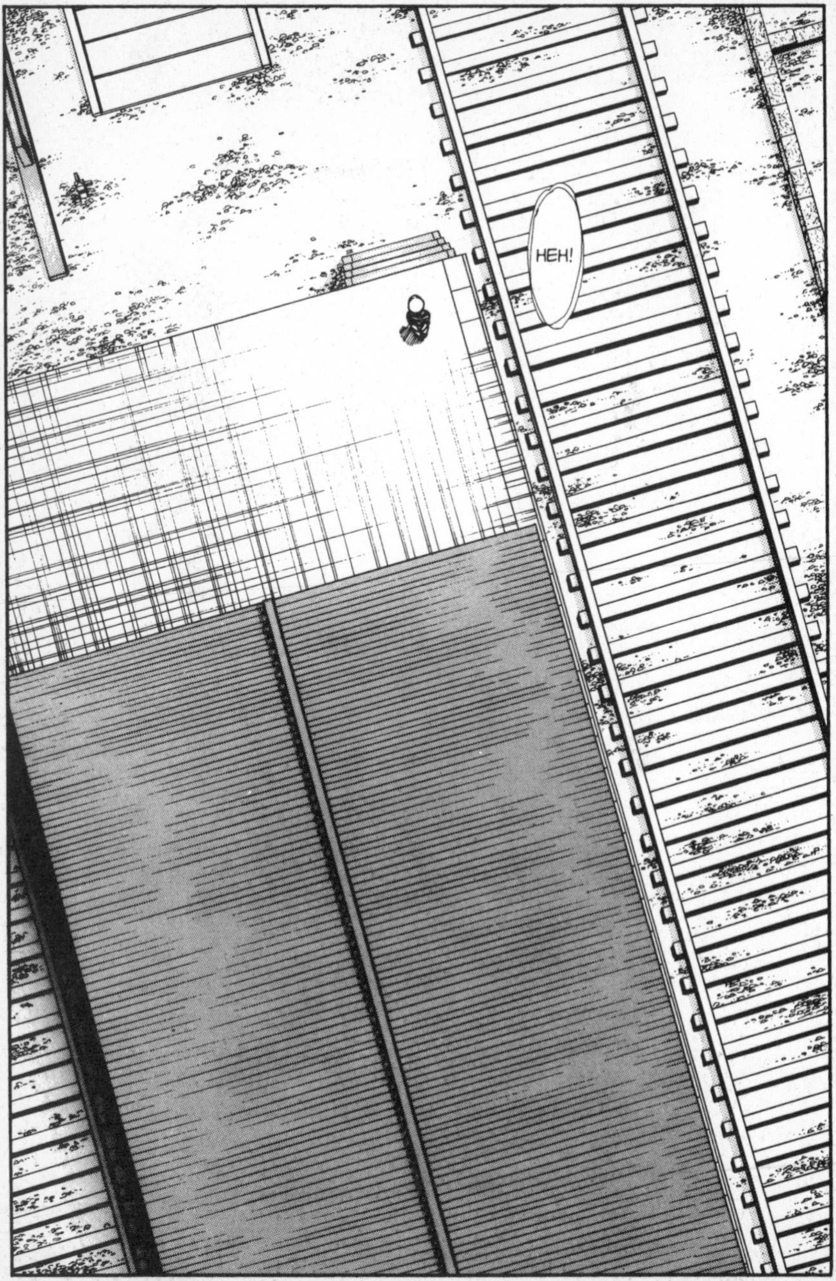
HEH!

PART I: END.

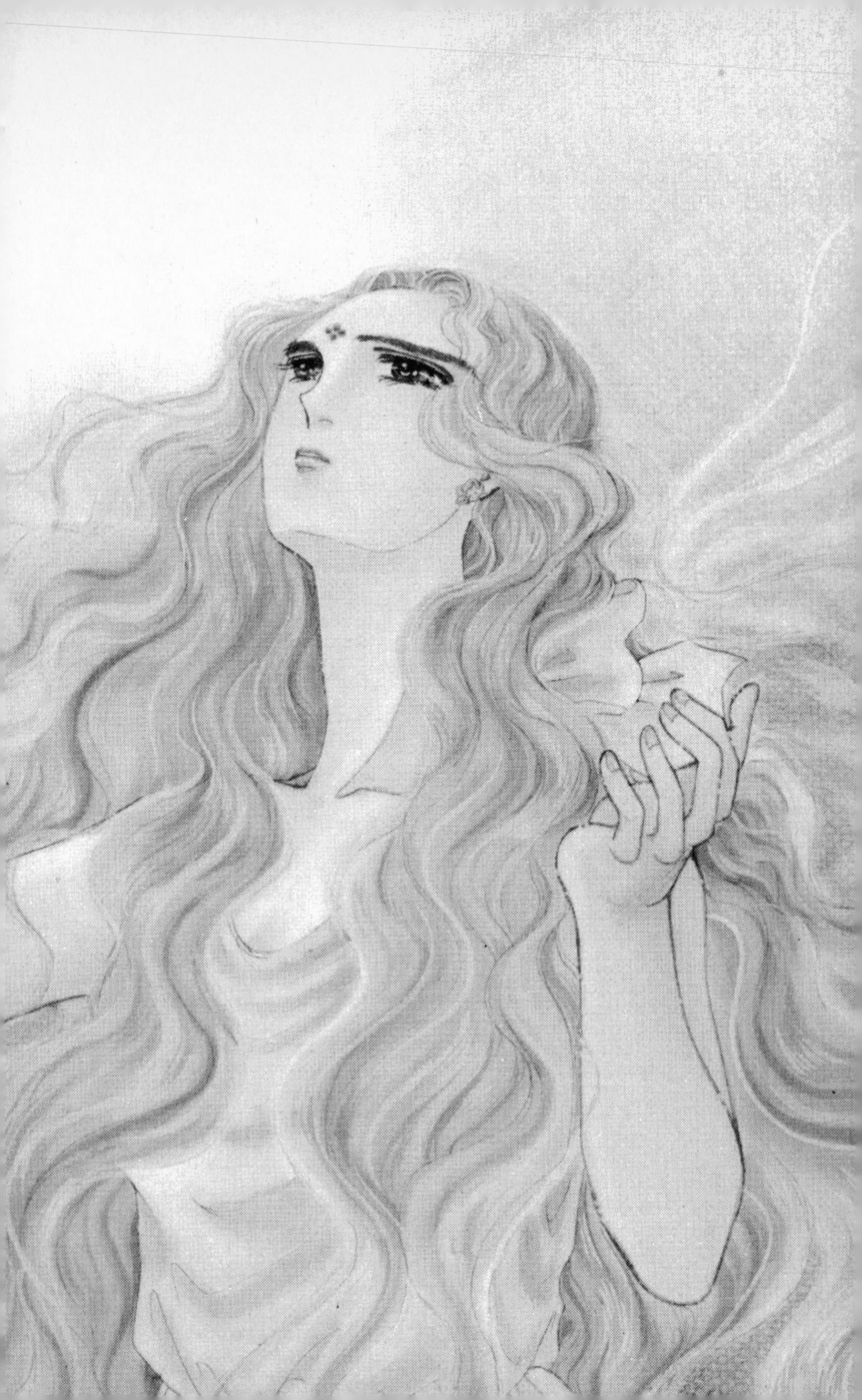

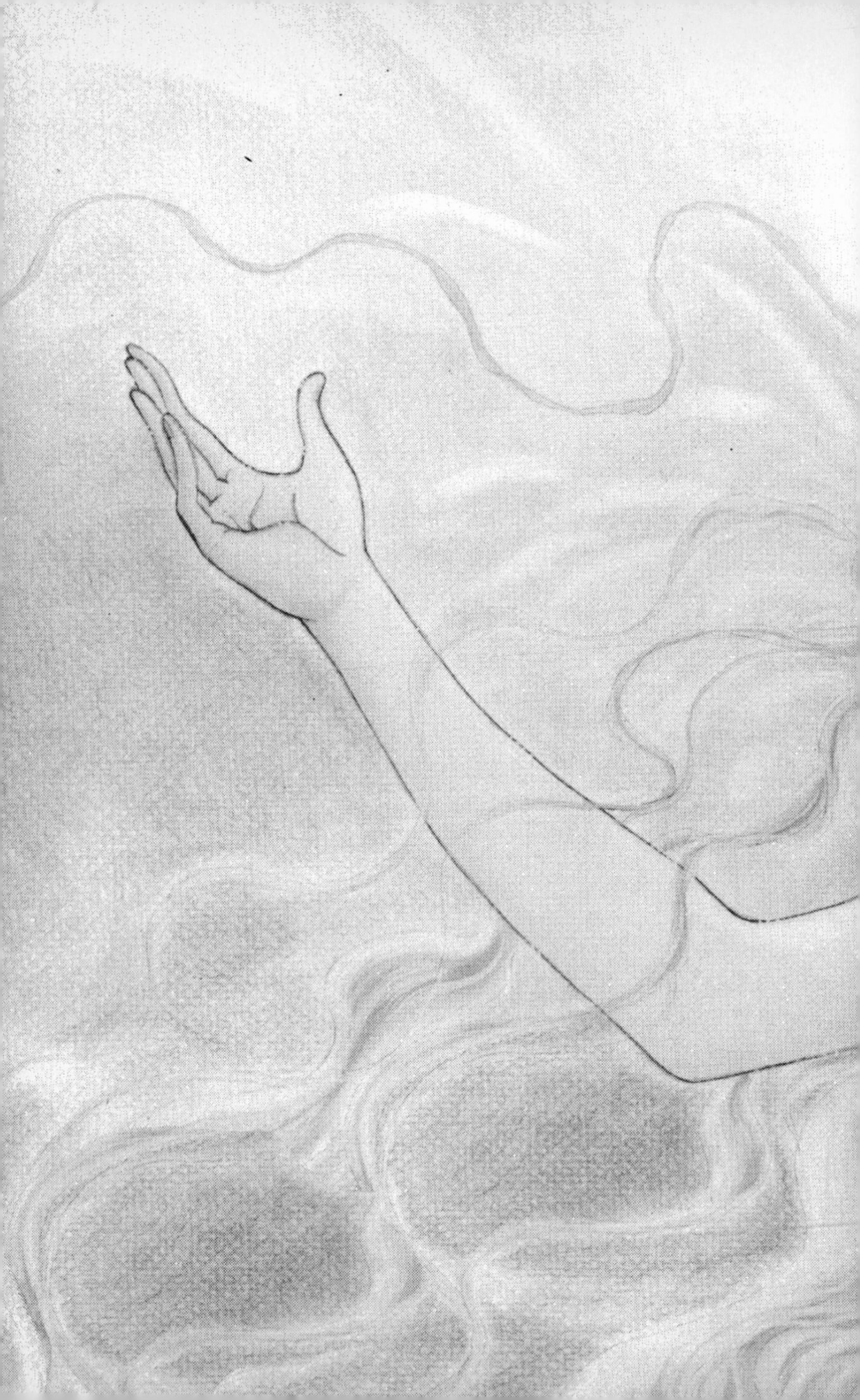

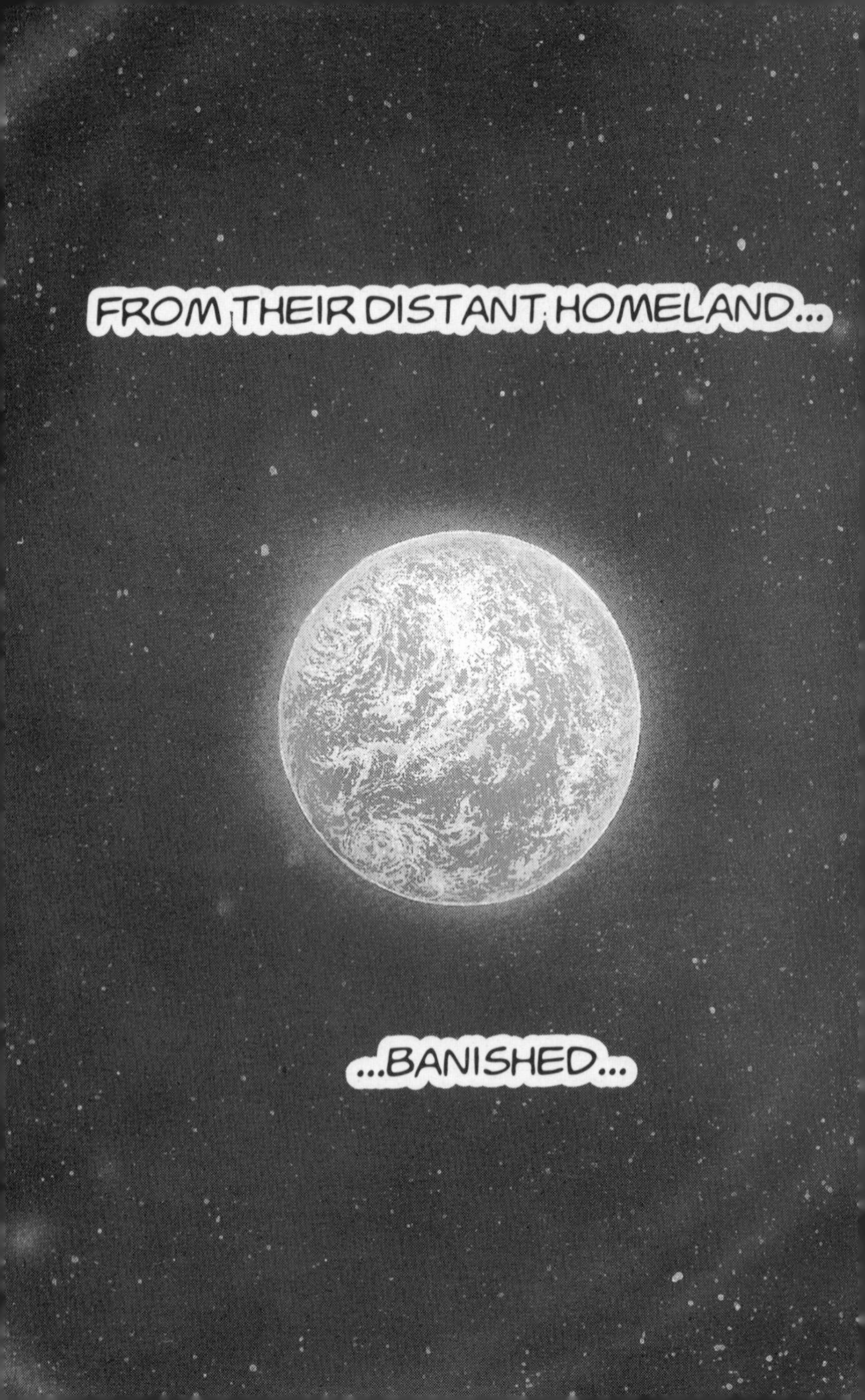
FROM THEIR DISTANT HOMELAND...
...BANISHED...

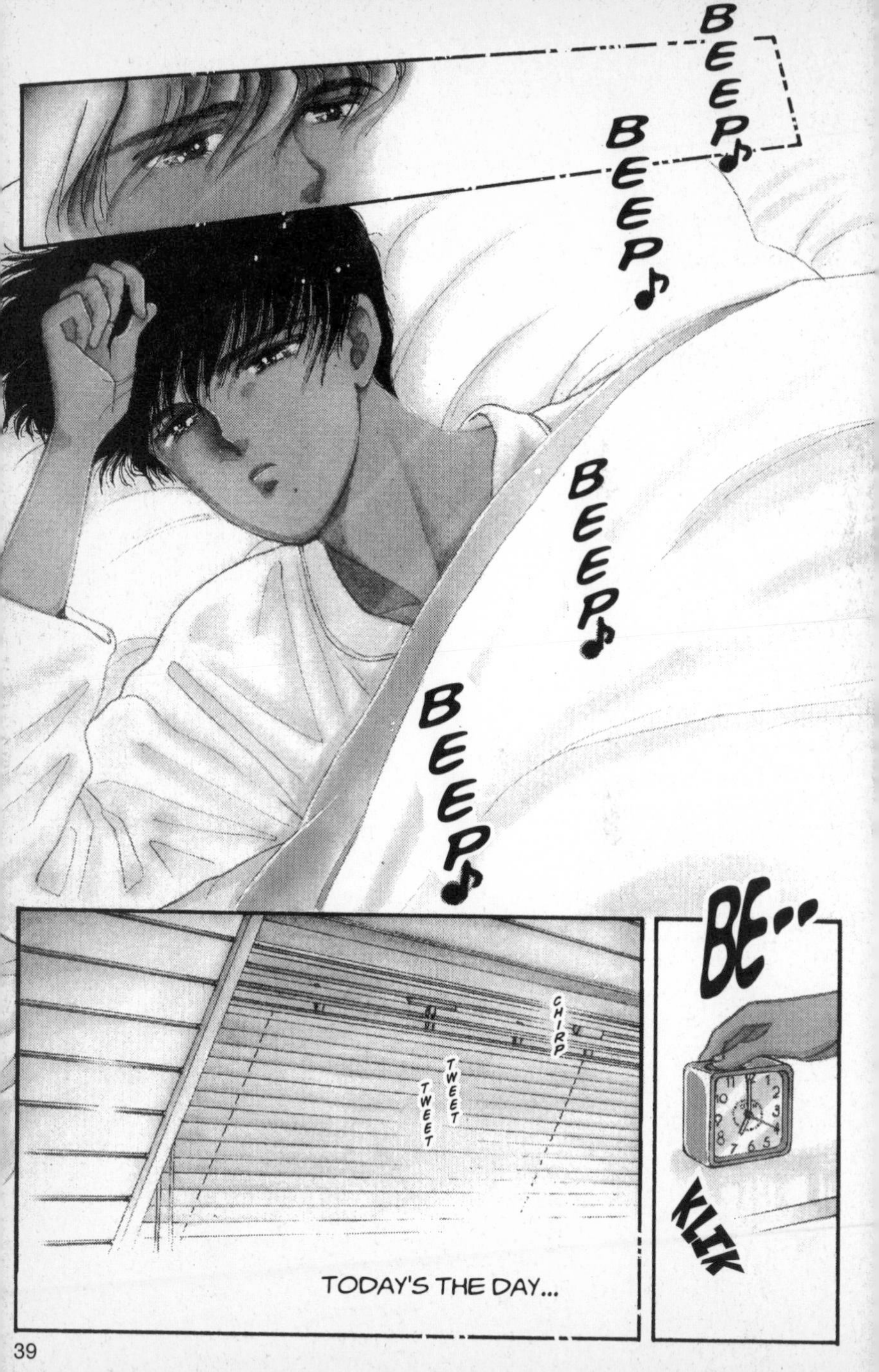
BEEP♪
BEEP♪
BEEP♪
BEEP♪
BE..
KLIK
CHIRP
TWEET
TWEET
TODAY'S THE DAY...

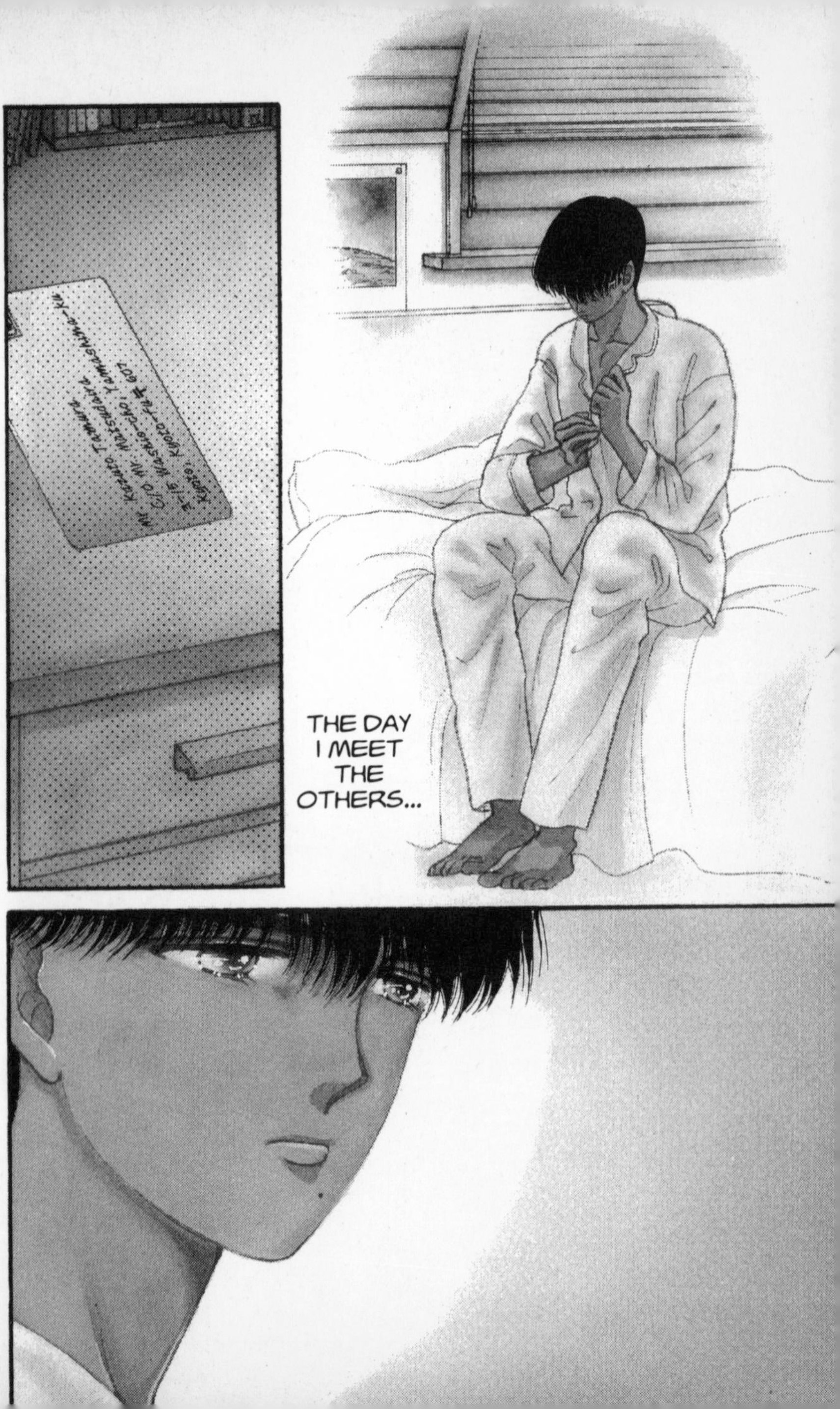
THE DAY I MEET THE OTHERS...
Mr. Kazuto Tamura
C/O Mr. Matsudaira

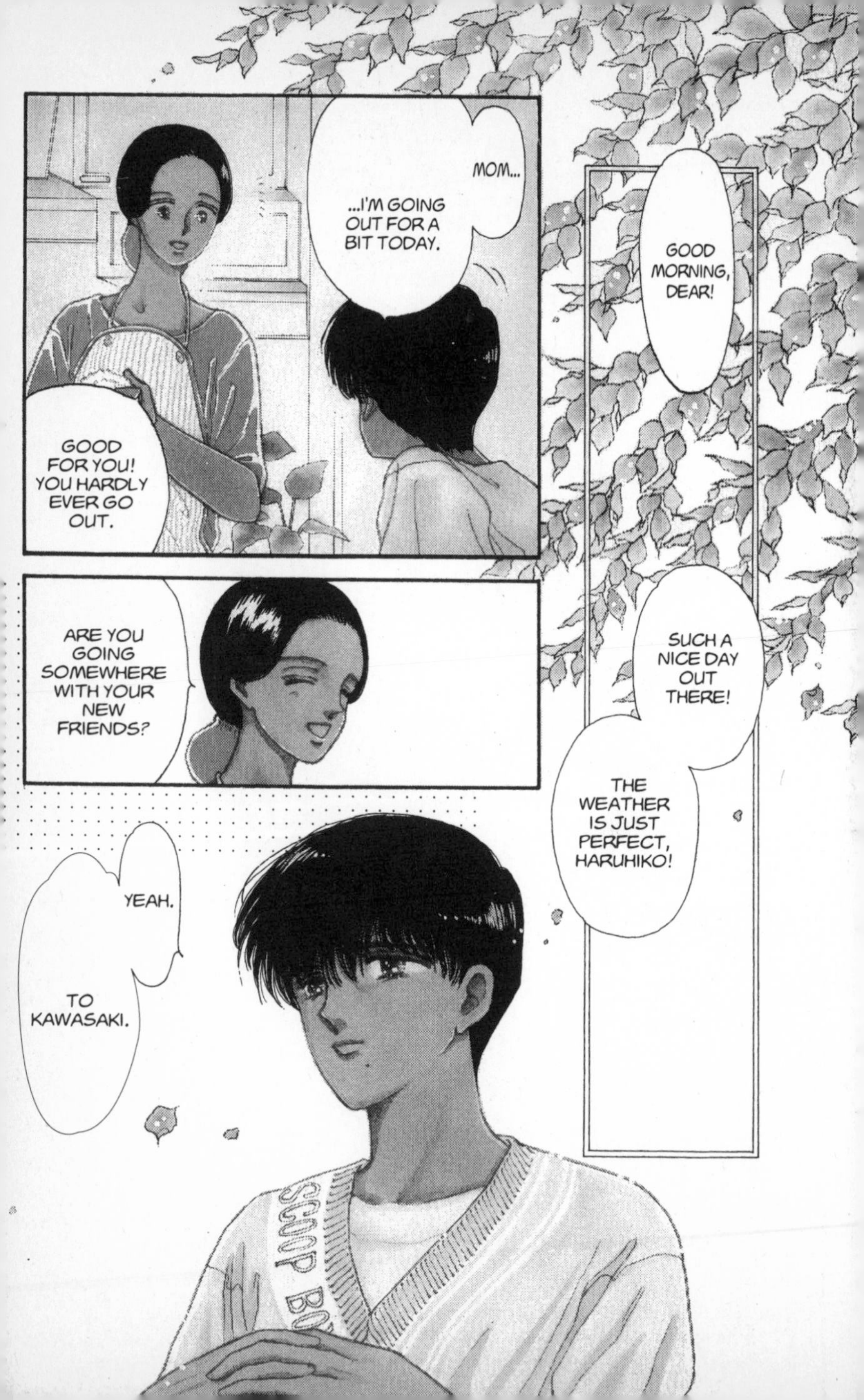
GOOD MORNING, DEAR!
SUCH A NICE DAY OUT THERE!
THE WEATHER IS JUST PERFECT, HARUHIKO!
MOM...
...I'M GOING OUT FOR A BIT TODAY.
GOOD FOR YOU! YOU HARDLY EVER GO OUT.
ARE YOU GOING SOMEWHERE WITH YOUR NEW FRIENDS?
YEAH.
TO KAWASAKI.

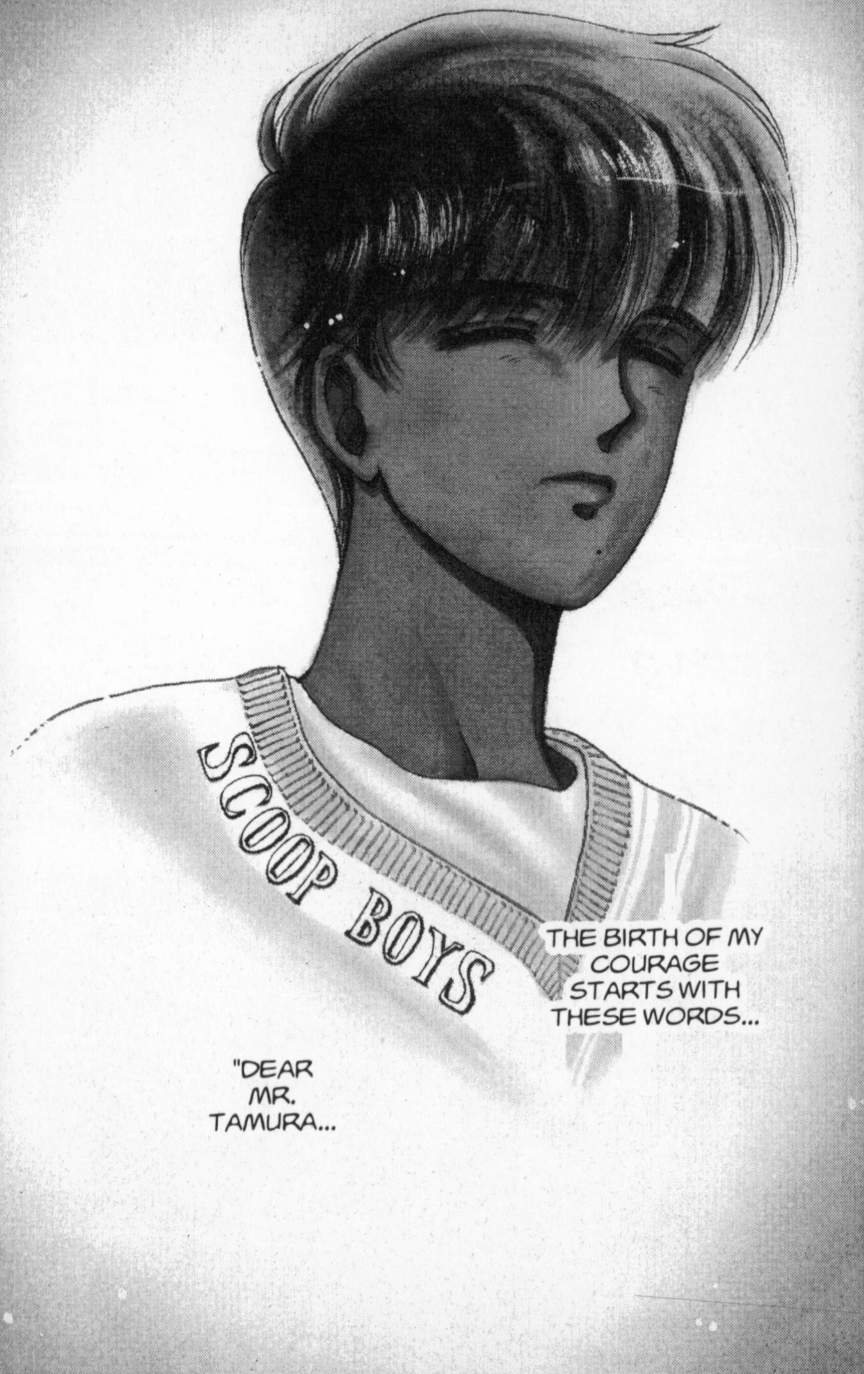

SCOOP BOYS
THE BIRTH OF MY COURAGE STARTS WITH THESE WORDS...
"DEAR MR. TAMURA...

_Here's the story I promise
you. What I'm about to
write took place in my
previous life. I've been
seeing it in my dreams,
since I was seven. I have
faith that you'll
understand._

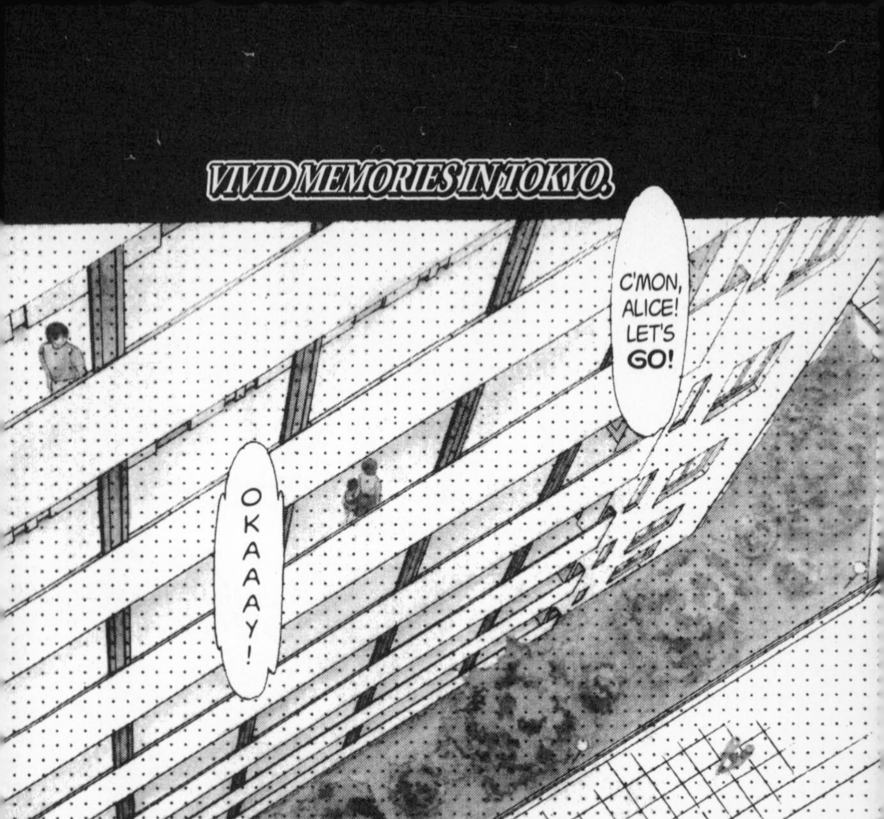
VIVID MEMORIES IN TOKYO.
C'MON, ALICE! LET'S GO!
OKAAAAY!

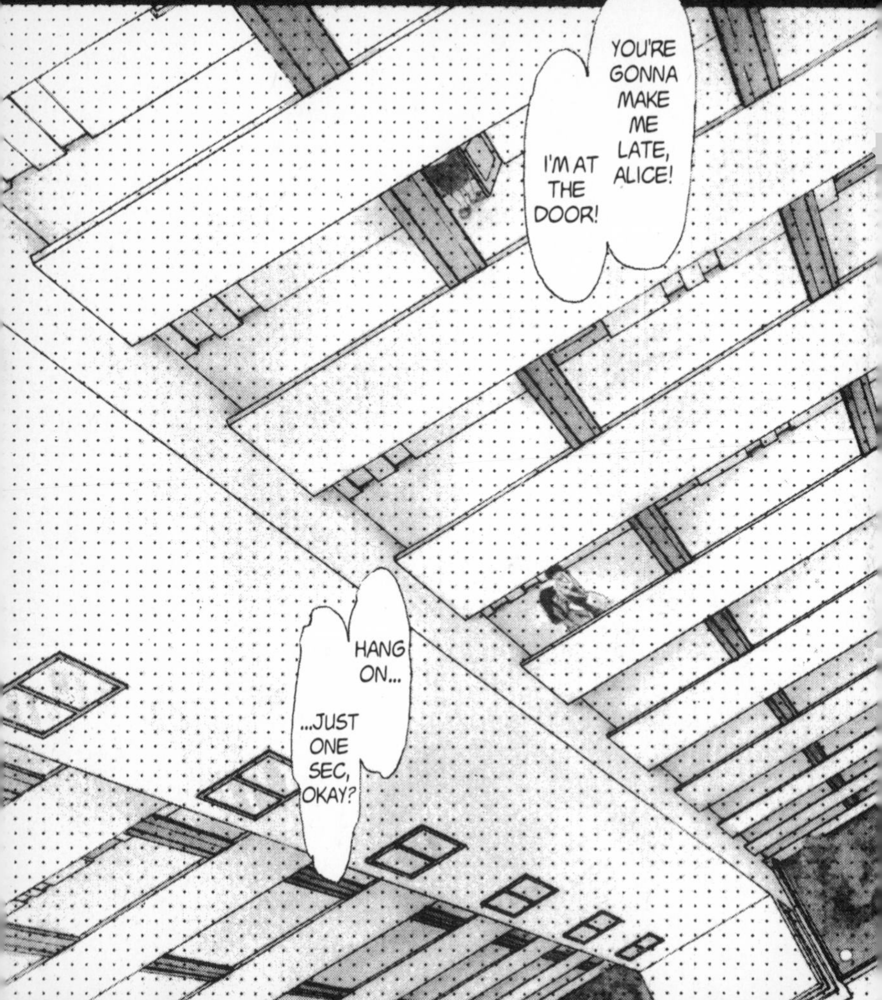
YOU'RE GONNA MAKE ME LATE, ALICE!
I'M AT THE DOOR!
HANG ON...
...JUST ONE SEC, OKAY?

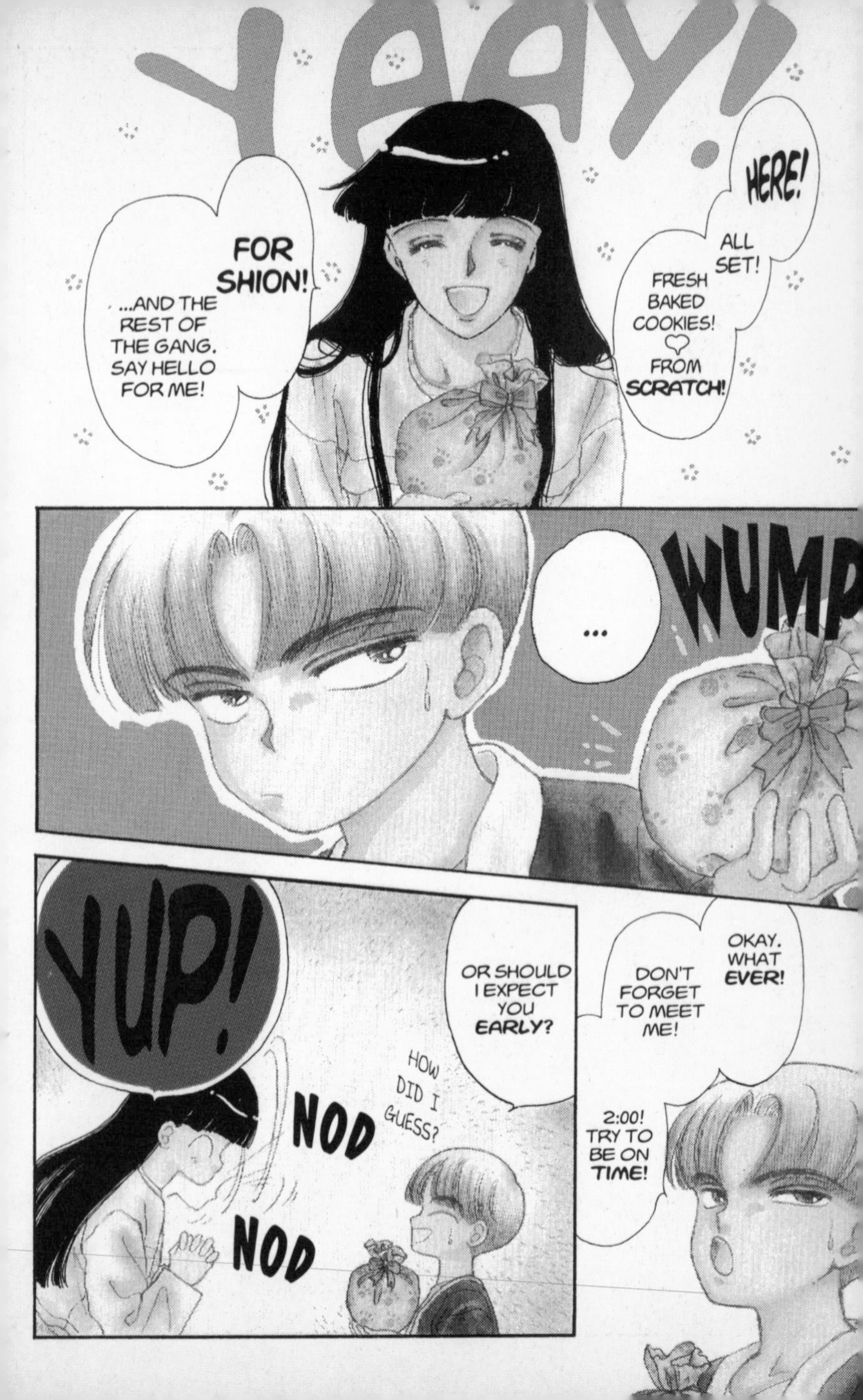
YAY!
HERE! ALL SET! FRESH BAKED COOKIES! FROM SCRATCH!
FOR SHION! ...AND THE REST OF THE GANG. SAY HELLO FOR ME!
WUMP
...
OKAY. WHATEVER!
DON'T FORGET TO MEET ME!
2:00! TRY TO BE ON TIME!
OR SHOULD I EXPECT YOU EARLY?
HOW DID I GUESS?
YUP!
NOD
NOD

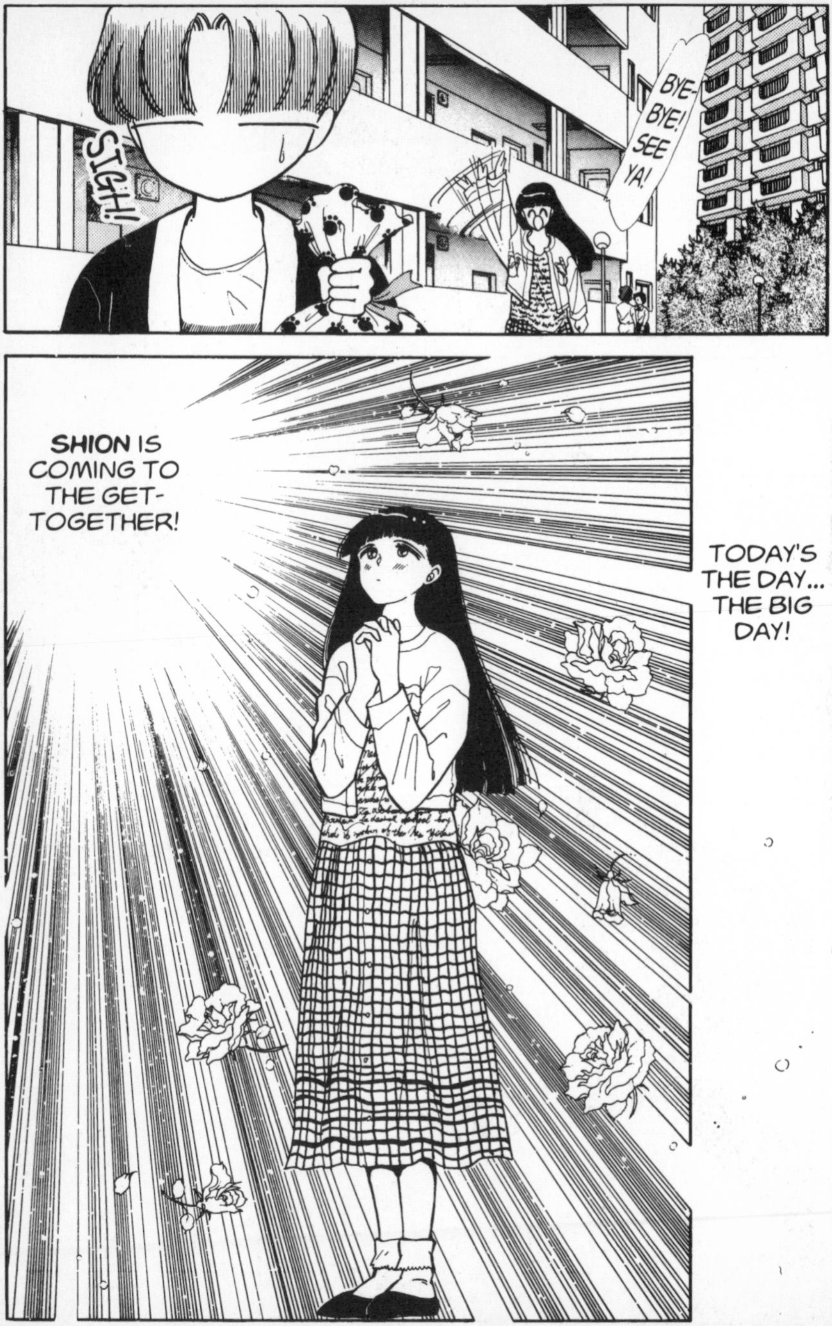
BYE-BYE! SEE YA!
SIGH!
TODAY'S THE DAY... THE BIG DAY!
SHION IS COMING TO THE GET-TOGETHER!

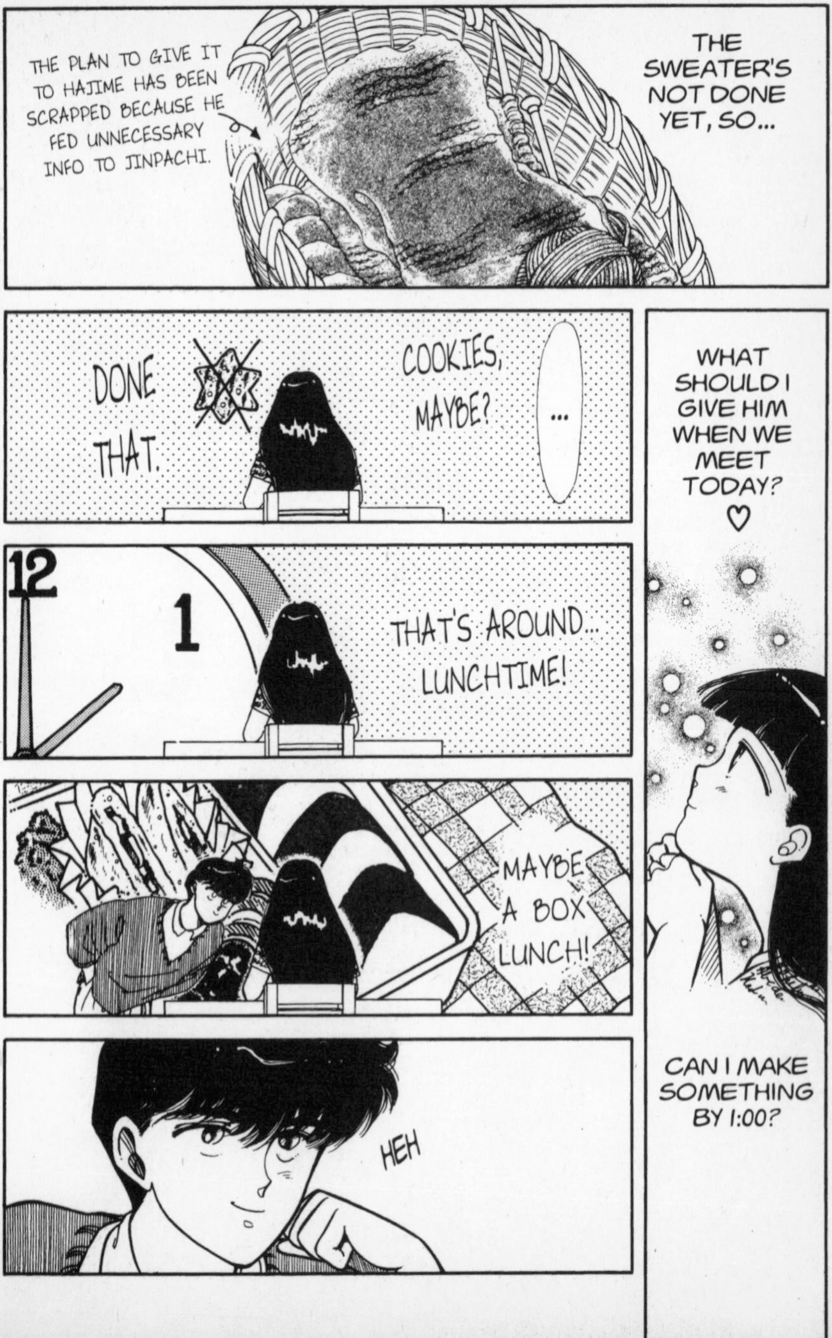
THE SWEATER'S NOT DONE YET, SO...
THE PLAN TO GIVE IT TO HAJIME HAS BEEN SCRAPPED BECAUSE HE FED UNNECESSARY INFO TO JINPACHI.
WHAT SHOULD I GIVE HIM WHEN WE MEET TODAY? ♡
CAN I MAKE SOMETHING BY 1:00?
...
COOKIES, MAYBE?
DONE THAT.
12
1
THAT'S AROUND... LUNCHTIME!
MAYBE A BOX LUNCH!
HEH

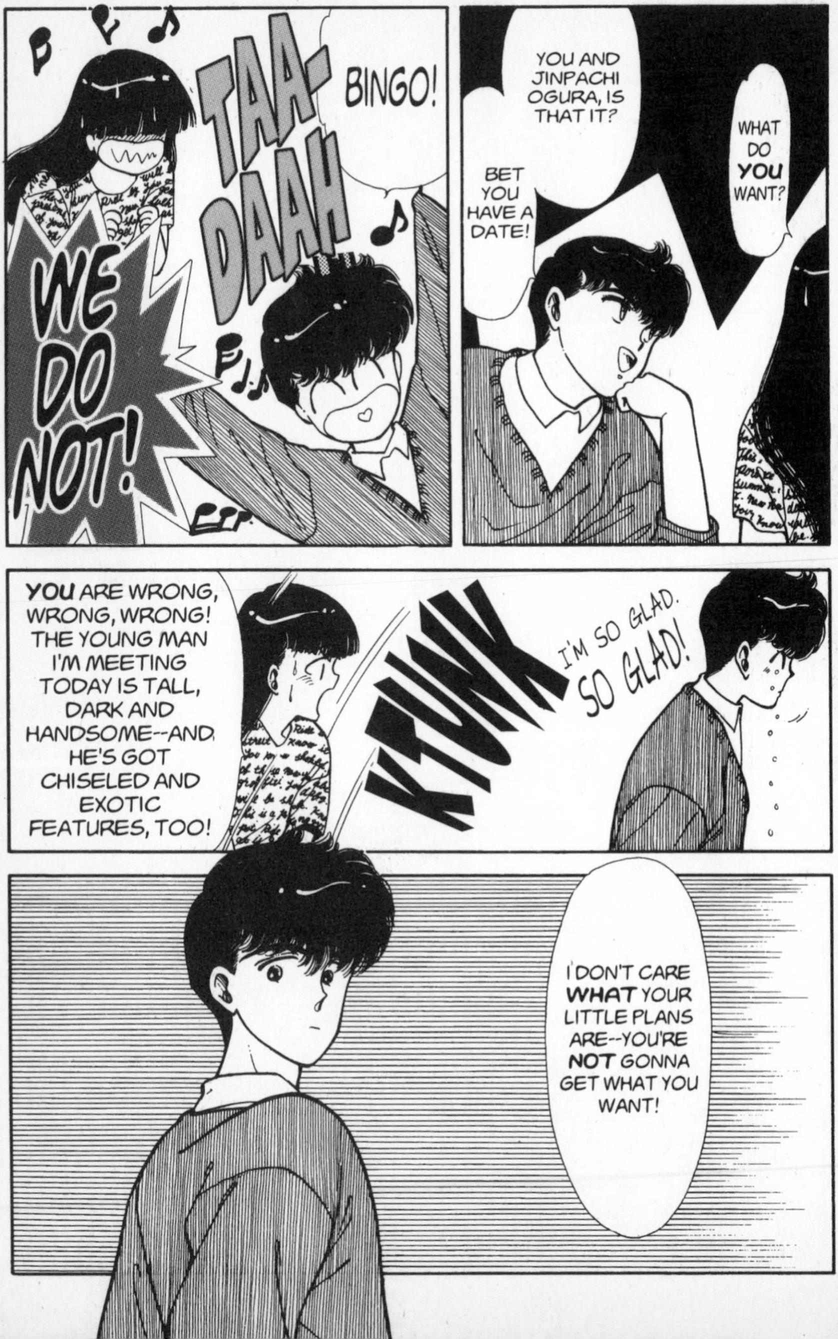
WHAT DO YOU WANT?
YOU AND JINPACHI OGURA, IS THAT IT?
BET YOU HAVE A DATE!
BINGO!
TAA-DAAH
WE DO NOT!
I'M SO GLAD. SO GLAD!
KTUNK
YOU ARE WRONG, WRONG, WRONG! THE YOUNG MAN I'M MEETING TODAY IS TALL, DARK AND HANDSOME--AND HE'S GOT CHISELED AND EXOTIC FEATURES, TOO!
I DON'T CARE WHAT YOUR LITTLE PLANS ARE--YOU'RE NOT GONNA GET WHAT YOU WANT!

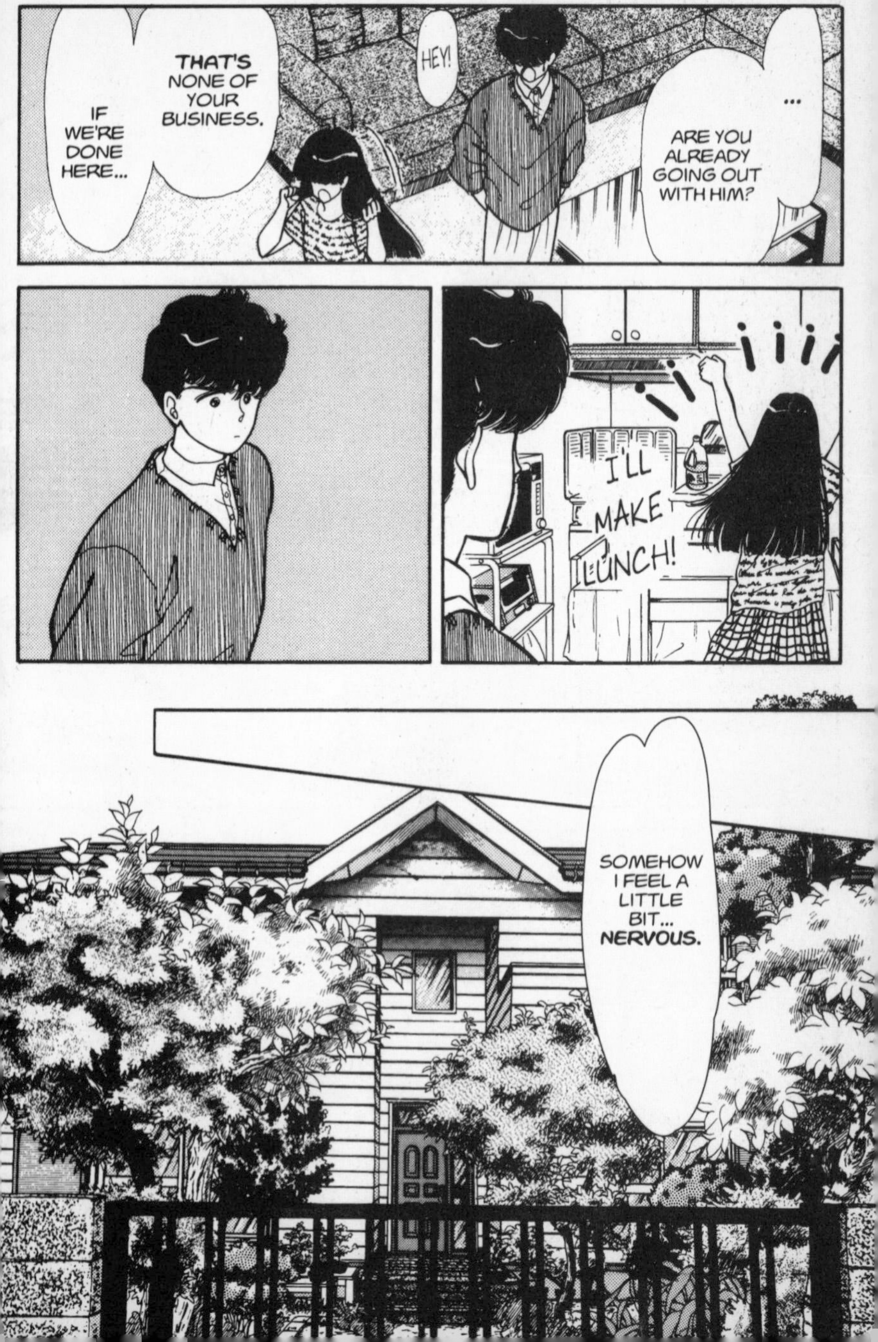
...
ARE YOU ALREADY GOING OUT WITH HIM?
HEY!
THAT'S NONE OF YOUR BUSINESS.
IF WE'RE DONE HERE...
I'LL MAKE LUNCH!
SOMEHOW I FEEL A LITTLE BIT... NERVOUS.

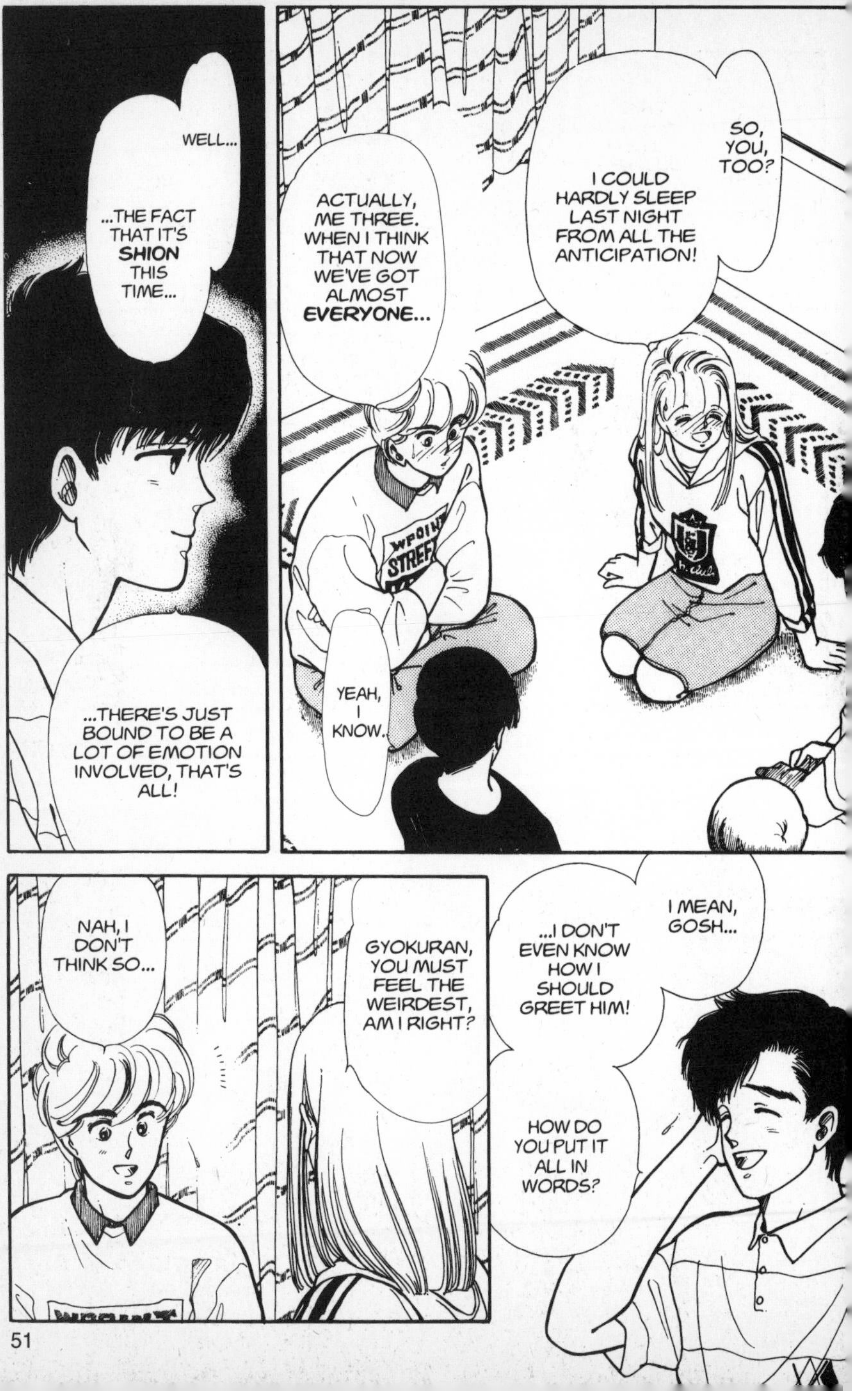
SO, YOU, TOO?
I COULD HARDLY SLEEP LAST NIGHT FROM ALL THE ANTICIPATION!
ACTUALLY, ME THREE. WHEN I THINK THAT NOW WE'VE GOT ALMOST **EVERYONE...**
YEAH, I KNOW.
WELL...
...THE FACT THAT IT'S **SHION** THIS TIME...
...THERE'S JUST BOUND TO BE A LOT OF EMOTION INVOLVED, THAT'S ALL!
I MEAN, GOSH...
...I DON'T EVEN KNOW HOW I SHOULD GREET HIM!
HOW DO YOU PUT IT ALL IN WORDS?
GYOKURAN, YOU MUST FEEL THE WEIRDEST, AM I RIGHT?
NAH, I DON'T THINK SO...

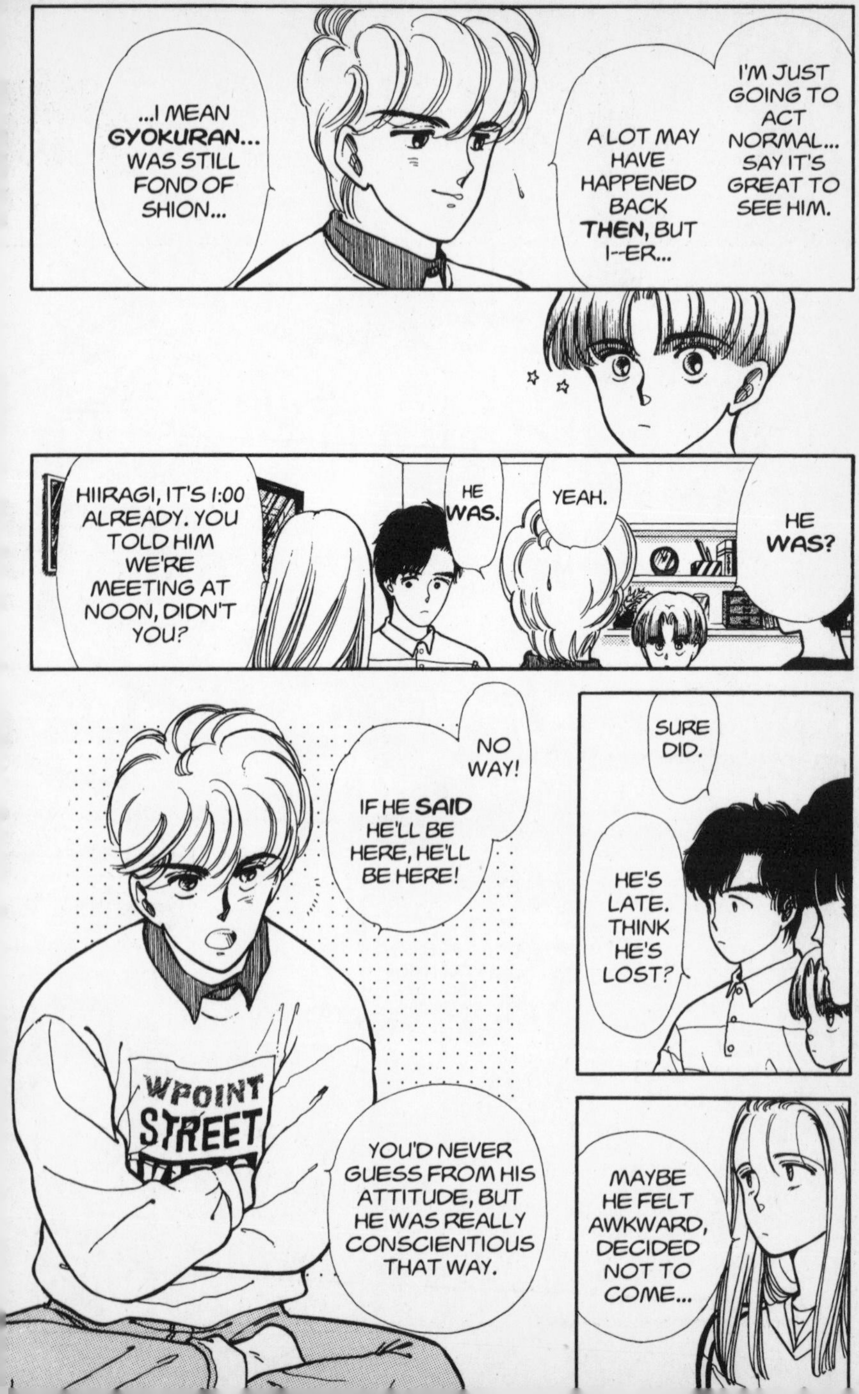
I'M JUST GOING TO ACT NORMAL... SAY IT'S GREAT TO SEE HIM.
A LOT MAY HAVE HAPPENED BACK **THEN**, BUT I--ER...
...I MEAN **GYOKURAN...** WAS STILL FOND OF SHION...
HE **WAS?**
YEAH.
HE **WAS.**
HIIRAGI, IT'S 1:00 ALREADY. YOU TOLD HIM WE'RE MEETING AT NOON, DIDN'T YOU?
SURE DID.
HE'S LATE. THINK HE'S LOST?
MAYBE HE FELT AWKWARD, DECIDED NOT TO COME...
NO WAY!
IF HE **SAID** HE'LL BE HERE, HE'LL BE HERE!
WPOINT STREET
YOU'D NEVER GUESS FROM HIS ATTITUDE, BUT HE WAS REALLY CONSCIENTIOUS THAT WAY.

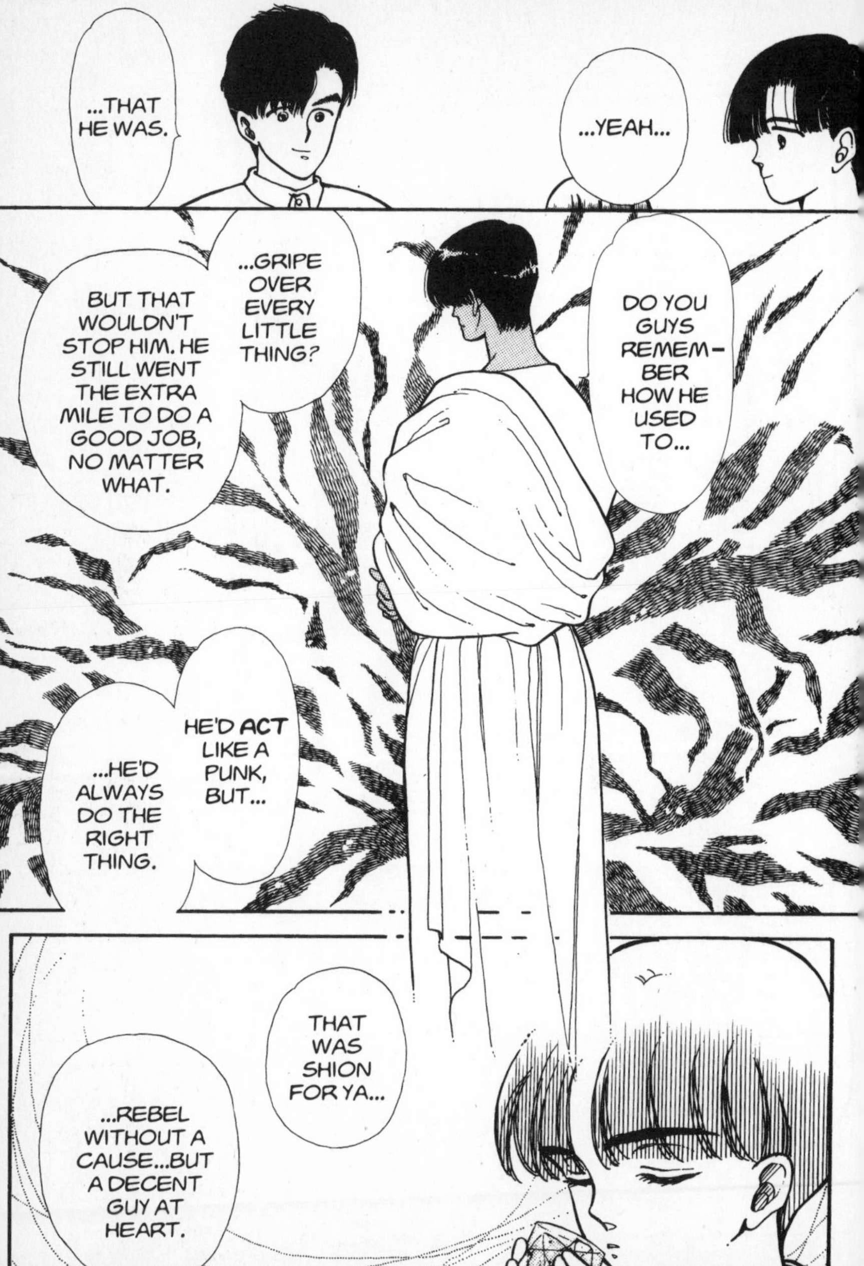
...YEAH...
...THAT HE WAS.
DO YOU GUYS REMEM-BER HOW HE USED TO...
...GRIPE OVER EVERY LITTLE THING?
BUT THAT WOULDN'T STOP HIM. HE STILL WENT THE EXTRA MILE TO DO A GOOD JOB, NO MATTER WHAT.
HE'D **ACT** LIKE A PUNK, BUT...
...HE'D ALWAYS DO THE RIGHT THING.
THAT WAS SHION FOR YA...
...REBEL WITHOUT A CAUSE...BUT A DECENT GUY AT HEART.

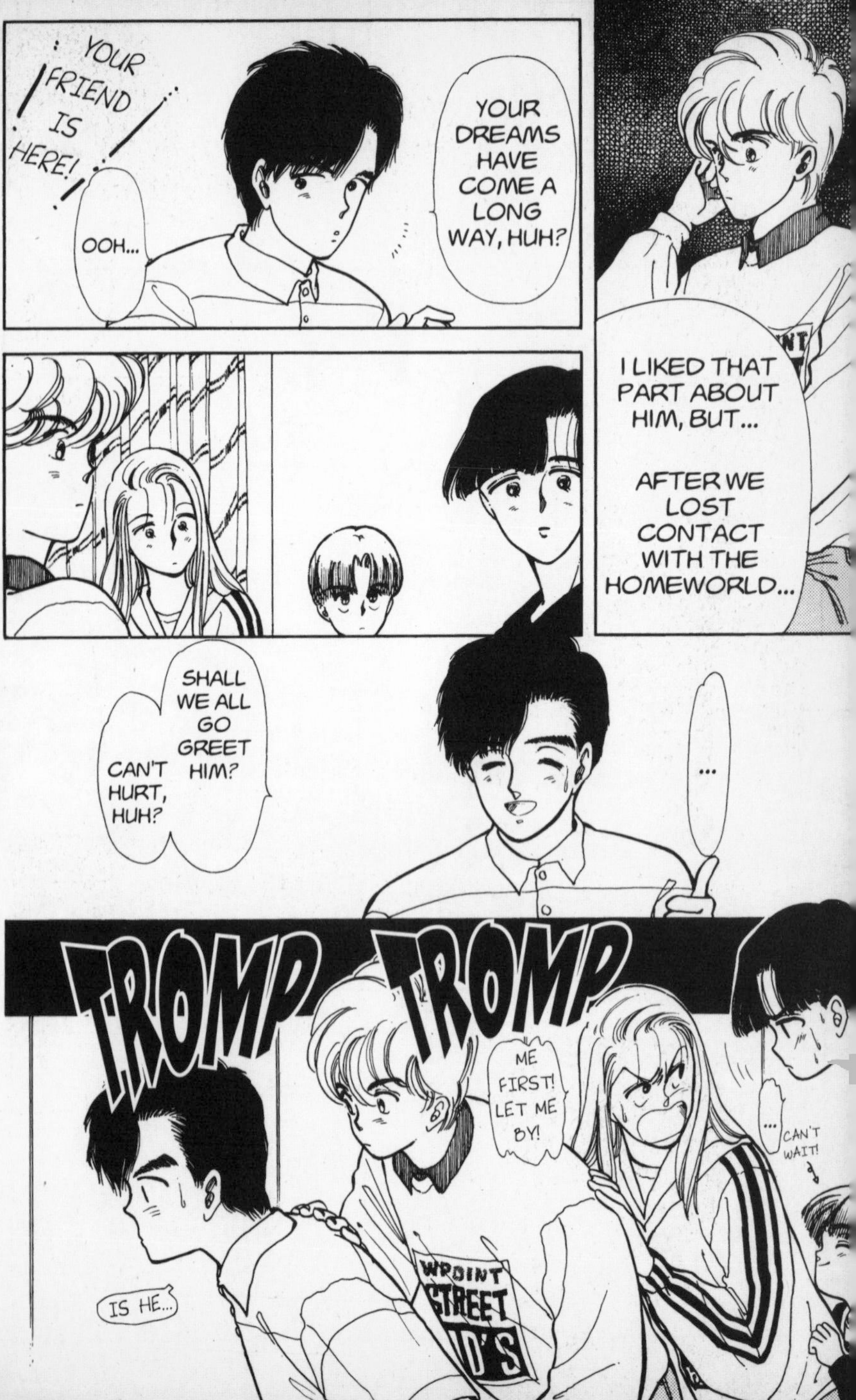
I LIKED THAT PART ABOUT HIM, BUT...
AFTER WE LOST CONTACT WITH THE HOMEWORLD...
YOUR DREAMS HAVE COME A LONG WAY, HUH?
YOUR FRIEND IS HERE!
OOH...
...
SHALL WE ALL GO GREET HIM?
CAN'T HURT, HUH?
TROMP
TROMP
... CAN'T WAIT!
ME FIRST! LET ME BY!
IS HE...

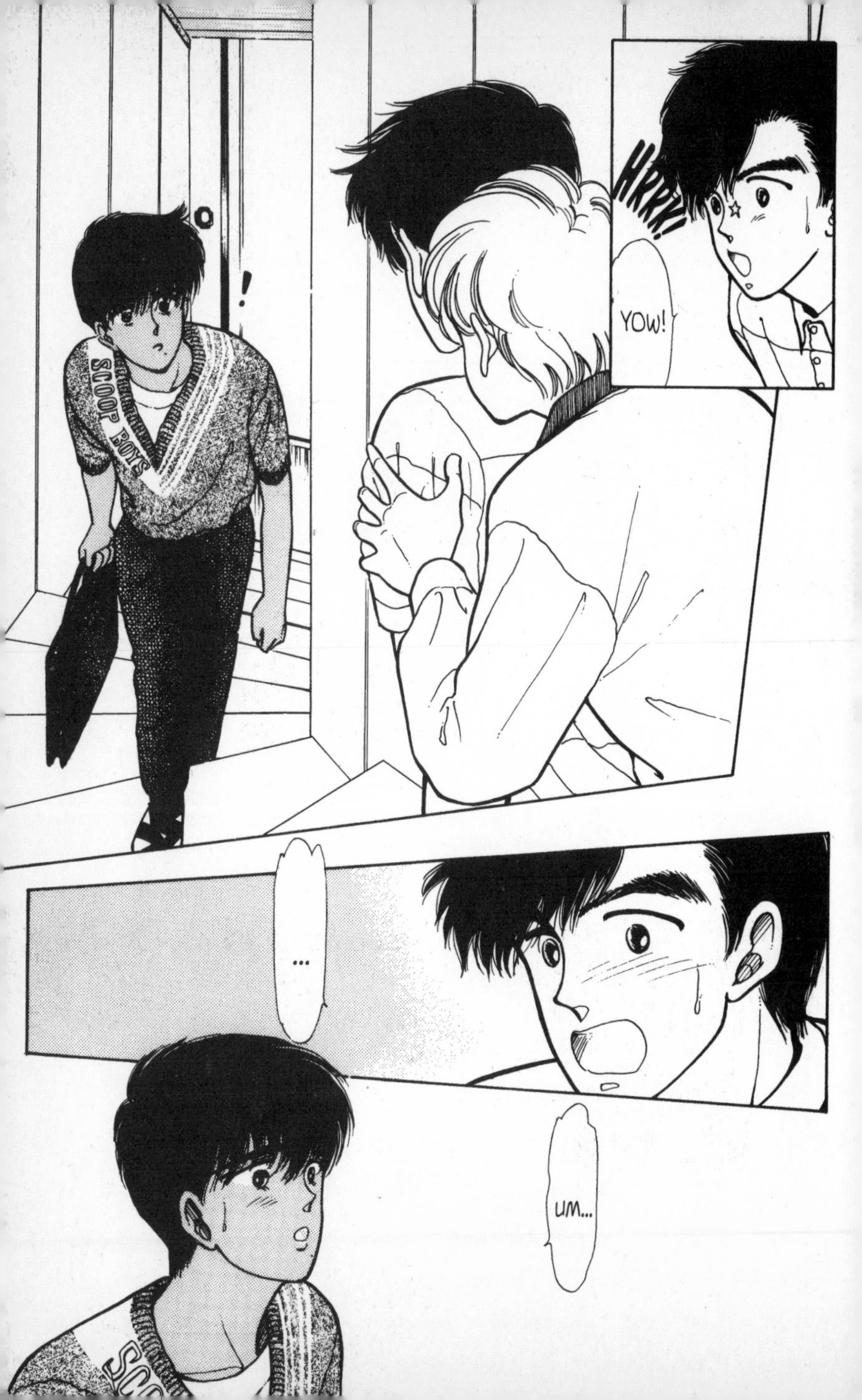
YOW!
...
UM...

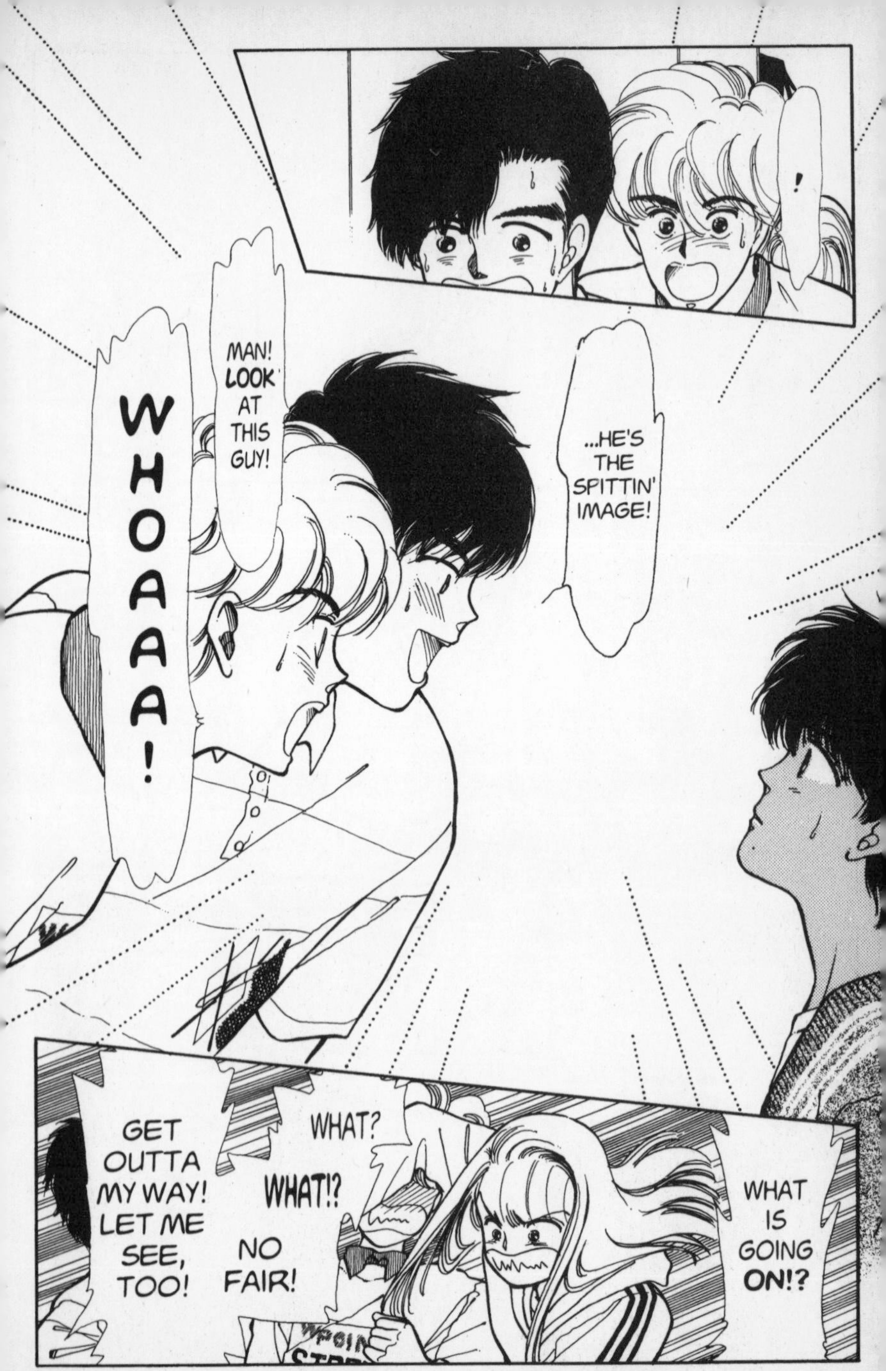
!
...HE'S THE SPITTIN' IMAGE!
MAN! LOOK AT THIS GUY!
WHOAAAA!
WHAT IS GOING ON!?
WHAT?
WHAT!?
NO FAIR!
GET OUTTA MY WAY! LET ME SEE, TOO!

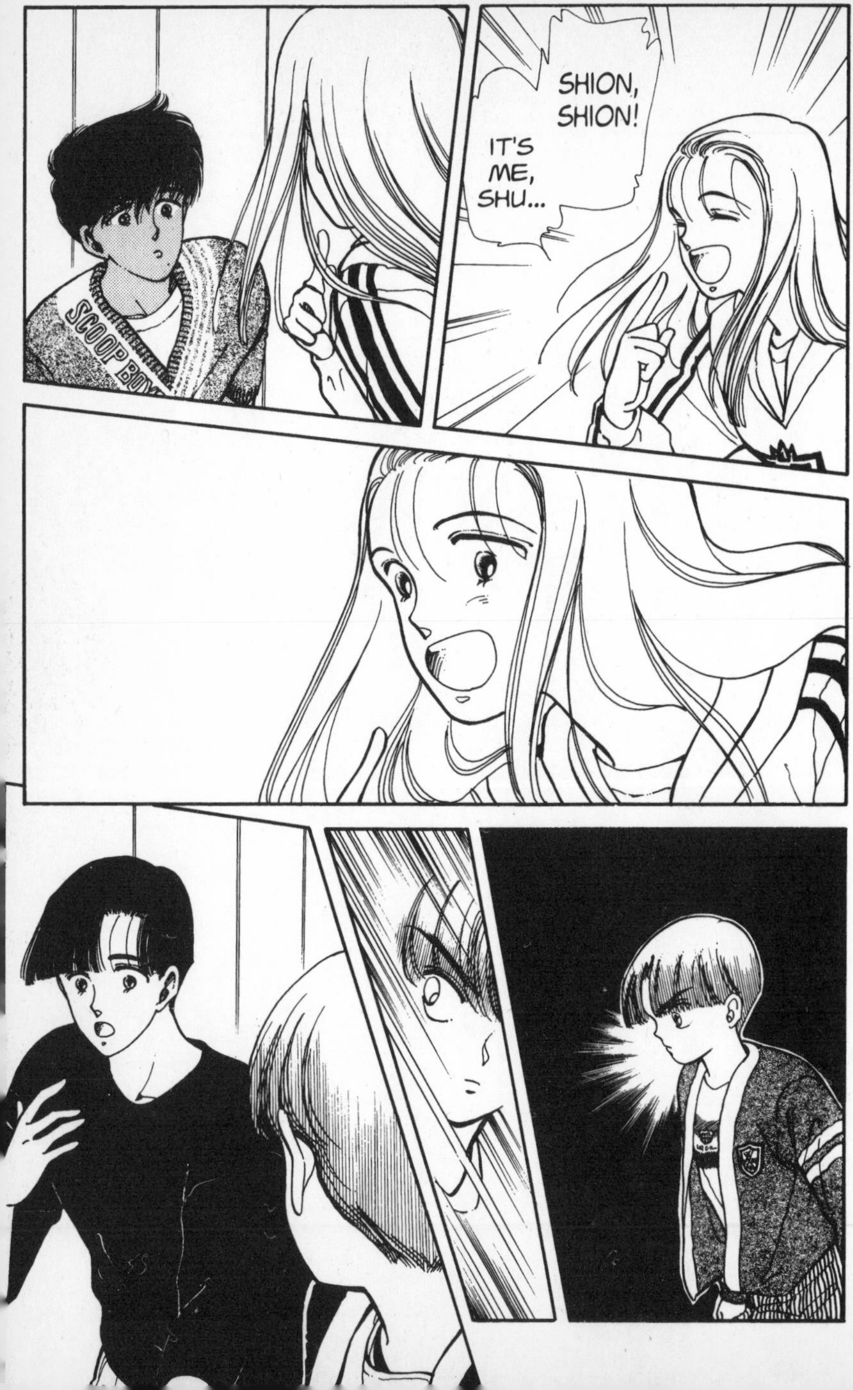
SHION, SHION!
IT'S ME, SHU...
SCOOP BOY

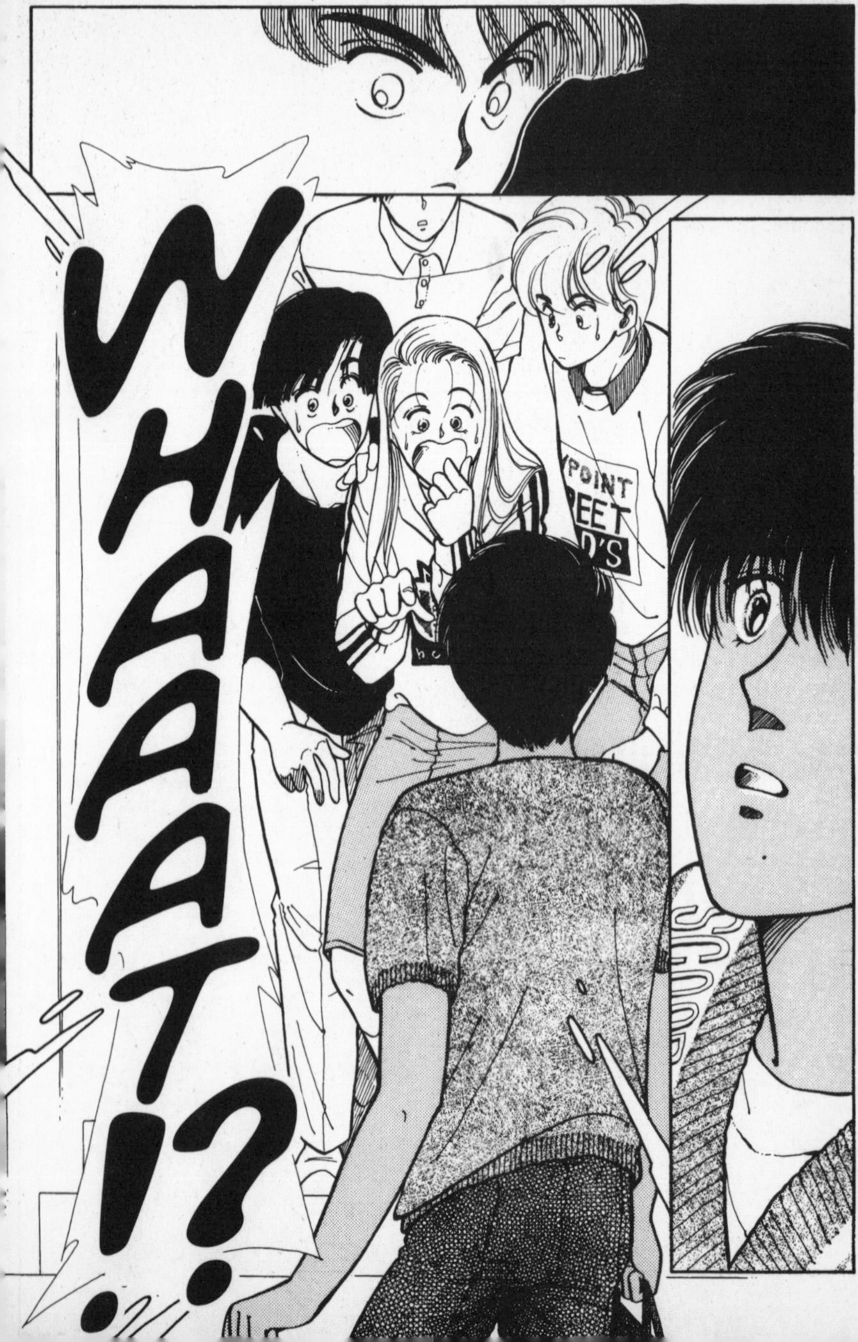
WHAAAT!?!

1/4 COLUMN NONSENSE

PART 2

As you're probably well aware, I recorded a toll-free telephone message to promote this album. Oh boy. I'm actually really shy, if I say so myself. It's true!

It was so embarrassing to go, "Hello! Thanks for calling!" like some DJ or radio personality.

I did two of them, and my friends thought I sounded angry in the first one. Ha, ha, ha, ha! I'm sorry I have such an ugly voice.

They printed so many pictures of me in the album insert...I'm sorry if any kind souls out there were disappointed that I didn't look like they imagined.

But if anyone was induced to vomiting, I'd like to give 'em a wallop!

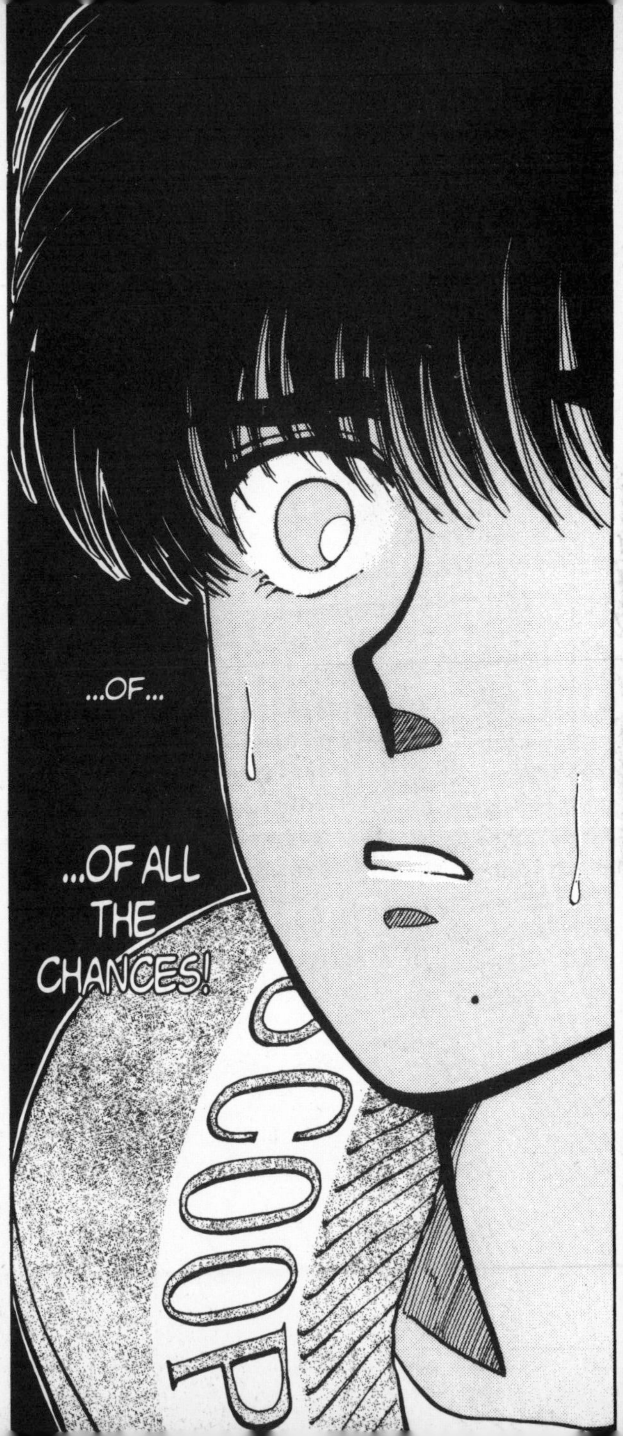
...OF...
...OF ALL THE CHANCES!

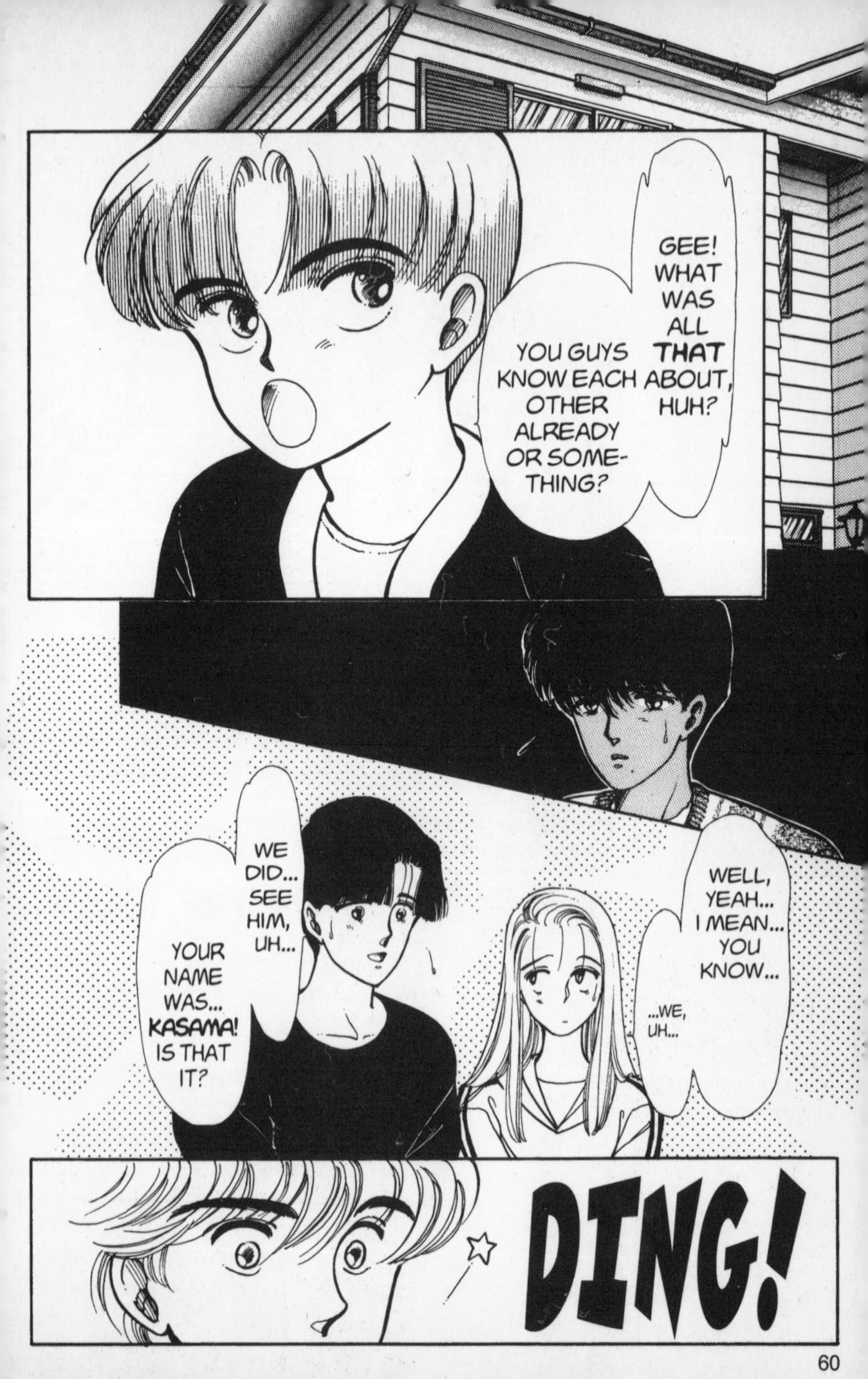
GEE! WHAT WAS ALL THAT ABOUT, HUH?
YOU GUYS KNOW EACH OTHER ALREADY OR SOME-THING?
WELL, YEAH... I MEAN... YOU KNOW...
...WE, UH...
WE DID... SEE HIM, UH...
YOUR NAME WAS... KASAMA! IS THAT IT?
DING!

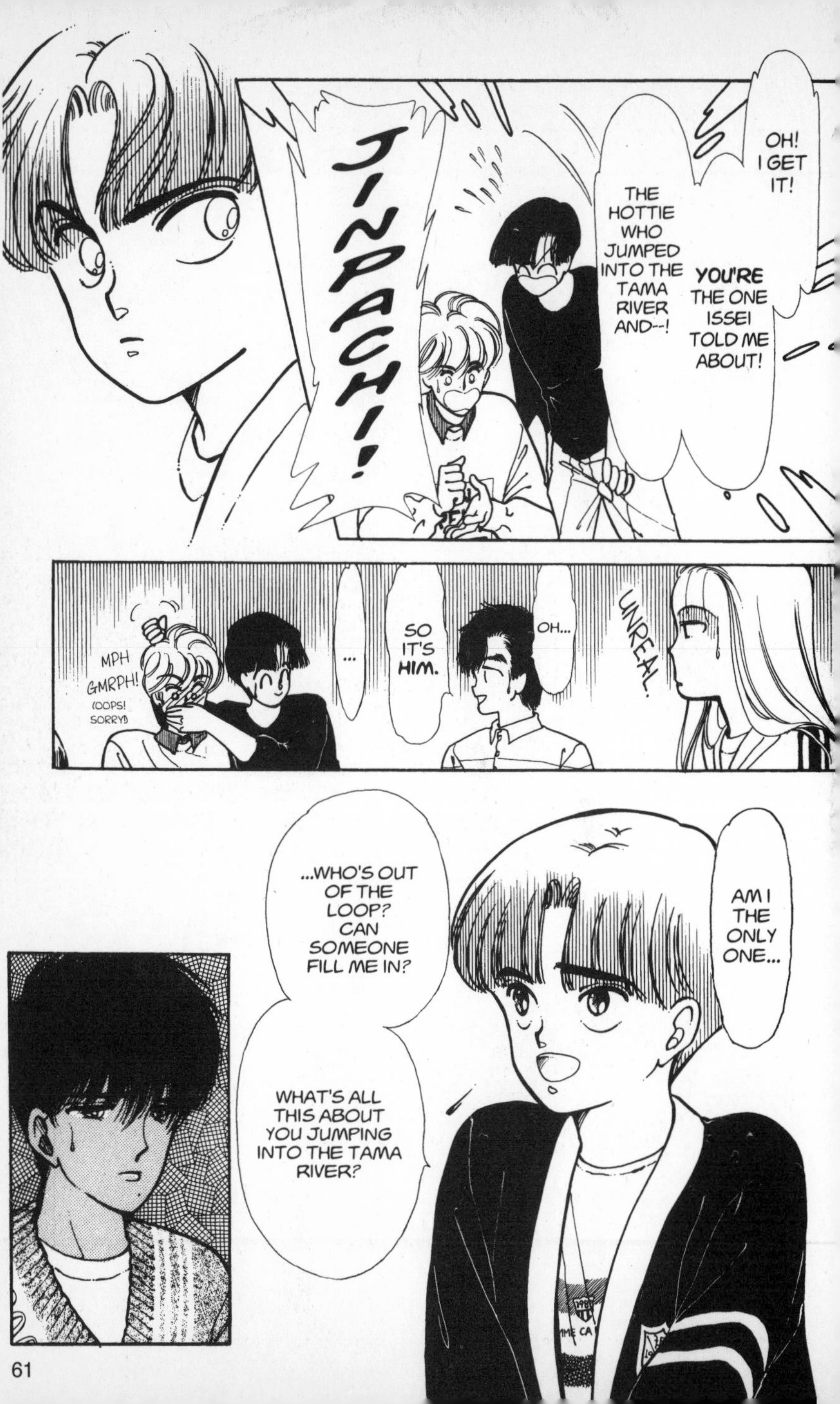
OH! I GET IT!
YOU'RE THE ONE ISSEI TOLD ME ABOUT!
THE HOTTIE WHO JUMPED INTO THE TAMA RIVER AND--!
JINPACHI!
UNREAL.
OH...
SO IT'S HIM.
...
MPH GMRPH!
(OOPS! SORRY)
AM I THE ONLY ONE...
...WHO'S OUT OF THE LOOP? CAN SOMEONE FILL ME IN?
WHAT'S ALL THIS ABOUT YOU JUMPING INTO THE TAMA RIVER?

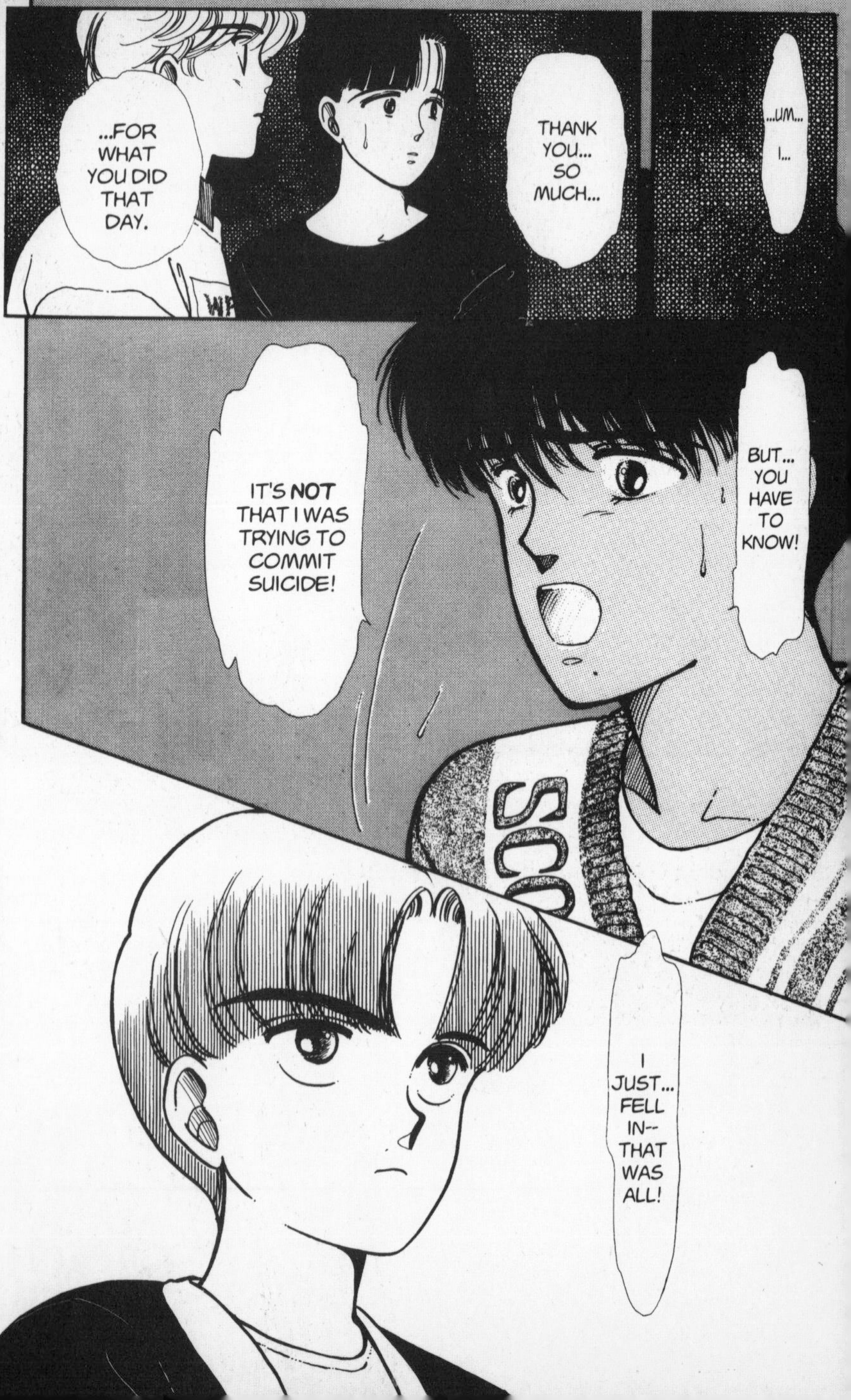
...UM... I...
THANK YOU... SO MUCH...
...FOR WHAT YOU DID THAT DAY.
BUT... YOU HAVE TO KNOW!
IT'S **NOT** THAT I WAS TRYING TO COMMIT SUICIDE!
I JUST... FELL IN-- THAT WAS ALL!

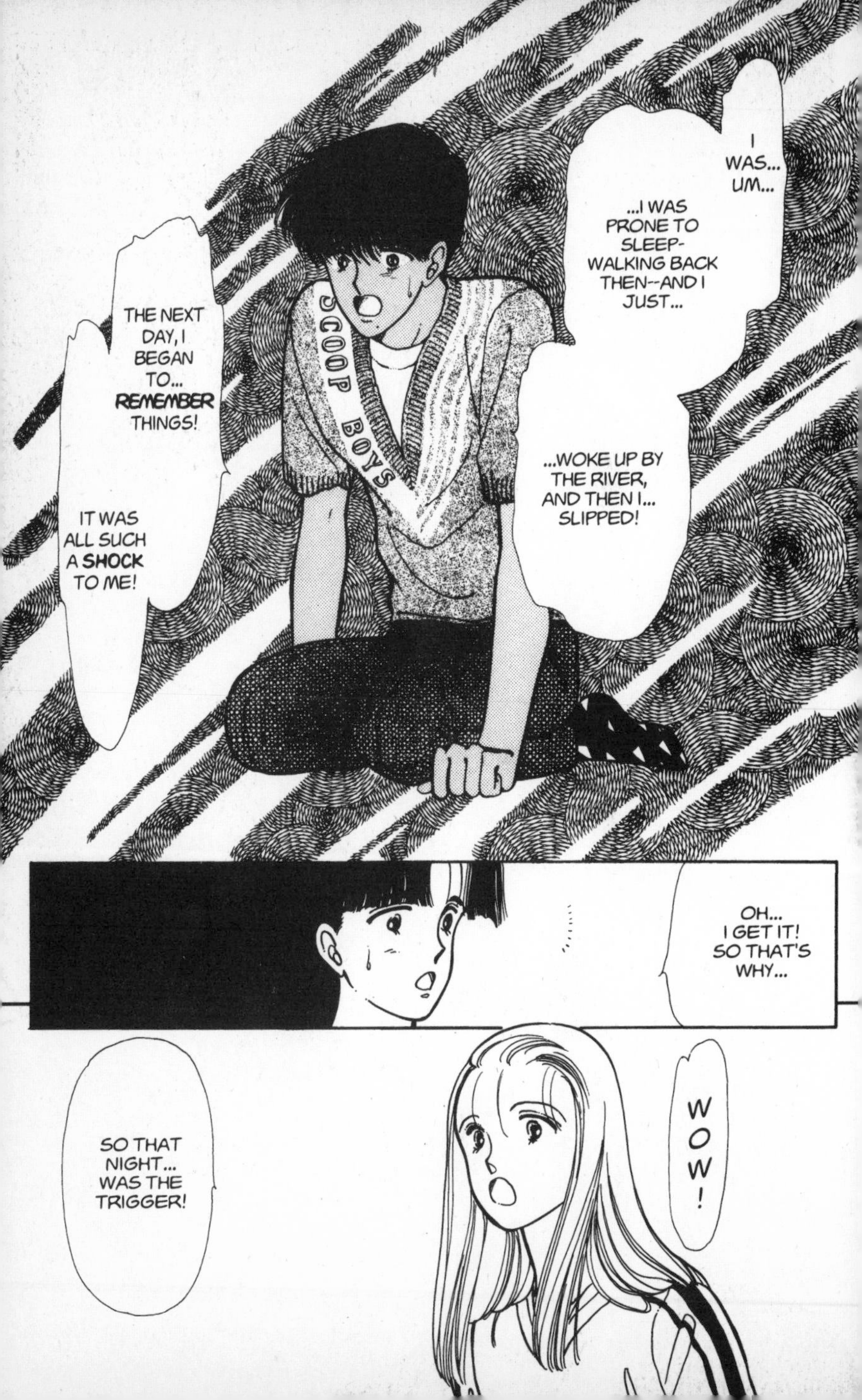
I WAS... UM...
...I WAS PRONE TO SLEEP-WALKING BACK THEN--AND I JUST...
...WOKE UP BY THE RIVER, AND THEN I... SLIPPED!
SCOOP BOYS
THE NEXT DAY, I BEGAN TO... REMEMBER THINGS!
IT WAS ALL SUCH A SHOCK TO ME!
OH... I GET IT! SO THAT'S WHY...
WOW!
SO THAT NIGHT... WAS THE TRIGGER!

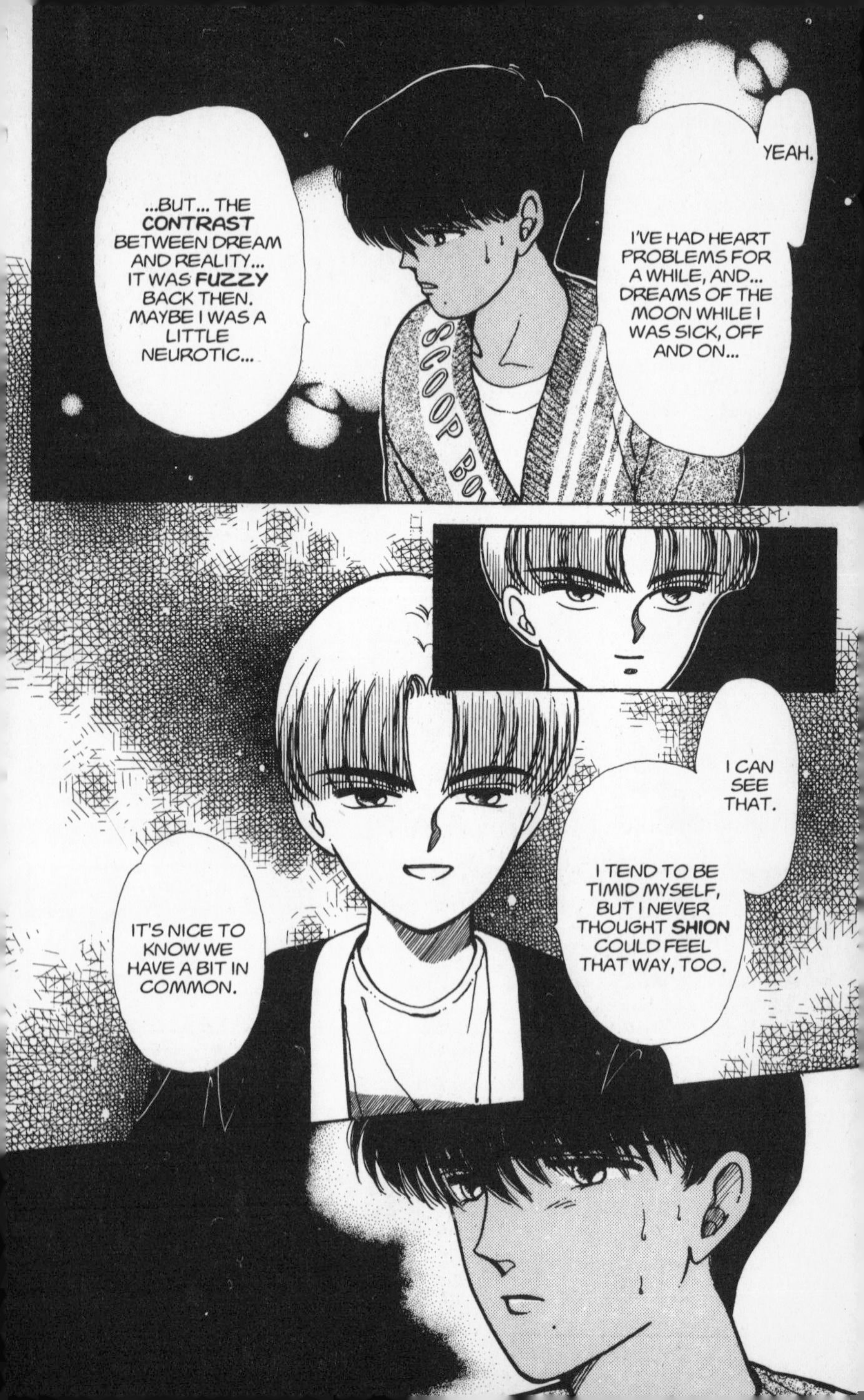
YEAH.
I'VE HAD HEART PROBLEMS FOR A WHILE, AND... DREAMS OF THE MOON WHILE I WAS SICK, OFF AND ON...
...BUT... THE **CONTRAST** BETWEEN DREAM AND REALITY... IT WAS **FUZZY** BACK THEN. MAYBE I WAS A LITTLE NEUROTIC...
I CAN SEE THAT.
I TEND TO BE TIMID MYSELF, BUT I NEVER THOUGHT **SHION** COULD FEEL THAT WAY, TOO.
IT'S NICE TO KNOW WE HAVE A BIT IN COMMON.

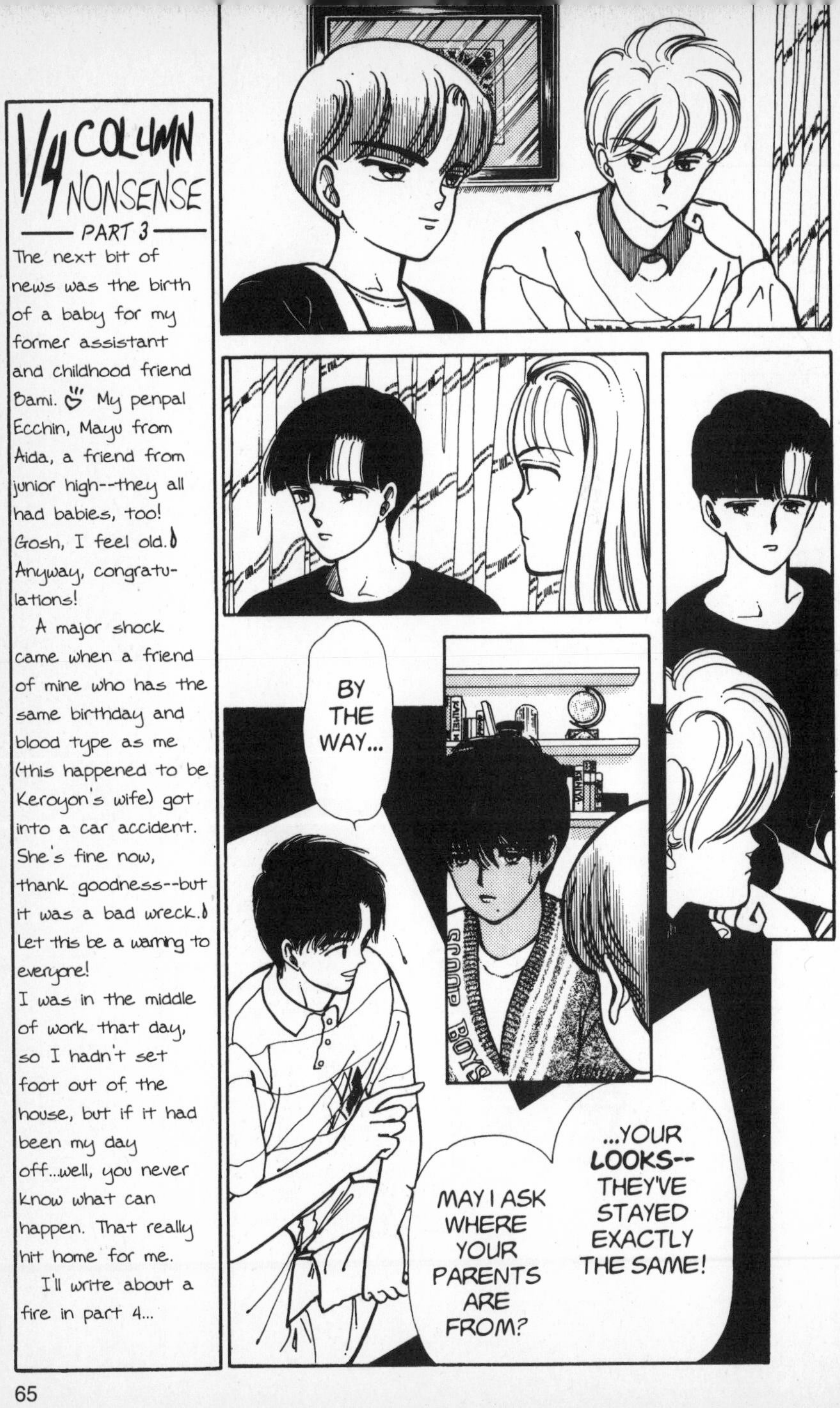
BY THE WAY...
...YOUR LOOKS--THEY'VE STAYED EXACTLY THE SAME!
MAY I ASK WHERE YOUR PARENTS ARE FROM?

1/4 COLUMN NONSENSE

PART 3

The next bit of news was the birth of a baby for my former assistant and childhood friend Bami. ♡ My penpal Ecchin, Mayu from Aida, a friend from junior high--they all had babies, too! Gosh, I feel old. Anyway, congratulations!

A major shock came when a friend of mine who has the same birthday and blood type as me (this happened to be Keroyon's wife) got into a car accident. She's fine now, thank goodness--but it was a bad wreck. Let this be a warning to everyone! I was in the middle of work that day, so I hadn't set foot out of the house, but if it had been my day off...well, you never know what can happen. That really hit home for me.

I'll write about a fire in part 4...

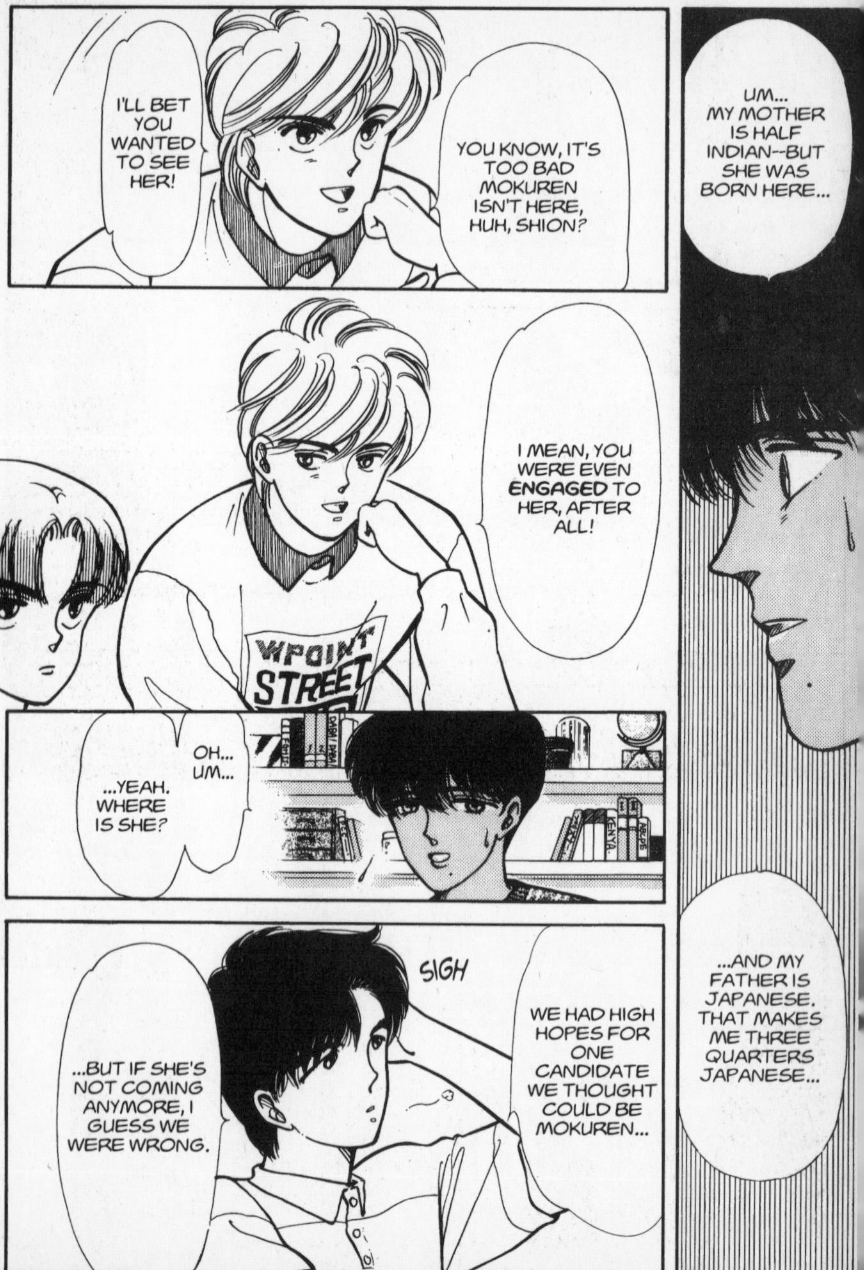
UM... MY MOTHER IS HALF INDIAN--BUT SHE WAS BORN HERE...
...AND MY FATHER IS JAPANESE. THAT MAKES ME THREE QUARTERS JAPANESE...
YOU KNOW, IT'S TOO BAD MOKUREN ISN'T HERE, HUH, SHION?
I'LL BET YOU WANTED TO SEE HER!
I MEAN, YOU WERE EVEN **ENGAGED** TO HER, AFTER ALL!
OH... UM...
...YEAH. WHERE IS SHE?
SIGH
WE HAD HIGH HOPES FOR ONE CANDIDATE WE THOUGHT COULD BE MOKUREN...
...BUT IF SHE'S NOT COMING ANYMORE, I GUESS WE WERE WRONG.

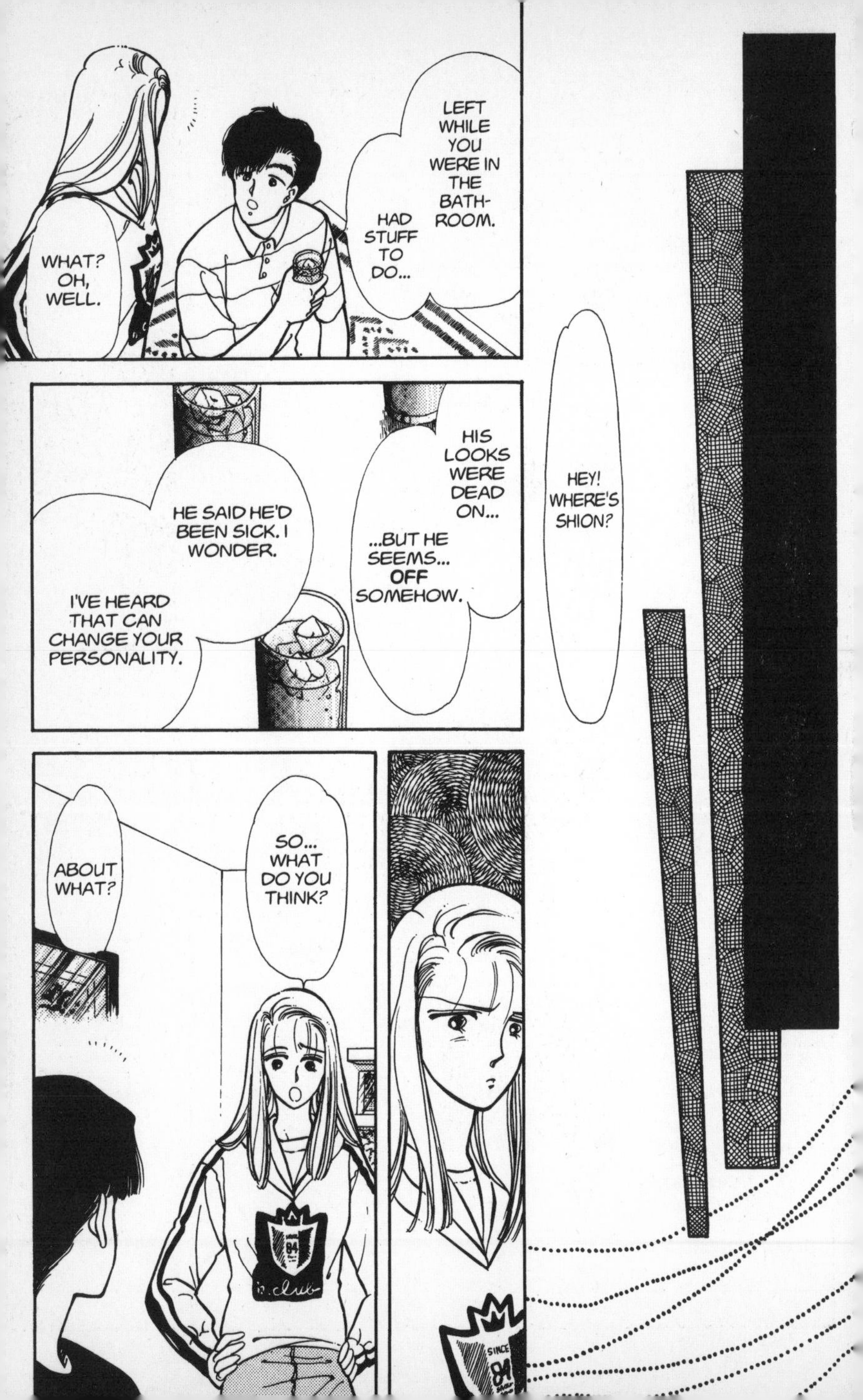
HEY! WHERE'S SHION?
LEFT WHILE YOU WERE IN THE BATH-ROOM.
HAD STUFF TO DO...
WHAT? OH, WELL.
HIS LOOKS WERE DEAD ON...
...BUT HE SEEMS... **OFF** SOMEHOW.
HE SAID HE'D BEEN SICK. I WONDER.
I'VE HEARD THAT CAN CHANGE YOUR PERSONALITY.
SO... WHAT DO YOU THINK?
ABOUT WHAT?

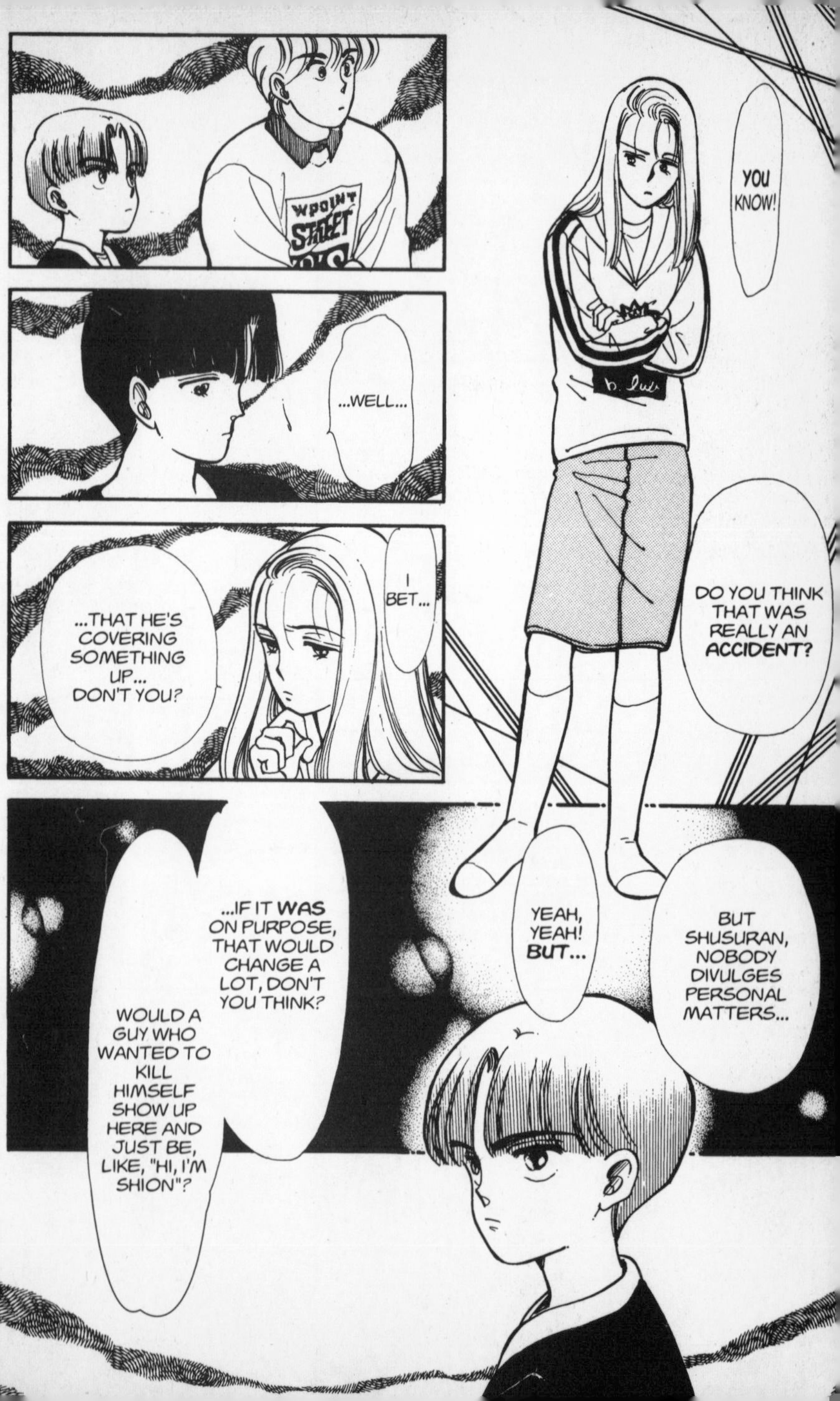
YOU KNOW!
DO YOU THINK THAT WAS REALLY AN ACCIDENT?
...WELL...
I BET...
...THAT HE'S COVERING SOMETHING UP... DON'T YOU?
BUT SHUSURAN, NOBODY DIVULGES PERSONAL MATTERS...
YEAH, YEAH! BUT...
...IF IT WAS ON PURPOSE, THAT WOULD CHANGE A LOT, DON'T YOU THINK?
WOULD A GUY WHO WANTED TO KILL HIMSELF SHOW UP HERE AND JUST BE, LIKE, "HI, I'M SHION"?

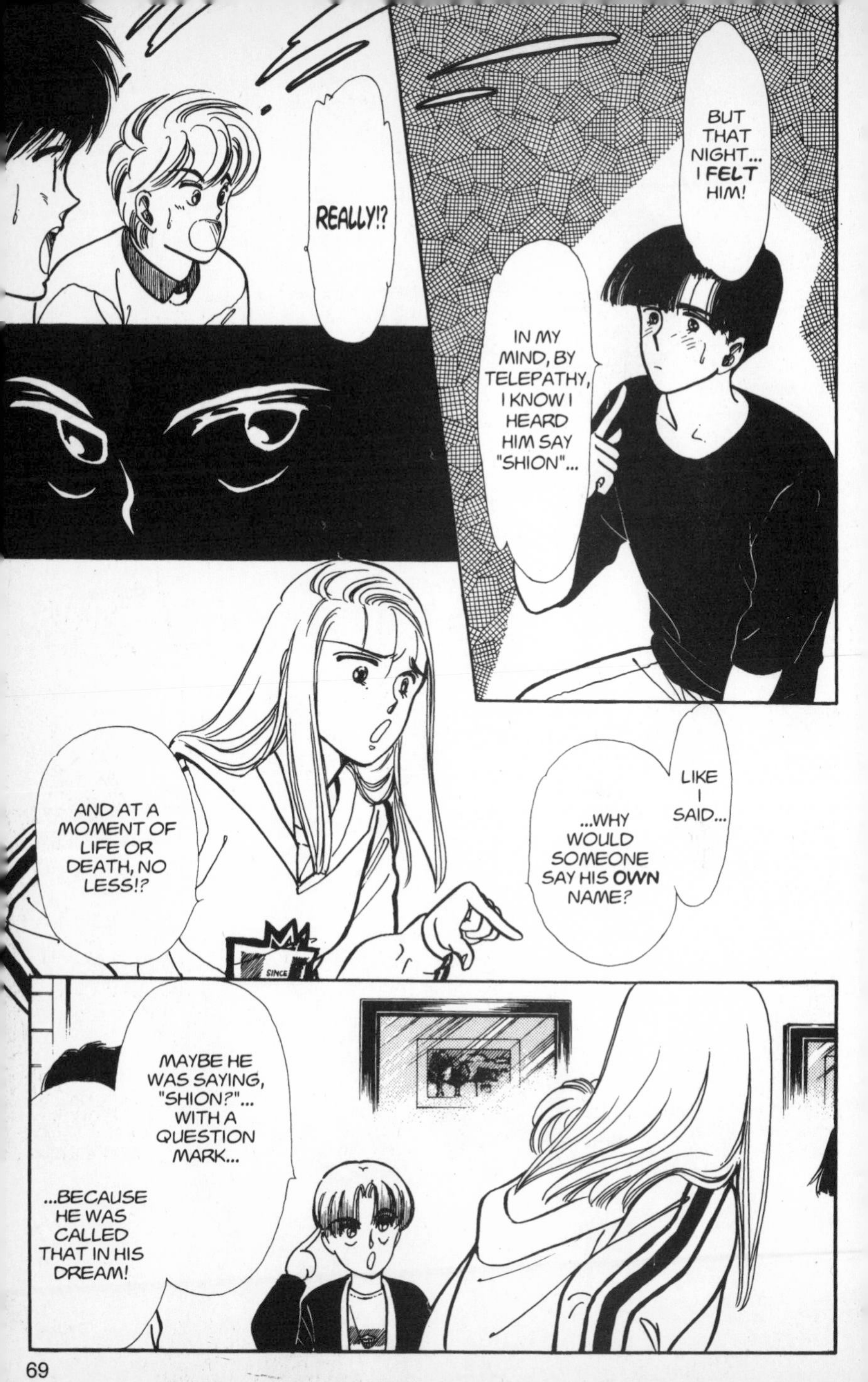
BUT THAT NIGHT... I **FELT** HIM!
IN MY MIND, BY TELEPATHY, I KNOW I HEARD HIM SAY "SHION"...
REALLY!?
LIKE I SAID...
...WHY WOULD SOMEONE SAY HIS **OWN** NAME?
AND AT A MOMENT OF LIFE OR DEATH, NO LESS!?
SINCE
MAYBE HE WAS SAYING, "SHION?"... WITH A QUESTION MARK...
...BECAUSE HE WAS CALLED THAT IN HIS DREAM!

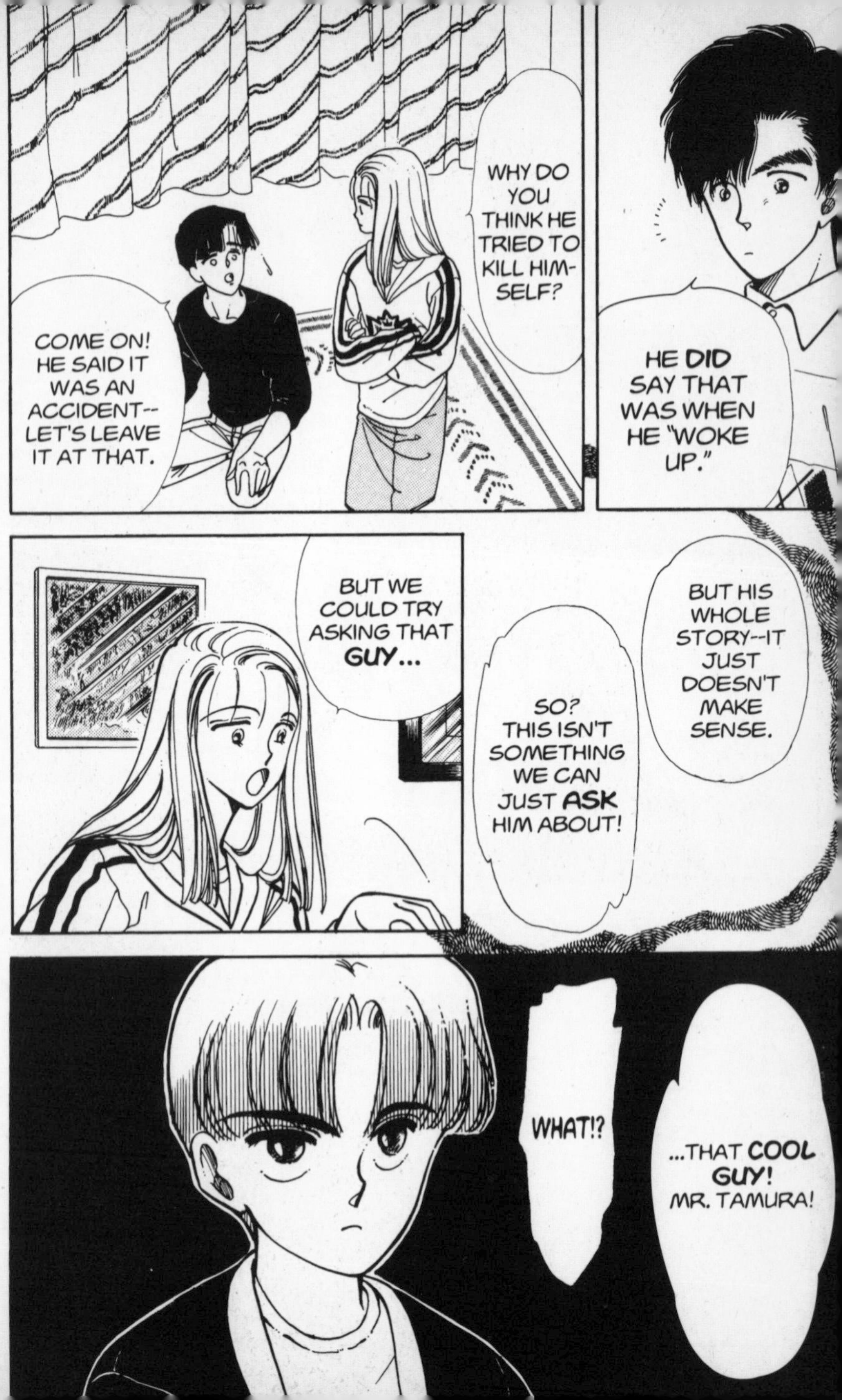
HE DID SAY THAT WAS WHEN HE "WOKE UP."
WHY DO YOU THINK HE TRIED TO KILL HIM-SELF?
COME ON! HE SAID IT WAS AN ACCIDENT-- LET'S LEAVE IT AT THAT.
BUT HIS WHOLE STORY--IT JUST DOESN'T MAKE SENSE.
SO? THIS ISN'T SOMETHING WE CAN JUST ASK HIM ABOUT!
BUT WE COULD TRY ASKING THAT GUY...
...THAT COOL GUY! MR. TAMURA!
WHAT!?

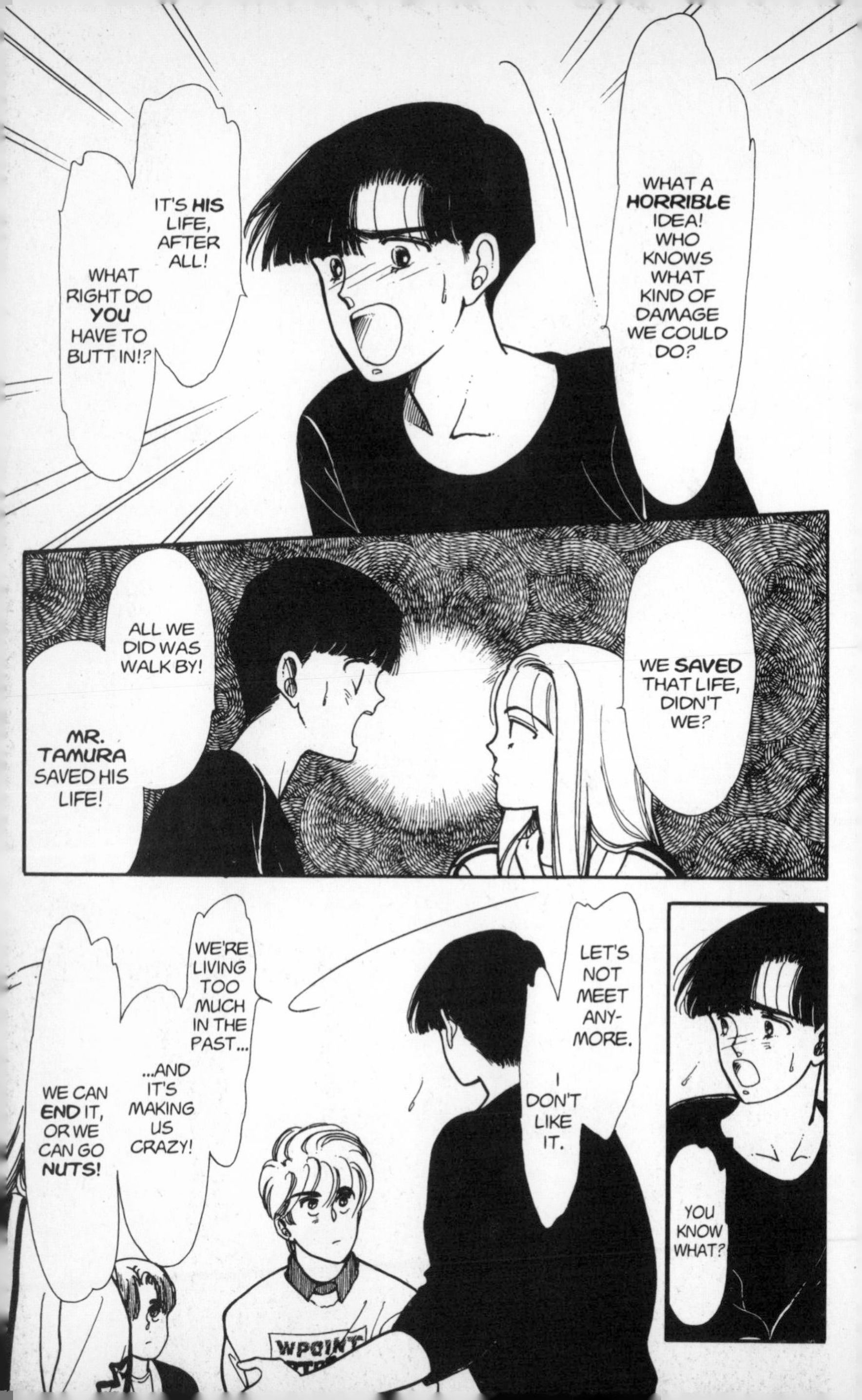
WHAT A HORRIBLE IDEA! WHO KNOWS WHAT KIND OF DAMAGE WE COULD DO?
IT'S HIS LIFE, AFTER ALL!
WHAT RIGHT DO YOU HAVE TO BUTT IN!?
WE SAVED THAT LIFE, DIDN'T WE?
ALL WE DID WAS WALK BY!
MR. TAMURA SAVED HIS LIFE!
YOU KNOW WHAT?
LET'S NOT MEET ANY-MORE.
I DON'T LIKE IT.
WE'RE LIVING TOO MUCH IN THE PAST...
...AND IT'S MAKING US CRAZY!
WE CAN END IT, OR WE CAN GO NUTS!

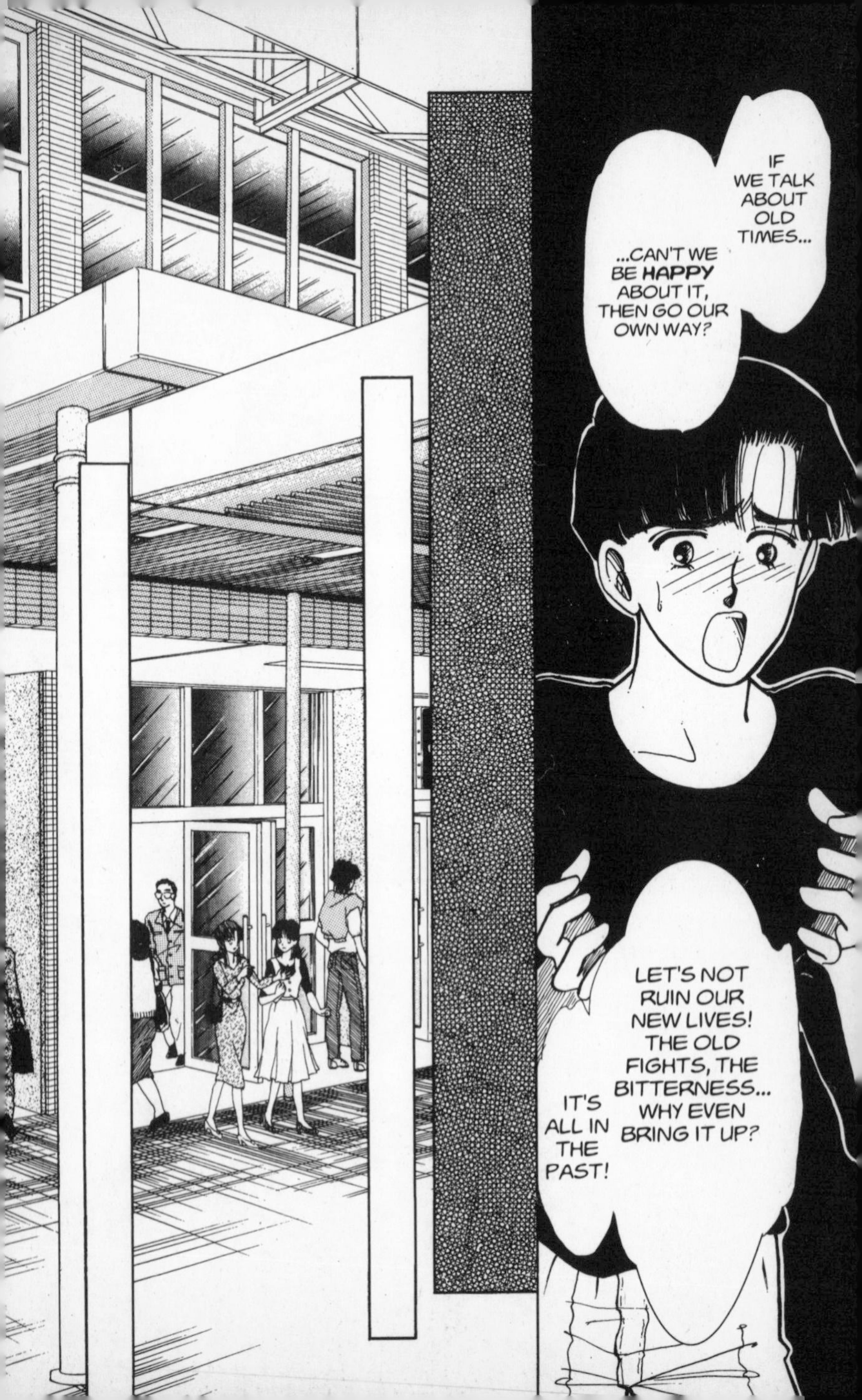
IF WE TALK ABOUT OLD TIMES...
...CAN'T WE BE **HAPPY** ABOUT IT, THEN GO OUR OWN WAY?
LET'S NOT RUIN OUR NEW LIVES! THE OLD FIGHTS, THE BITTERNESS... WHY EVEN BRING IT UP?
IT'S ALL IN THE PAST!

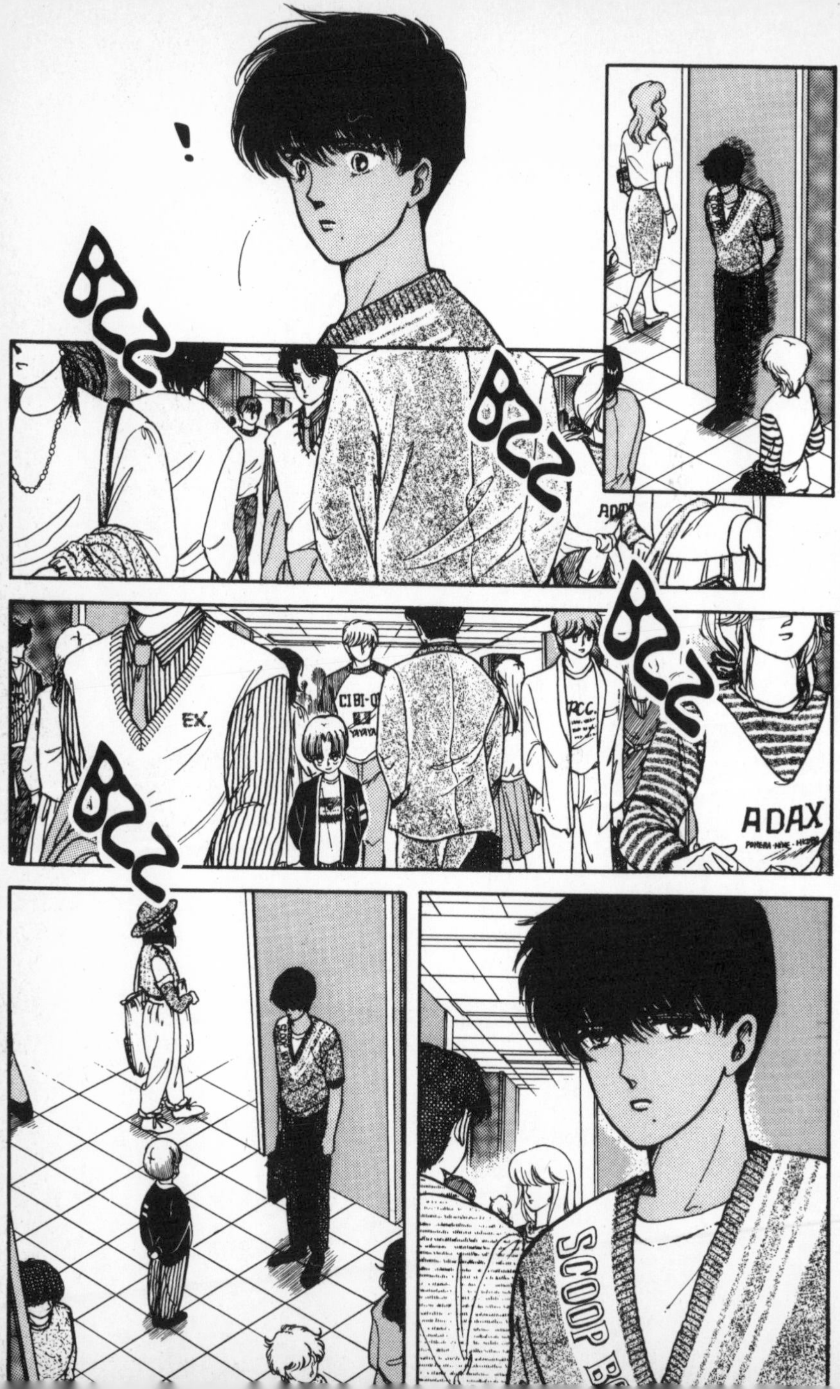
!
BZZ
BZZ
ADAX
BZZ
ADAX
EX.
BZZ
SCOOP B

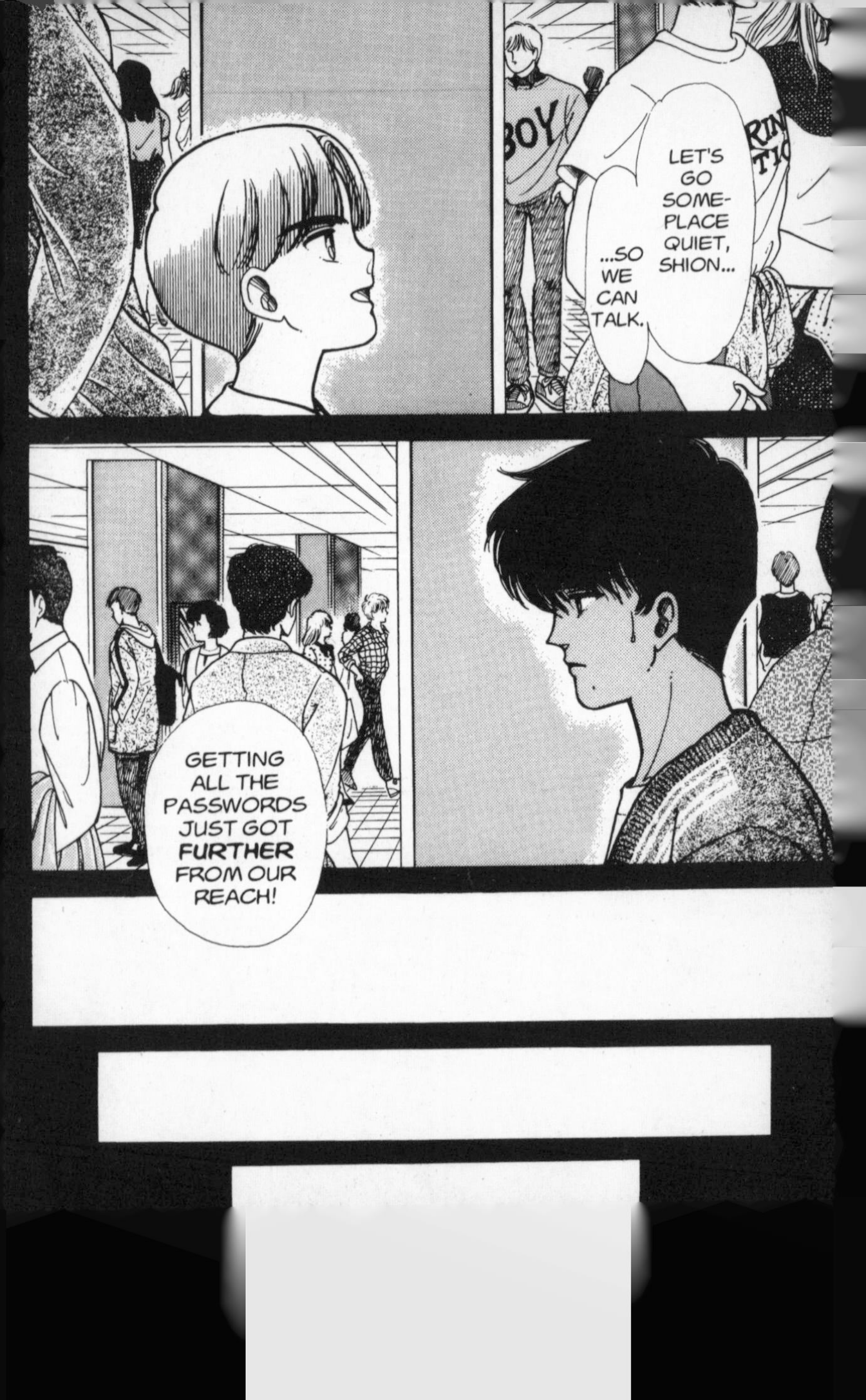
LET'S GO SOME-PLACE QUIET, SHION...
...SO WE CAN TALK.
GETTING ALL THE PASSWORDS JUST GOT **FURTHER** FROM OUR REACH!

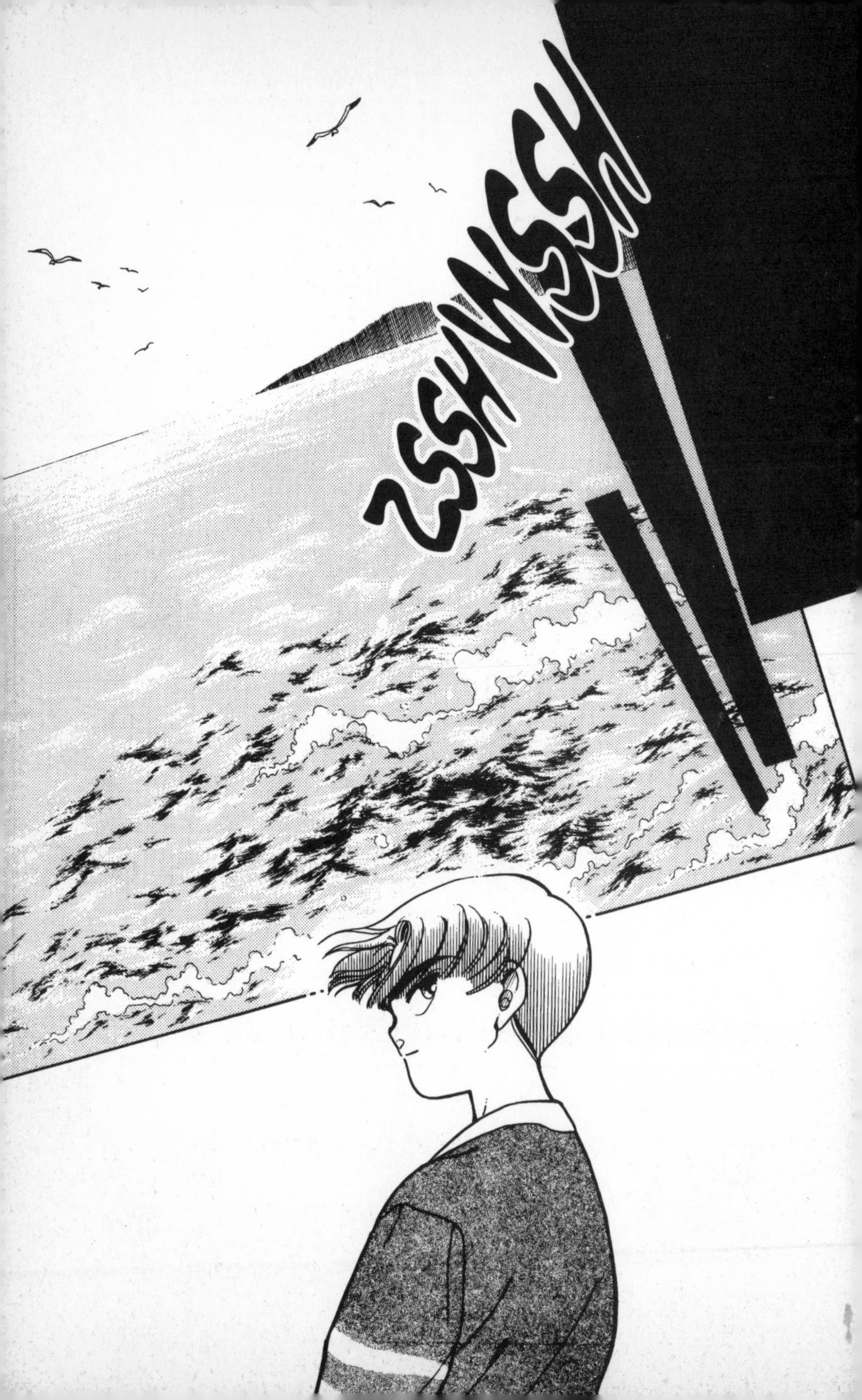
ZSSHWSSH

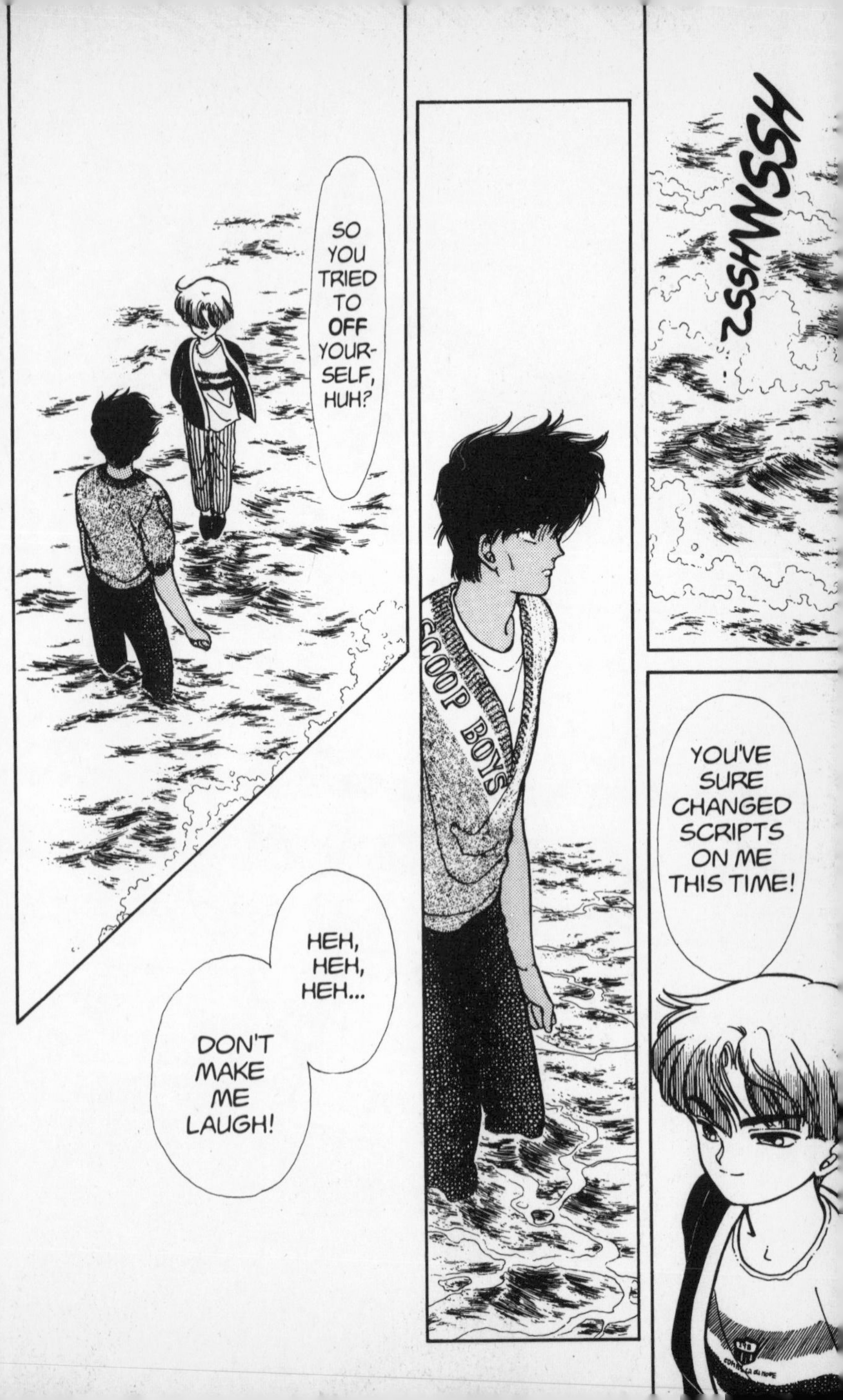
HSSMHSSZ
YOU'VE SURE CHANGED SCRIPTS ON ME THIS TIME!
HEH, HEH, HEH...
DON'T MAKE ME LAUGH!
SO YOU TRIED TO OFF YOURSELF, HUH?

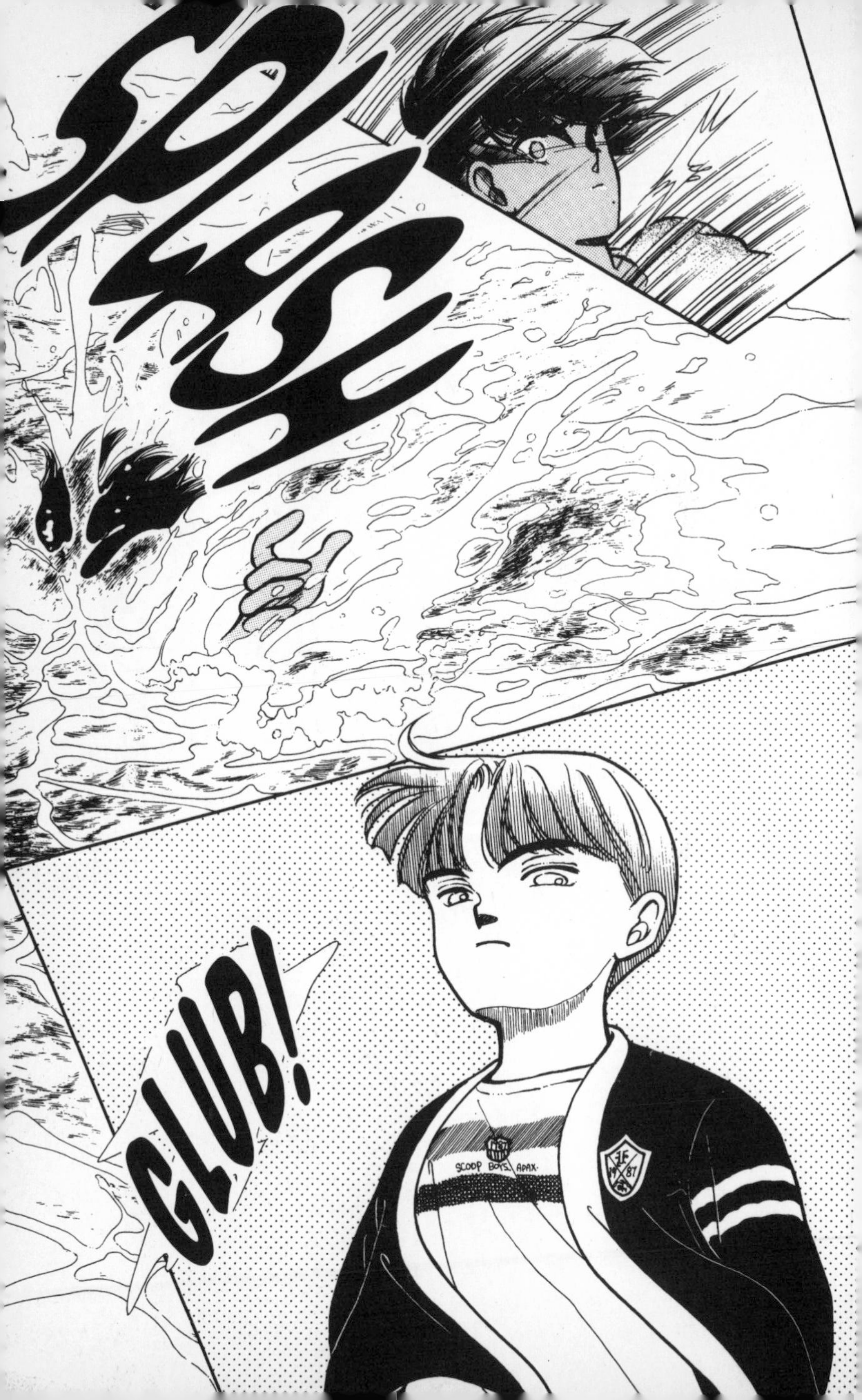
SPLASH
GLUB!
SCOOP BOYS APAX·

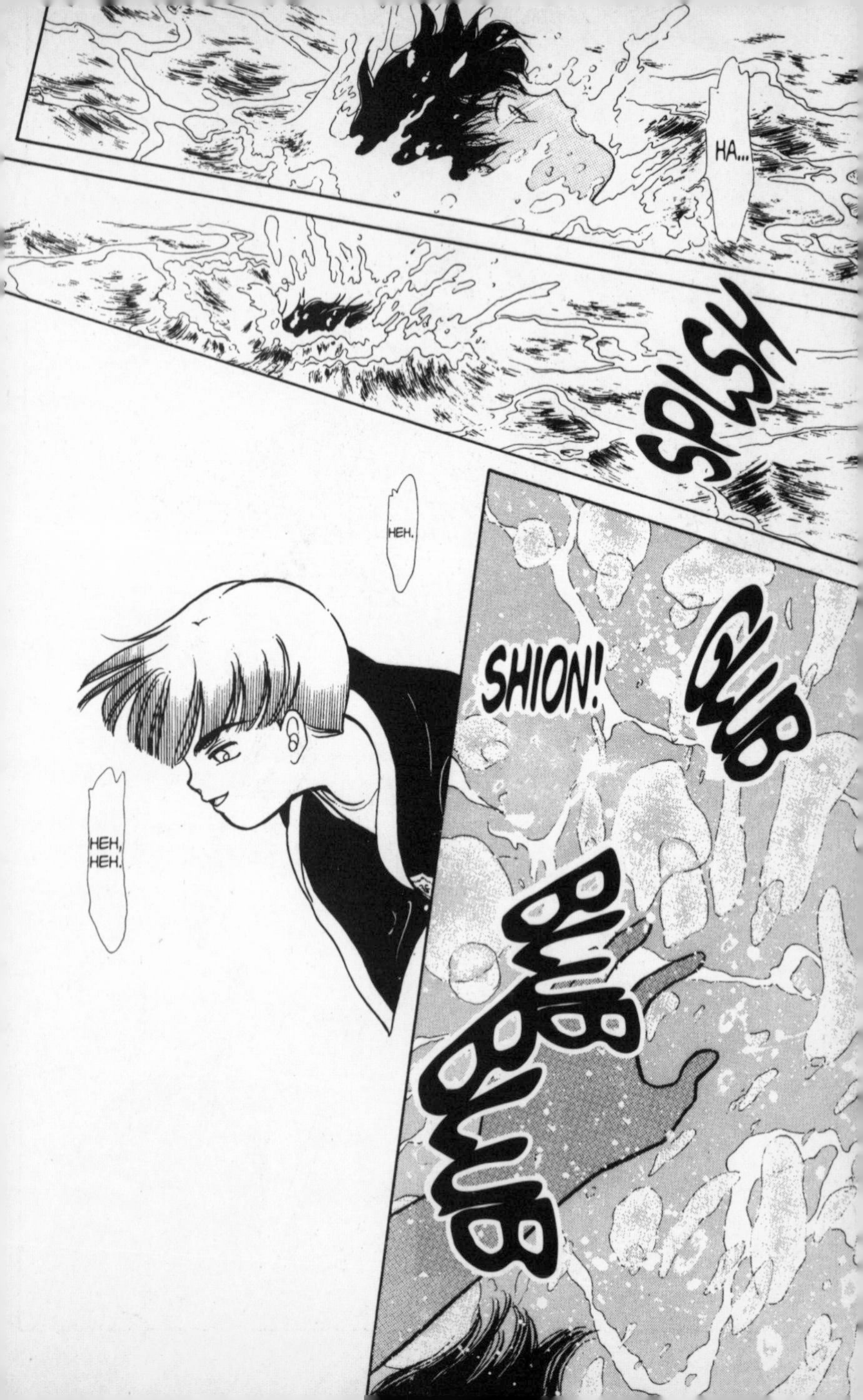
HA...
SPLSH
HEH.
HEH, HEH.
SHION!
GLUB
BLUB BLUB

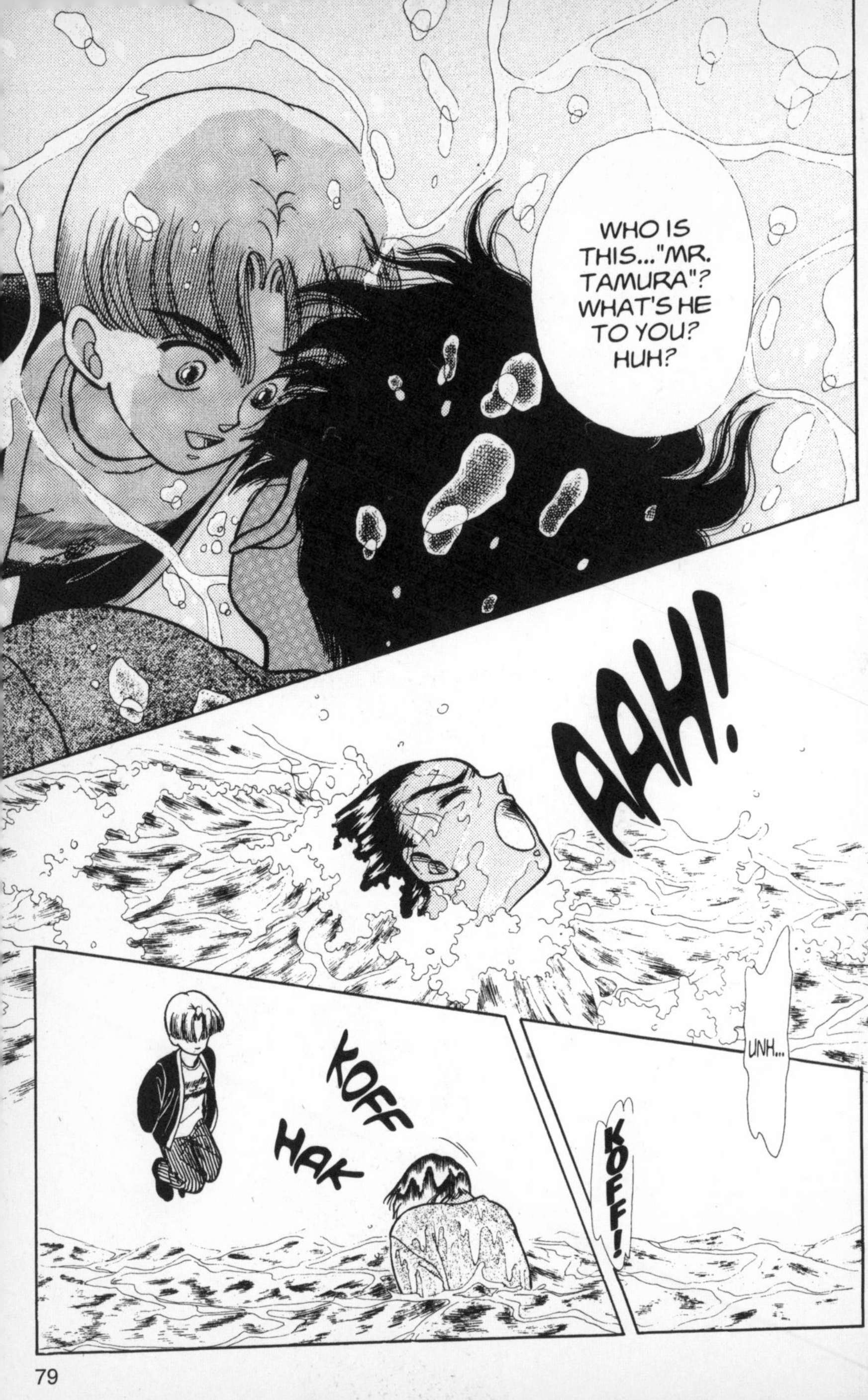
WHO IS THIS..."MR. TAMURA"? WHAT'S HE TO YOU? HUH?
AAH!
UNH...
KOFF!
KOFF
HAK

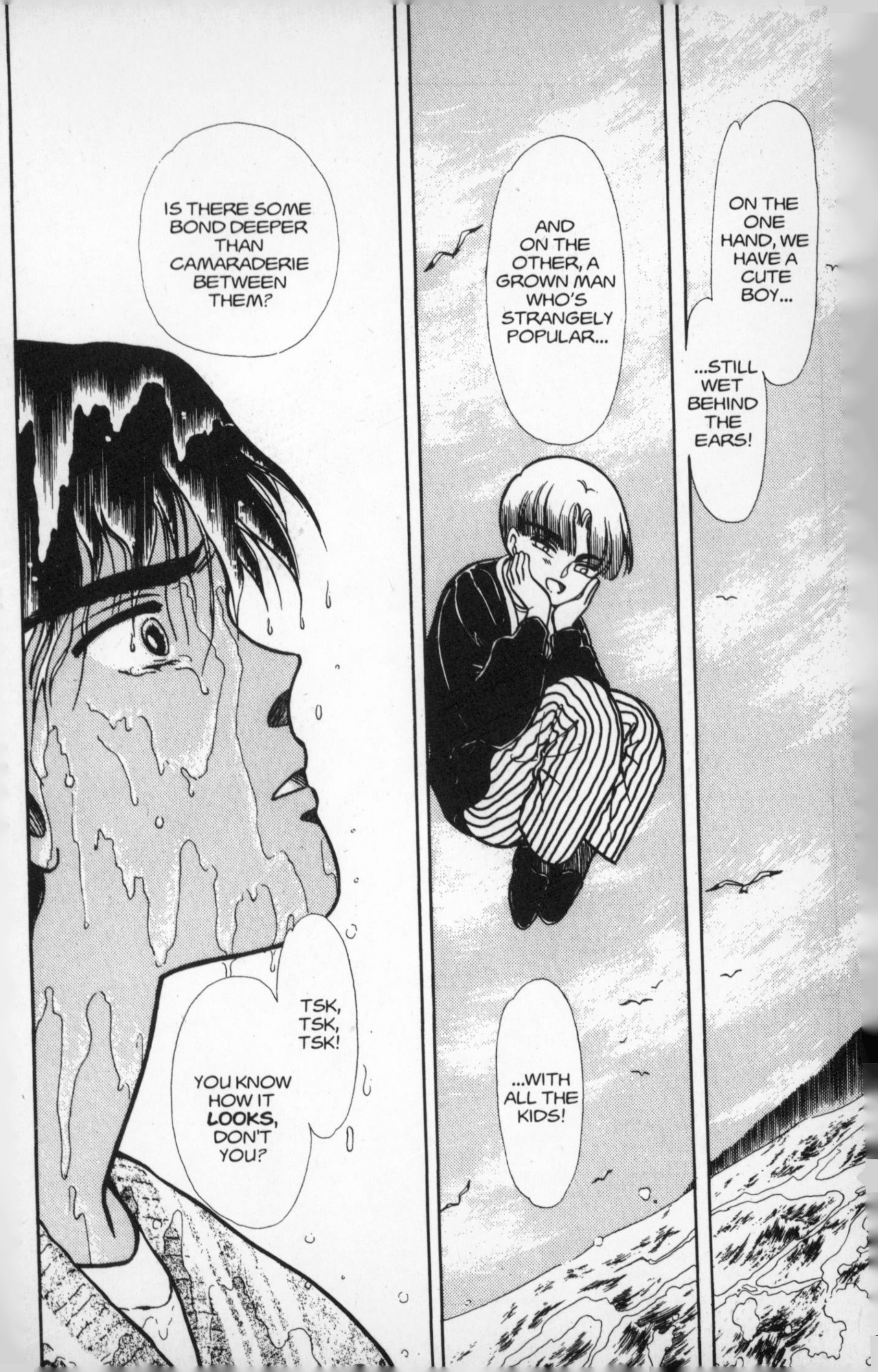
ON THE ONE HAND, WE HAVE A CUTE BOY...
...STILL WET BEHIND THE EARS!
AND ON THE OTHER, A GROWN MAN WHO'S STRANGELY POPULAR...
...WITH ALL THE KIDS!
IS THERE SOME BOND DEEPER THAN CAMARADERIE BETWEEN THEM?
TSK, TSK, TSK!
YOU KNOW HOW IT **LOOKS**, DON'T YOU?

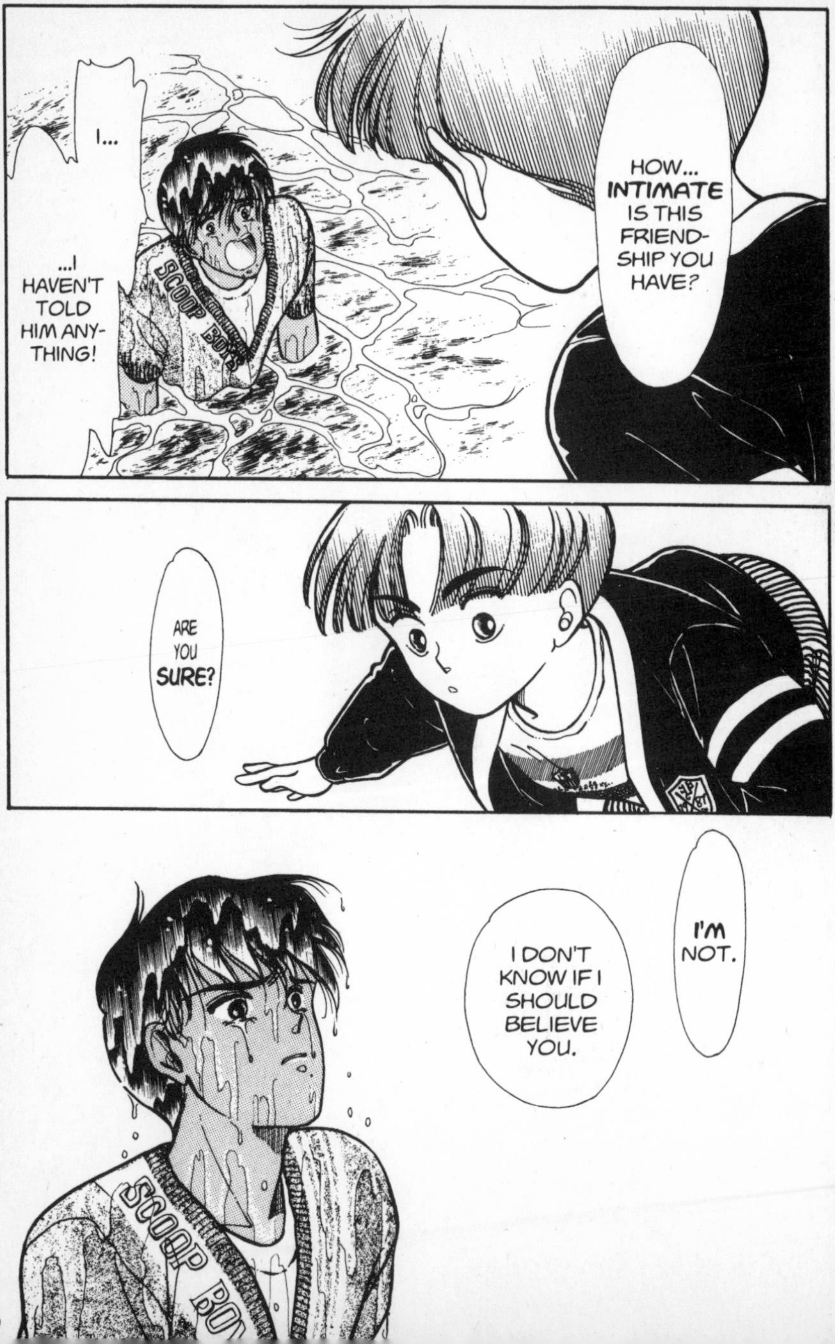
HOW... INTIMATE IS THIS FRIEND-SHIP YOU HAVE?
I...
...I HAVEN'T TOLD HIM ANY-THING!
SCOOP BOYS
ARE YOU SURE?
I'M NOT.
I DON'T KNOW IF I SHOULD BELIEVE YOU.
SCOOP BOY

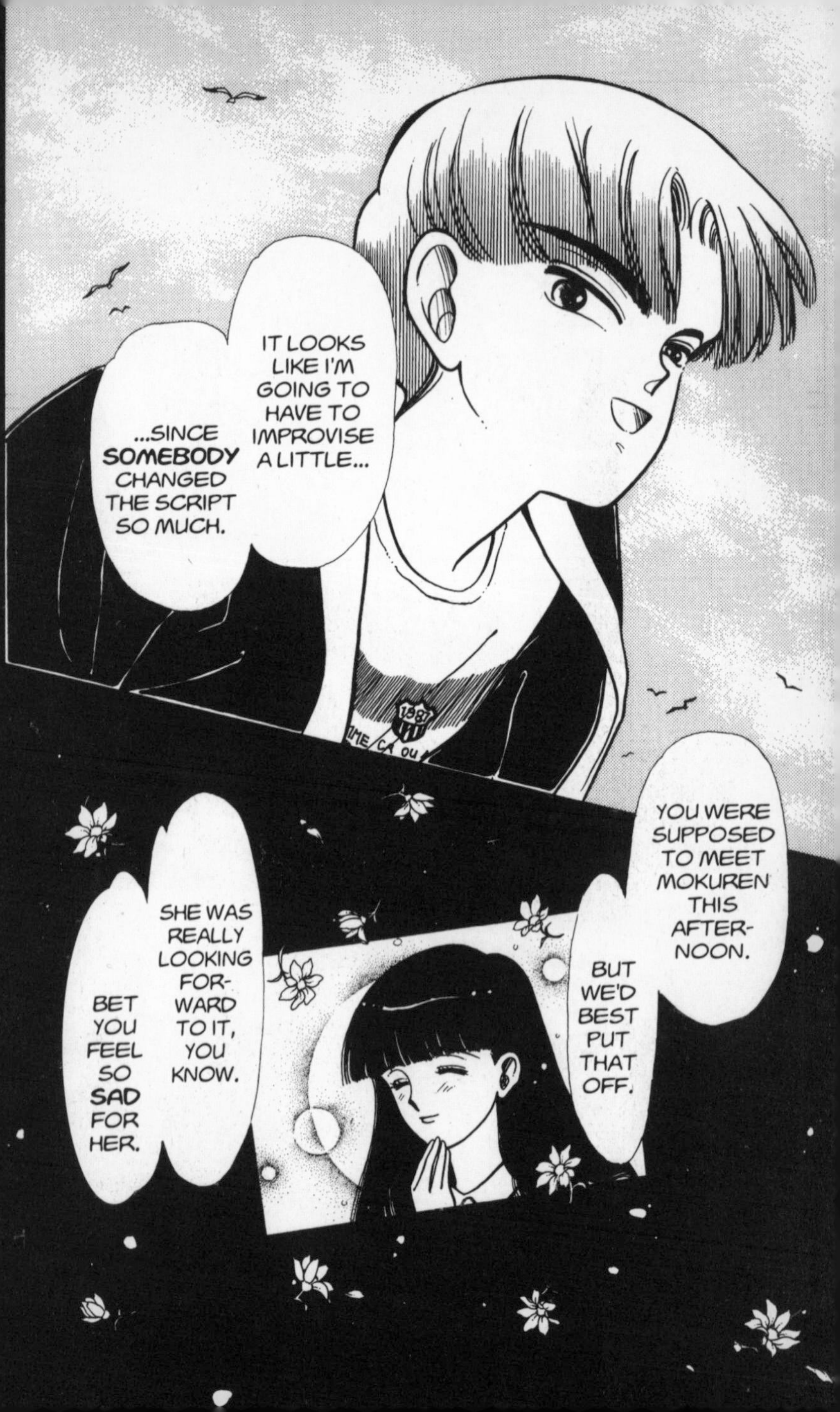
IT LOOKS LIKE I'M GOING TO HAVE TO IMPROVISE A LITTLE...
...SINCE **SOMEBODY** CHANGED THE SCRIPT SO MUCH.
YOU WERE SUPPOSED TO MEET MOKUREN THIS AFTER-NOON.
BUT WE'D BEST PUT THAT OFF.
SHE WAS REALLY LOOKING FOR-WARD TO IT, YOU KNOW.
BET YOU FEEL SO **SAD** FOR HER.

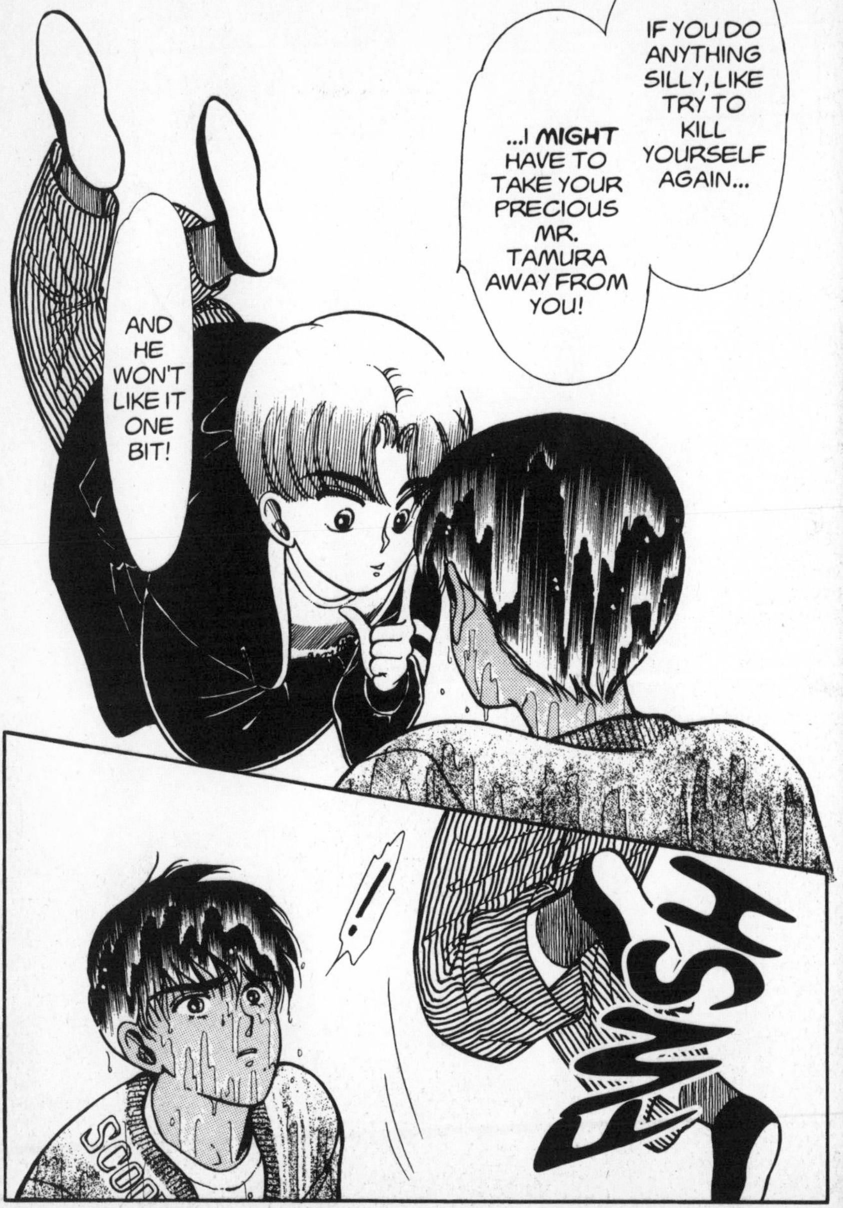
IF YOU DO ANYTHING SILLY, LIKE TRY TO KILL YOURSELF AGAIN...
...I **MIGHT** HAVE TO TAKE YOUR PRECIOUS MR. TAMURA AWAY FROM YOU!
AND HE WON'T LIKE IT ONE BIT!
!
SWISH

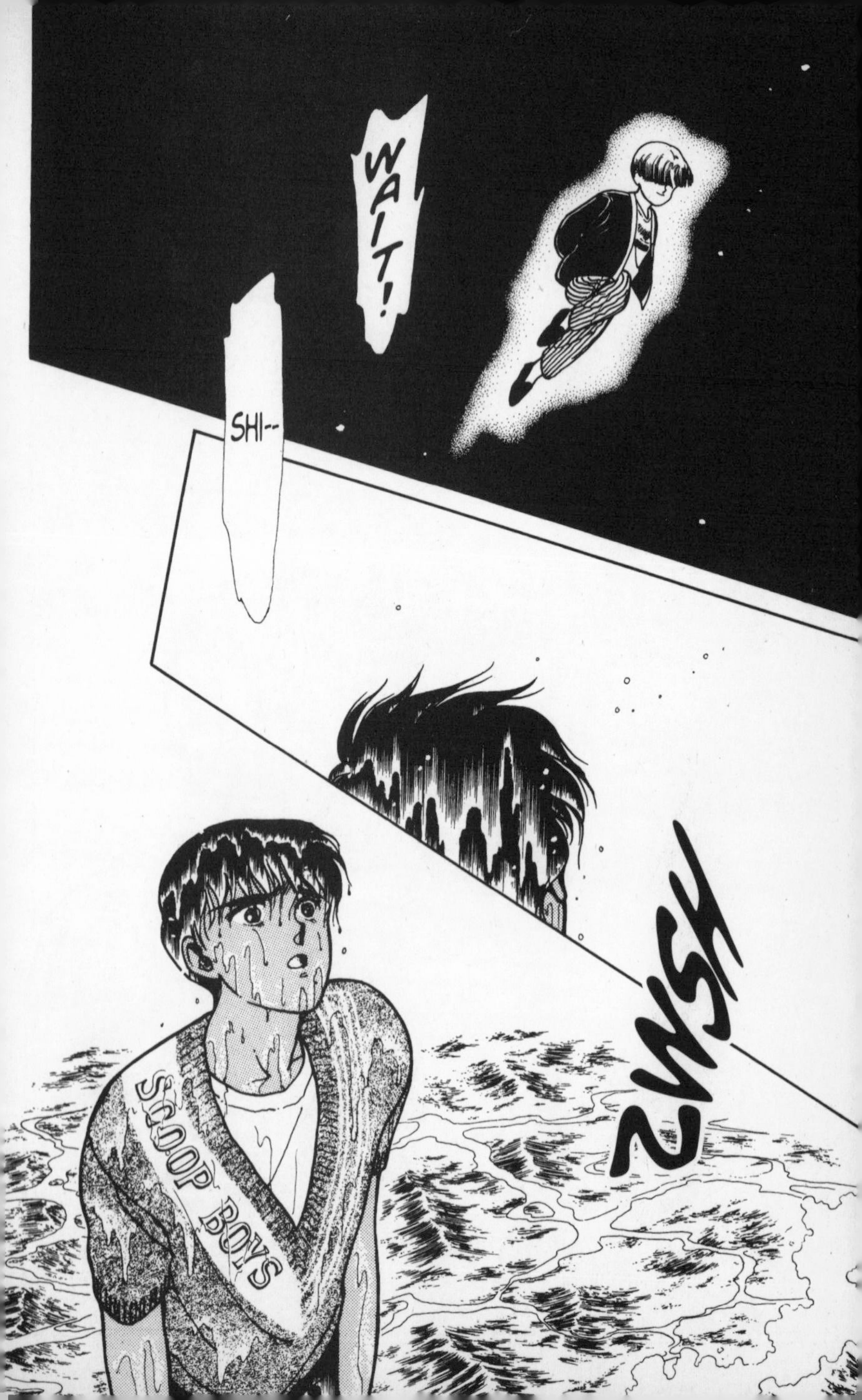
WAIT!
SHI--
ZWSH
SCOOP BOYS

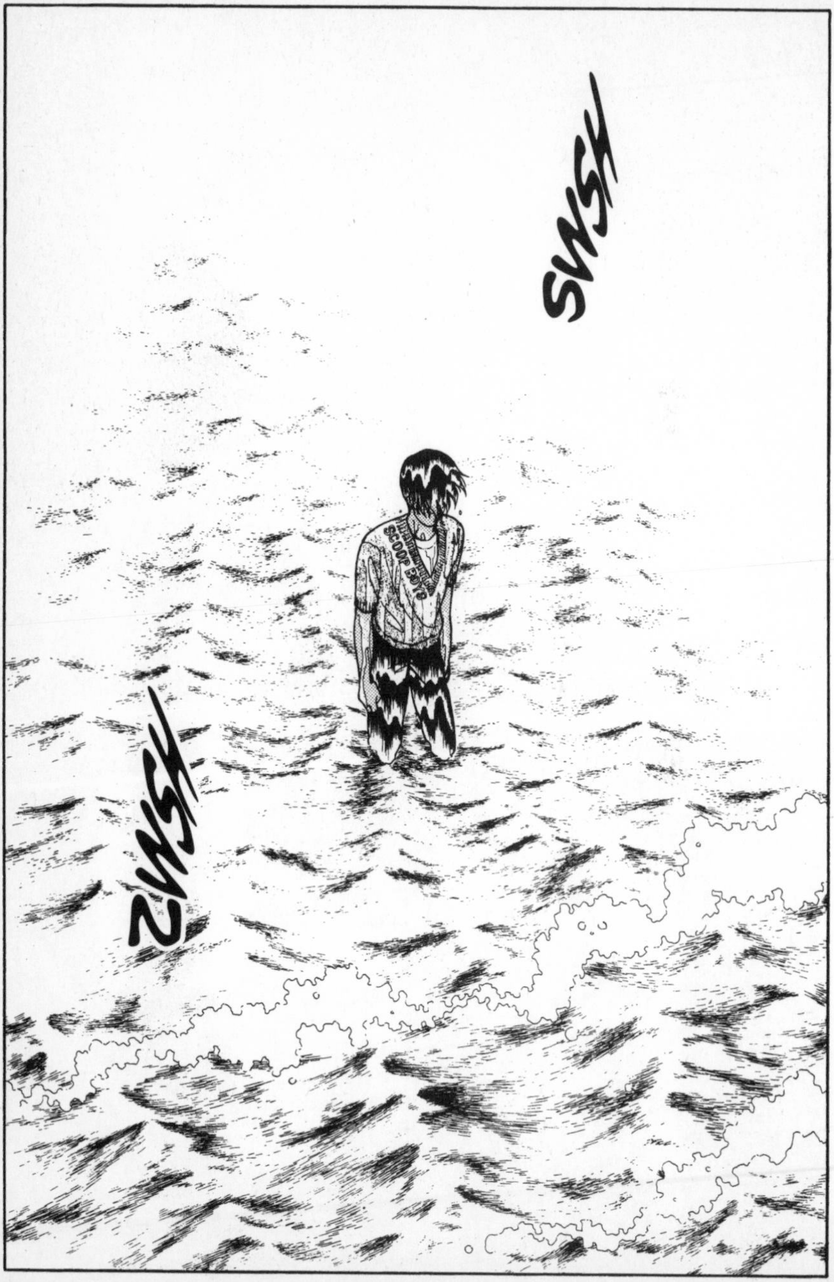
SWSH
SCOOP BOYS
SWSH

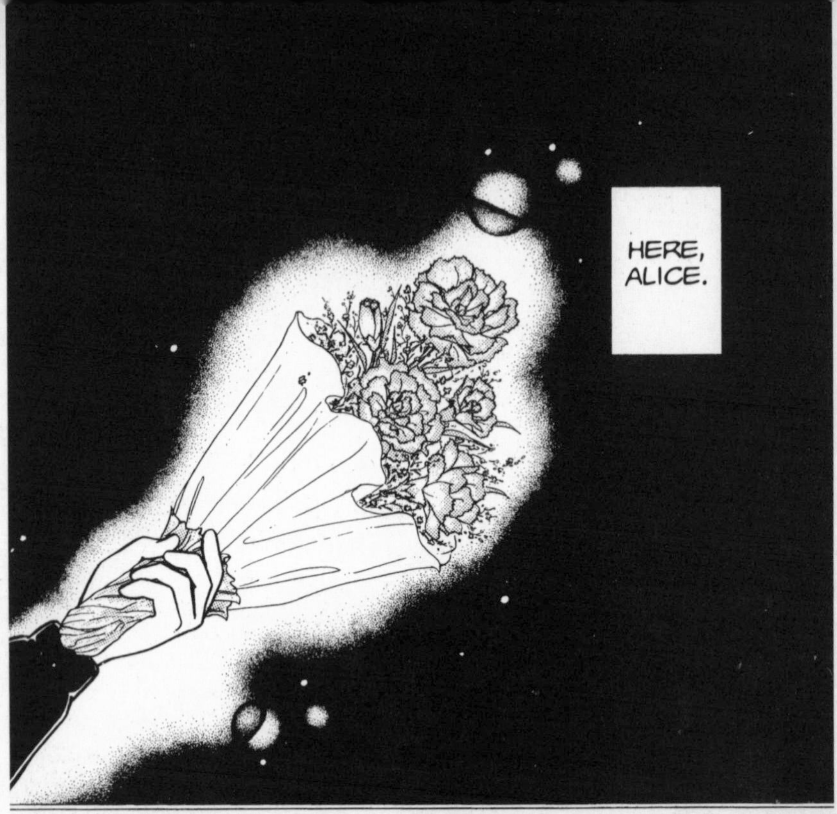
HERE, ALICE.

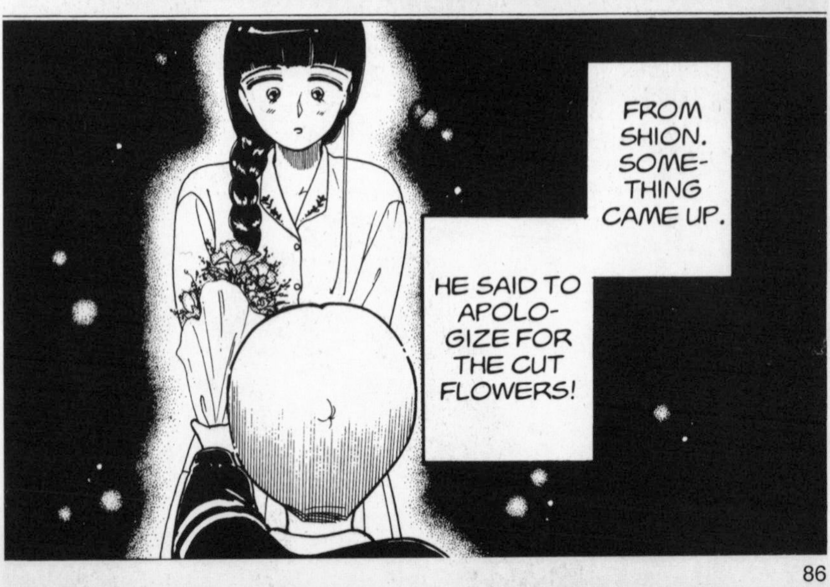
FROM SHION. SOME-THING CAME UP.
HE SAID TO APOLO-GIZE FOR THE CUT FLOWERS!

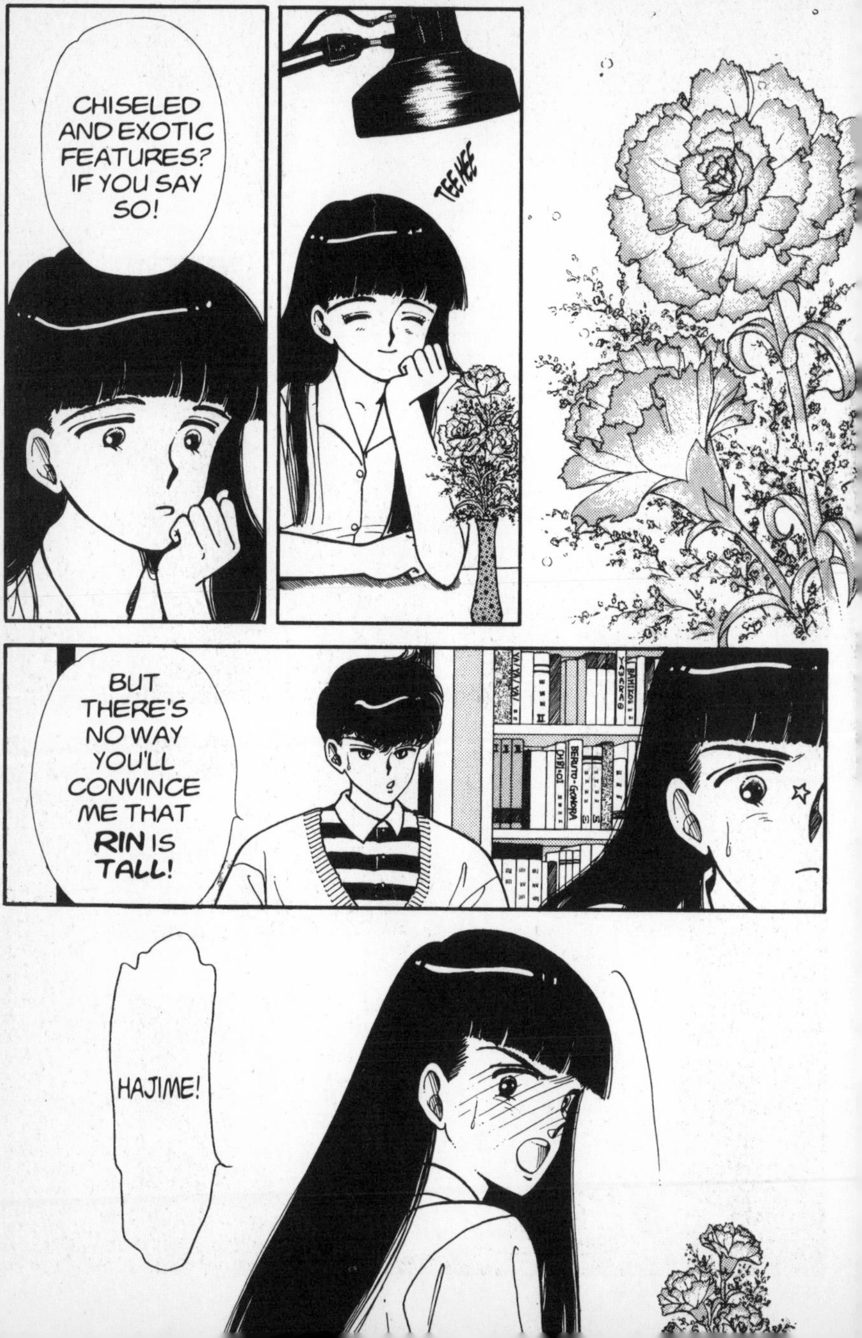
TEE HEE
CHISELED AND EXOTIC FEATURES? IF YOU SAY SO!
BUT THERE'S NO WAY YOU'LL CONVINCE ME THAT **RIN** IS **TALL**!
HAJIME!

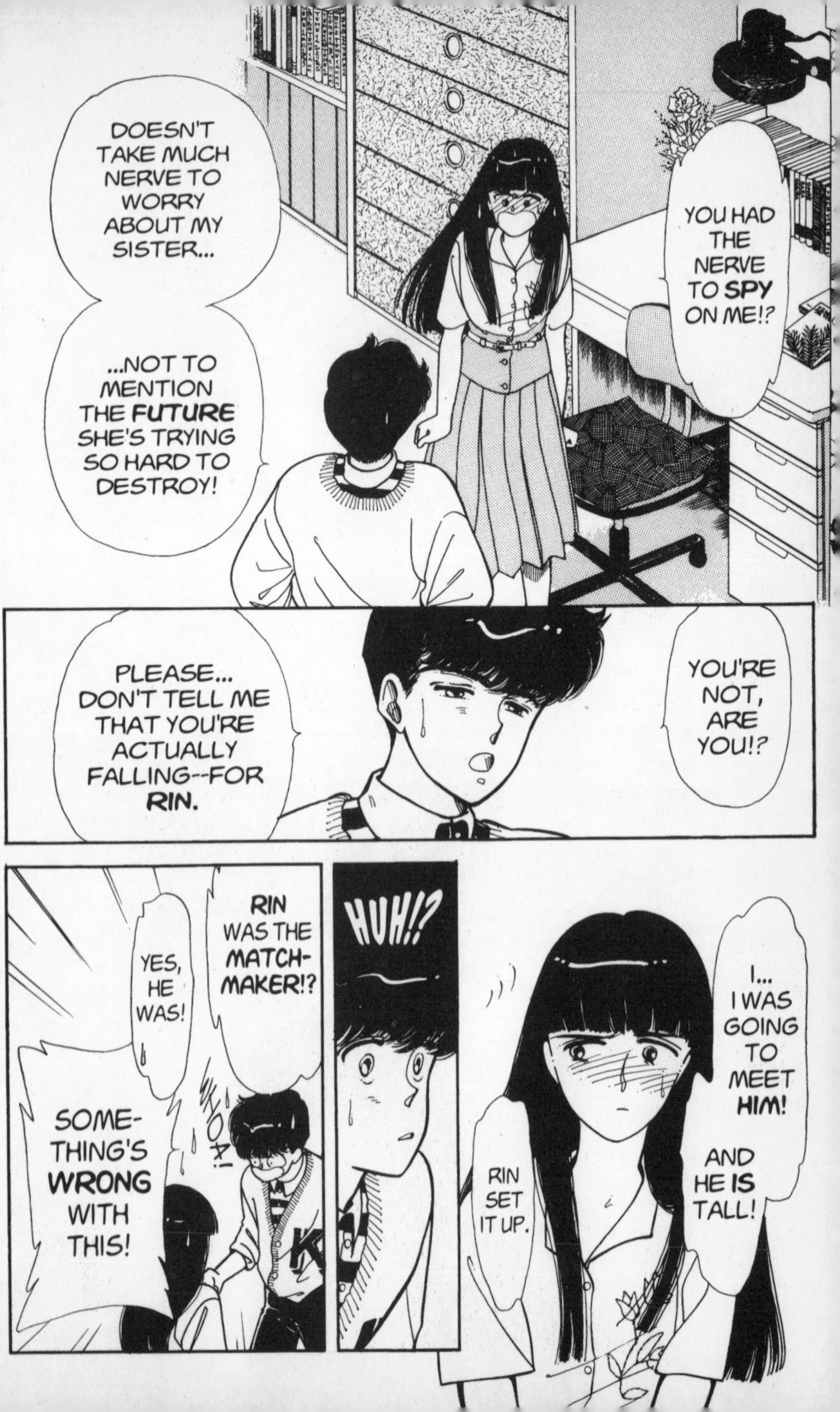

YOU HAD THE NERVE TO **SPY** ON ME!?
DOESN'T TAKE MUCH NERVE TO WORRY ABOUT MY SISTER...
...NOT TO MENTION THE **FUTURE** SHE'S TRYING SO HARD TO DESTROY!
YOU'RE NOT, ARE YOU!?
PLEASE... DON'T TELL ME THAT YOU'RE ACTUALLY FALLING--FOR **RIN**.
I... I WAS GOING TO MEET **HIM**!
AND HE **IS** TALL!
RIN SET IT UP.
HUH!?
RIN WAS THE **MATCH-MAKER**!?
YES, HE WAS!
WHOA!
SOME-THING'S **WRONG** WITH THIS!

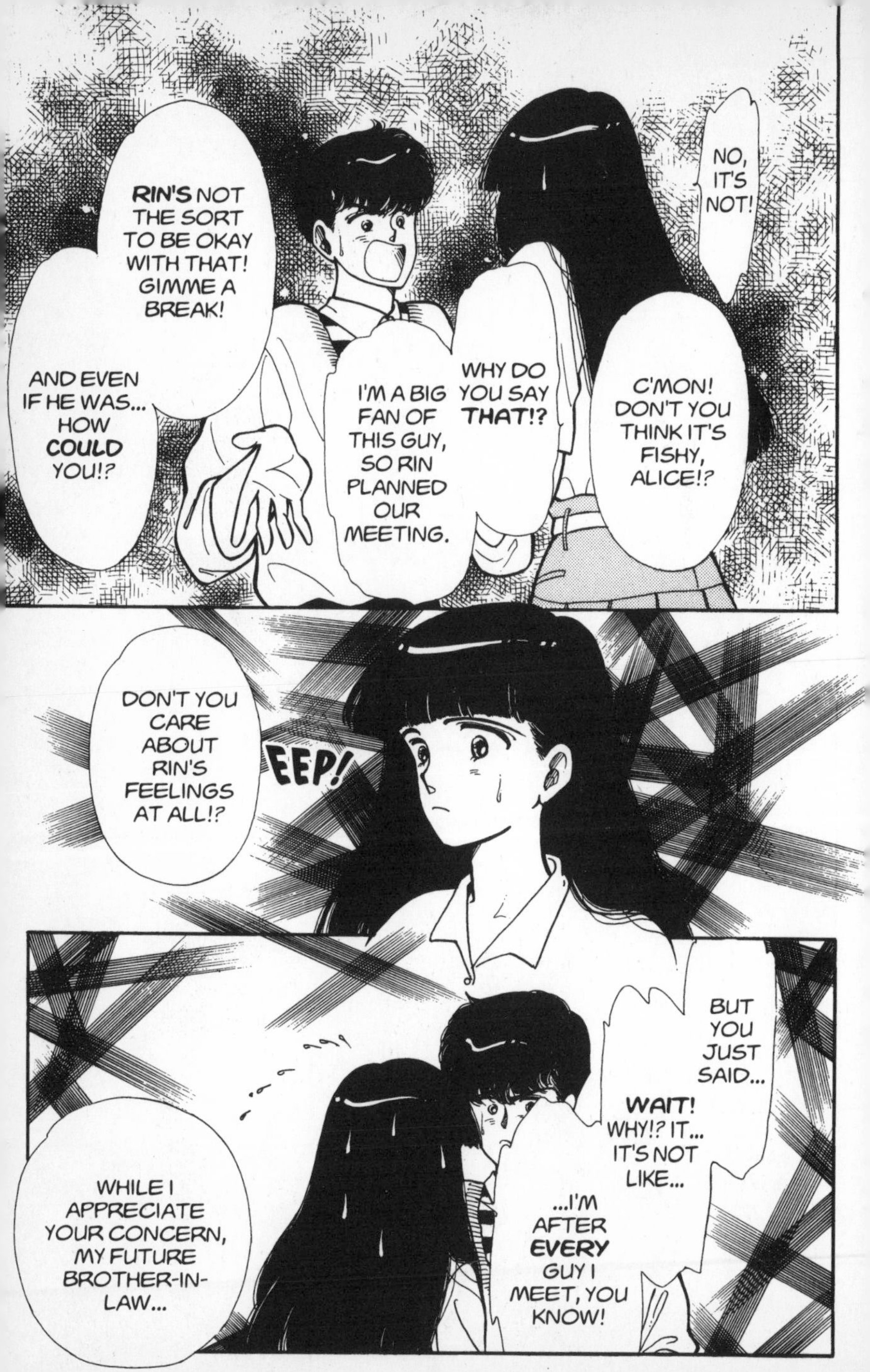
NO, IT'S NOT!
C'MON! DON'T YOU THINK IT'S FISHY, ALICE!?
WHY DO YOU SAY THAT!?
I'M A BIG FAN OF THIS GUY, SO RIN PLANNED OUR MEETING.
RIN'S NOT THE SORT TO BE OKAY WITH THAT! GIMME A BREAK!
AND EVEN IF HE WAS... HOW COULD YOU!?
EEP!
DON'T YOU CARE ABOUT RIN'S FEELINGS AT ALL!?
BUT YOU JUST SAID... WAIT! WHY!? IT... IT'S NOT LIKE...
...I'M AFTER EVERY GUY I MEET, YOU KNOW!
WHILE I APPRECIATE YOUR CONCERN, MY FUTURE BROTHER-IN-LAW...

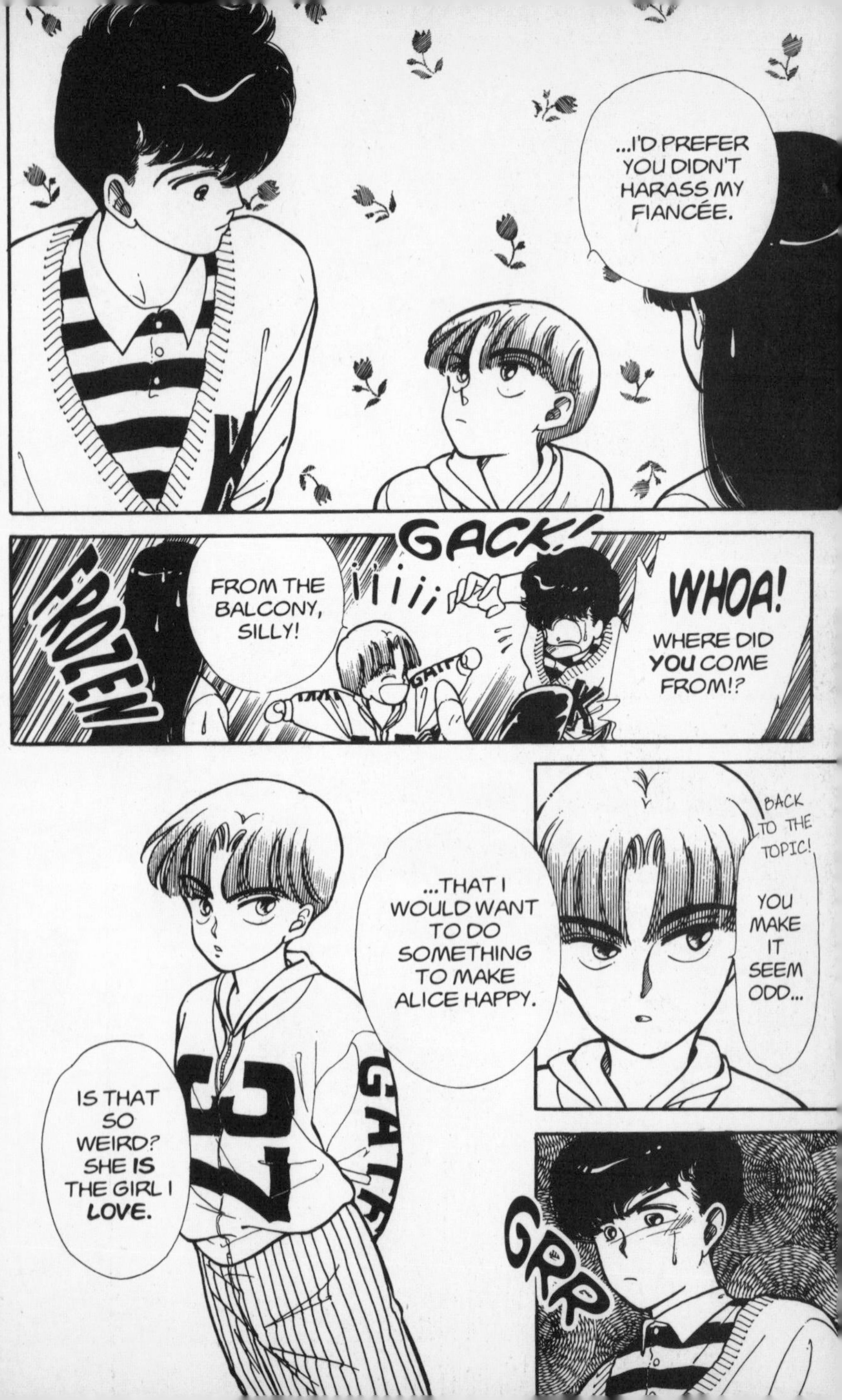
...I'D PREFER YOU DIDN'T HARASS MY FIANCÉE.
WHOA! WHERE DID YOU COME FROM!?
GACK!
FROM THE BALCONY, SILLY!
FROZEN
BACK TO THE TOPIC!
YOU MAKE IT SEEM ODD...
...THAT I WOULD WANT TO DO SOMETHING TO MAKE ALICE HAPPY.
IS THAT SO WEIRD? SHE IS THE GIRL I LOVE.
GRR

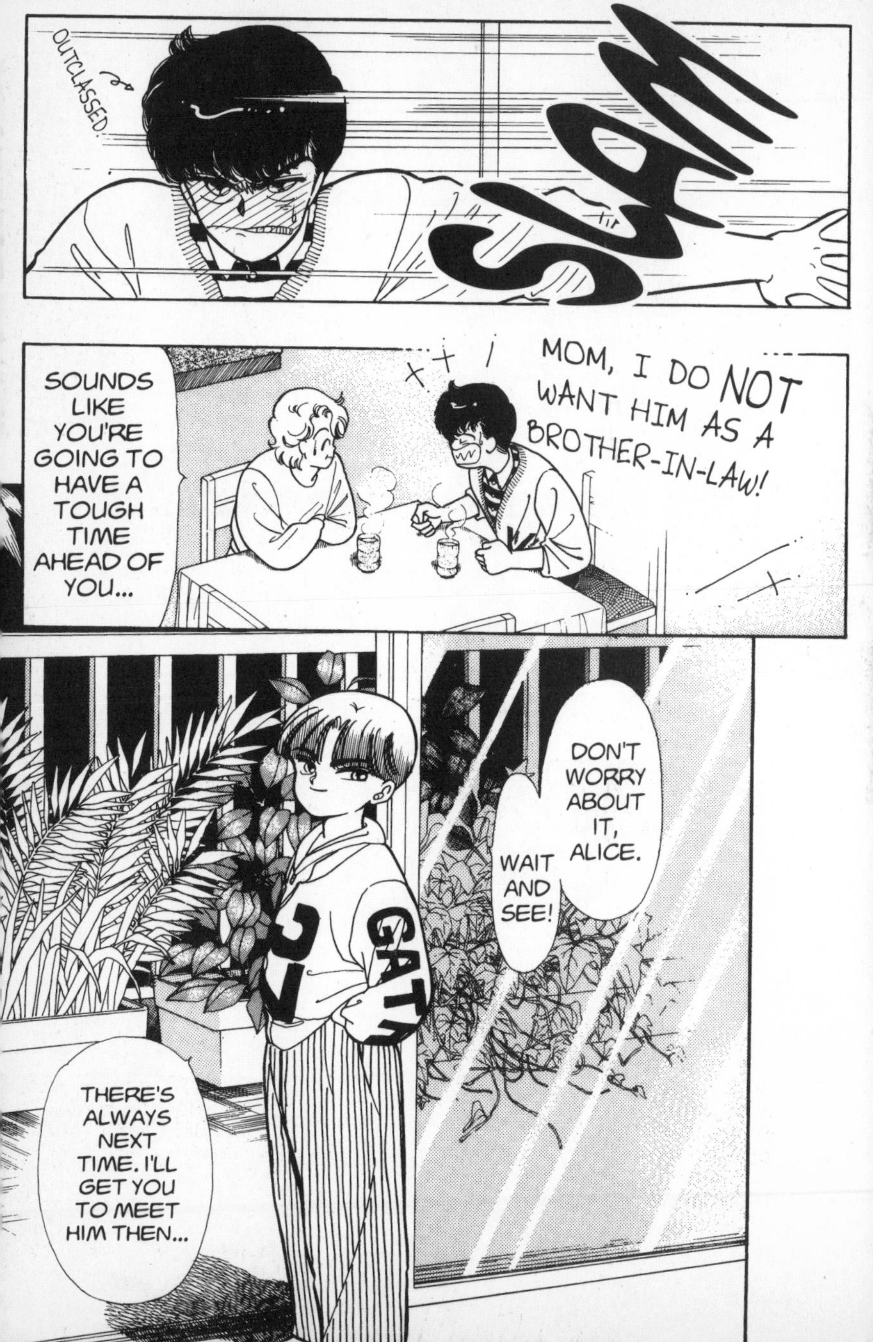
SLAM
OUTCLASSED
MOM, I DO NOT WANT HIM AS A BROTHER-IN-LAW!
SOUNDS LIKE YOU'RE GOING TO HAVE A TOUGH TIME AHEAD OF YOU...
DON'T WORRY ABOUT IT, ALICE.
WAIT AND SEE!
THERE'S ALWAYS NEXT TIME. I'LL GET YOU TO MEET HIM THEN...

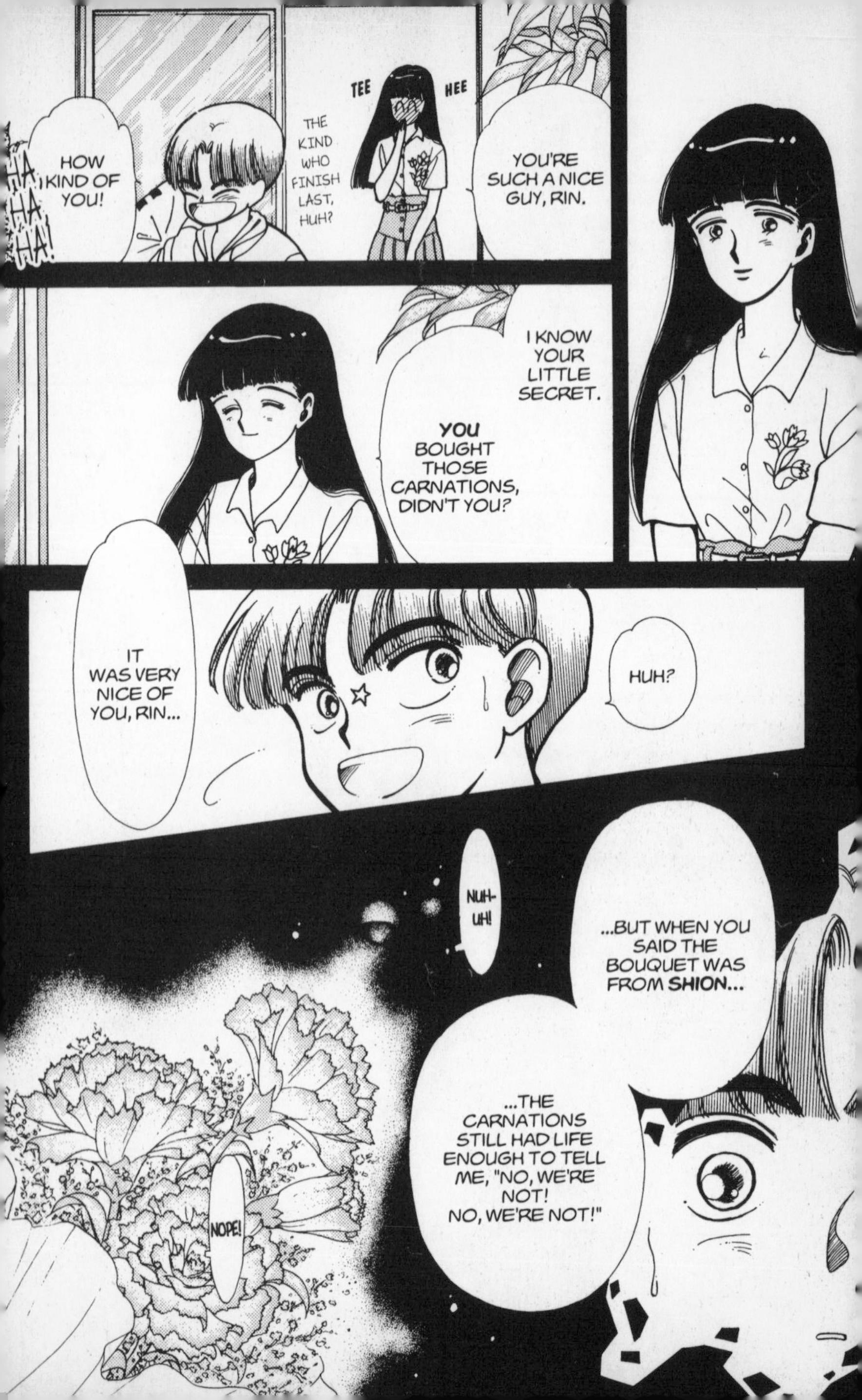

YOU'RE SUCH A NICE GUY, RIN.
TEE HEE
THE KIND WHO FINISH LAST, HUH?
HOW KIND OF YOU!
HA HA HA!
I KNOW YOUR LITTLE SECRET.
YOU BOUGHT THOSE CARNATIONS, DIDN'T YOU?
HUH?
IT WAS VERY NICE OF YOU, RIN...
...BUT WHEN YOU SAID THE BOUQUET WAS FROM SHION...
...THE CARNATIONS STILL HAD LIFE ENOUGH TO TELL ME, "NO, WE'RE NOT! NO, WE'RE NOT!"
NUH-UH!
NOPE!

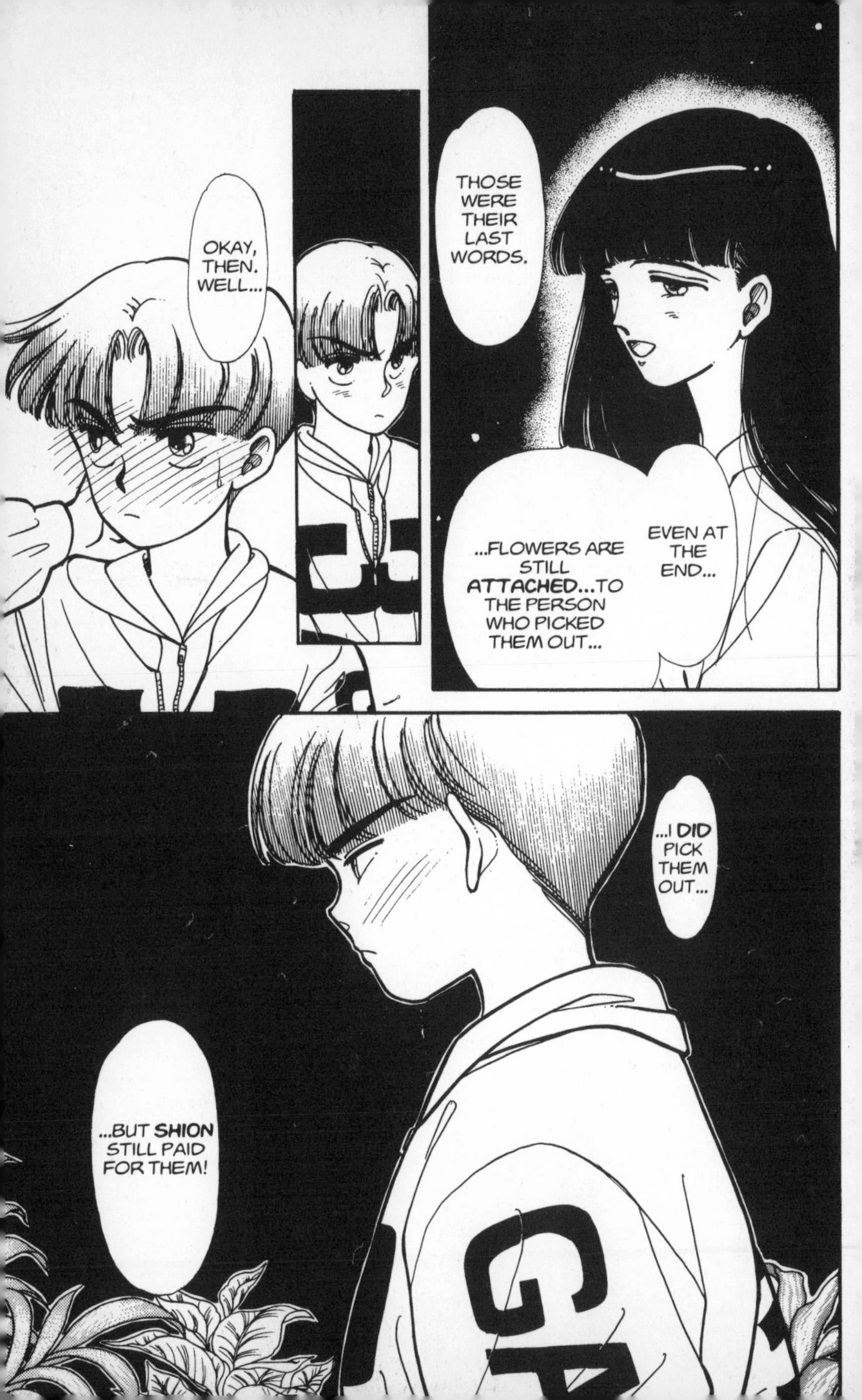
THOSE WERE THEIR LAST WORDS.
EVEN AT THE END...
...FLOWERS ARE STILL ATTACHED...TO THE PERSON WHO PICKED THEM OUT...
OKAY, THEN. WELL...
...I DID PICK THEM OUT...
...BUT SHION STILL PAID FOR THEM!

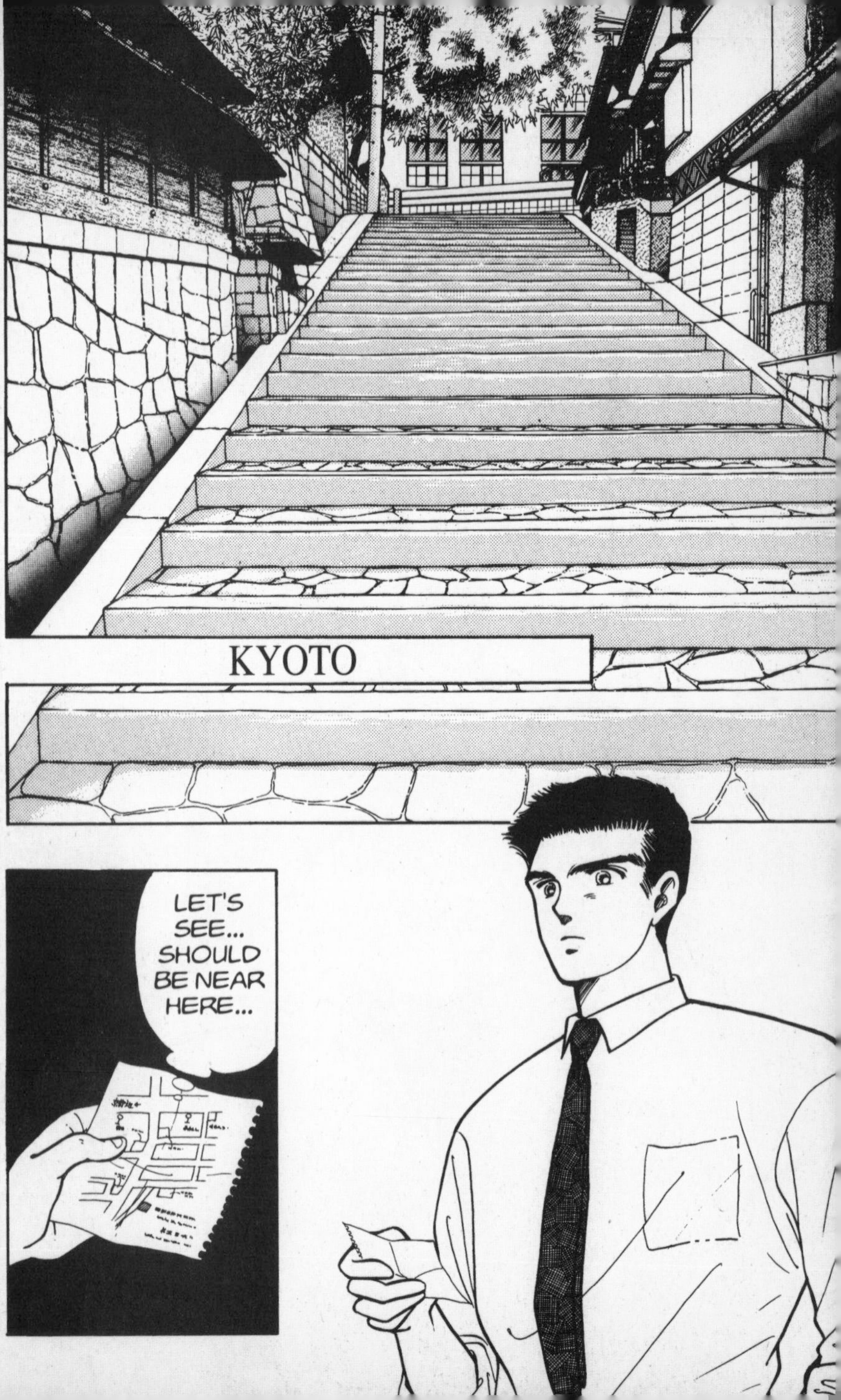
KYOTO
LET'S SEE... SHOULD BE NEAR HERE...

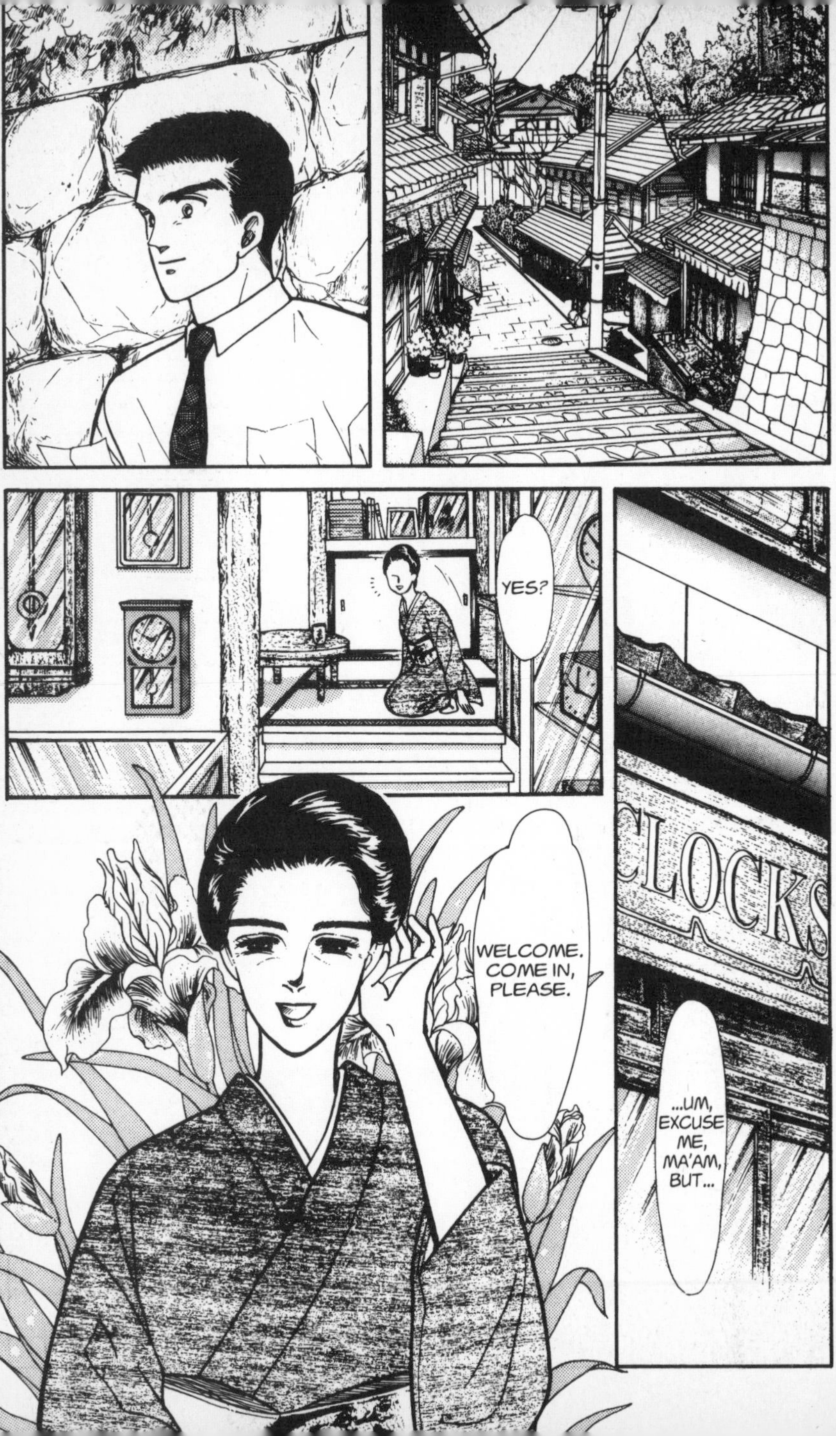
CLOCKS
...UM, EXCUSE ME, MA'AM, BUT...
YES?
WELCOME. COME IN, PLEASE.

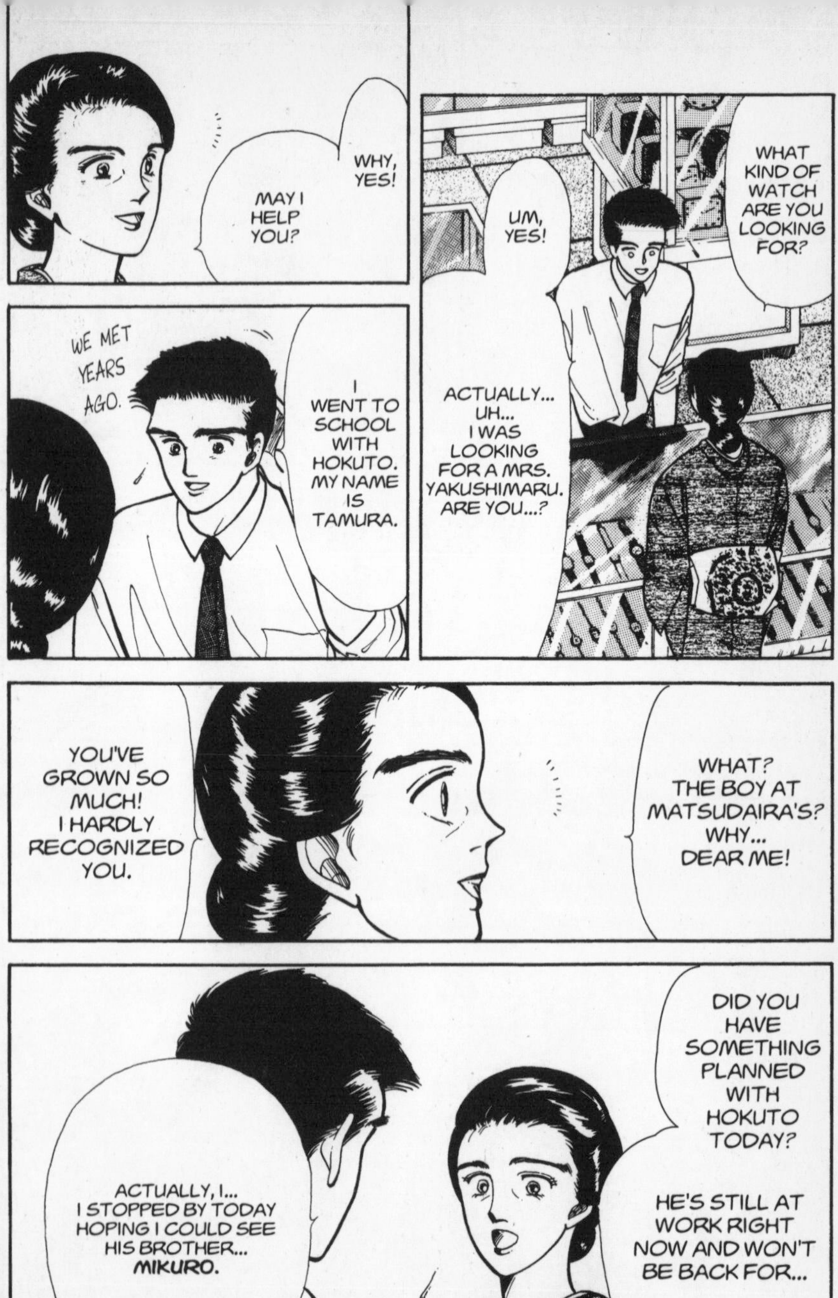
WHAT KIND OF WATCH ARE YOU LOOKING FOR?
UM, YES!
ACTUALLY... UH... I WAS LOOKING FOR A MRS. YAKUSHIMARU. ARE YOU...?
WHY, YES!
MAY I HELP YOU?
I WENT TO SCHOOL WITH HOKUTO. MY NAME IS TAMURA.
WE MET YEARS AGO.
WHAT? THE BOY AT MATSUDAIRA'S? WHY... DEAR ME!
YOU'VE GROWN SO MUCH! I HARDLY RECOGNIZED YOU.
DID YOU HAVE SOMETHING PLANNED WITH HOKUTO TODAY?
HE'S STILL AT WORK RIGHT NOW AND WON'T BE BACK FOR...
ACTUALLY, I... I STOPPED BY TODAY HOPING I COULD SEE HIS BROTHER... **MIKURO.**

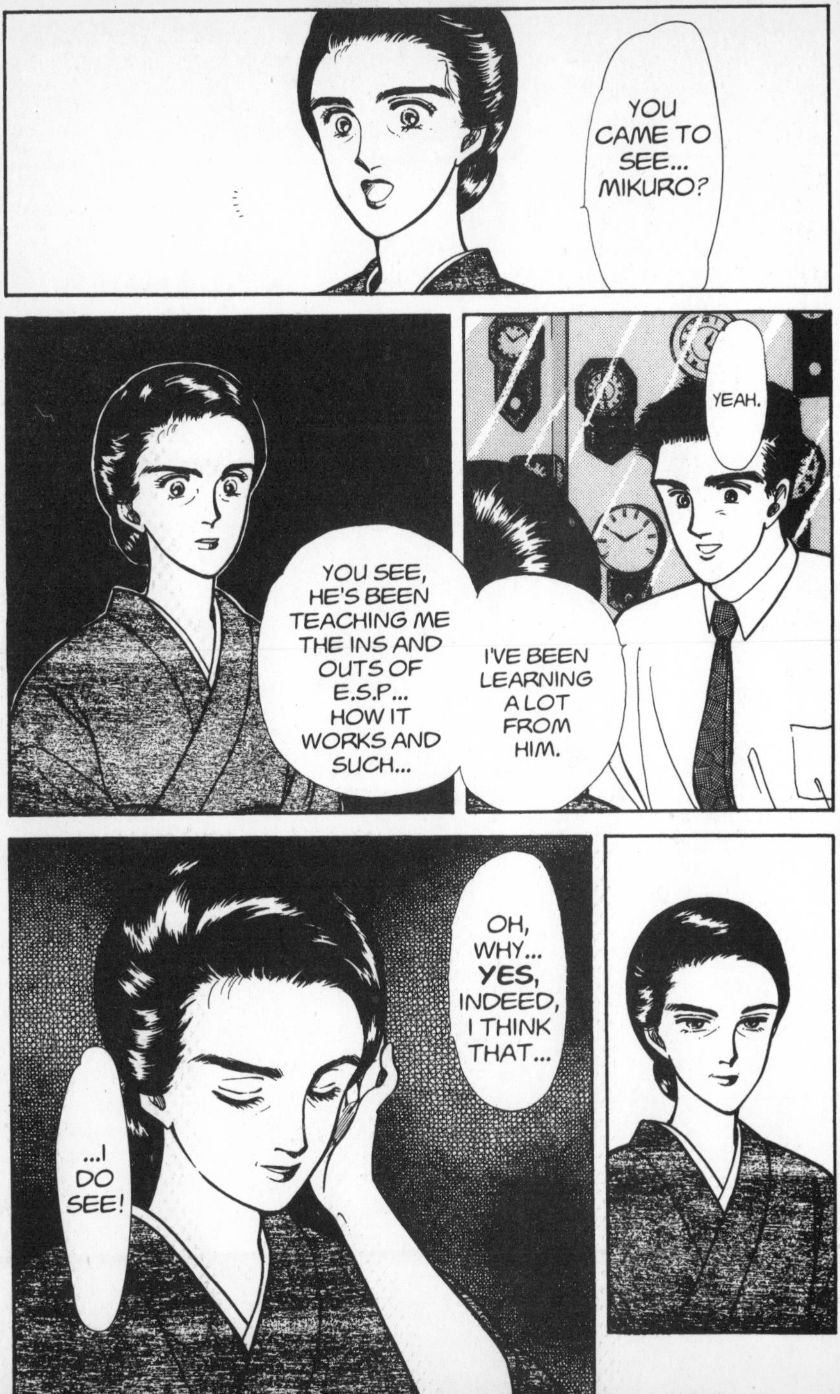
YOU CAME TO SEE... MIKURO?
YEAH.
I'VE BEEN LEARNING A LOT FROM HIM.
YOU SEE, HE'S BEEN TEACHING ME THE INS AND OUTS OF E.S.P... HOW IT WORKS AND SUCH...
OH, WHY... **YES,** INDEED, I THINK THAT...
...I DO SEE!

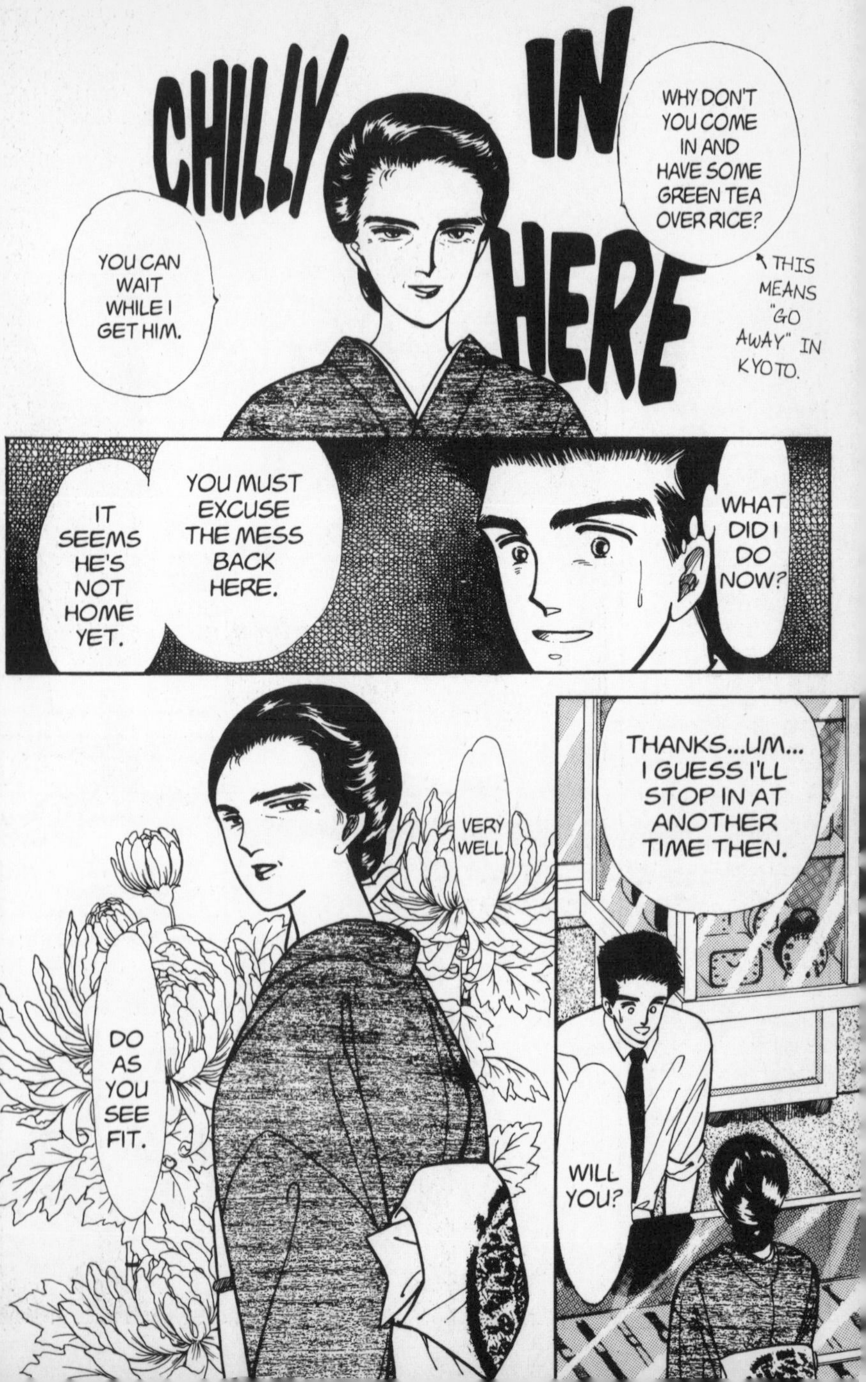
WHY DON'T YOU COME IN AND HAVE SOME GREEN TEA OVER RICE?
THIS MEANS "GO AWAY" IN KYOTO.
CHILLY IN HERE
YOU CAN WAIT WHILE I GET HIM.
WHAT DID I DO NOW?
YOU MUST EXCUSE THE MESS BACK HERE.
IT SEEMS HE'S NOT HOME YET.
THANKS...UM... I GUESS I'LL STOP IN AT ANOTHER TIME THEN.
WILL YOU?
VERY WELL.
DO AS YOU SEE FIT.

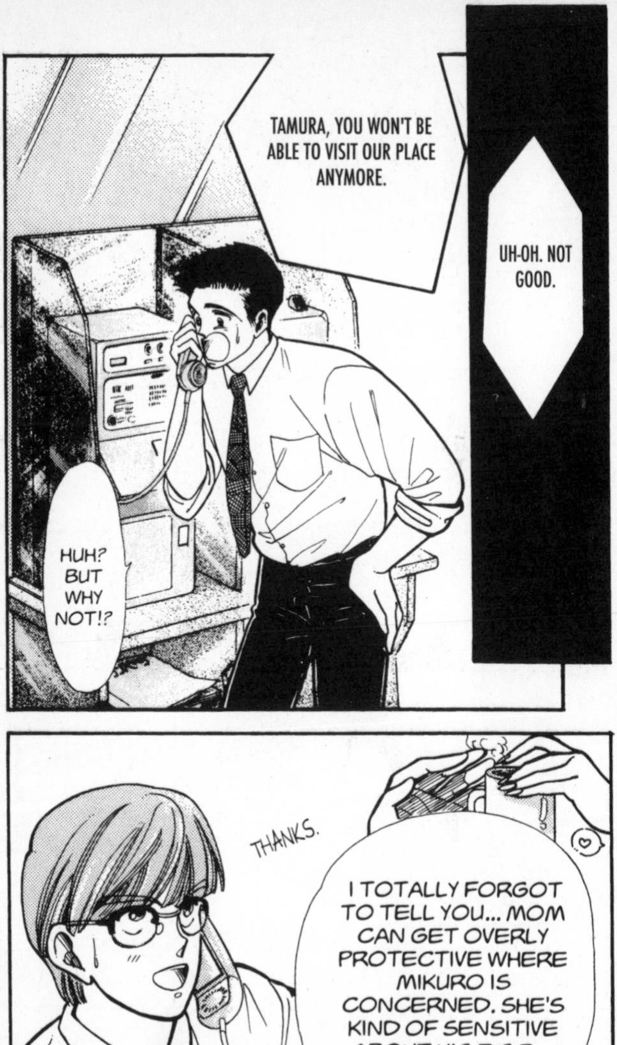
TAMURA, YOU WON'T BE ABLE TO VISIT OUR PLACE ANYMORE.
UH-OH. NOT GOOD.
HUH? BUT WHY NOT!?
THANKS.
I TOTALLY FORGOT TO TELL YOU... MOM CAN GET OVERLY PROTECTIVE WHERE MIKURO IS CONCERNED. SHE'S KIND OF SENSITIVE ABOUT HIS E.S.P....
...DOESN'T WANT HER SON TO BE SOME KIND OF FREAKSHOW. SHE HATES IT WHEN PEOPLE PRY OUT OF CURIOSITY.

1/4 COLUMN NONSENSE

PART 4

I'm not sure if this was in August (I forget), but it happened one evening as I was walking home from my studio. Someone yelled, "You there, walking down the street!" I turned to see if she was talking to me, and I saw a woman--maybe a housewife--leaning out a window a few houses down. "Is that apartment next to you on fire!?" Indeed, there was black smoke pouring out from the first floor window...

I won't go into details, because it would get too long, but utter chaos ensued. I wound up covered in fire extinguishing powder and soot--but I helped to put out a fire for the first time in my life. It was scary. **Boy,** was it scary. I guess it was only a small fire in scale, but I was absolutely terrified when I opened the door to the bathroom, the source of the smoke! (Never heat an empty bathtub!)

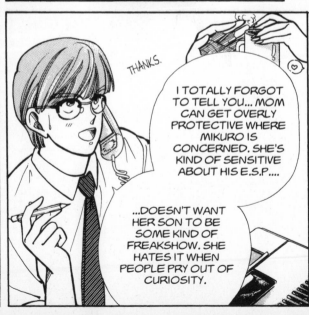

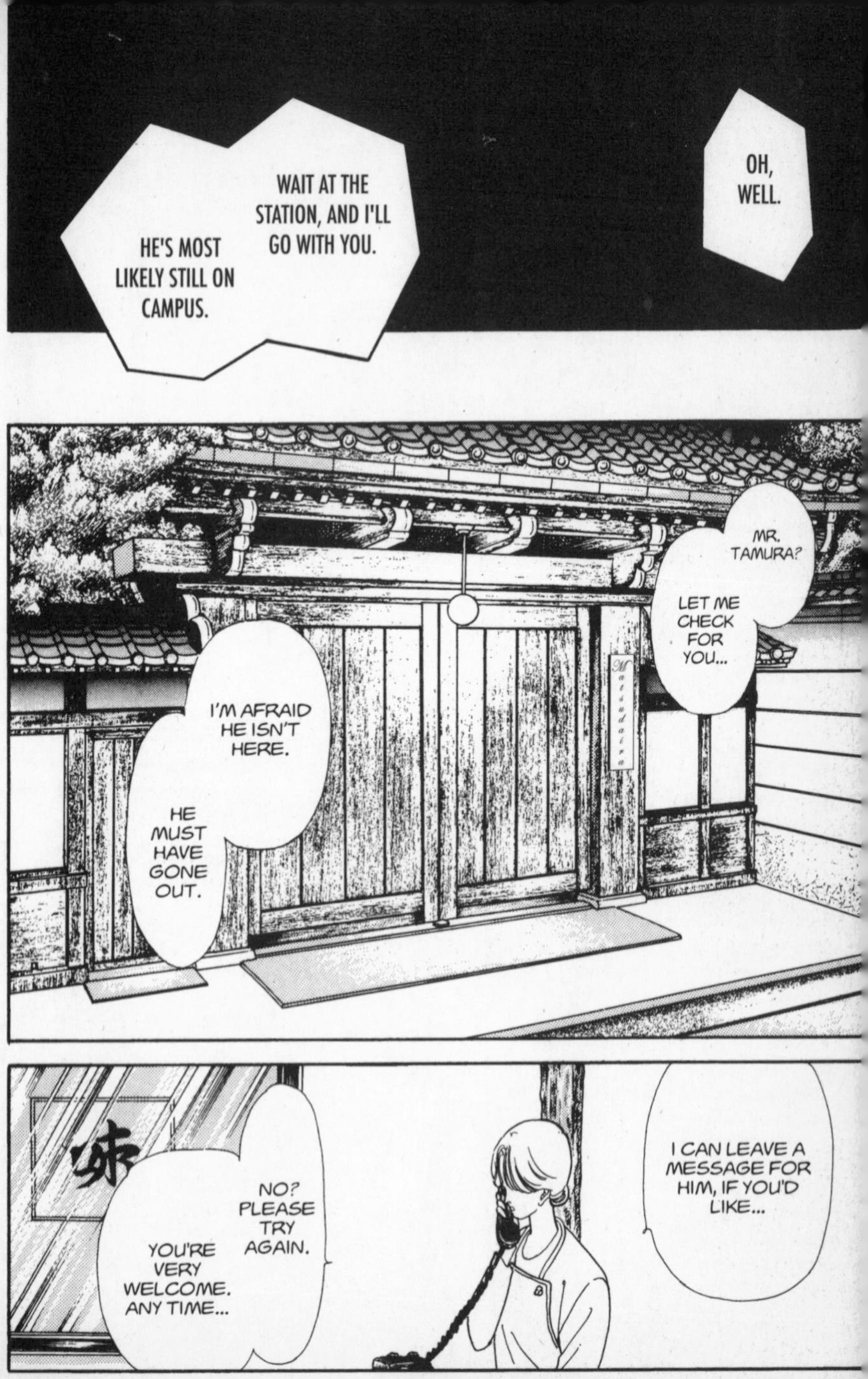
OH, WELL.
WAIT AT THE STATION, AND I'LL GO WITH YOU.
HE'S MOST LIKELY STILL ON CAMPUS.
MR. TAMURA?
LET ME CHECK FOR YOU...
I'M AFRAID HE ISN'T HERE.
HE MUST HAVE GONE OUT.
I CAN LEAVE A MESSAGE FOR HIM, IF YOU'D LIKE...
NO? PLEASE TRY AGAIN.
YOU'RE VERY WELCOME. ANY TIME...

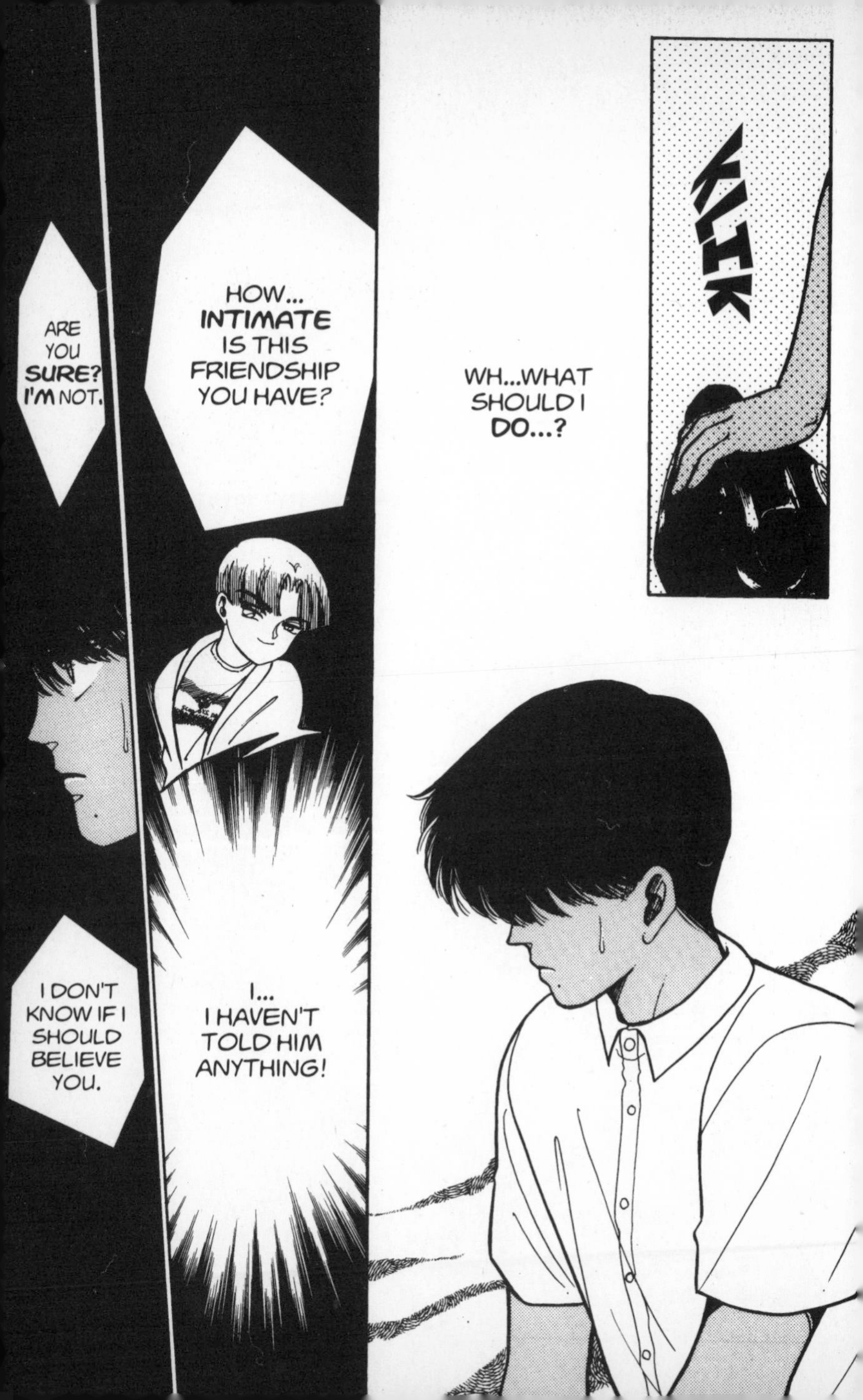
KLIK
WH...WHAT SHOULD I DO...?
HOW... INTIMATE IS THIS FRIENDSHIP YOU HAVE?
I... I HAVEN'T TOLD HIM ANYTHING!
ARE YOU SURE? I'M NOT.
I DON'T KNOW IF I SHOULD BELIEVE YOU.

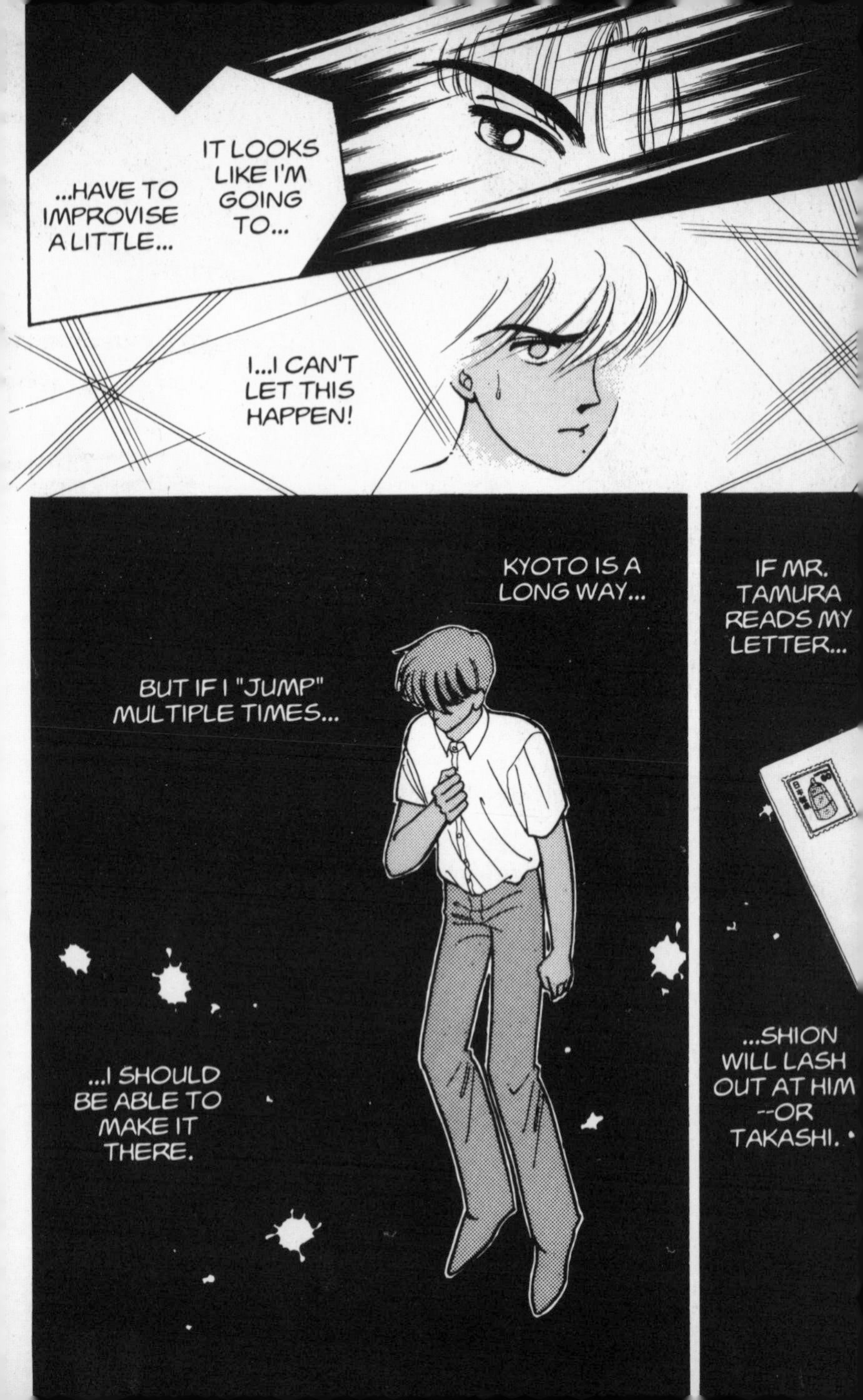
IT LOOKS LIKE I'M GOING TO...
...HAVE TO IMPROVISE A LITTLE...
I...I CAN'T LET THIS HAPPEN!
IF MR. TAMURA READS MY LETTER...
...SHION WILL LASH OUT AT HIM --OR TAKASHI.
KYOTO IS A LONG WAY...
BUT IF I "JUMP" MULTIPLE TIMES...
...I SHOULD BE ABLE TO MAKE IT THERE.

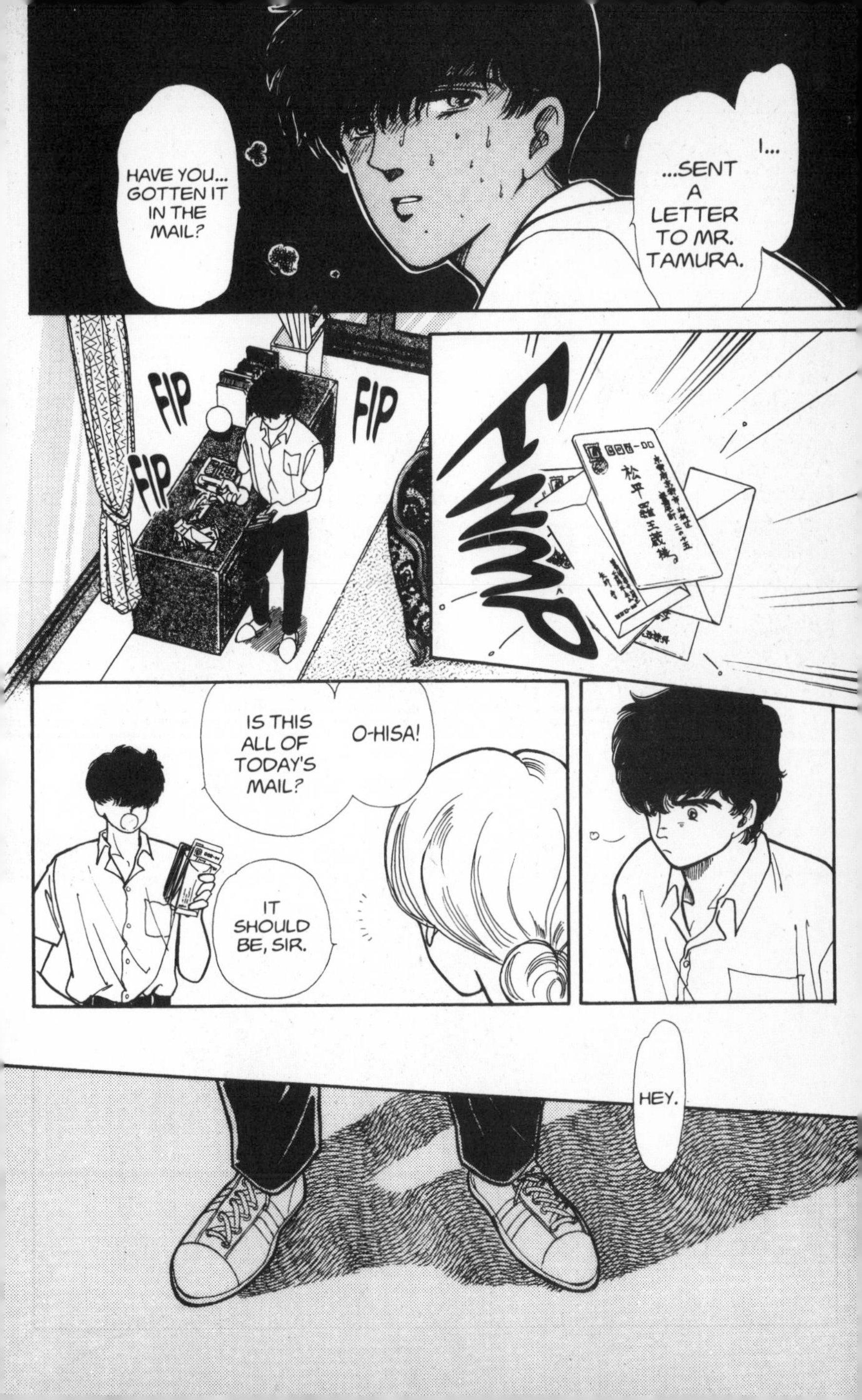
I... ...SENT A LETTER TO MR. TAMURA.
HAVE YOU... GOTTEN IT IN THE MAIL?
FWMP
FIP
FIP
FIP
O-HISA!
IS THIS ALL OF TODAY'S MAIL?
IT SHOULD BE, SIR.
HEY.

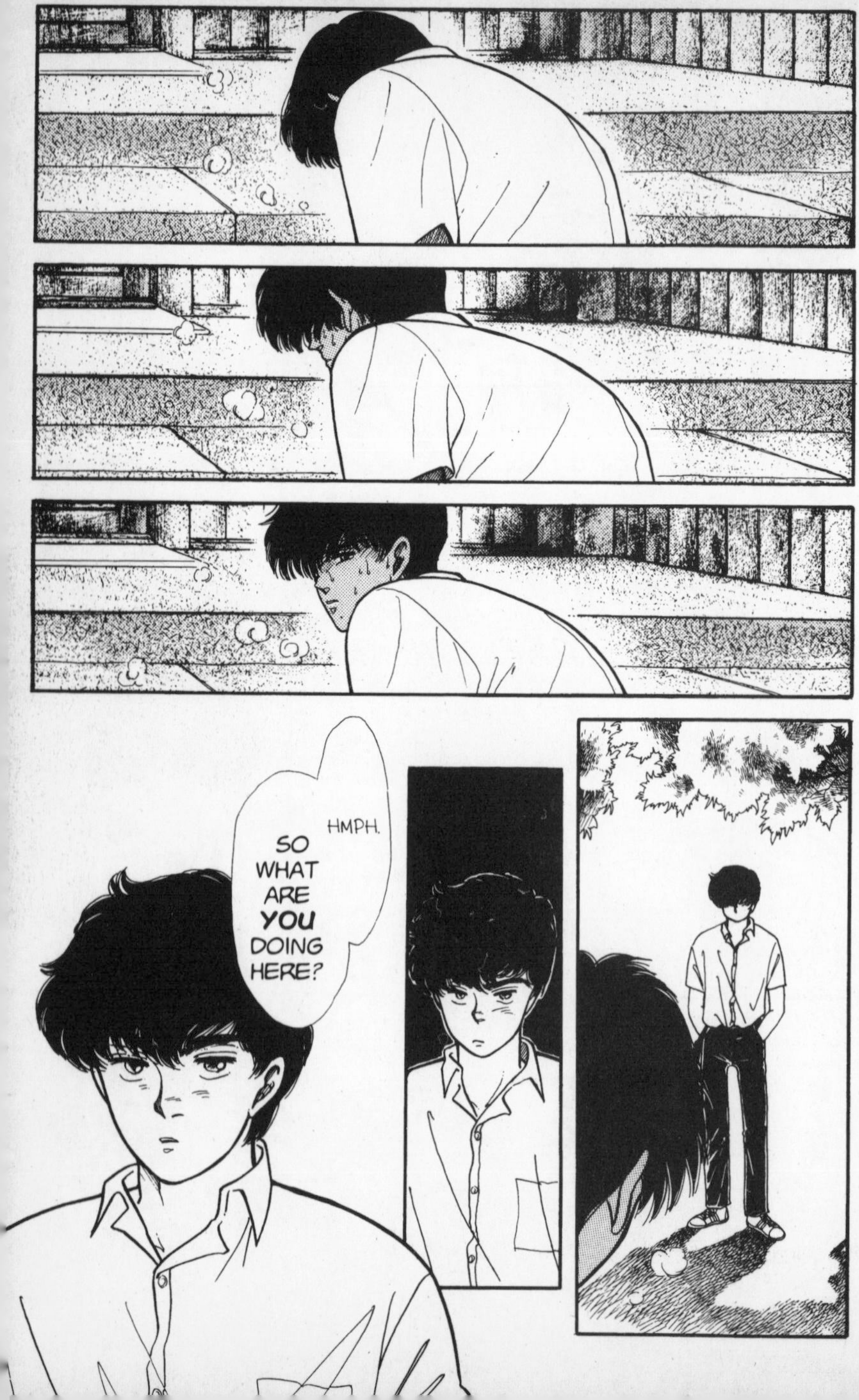
HMPH.
SO WHAT ARE YOU DOING HERE?

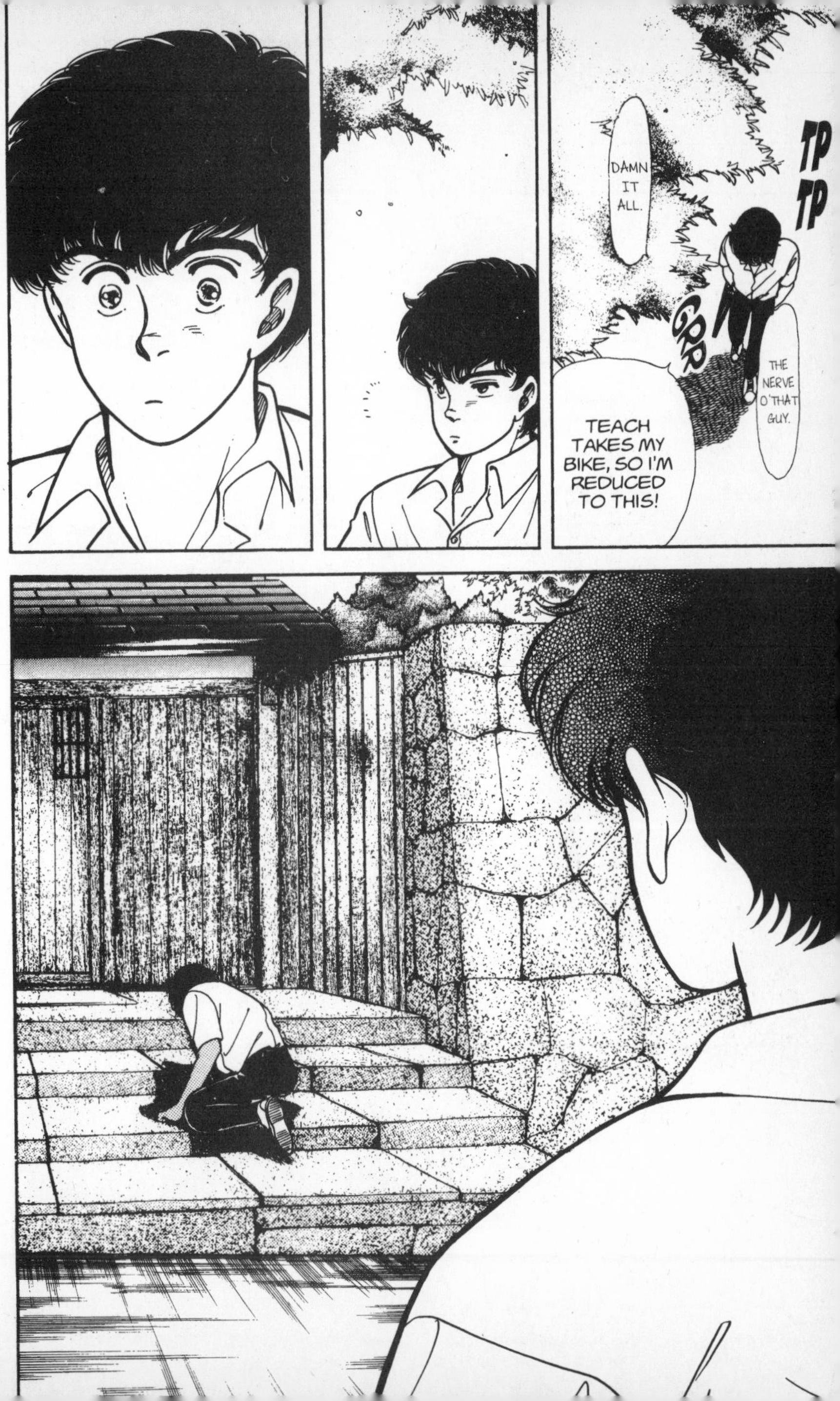
TP TP
DAMN IT ALL.
GRR
THE NERVE O'THAT GUY.
TEACH TAKES MY BIKE, SO I'M REDUCED TO THIS!

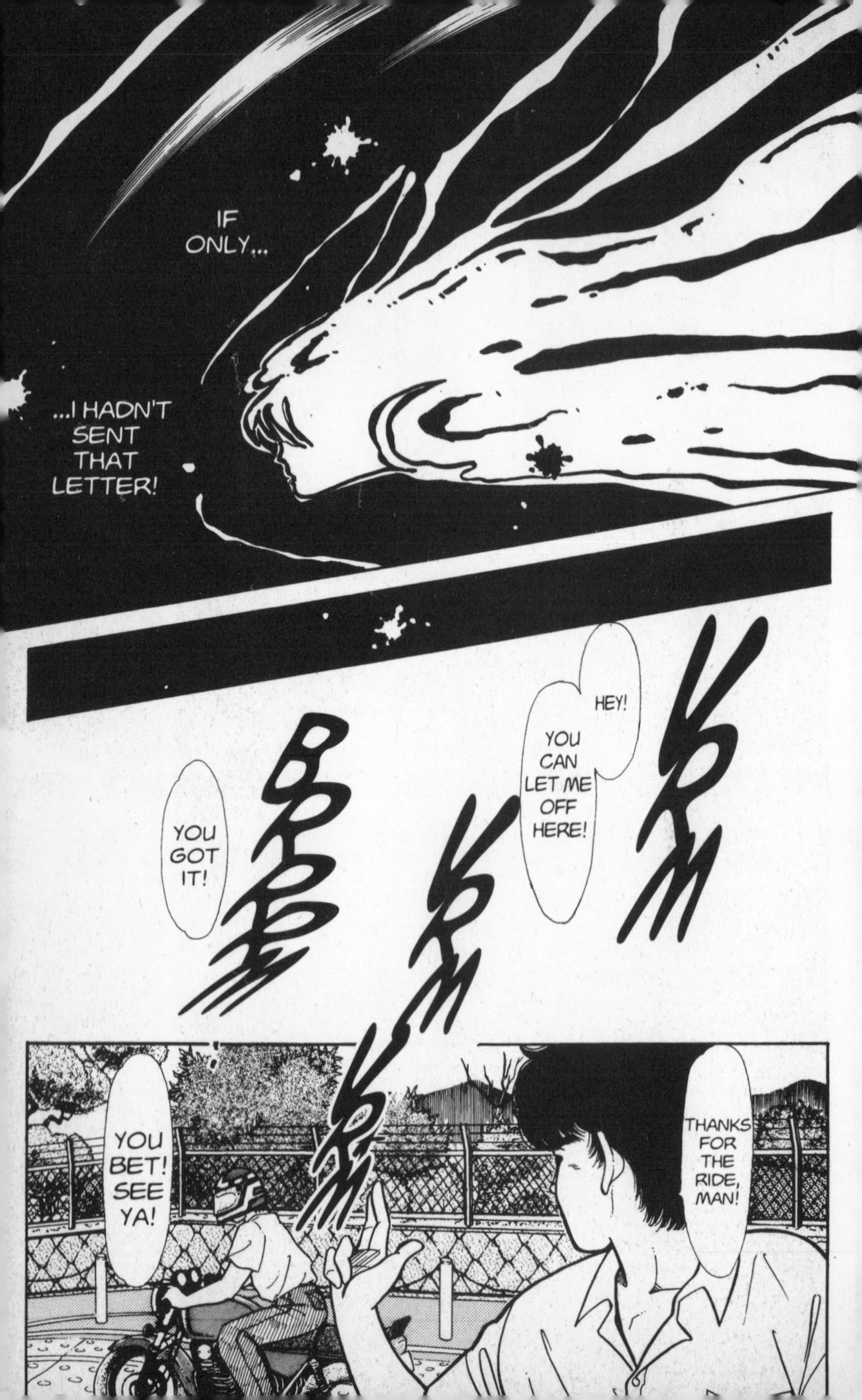
IF ONLY...
...I HADN'T SENT THAT LETTER!
HEY! YOU CAN LET ME OFF HERE!
YOU GOT IT!
THANKS FOR THE RIDE, MAN!
YOU BET! SEE YA!

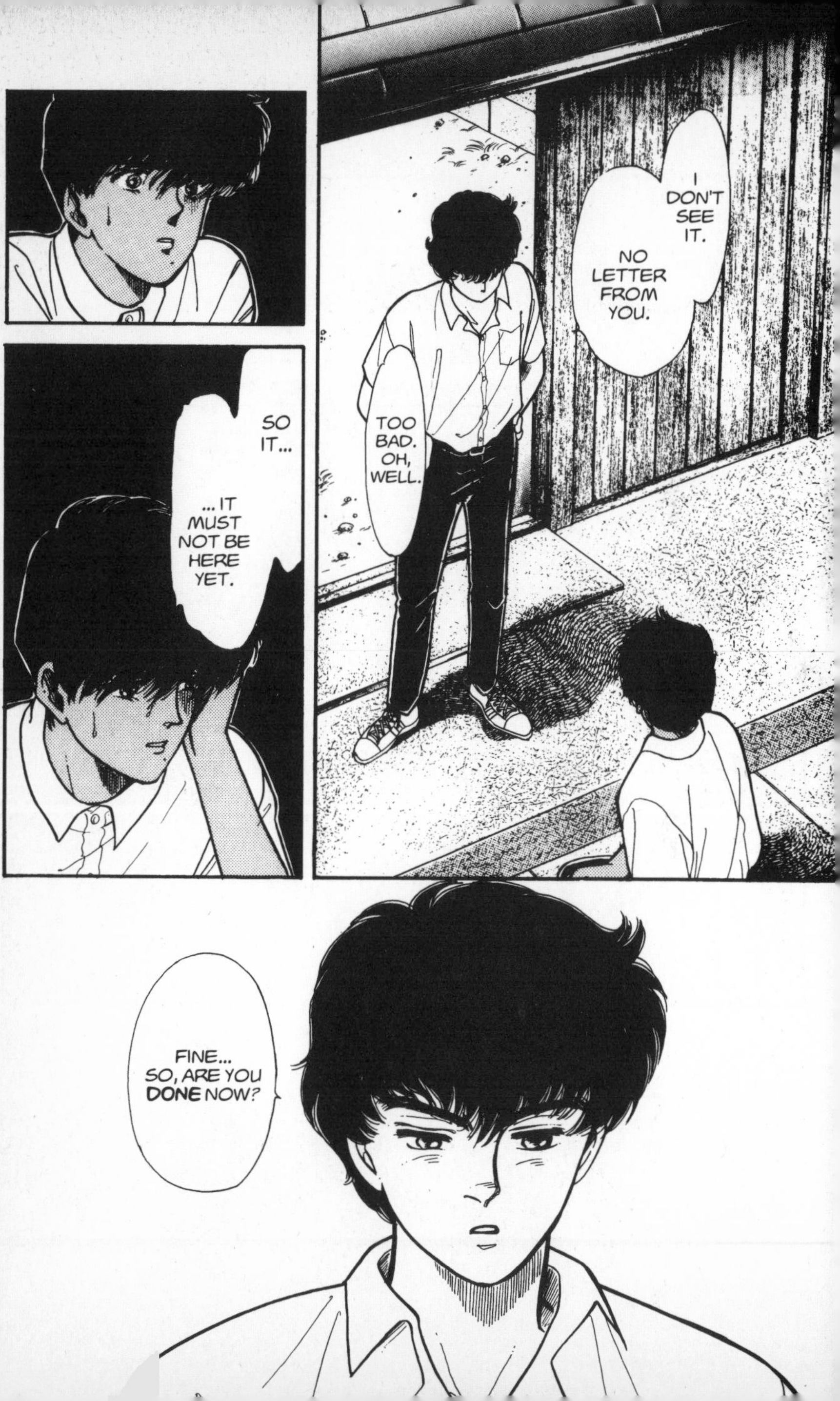
I DON'T SEE IT.
NO LETTER FROM YOU.
TOO BAD. OH, WELL.
SO IT...
...IT MUST NOT BE HERE YET.
FINE... SO, ARE YOU **DONE** NOW?

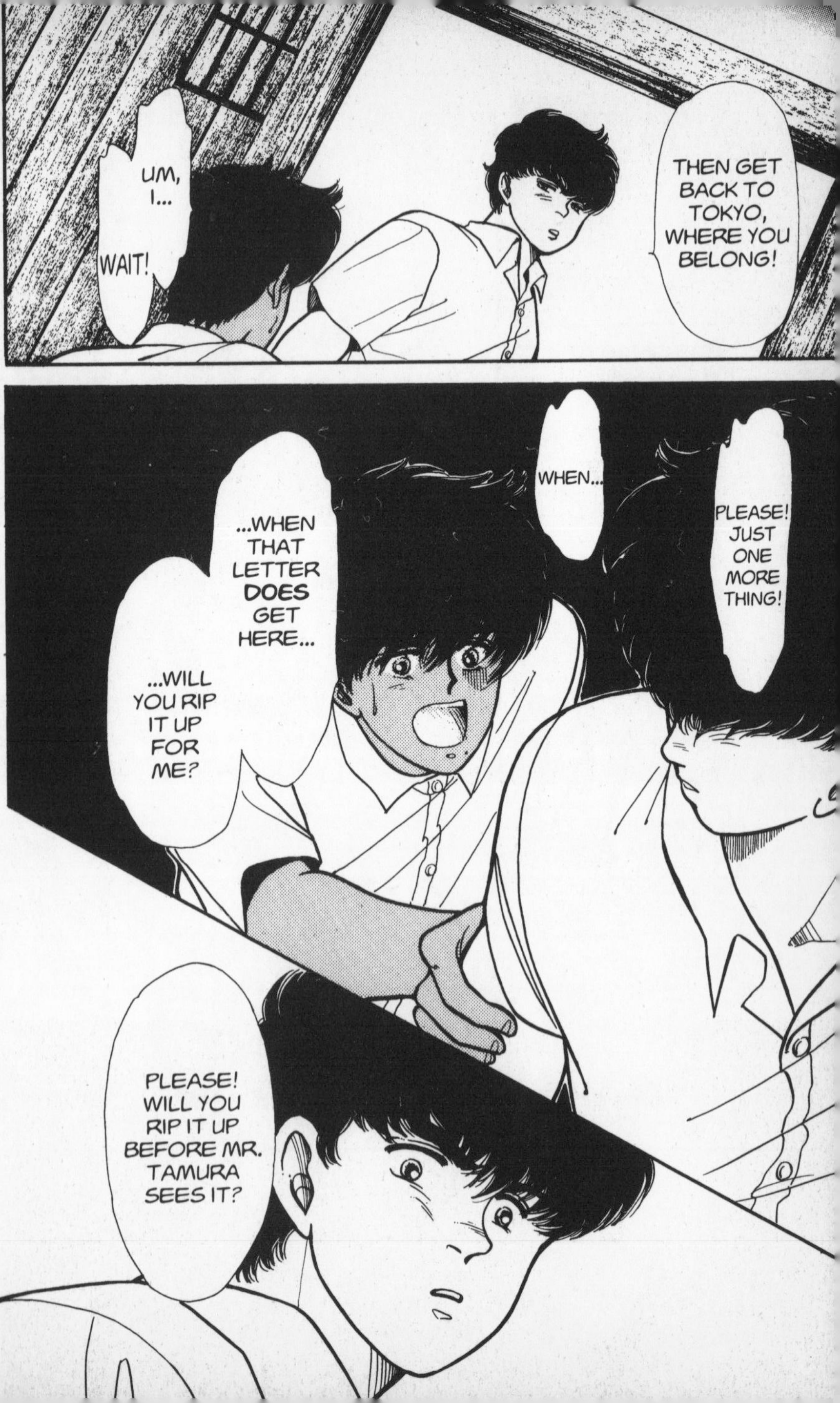
THEN GET BACK TO TOKYO, WHERE YOU BELONG!
UM, I...
WAIT!
PLEASE! JUST ONE MORE THING!
WHEN...
...WHEN THAT LETTER **DOES** GET HERE...
...WILL YOU RIP IT UP FOR ME?
PLEASE! WILL YOU RIP IT UP BEFORE MR. TAMURA SEES IT?

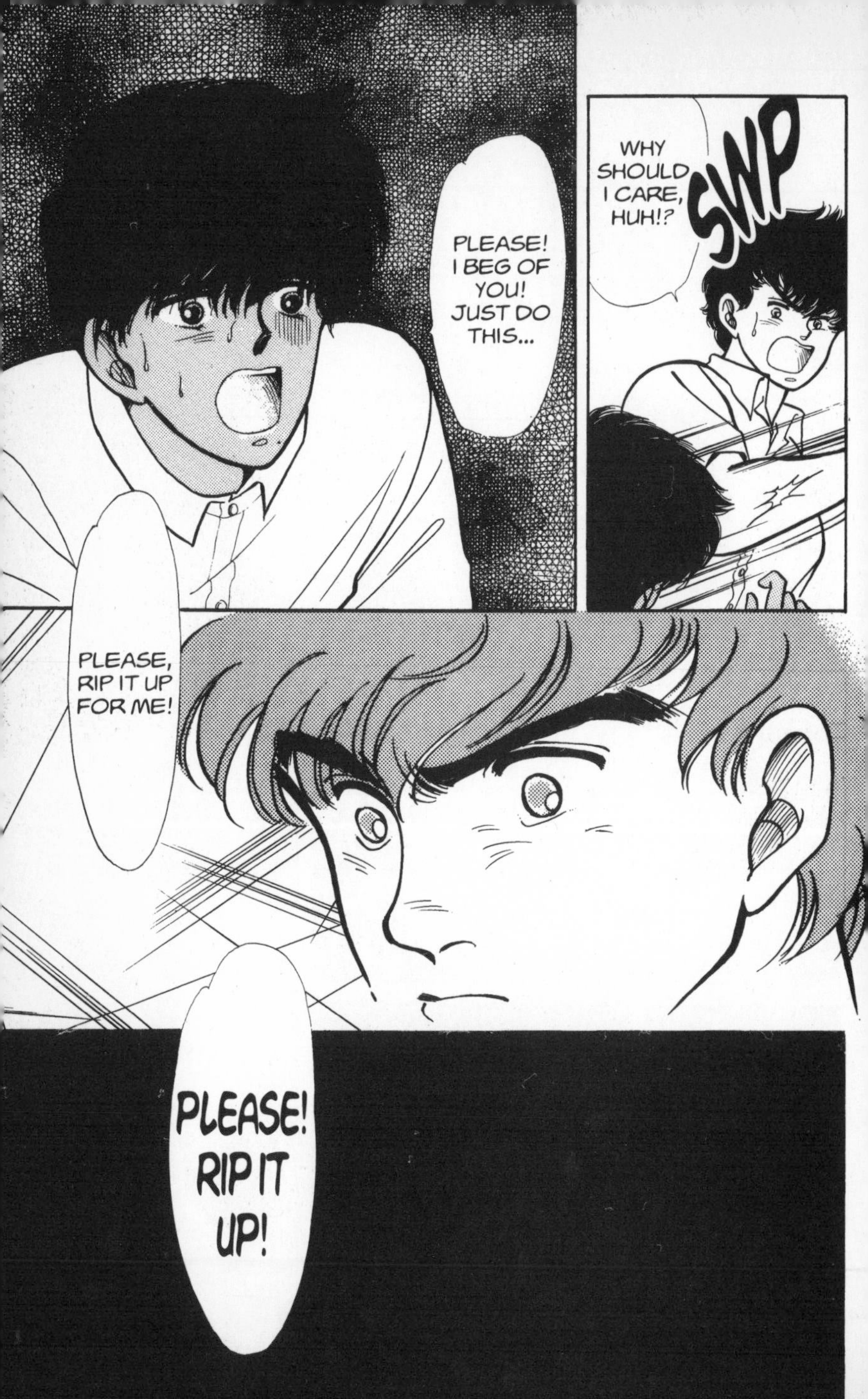
WHY SHOULD I CARE, HUH!?
SWP
PLEASE! I BEG OF YOU! JUST DO THIS...
PLEASE, RIP IT UP FOR ME!
PLEASE! RIP IT UP!

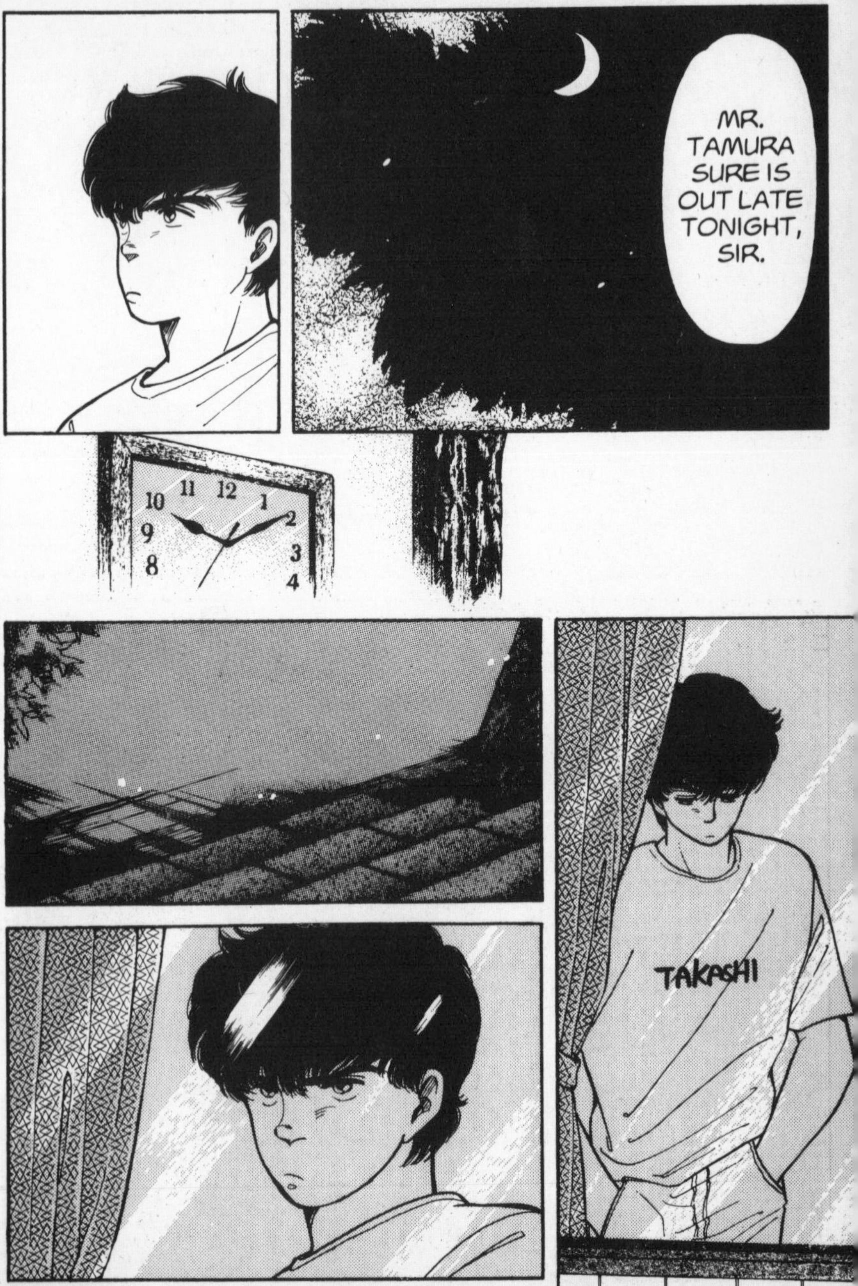
MR. TAMURA SURE IS OUT LATE TONIGHT, SIR.
TAKASHI

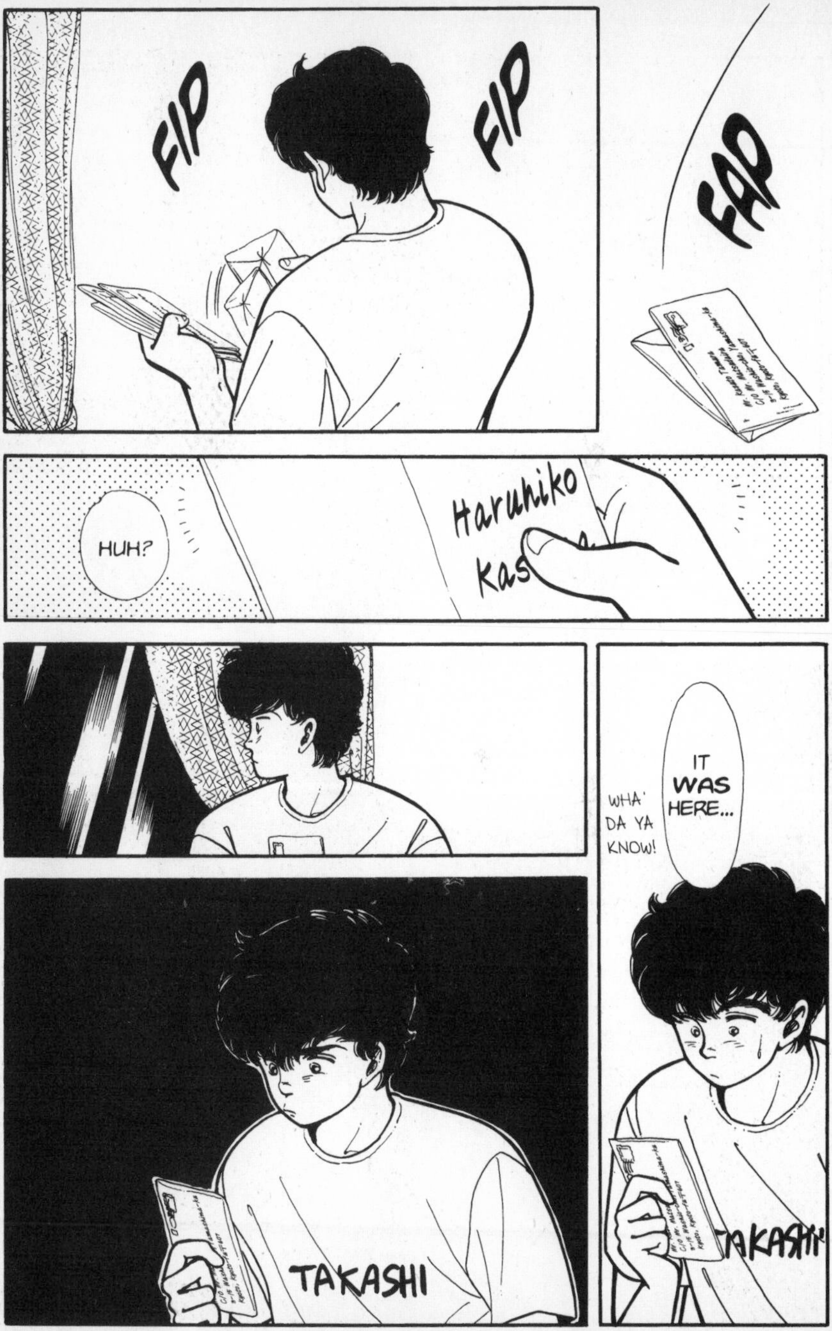
FAP
FIP
FIP
HUH?
Haruhiko Kas
IT WAS HERE...
WHA' DA YA KNOW!
TAKASHI
TAKASHI

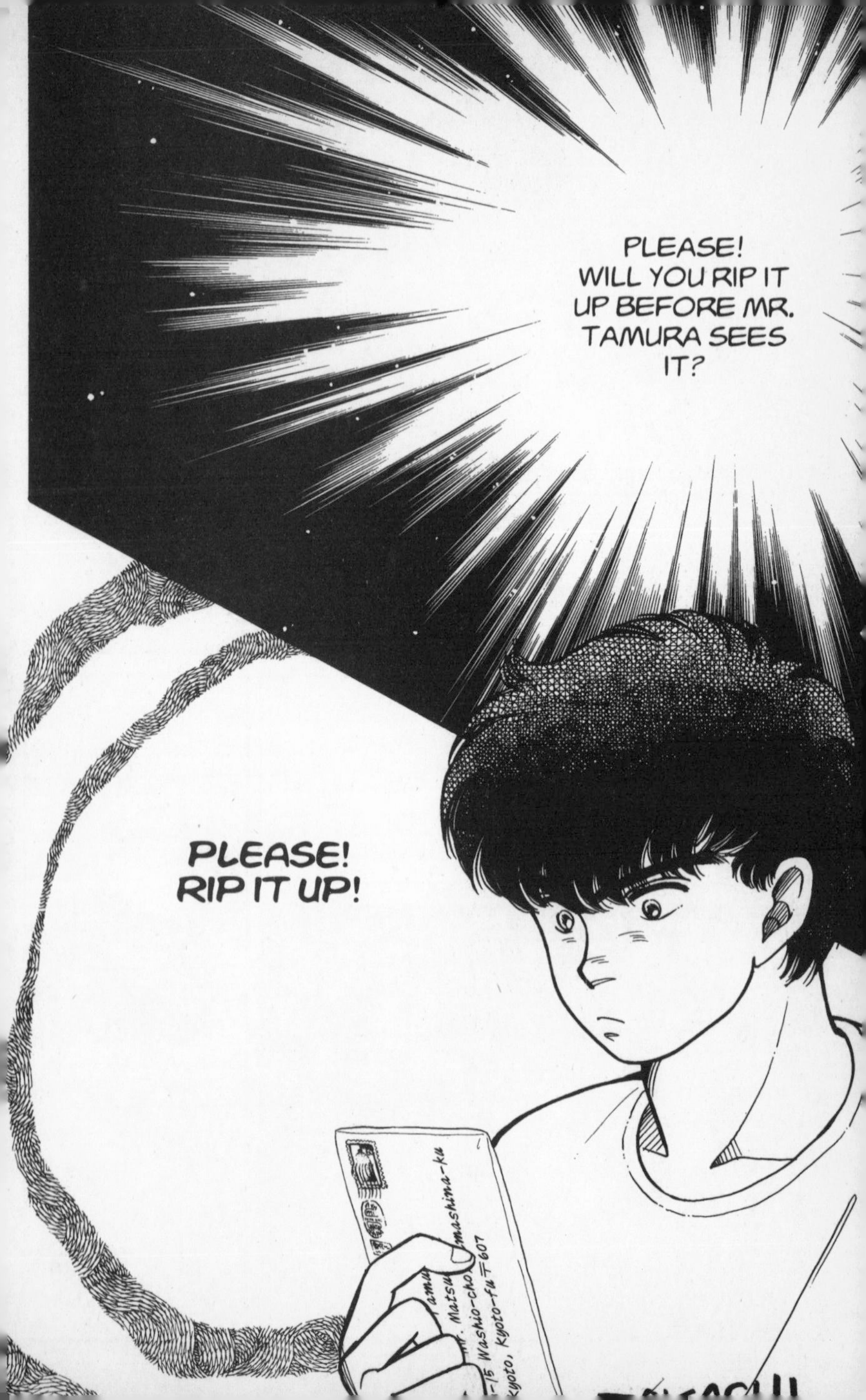
PLEASE! WILL YOU RIP IT UP BEFORE MR. TAMURA SEES IT?
PLEASE! RIP IT UP!

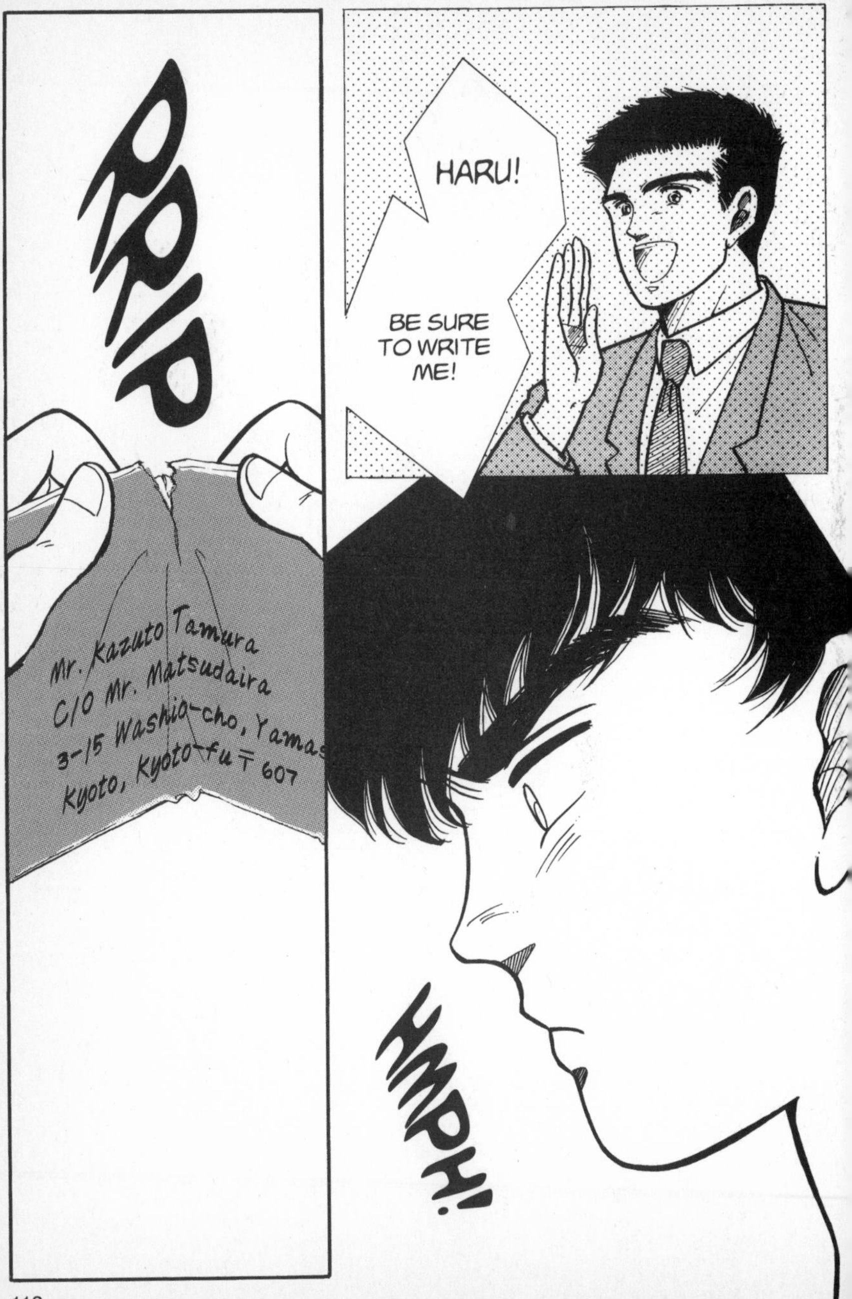
HARU!
BE SURE TO WRITE ME!
HMPH!
RRRIP
Mr. Kazuto Tamura
C/O Mr. Matsudaira
3-15 Washio-cho, Yamas
Kyoto, Kyoto-fu 〒 607

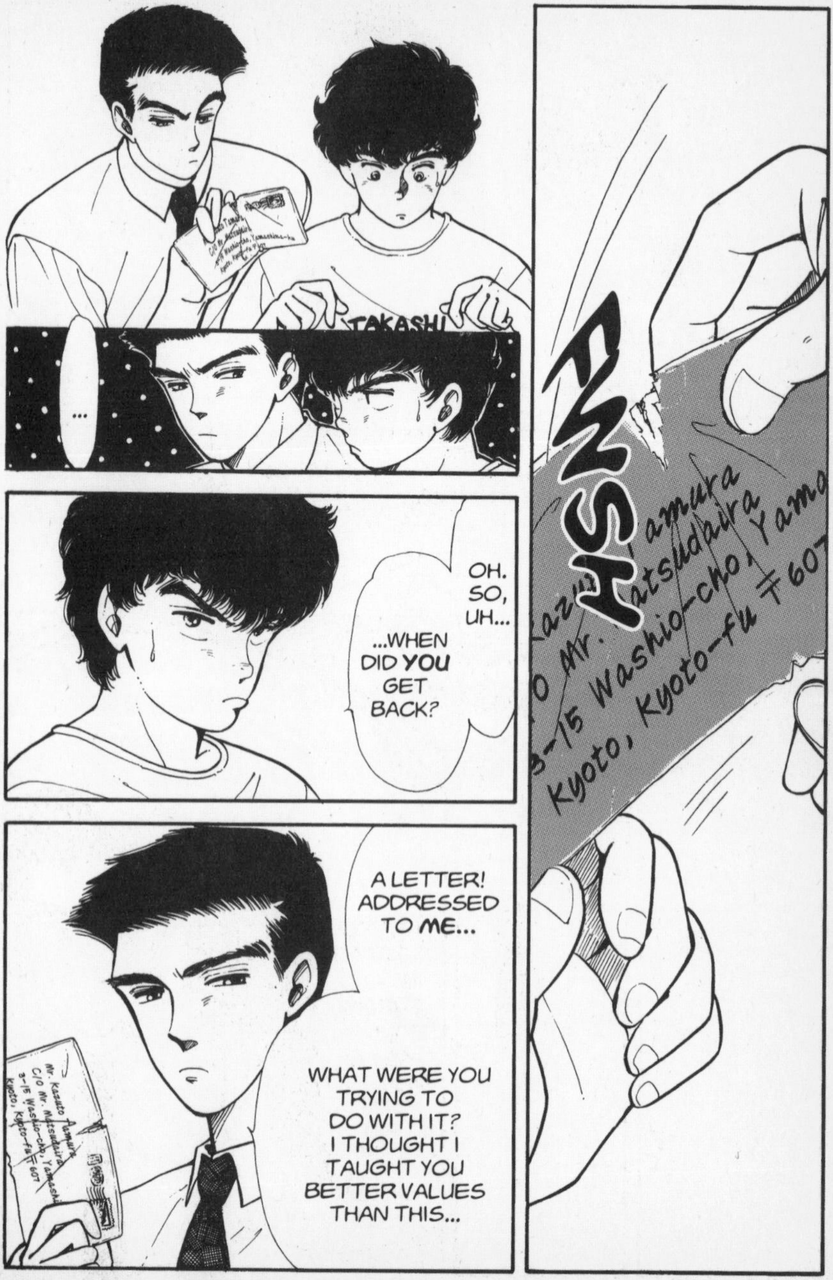
FWSH
3-15 Washio-cho,
Kyoto, Kyoto-fu 〒607
TAKASHI
...
OH. SO, UH...
...WHEN DID YOU GET BACK?
A LETTER! ADDRESSED TO ME...
WHAT WERE YOU TRYING TO DO WITH IT? I THOUGHT I TAUGHT YOU BETTER VALUES THAN THIS...

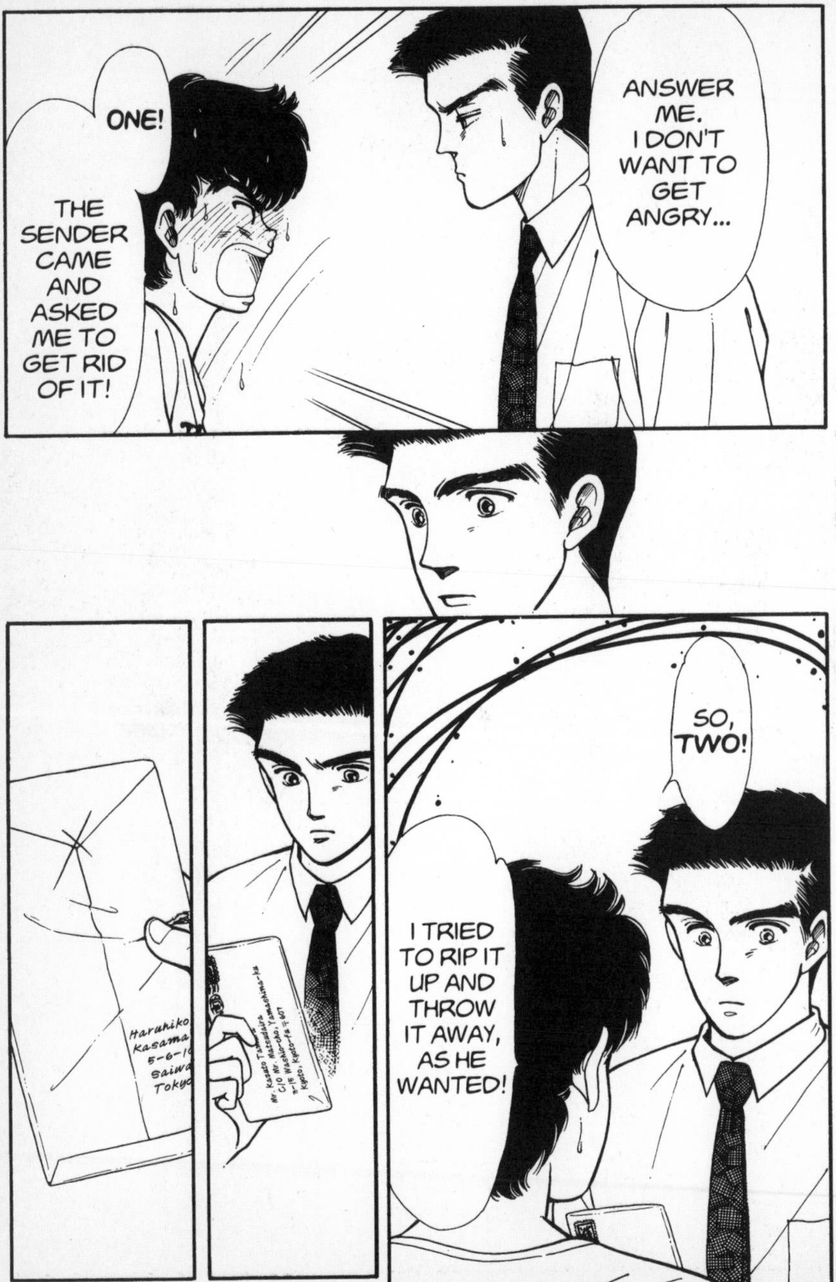
ANSWER ME. I DON'T WANT TO GET ANGRY...
ONE!
THE SENDER CAME AND ASKED ME TO GET RID OF IT!
SO, TWO!
I TRIED TO RIP IT UP AND THROW IT AWAY, AS HE WANTED!

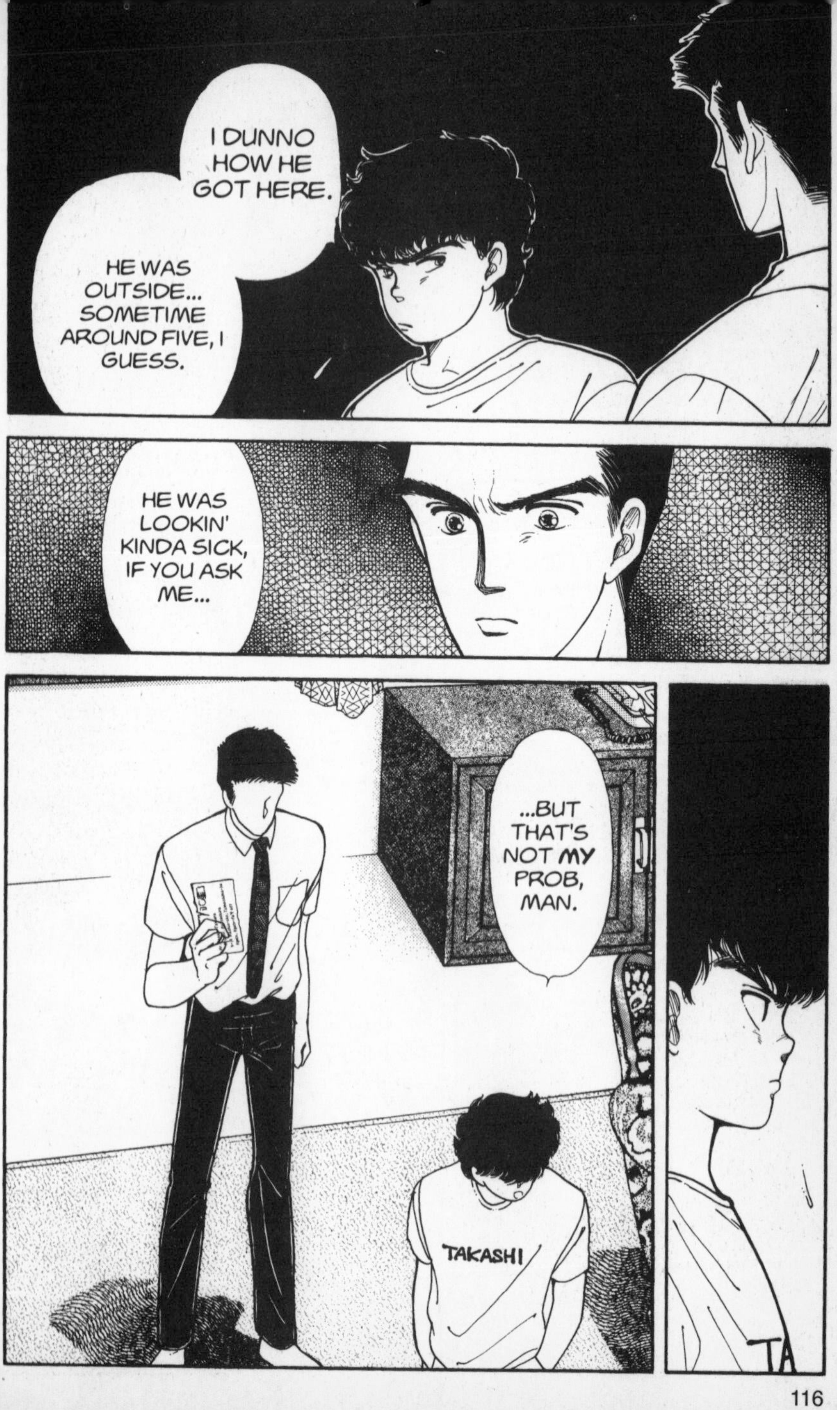
I DUNNO HOW HE GOT HERE.
HE WAS OUTSIDE... SOMETIME AROUND FIVE, I GUESS.
HE WAS LOOKIN' KINDA SICK, IF YOU ASK ME...
TA
...BUT THAT'S NOT **MY** PROB, MAN.
TAKASHI

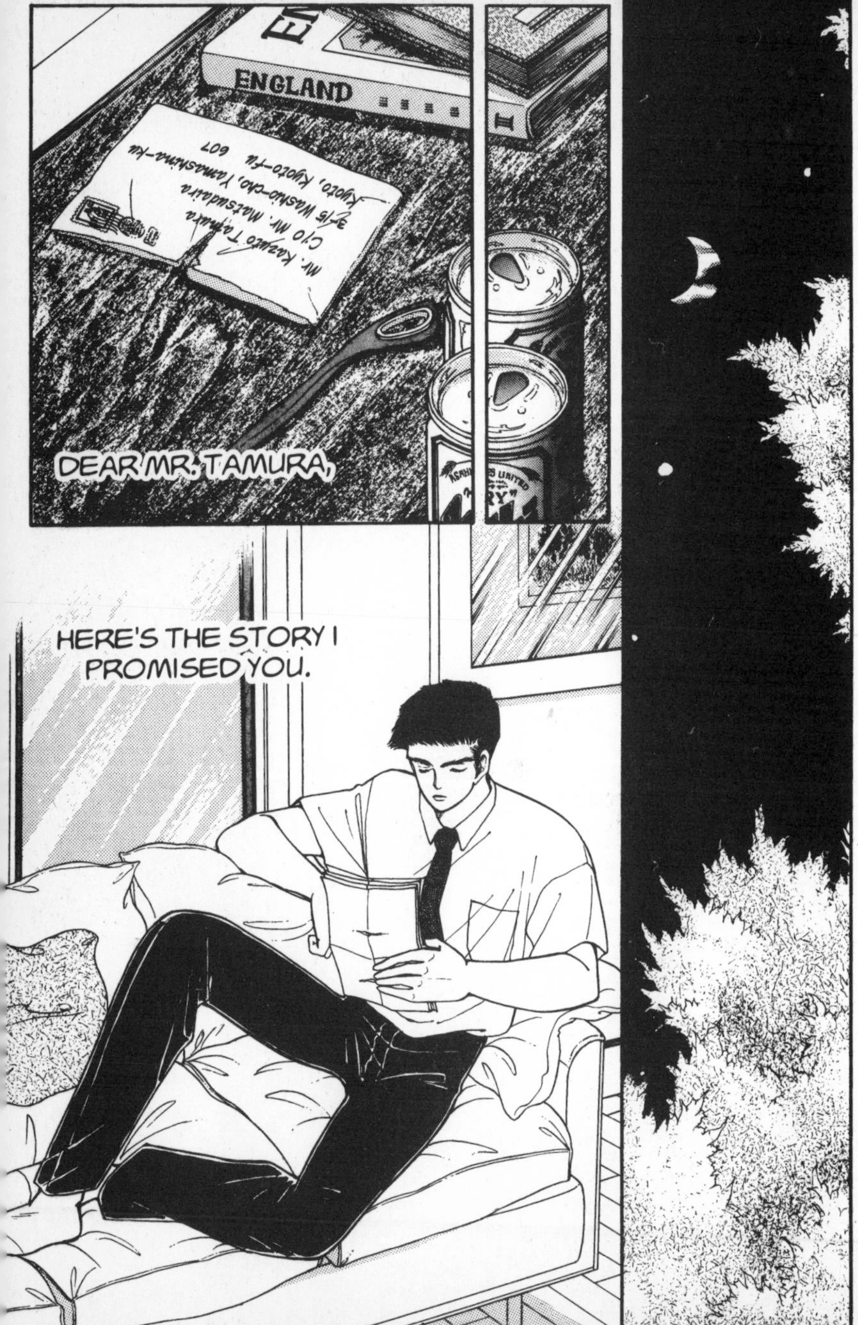
ENGLAND
Mr. Kazuto Tamura
c/o Mr. Matsudaira
3/5 Washio-cho, Yamashina-ku
Kyoto, Kyoto-Fu 607
DEAR MR. TAMURA,
HERE'S THE STORY I PROMISED YOU.

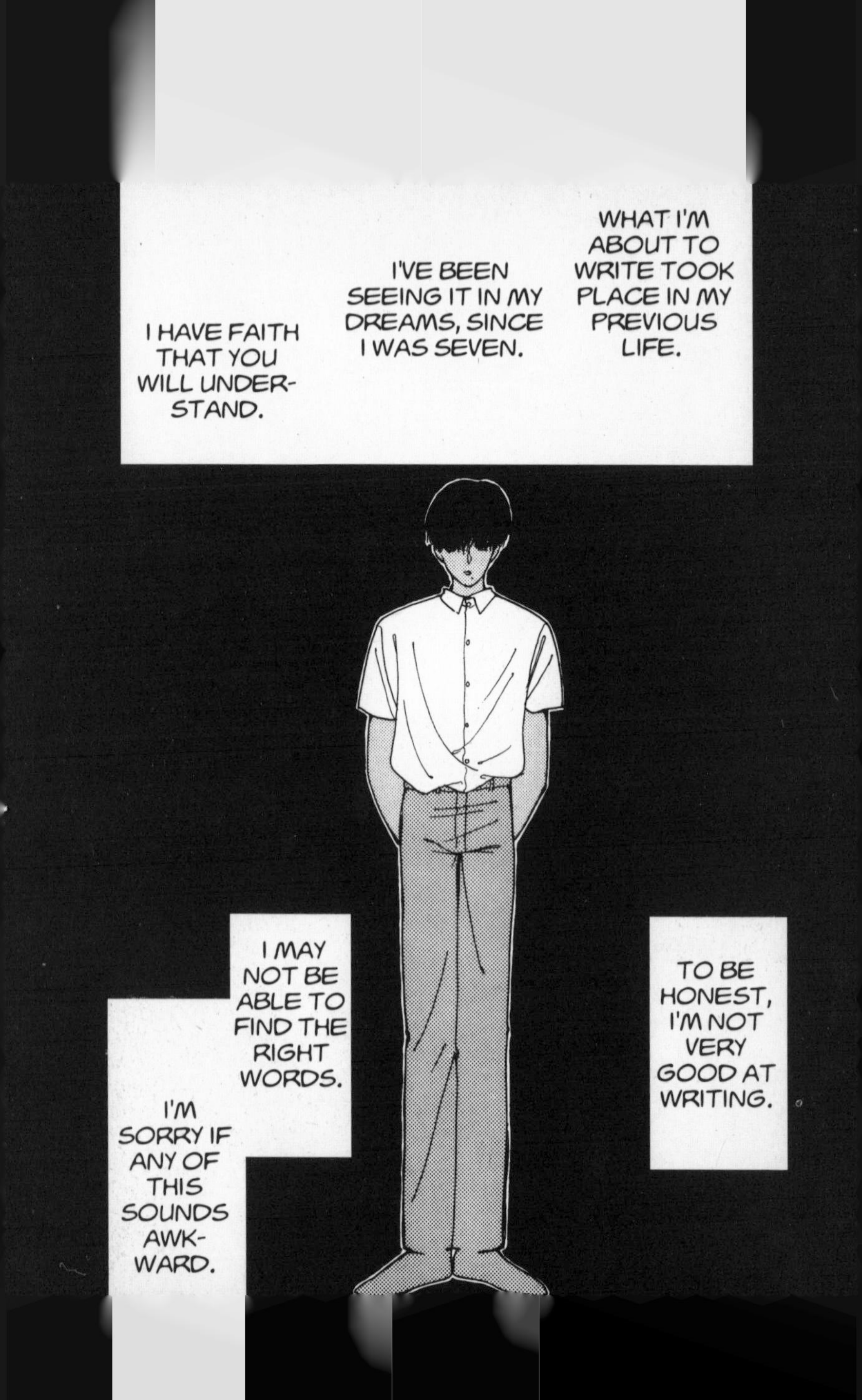
WHAT I'M ABOUT TO WRITE TOOK PLACE IN MY PREVIOUS LIFE.
I'VE BEEN SEEING IT IN MY DREAMS, SINCE I WAS SEVEN.
I HAVE FAITH THAT YOU WILL UNDER-STAND.
TO BE HONEST, I'M NOT VERY GOOD AT WRITING.
I MAY NOT BE ABLE TO FIND THE RIGHT WORDS.
I'M SORRY IF ANY OF THIS SOUNDS AWK-WARD.

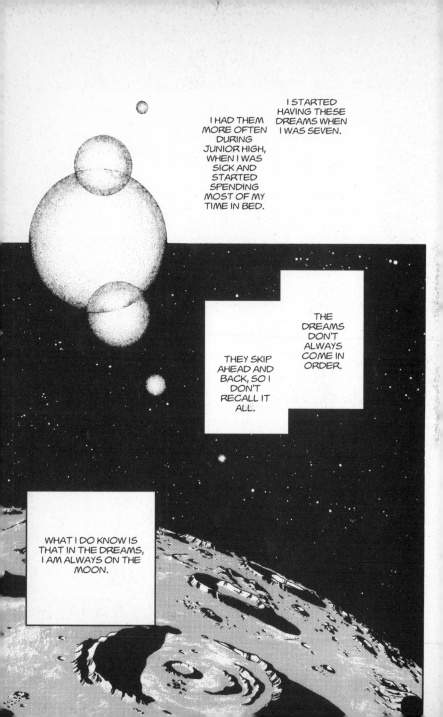

I STARTED HAVING THESE DREAMS WHEN I WAS SEVEN.

I HAD THEM MORE OFTEN DURING JUNIOR HIGH, WHEN I WAS SICK AND STARTED SPENDING MOST OF MY TIME IN BED.

THE DREAMS DON'T ALWAYS COME IN ORDER.

THEY SKIP AHEAD AND BACK, SO I DON'T RECALL IT ALL.

WHAT I DO KNOW IS THAT IN THE DREAMS, I AM ALWAYS ON THE MOON.

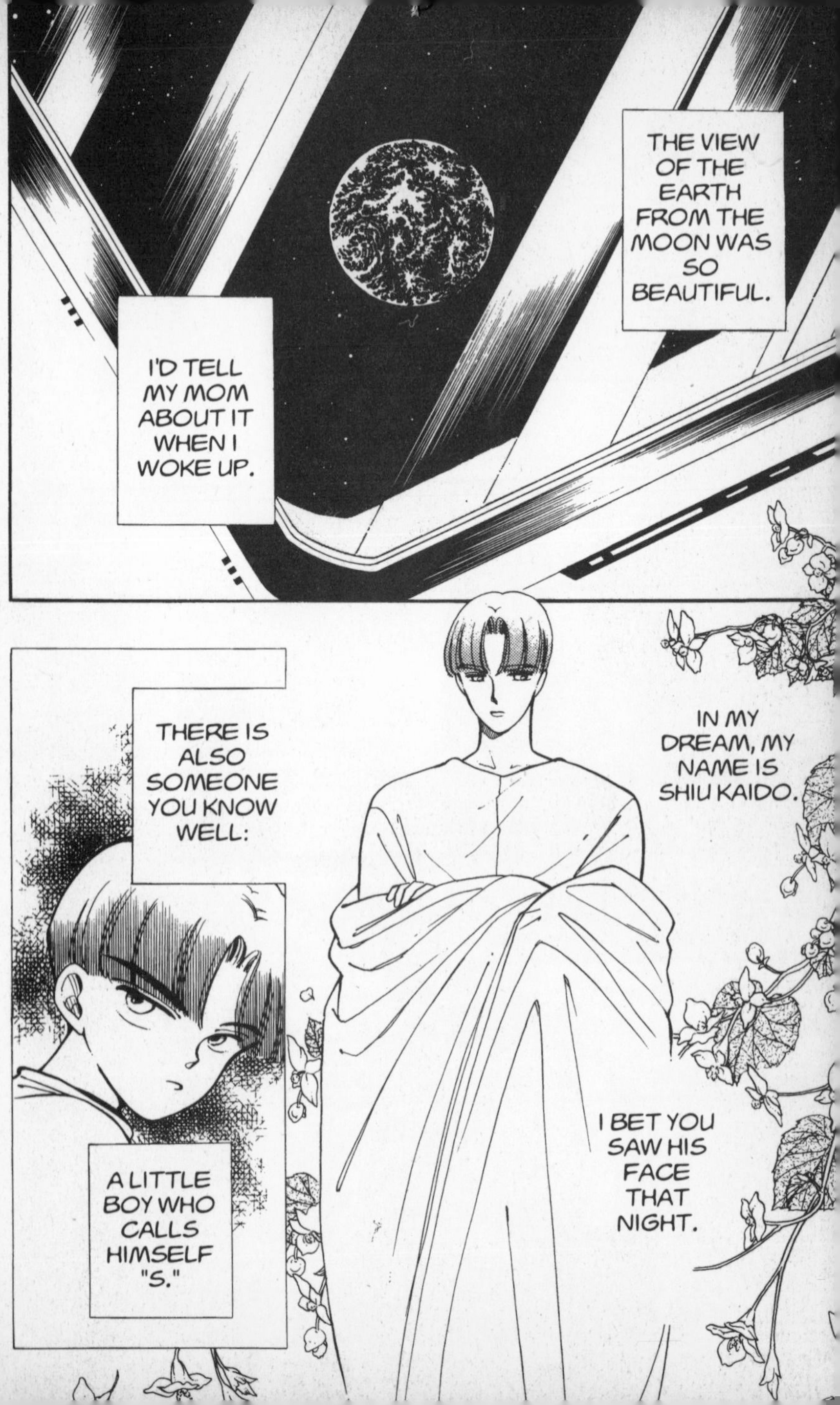
THE VIEW OF THE EARTH FROM THE MOON WAS SO BEAUTIFUL.
I'D TELL MY MOM ABOUT IT WHEN I WOKE UP.
IN MY DREAM, MY NAME IS SHIU KAIDO.
I BET YOU SAW HIS FACE THAT NIGHT.
THERE IS ALSO SOMEONE YOU KNOW WELL:
A LITTLE BOY WHO CALLS HIMSELF "S."

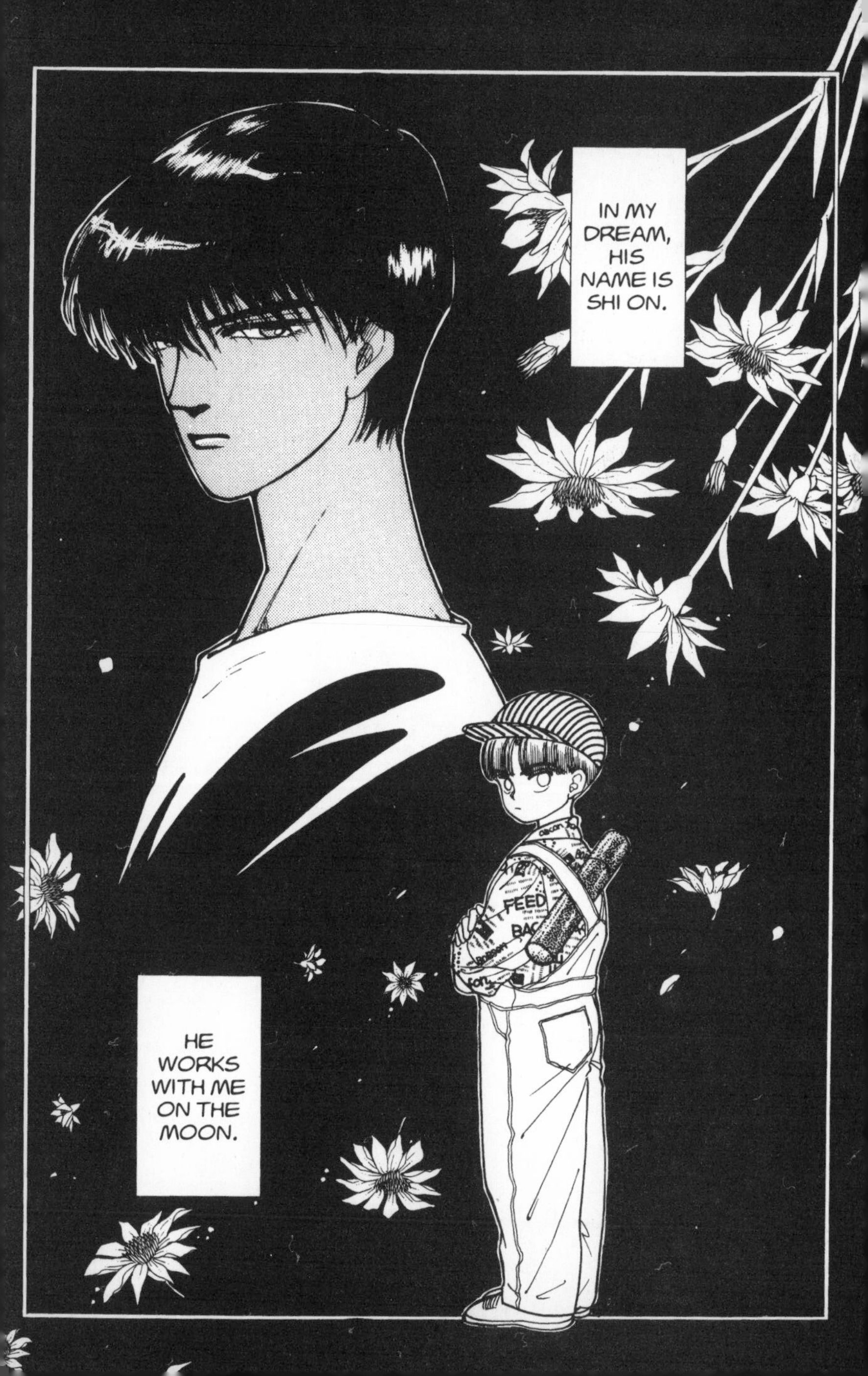
IN MY DREAM, HIS NAME IS SHI ON.
HE WORKS WITH ME ON THE MOON.

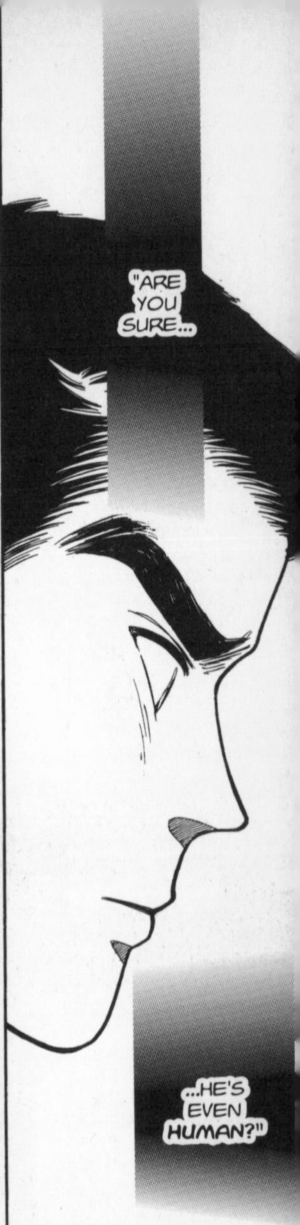
"ARE YOU SURE...
...HE'S EVEN HUMAN?"
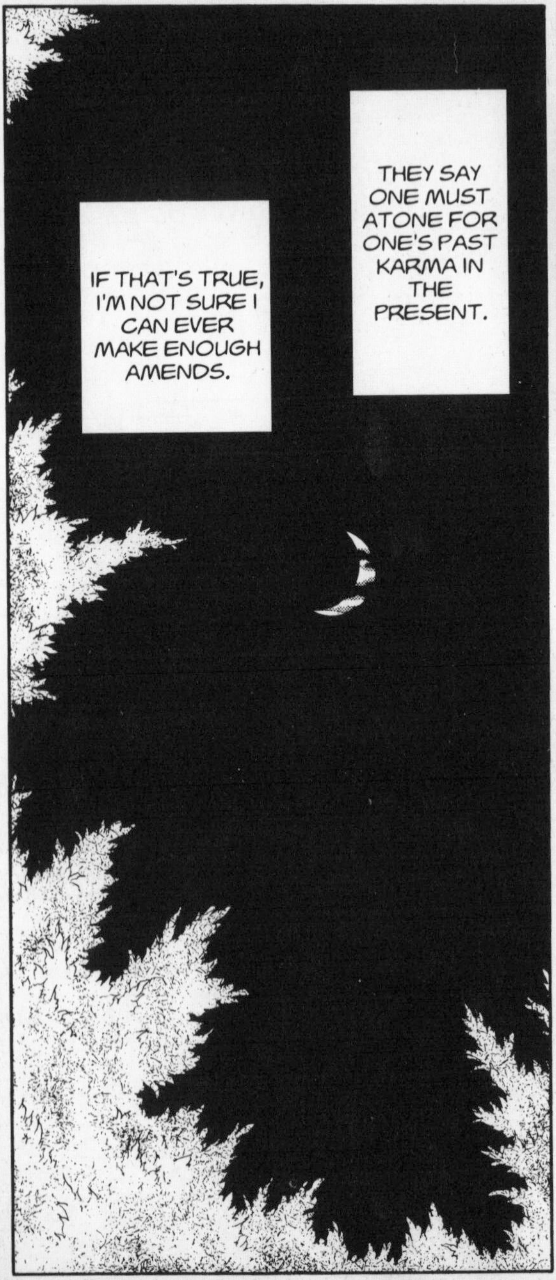
THEY SAY ONE MUST ATONE FOR ONE'S PAST KARMA IN THE PRESENT.
IF THAT'S TRUE, I'M NOT SURE I CAN EVER MAKE ENOUGH AMENDS.

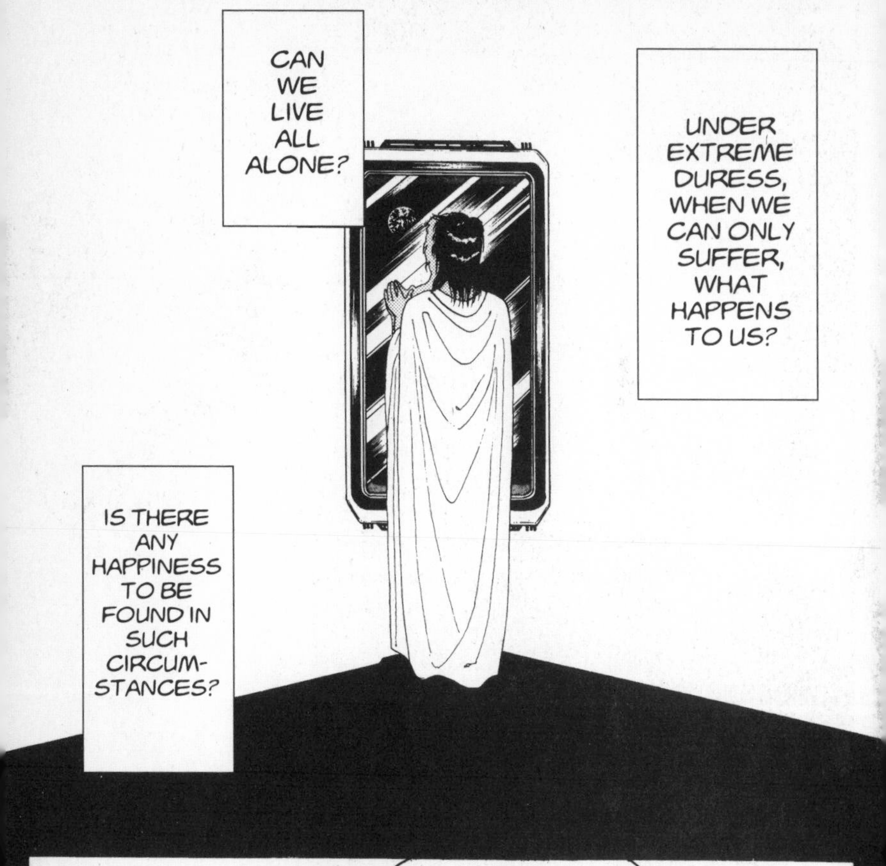
UNDER EXTREME DURESS, WHEN WE CAN ONLY SUFFER, WHAT HAPPENS TO US?
CAN WE LIVE ALL ALONE?
IS THERE ANY HAPPINESS TO BE FOUND IN SUCH CIRCUM-STANCES?

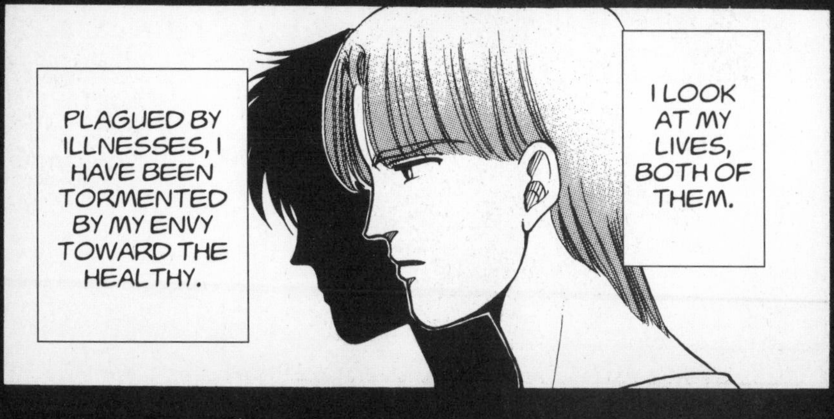
I LOOK AT MY LIVES, BOTH OF THEM.
PLAGUED BY ILLNESSES, I HAVE BEEN TORMENTED BY MY ENVY TOWARD THE HEALTHY.

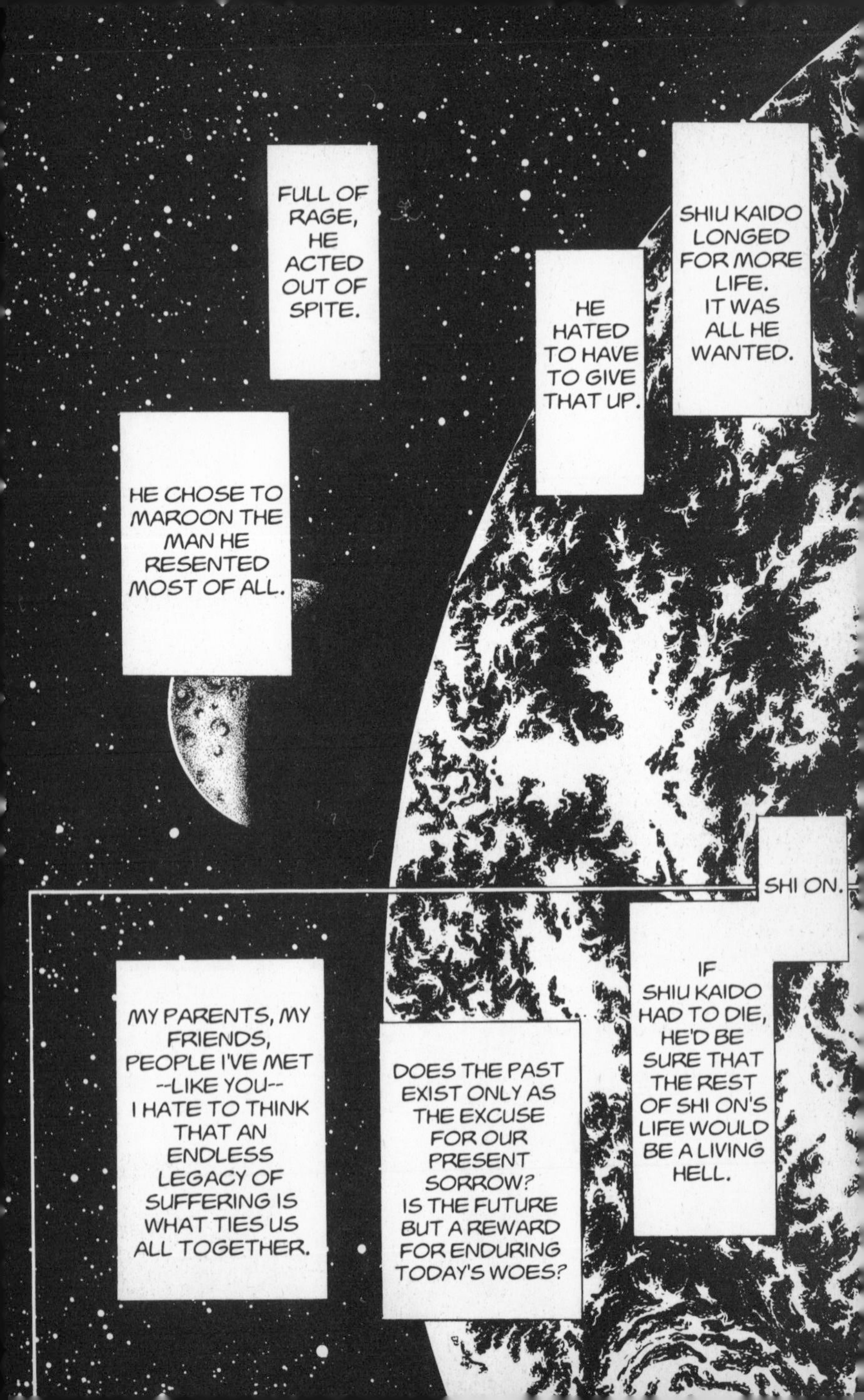
SHIU KAIDO LONGED FOR MORE LIFE. IT WAS ALL HE WANTED.
HE HATED TO HAVE TO GIVE THAT UP.
FULL OF RAGE, HE ACTED OUT OF SPITE.
HE CHOSE TO MAROON THE MAN HE RESENTED MOST OF ALL.
SHI ON.
IF SHIU KAIDO HAD TO DIE, HE'D BE SURE THAT THE REST OF SHI ON'S LIFE WOULD BE A LIVING HELL.
DOES THE PAST EXIST ONLY AS THE EXCUSE FOR OUR PRESENT SORROW? IS THE FUTURE BUT A REWARD FOR ENDURING TODAY'S WOES?
MY PARENTS, MY FRIENDS, PEOPLE I'VE MET --LIKE YOU-- I HATE TO THINK THAT AN ENDLESS LEGACY OF SUFFERING IS WHAT TIES US ALL TOGETHER.

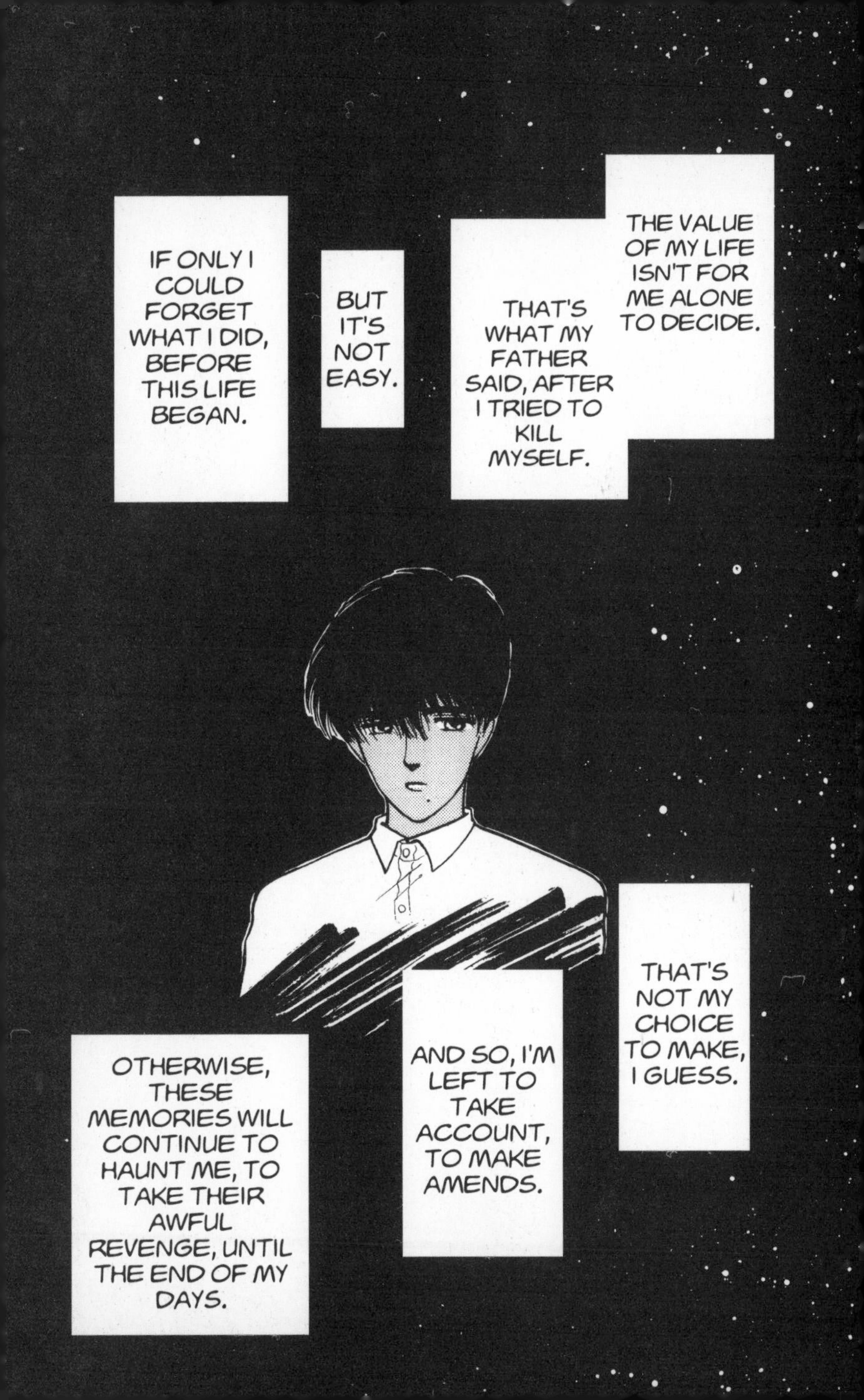
THE VALUE OF MY LIFE ISN'T FOR ME ALONE TO DECIDE.
THAT'S WHAT MY FATHER SAID, AFTER I TRIED TO KILL MYSELF.
BUT IT'S NOT EASY.
IF ONLY I COULD FORGET WHAT I DID, BEFORE THIS LIFE BEGAN.
THAT'S NOT MY CHOICE TO MAKE, I GUESS.
AND SO, I'M LEFT TO TAKE ACCOUNT, TO MAKE AMENDS.
OTHERWISE, THESE MEMORIES WILL CONTINUE TO HAUNT ME, TO TAKE THEIR AWFUL REVENGE, UNTIL THE END OF MY DAYS.

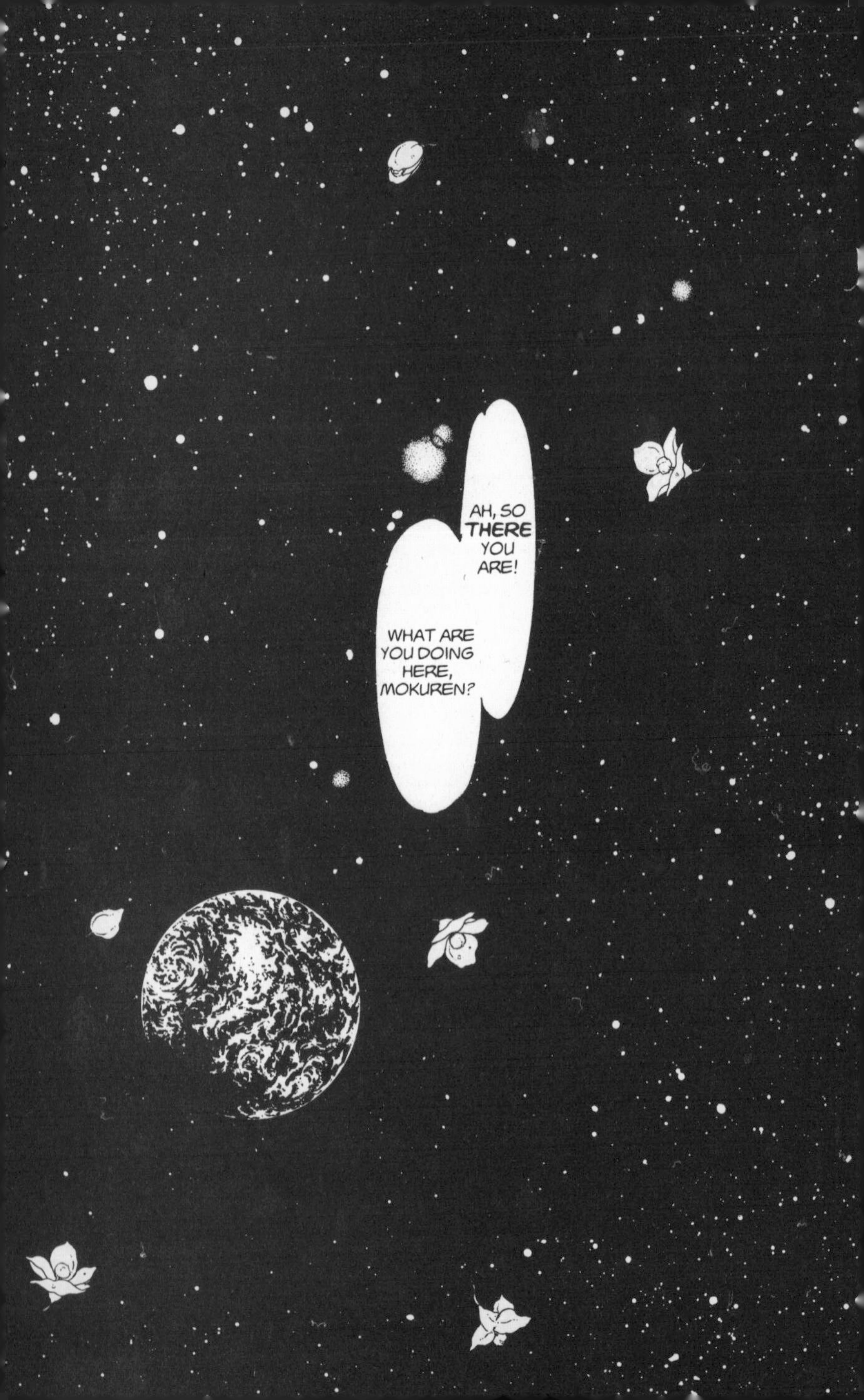
AH, SO THERE YOU ARE!
WHAT ARE YOU DOING HERE, MOKUREN?

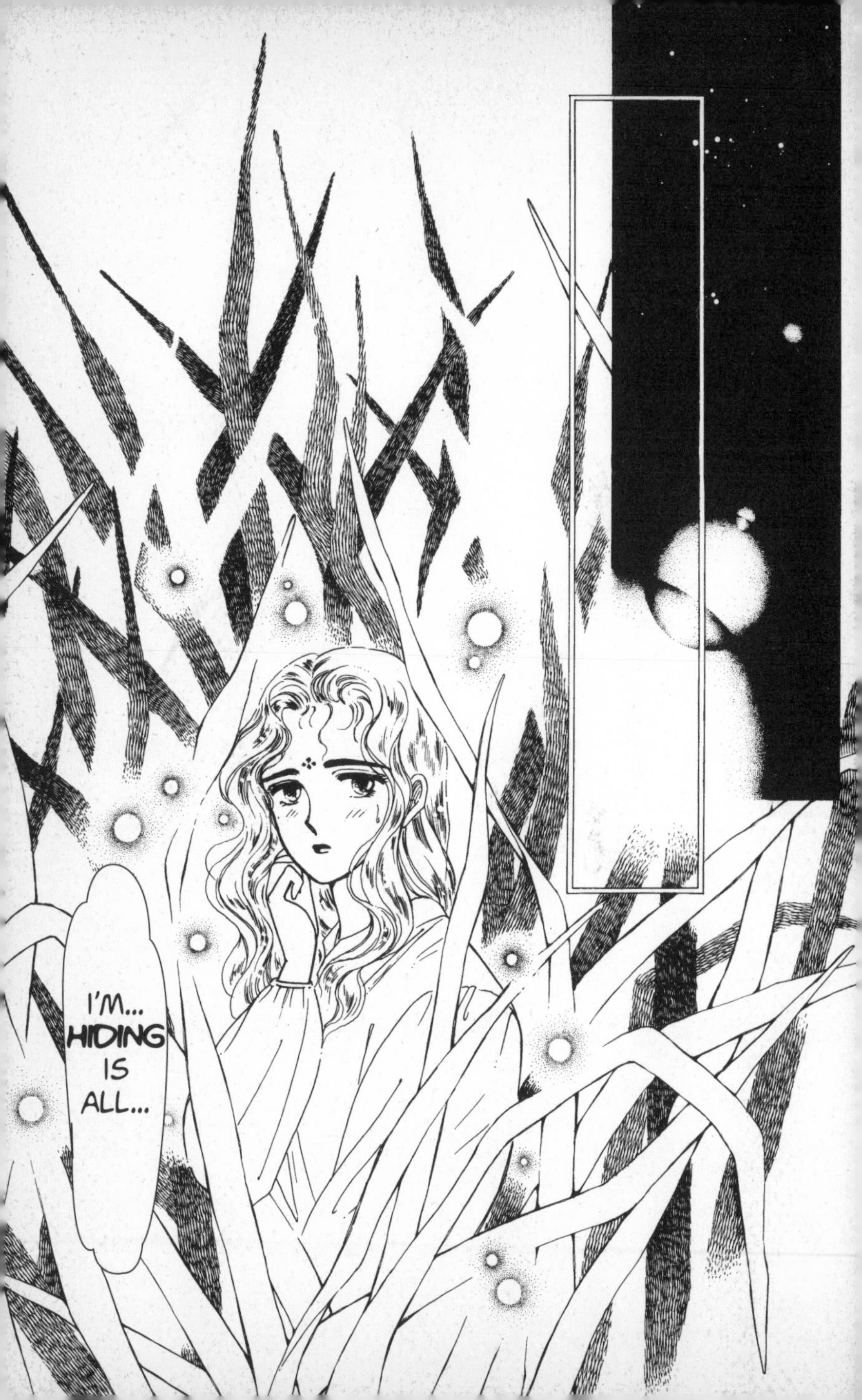
I'M... HIDING IS ALL...

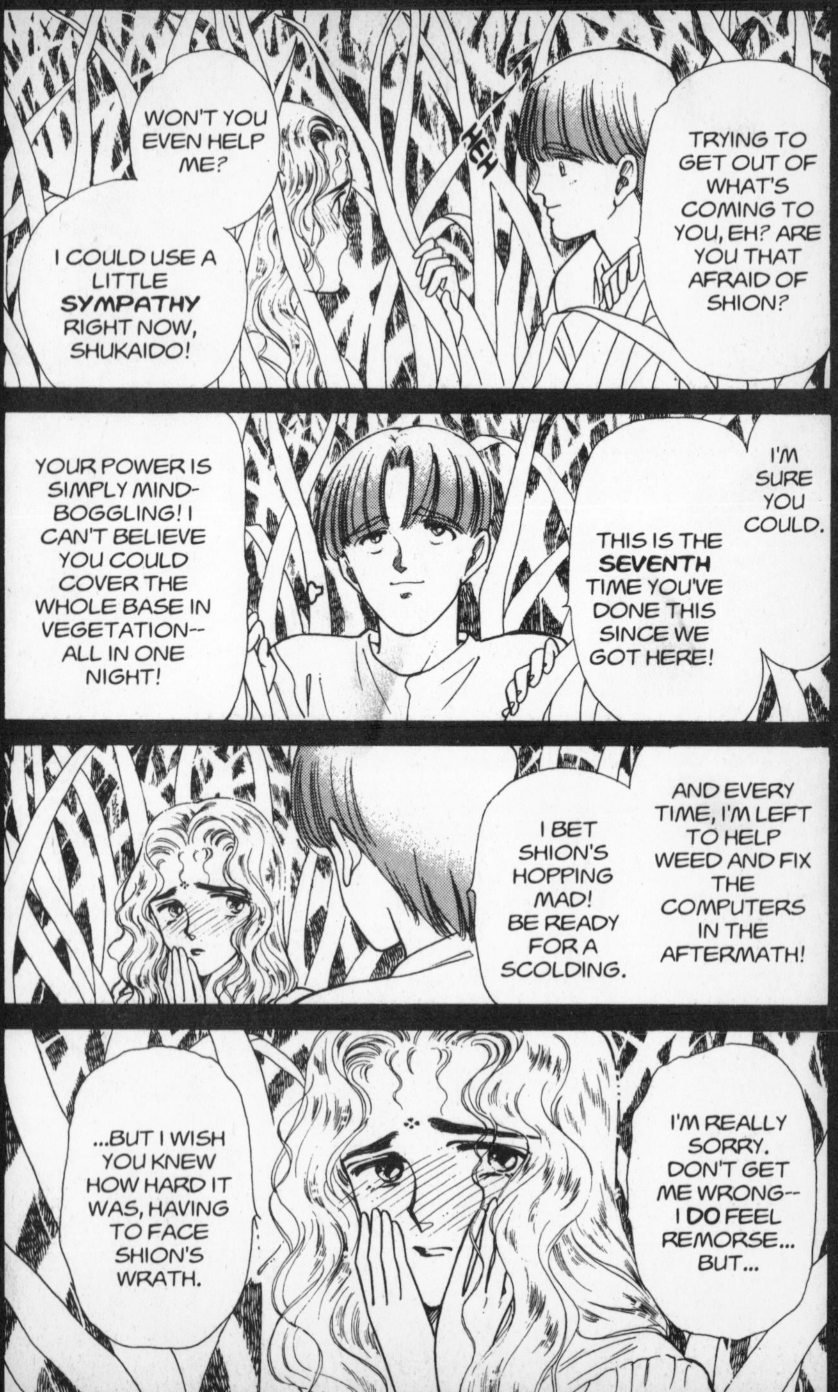
HEH
TRYING TO GET OUT OF WHAT'S COMING TO YOU, EH? ARE YOU THAT AFRAID OF SHION?
WON'T YOU EVEN HELP ME?
I COULD USE A LITTLE **SYMPATHY** RIGHT NOW, SHUKAIDO!
I'M SURE YOU COULD.
THIS IS THE **SEVENTH** TIME YOU'VE DONE THIS SINCE WE GOT HERE!
YOUR POWER IS SIMPLY MIND-BOGGLING! I CAN'T BELIEVE YOU COULD COVER THE WHOLE BASE IN VEGETATION-- ALL IN ONE NIGHT!
AND EVERY TIME, I'M LEFT TO HELP WEED AND FIX THE COMPUTERS IN THE AFTERMATH!
I BET SHION'S HOPPING MAD! BE READY FOR A SCOLDING.
I'M REALLY SORRY. DON'T GET ME WRONG-- I **DO** FEEL REMORSE... BUT...
...BUT I WISH YOU KNEW HOW HARD IT WAS, HAVING TO FACE SHION'S WRATH.

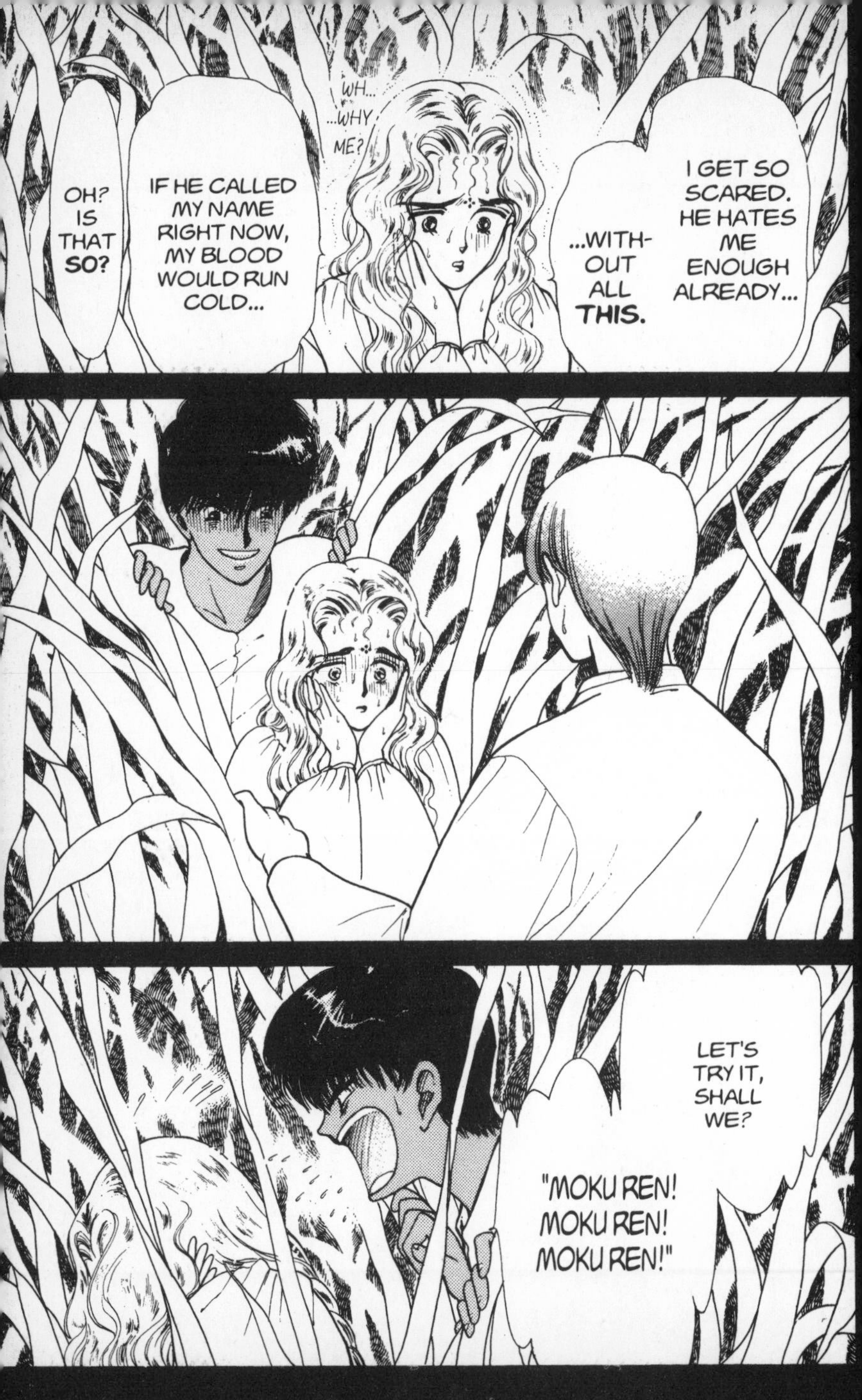
I GET SO SCARED. HE HATES ME ENOUGH ALREADY...
...WITH-OUT ALL THIS.
WH... ...WHY ME?
IF HE CALLED MY NAME RIGHT NOW, MY BLOOD WOULD RUN COLD...
OH? IS THAT SO?
LET'S TRY IT, SHALL WE?
"MOKU REN! MOKU REN! MOKU REN!"

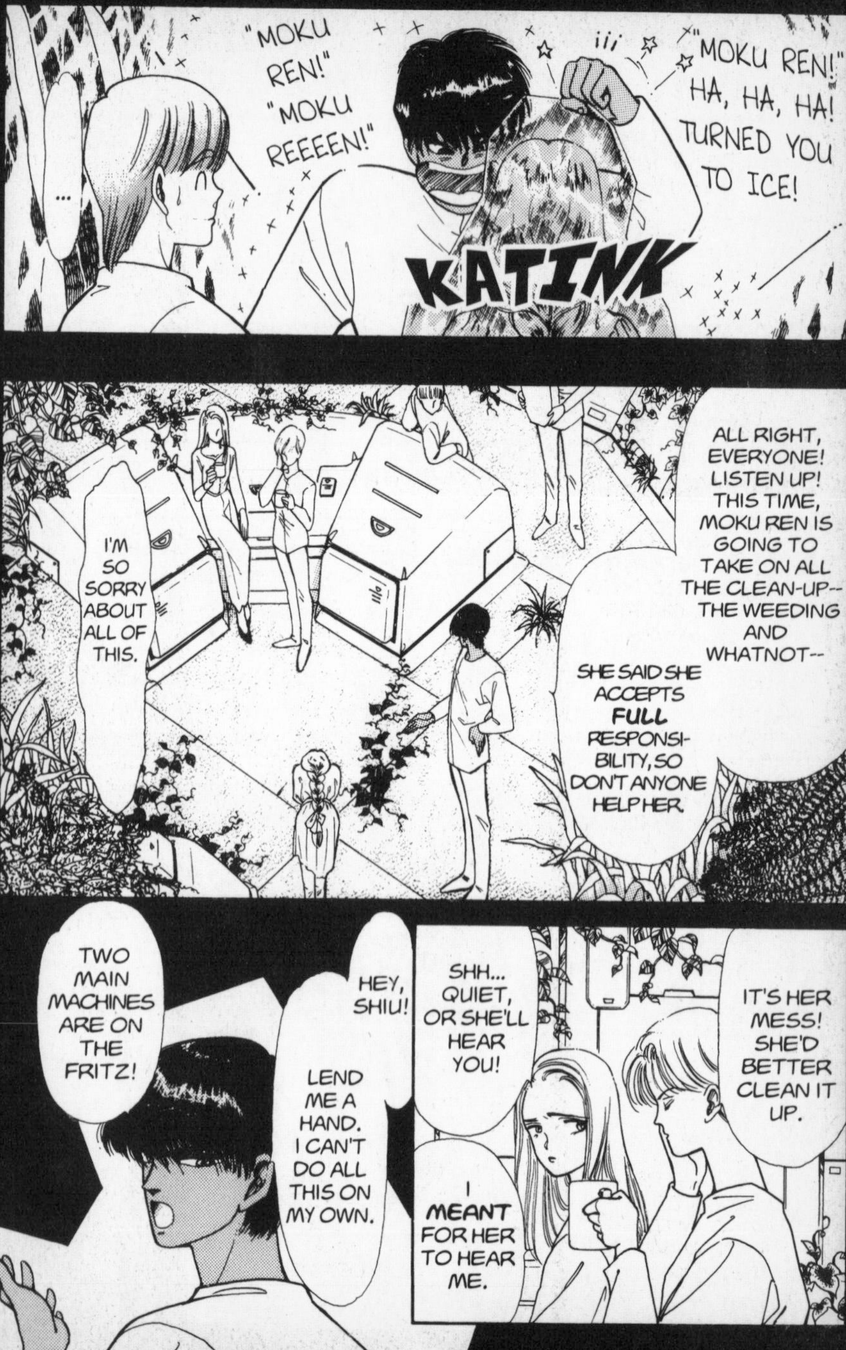
"MOKU REN!" HA, HA, HA! TURNED YOU TO ICE!
"MOKU REN!" "MOKU REEEEN!"
KATINK
...
ALL RIGHT, EVERYONE! LISTEN UP! THIS TIME, MOKU REN IS GOING TO TAKE ON ALL THE CLEAN-UP-- THE WEEDING AND WHATNOT--
SHE SAID SHE ACCEPTS **FULL** RESPONSI-BILITY, SO DON'T ANYONE HELP HER.
I'M SO SORRY ABOUT ALL OF THIS.
IT'S HER MESS! SHE'D BETTER CLEAN IT UP.
SHH... QUIET, OR SHE'LL HEAR YOU!
I **MEANT** FOR HER TO HEAR ME.
HEY, SHIU!
TWO MAIN MACHINES ARE ON THE FRITZ!
LEND ME A HAND. I CAN'T DO ALL THIS ON MY OWN.

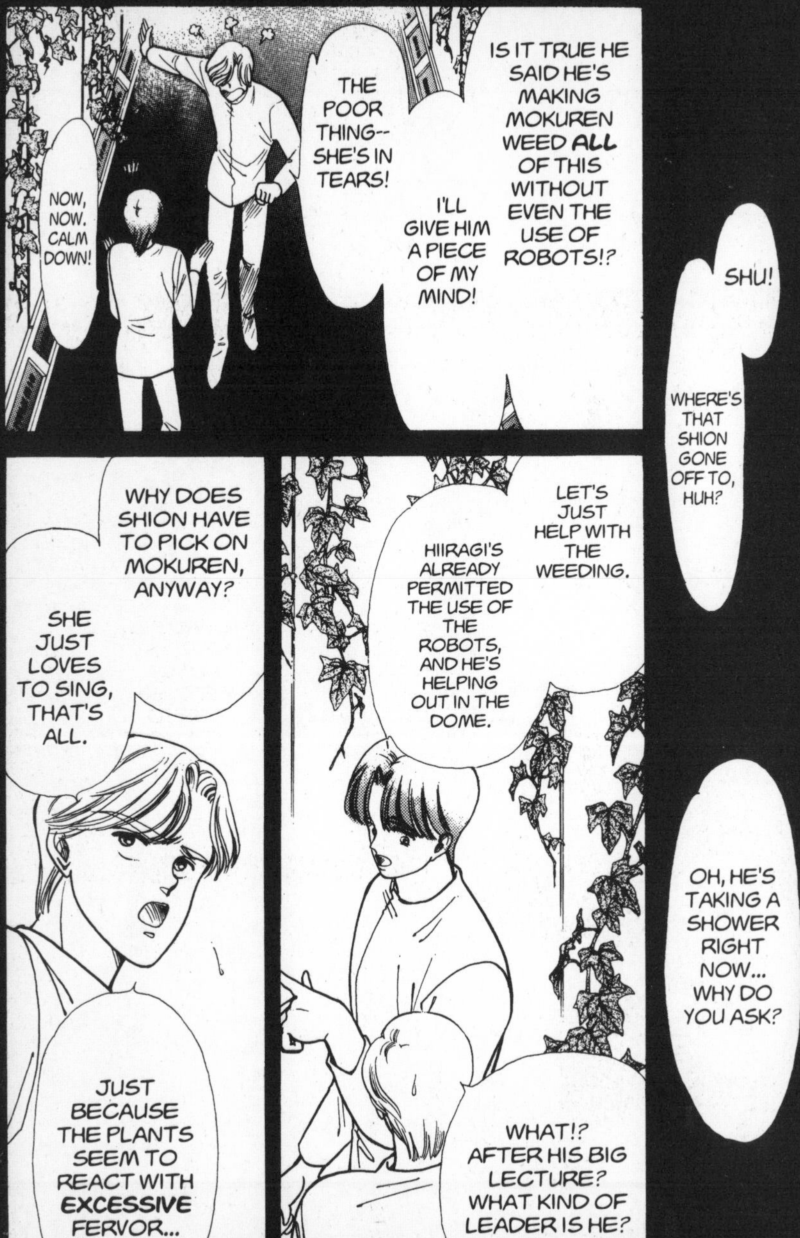
IS IT TRUE HE SAID HE'S MAKING MOKUREN WEED ALL OF THIS WITHOUT EVEN THE USE OF ROBOTS!?
THE POOR THING-- SHE'S IN TEARS!
I'LL GIVE HIM A PIECE OF MY MIND!
NOW, NOW. CALM DOWN!
SHU!
WHERE'S THAT SHION GONE OFF TO, HUH?
OH, HE'S TAKING A SHOWER RIGHT NOW... WHY DO YOU ASK?
LET'S JUST HELP WITH THE WEEDING.
HIIRAGI'S ALREADY PERMITTED THE USE OF THE ROBOTS, AND HE'S HELPING OUT IN THE DOME.
WHAT!? AFTER HIS BIG LECTURE? WHAT KIND OF LEADER IS HE?
WHY DOES SHION HAVE TO PICK ON MOKUREN, ANYWAY?
SHE JUST LOVES TO SING, THAT'S ALL.
JUST BECAUSE THE PLANTS SEEM TO REACT WITH EXCESSIVE FERVOR...

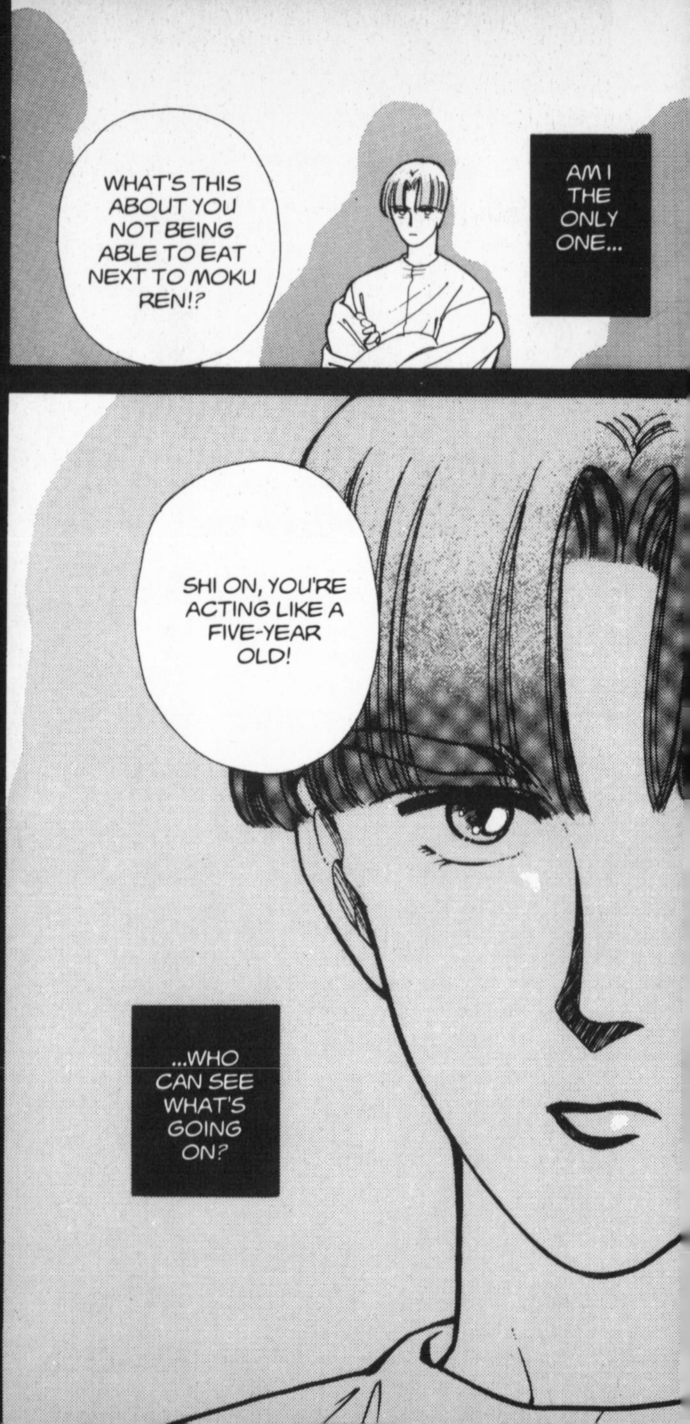
AM I THE ONLY ONE...
WHAT'S THIS ABOUT YOU NOT BEING ABLE TO EAT NEXT TO MOKU REN!?
SHI ON, YOU'RE ACTING LIKE A FIVE-YEAR OLD!
...WHO CAN SEE WHAT'S GOING ON?

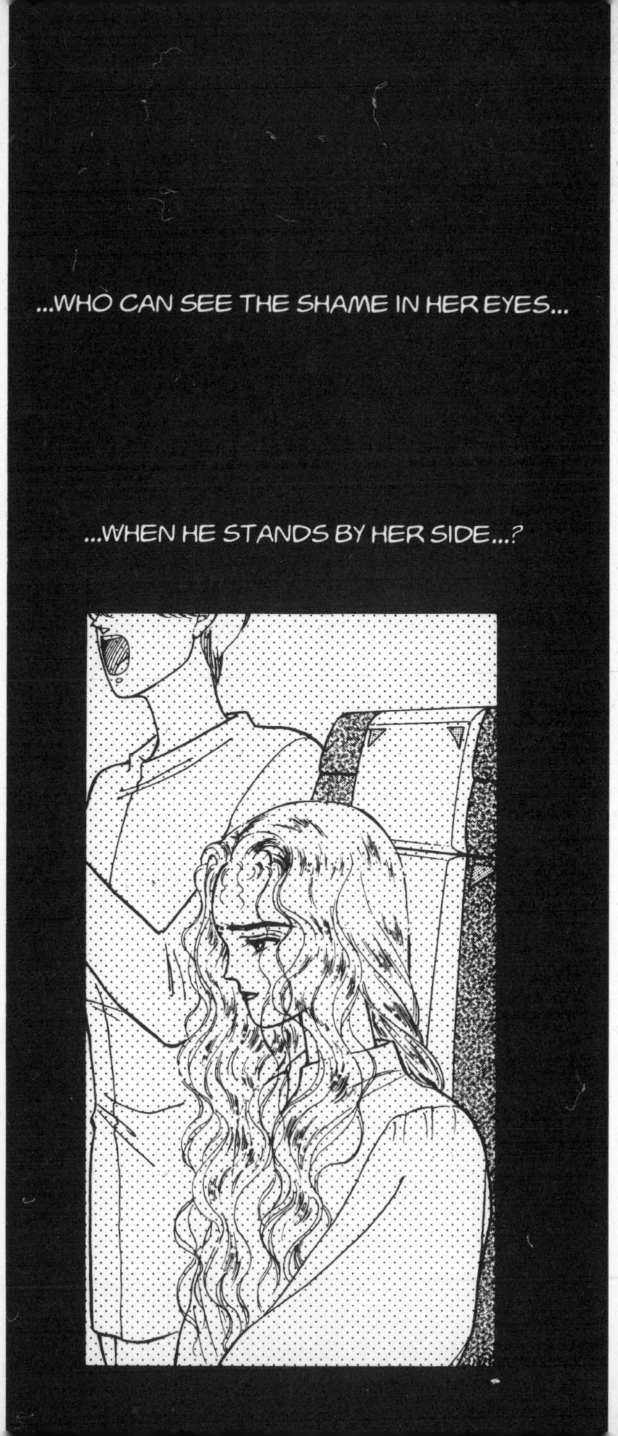
...WHO CAN SEE THE SHAME IN HER EYES...
...WHEN HE STANDS BY HER SIDE...?

1/4 COLUMN NONSENSE

—PART 5—

Three kids were in the house at the time--a boy about Rin's age, a much younger boy, and a baby. The older boy came to the door when I rang the bell and whimpered, "The fire in the bathroom won't go out." I think he was more frightened than I was. After it was all over and the adults started to make a fuss, I turned to talk to the boys. He looked up at me, and his eyes... I'll probably never forget the "look" he had. It couldn't be described with words... Well, that's probably a hated cliché.

How to put it... It was an expression impossible for an adult--a fleeting look that reflected wisdom beyond years... Hmm, I just can't write. My vocabulary is so inadequate! Well... I guess Rin, or a young Mikuro could pull off a look like that.

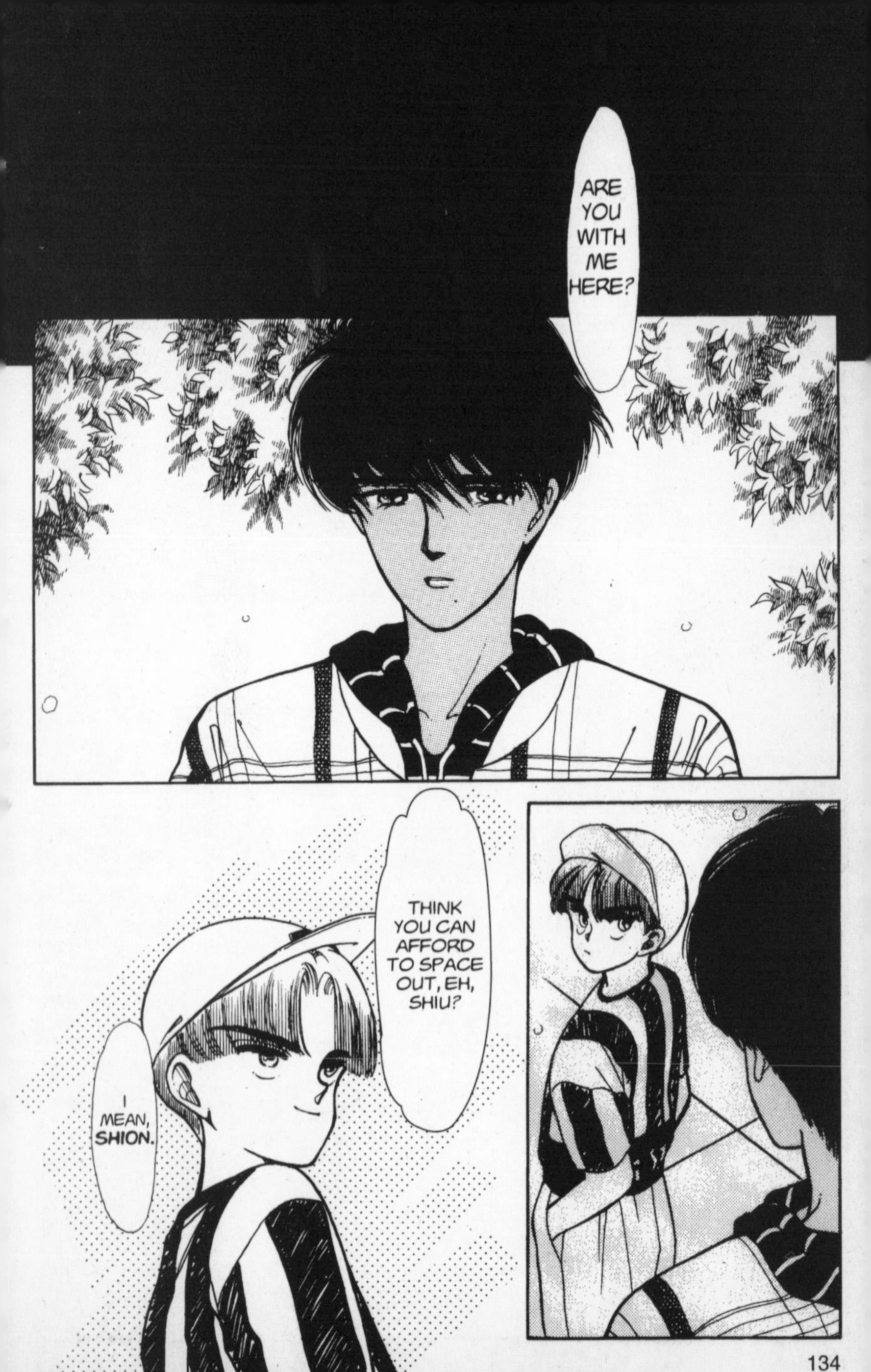
ARE YOU WITH ME HERE?
THINK YOU CAN AFFORD TO SPACE OUT, EH, SHIU?
I MEAN, SHION.

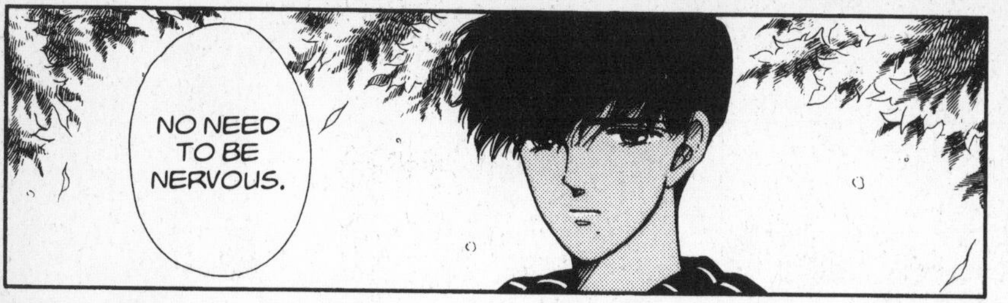
NO NEED TO BE NERVOUS.

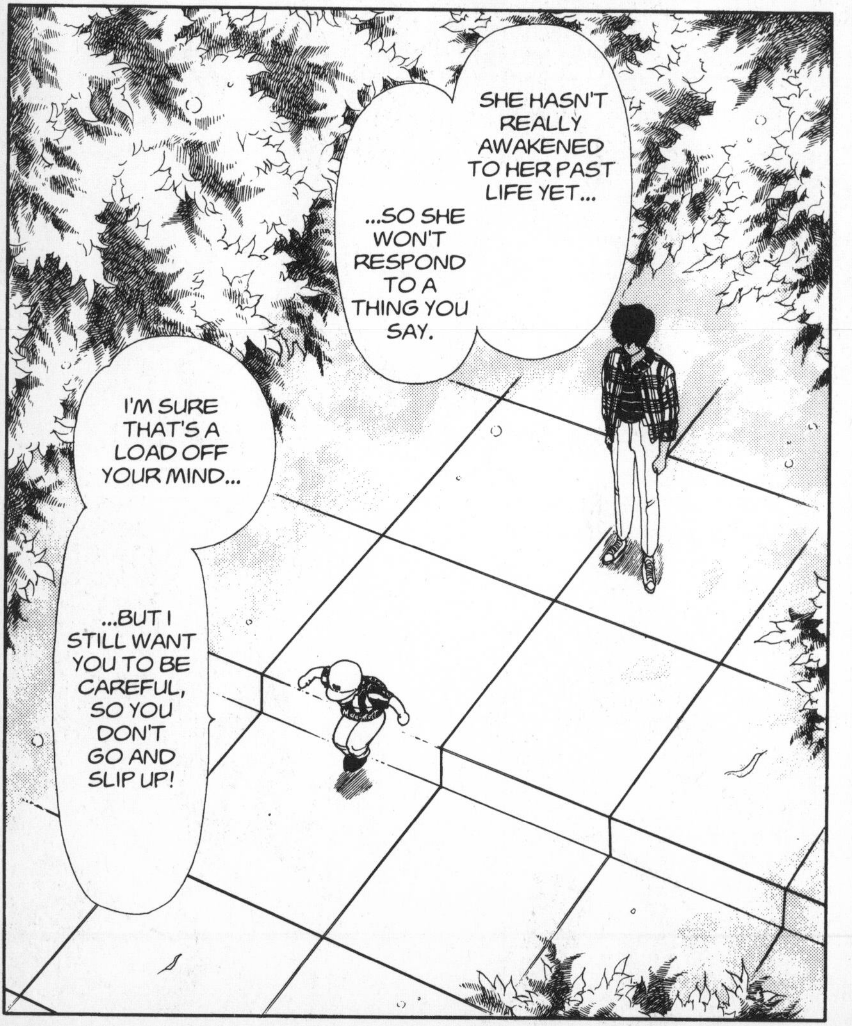
SHE HASN'T REALLY AWAKENED TO HER PAST LIFE YET...
...SO SHE WON'T RESPOND TO A THING YOU SAY.
I'M SURE THAT'S A LOAD OFF YOUR MIND...
...BUT I STILL WANT YOU TO BE CAREFUL, SO YOU DON'T GO AND SLIP UP!

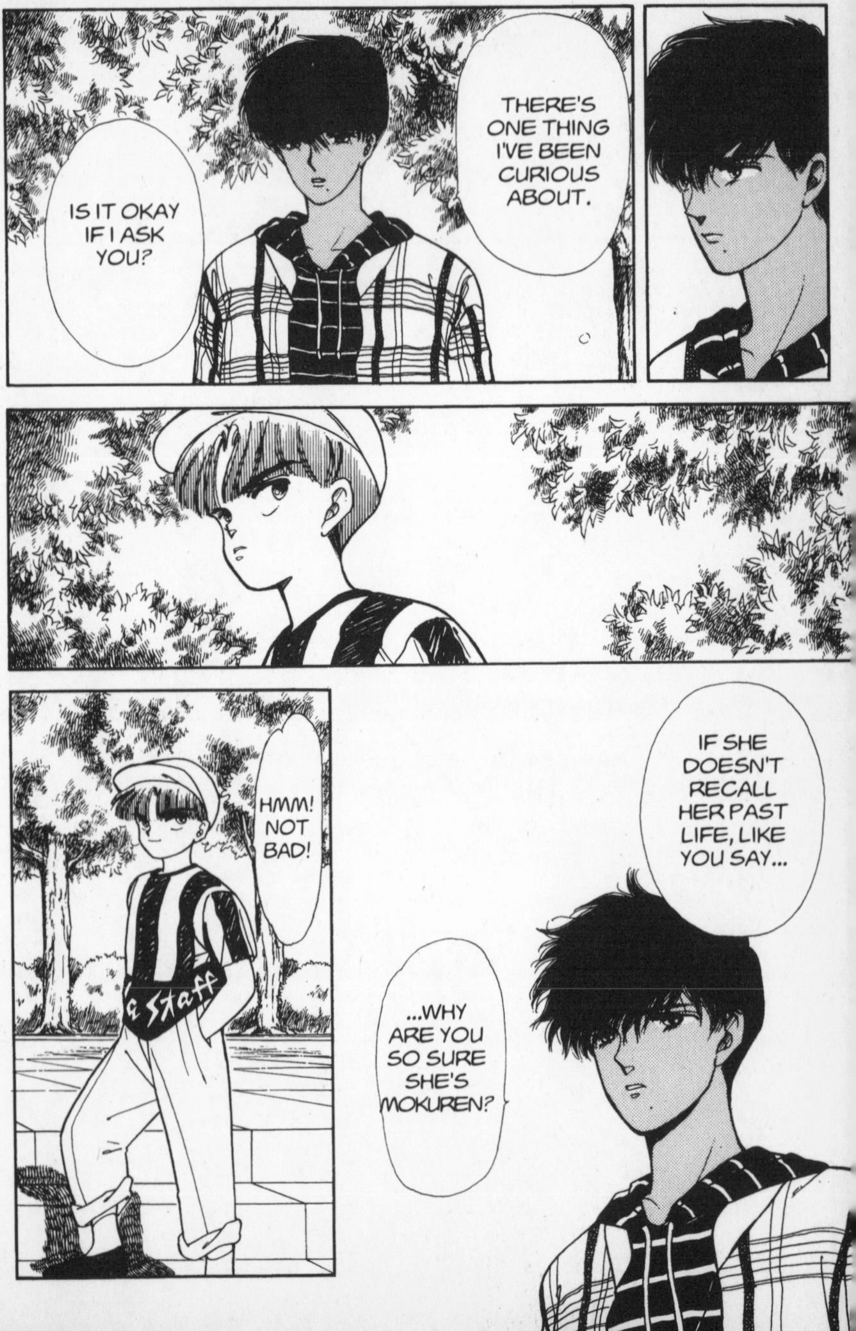
THERE'S ONE THING I'VE BEEN CURIOUS ABOUT.
IS IT OKAY IF I ASK YOU?
IF SHE DOESN'T RECALL HER PAST LIFE, LIKE YOU SAY...
...WHY ARE YOU SO SURE SHE'S MOKUREN?
HMM! NOT BAD!

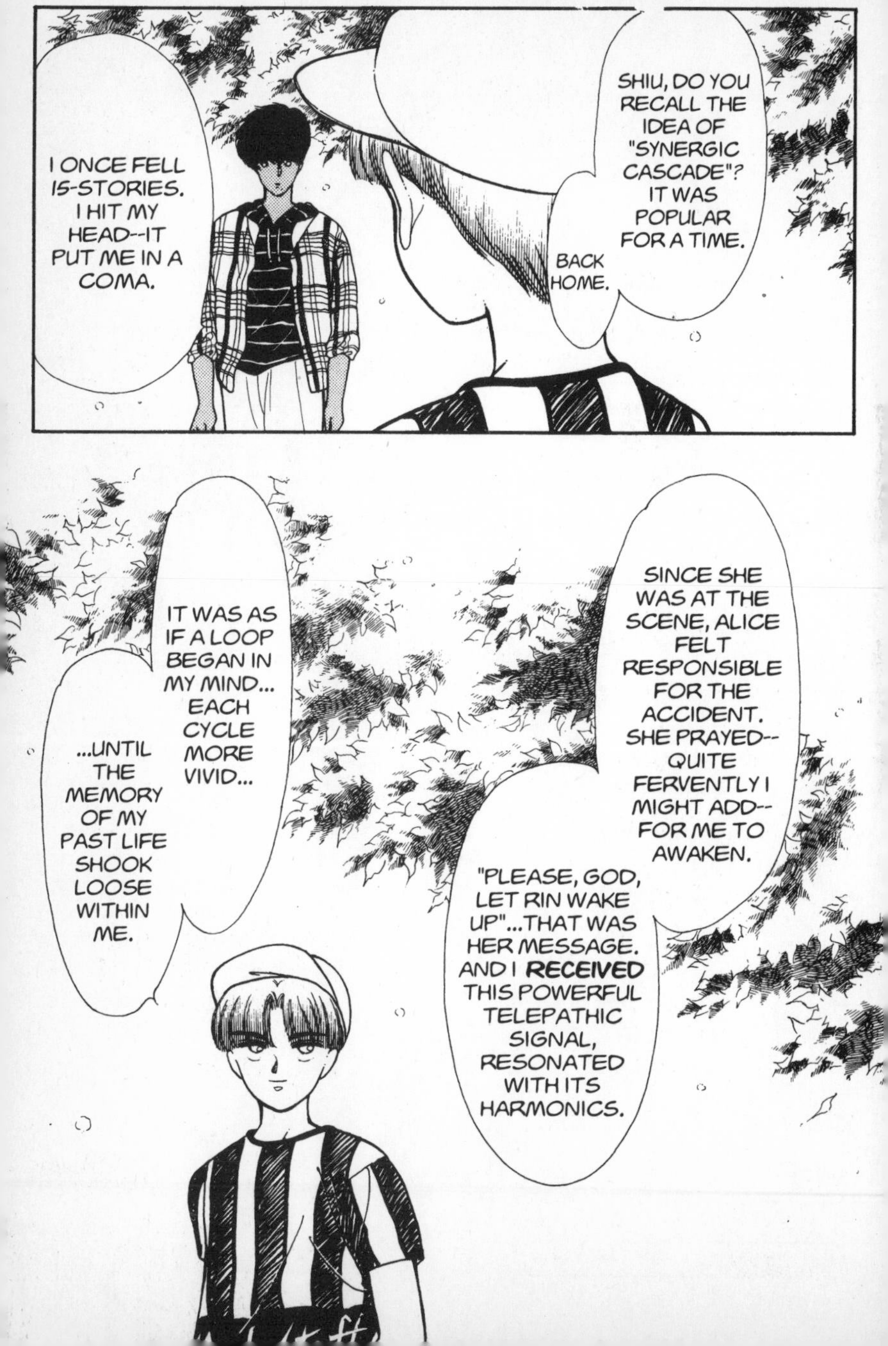
SHIU, DO YOU RECALL THE IDEA OF "SYNERGIC CASCADE"? IT WAS POPULAR FOR A TIME.
BACK HOME.
I ONCE FELL 15-STORIES. I HIT MY HEAD--IT PUT ME IN A COMA.
SINCE SHE WAS AT THE SCENE, ALICE FELT RESPONSIBLE FOR THE ACCIDENT. SHE PRAYED--QUITE FERVENTLY I MIGHT ADD--FOR ME TO AWAKEN.
"PLEASE, GOD, LET RIN WAKE UP"...THAT WAS HER MESSAGE. AND I **RECEIVED** THIS POWERFUL TELEPATHIC SIGNAL, RESONATED WITH ITS HARMONICS.
IT WAS AS IF A LOOP BEGAN IN MY MIND... EACH CYCLE MORE VIVID...
...UNTIL THE MEMORY OF MY PAST LIFE SHOOK LOOSE WITHIN ME.

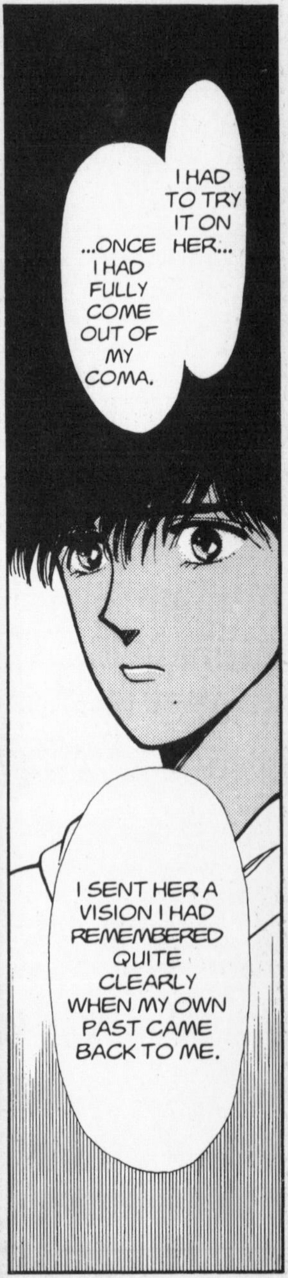
I HAD TO TRY IT ON HER...
...ONCE I HAD FULLY COME OUT OF MY COMA.
I SENT HER A VISION I HAD REMEMBERED QUITE CLEARLY WHEN MY OWN PAST CAME BACK TO ME.

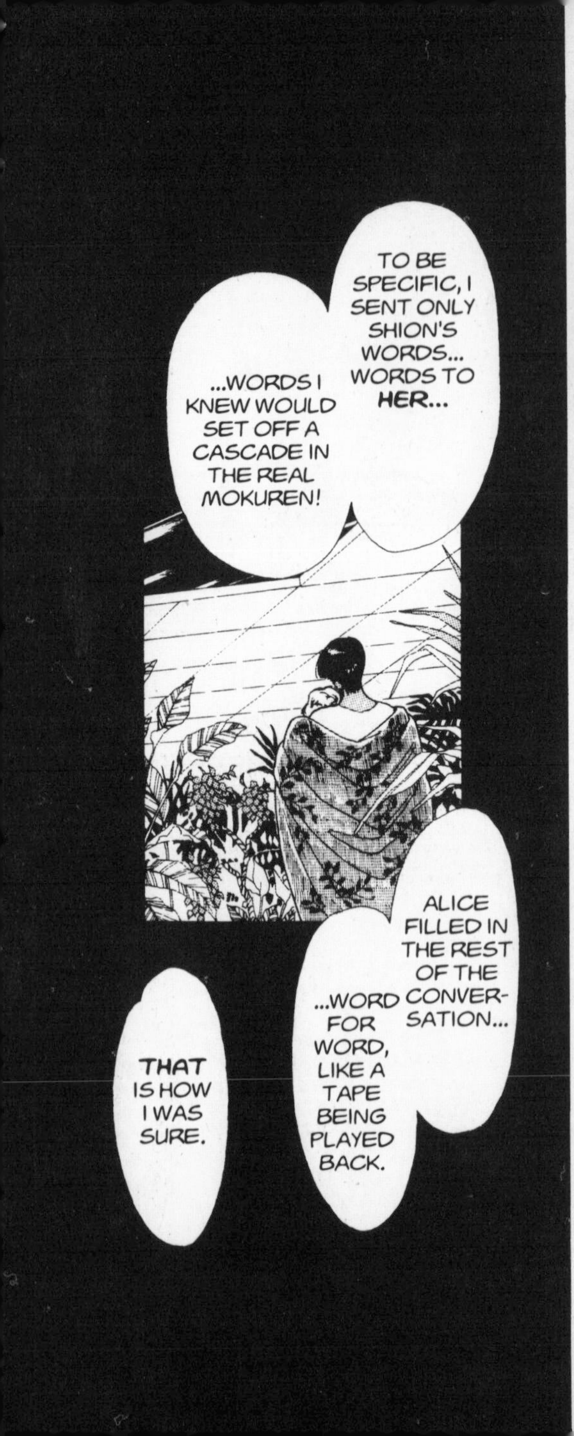
TO BE SPECIFIC, I SENT ONLY SHION'S WORDS... WORDS TO **HER**...
...WORDS I KNEW WOULD SET OFF A CASCADE IN THE REAL MOKUREN!
ALICE FILLED IN THE REST OF THE CONVERSATION...
...WORD FOR WORD, LIKE A TAPE BEING PLAYED BACK.
THAT IS HOW I WAS SURE.

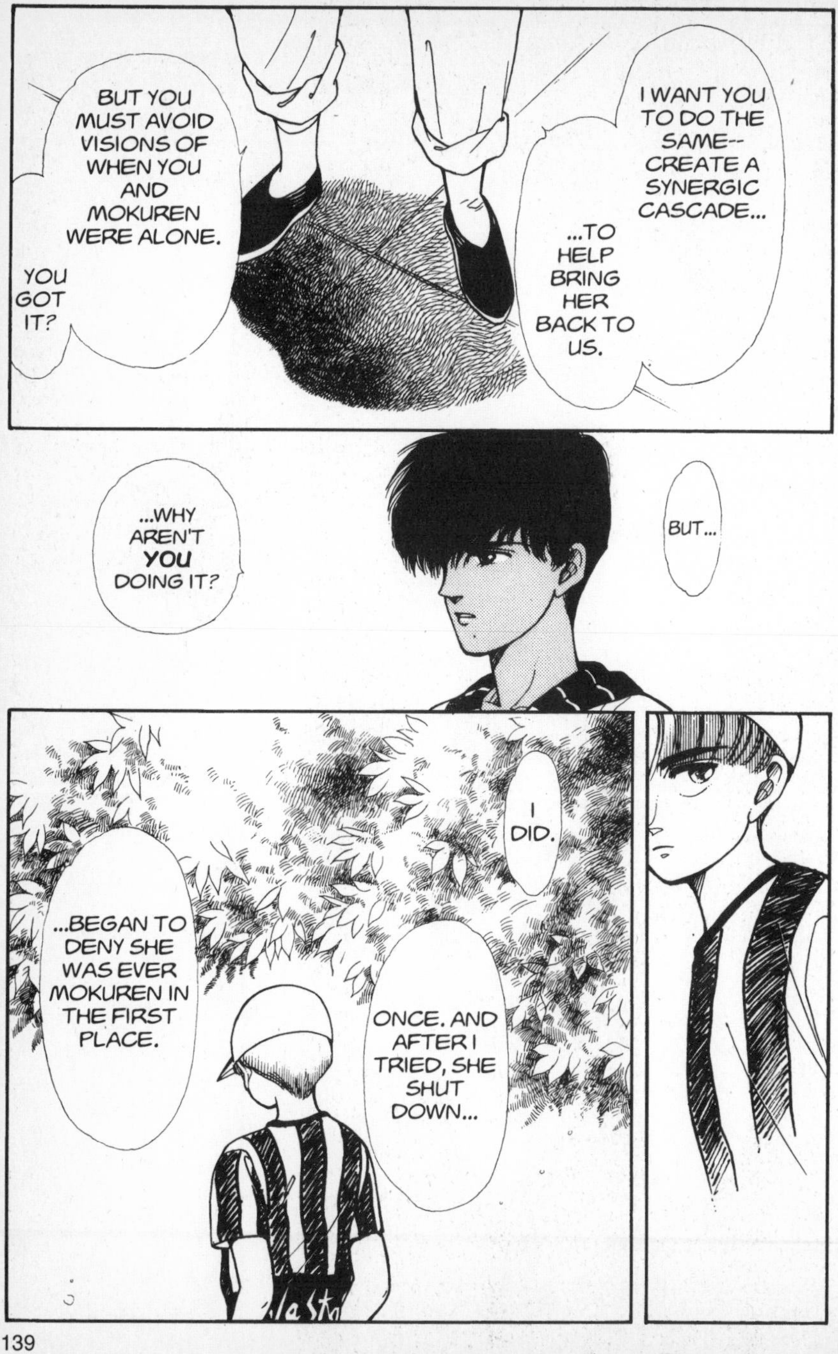
I WANT YOU TO DO THE SAME-- CREATE A SYNERGIC CASCADE...
...TO HELP BRING HER BACK TO US.
BUT YOU MUST AVOID VISIONS OF WHEN YOU AND MOKUREN WERE ALONE.
YOU GOT IT?
BUT...
...WHY AREN'T **YOU** DOING IT?
I DID.
ONCE. AND AFTER I TRIED, SHE SHUT DOWN...
...BEGAN TO DENY SHE WAS EVER MOKUREN IN THE FIRST PLACE.

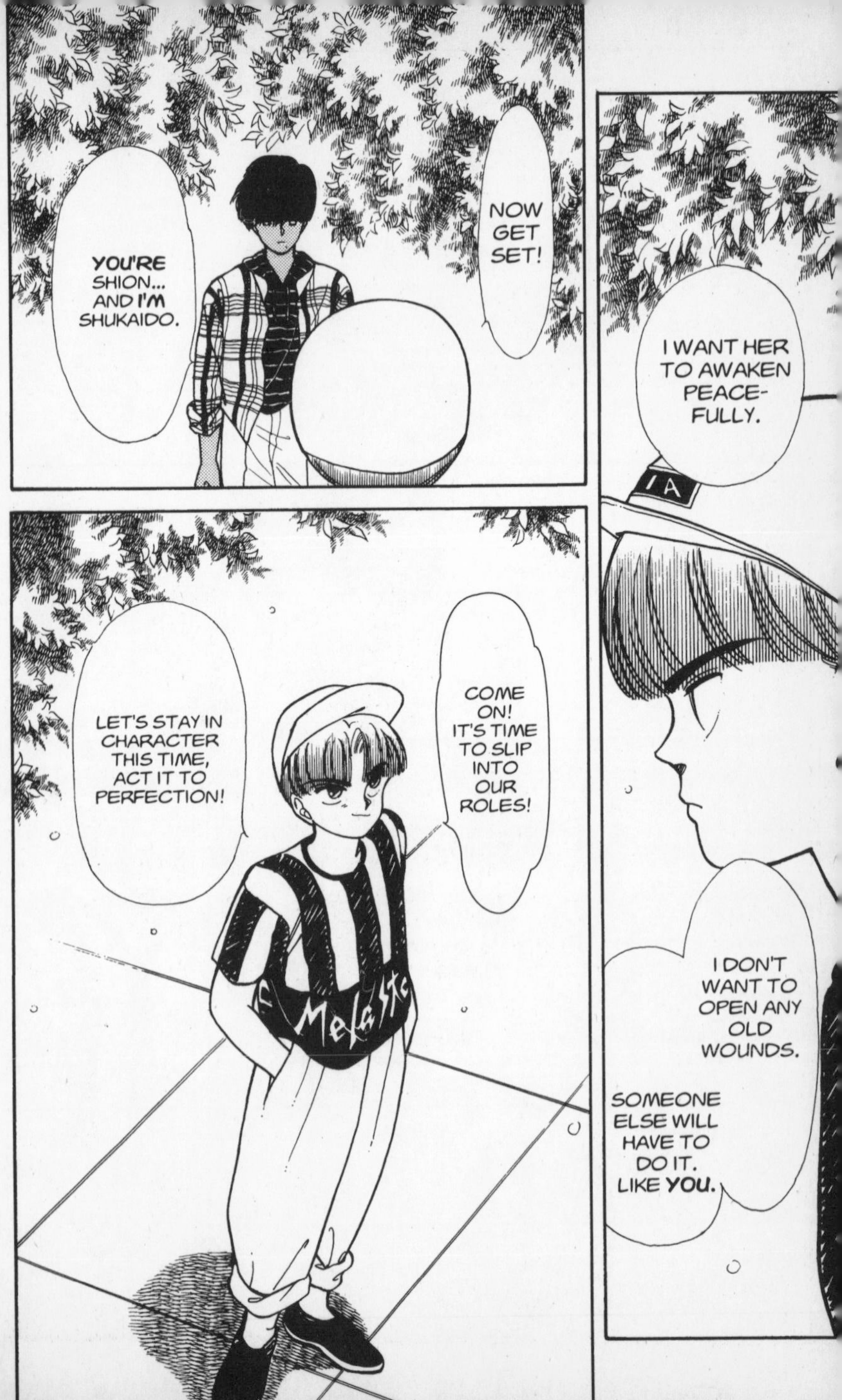
I WANT HER TO AWAKEN PEACEFULLY.
I DON'T WANT TO OPEN ANY OLD WOUNDS.
SOMEONE ELSE WILL HAVE TO DO IT. LIKE YOU.
NOW GET SET!
YOU'RE SHION... AND I'M SHUKAIDO.
COME ON! IT'S TIME TO SLIP INTO OUR ROLES!
LET'S STAY IN CHARACTER THIS TIME, ACT IT TO PERFECTION!

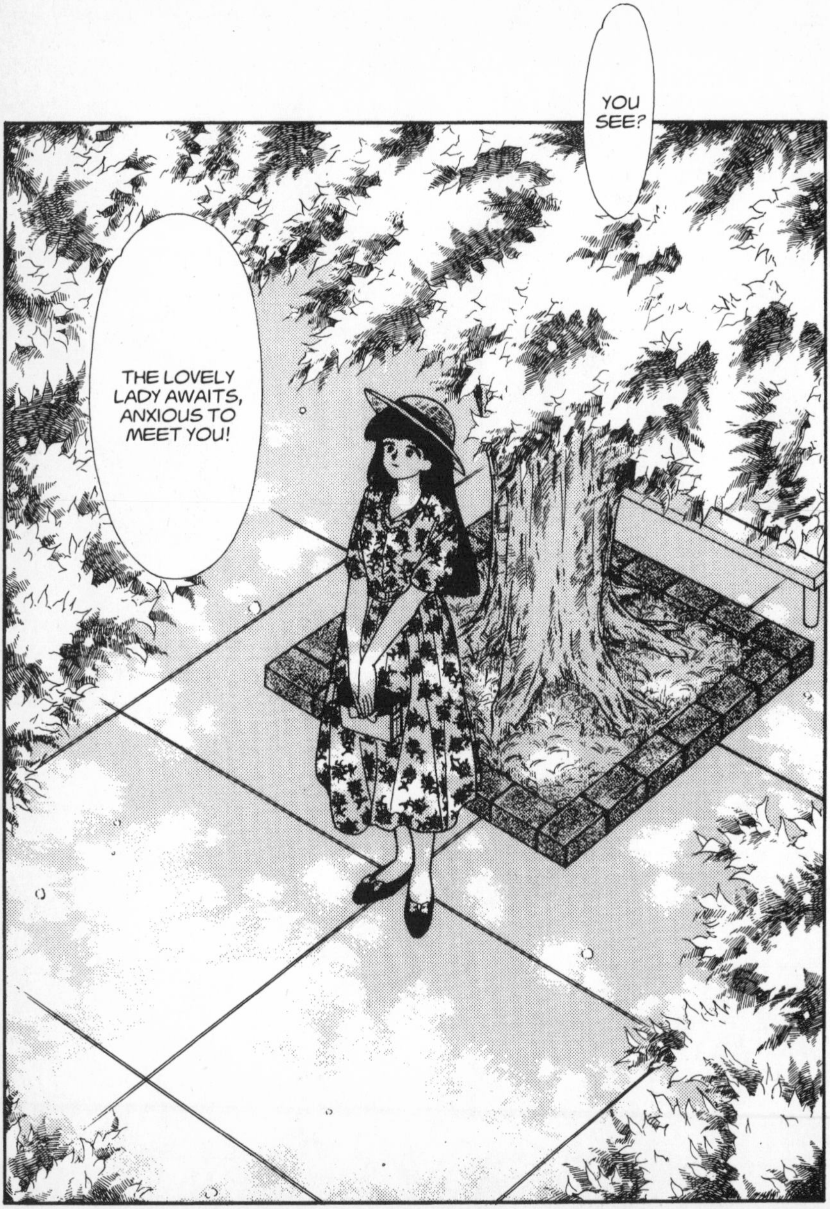
YOU SEE?
THE LOVELY LADY AWAITS, ANXIOUS TO MEET YOU!

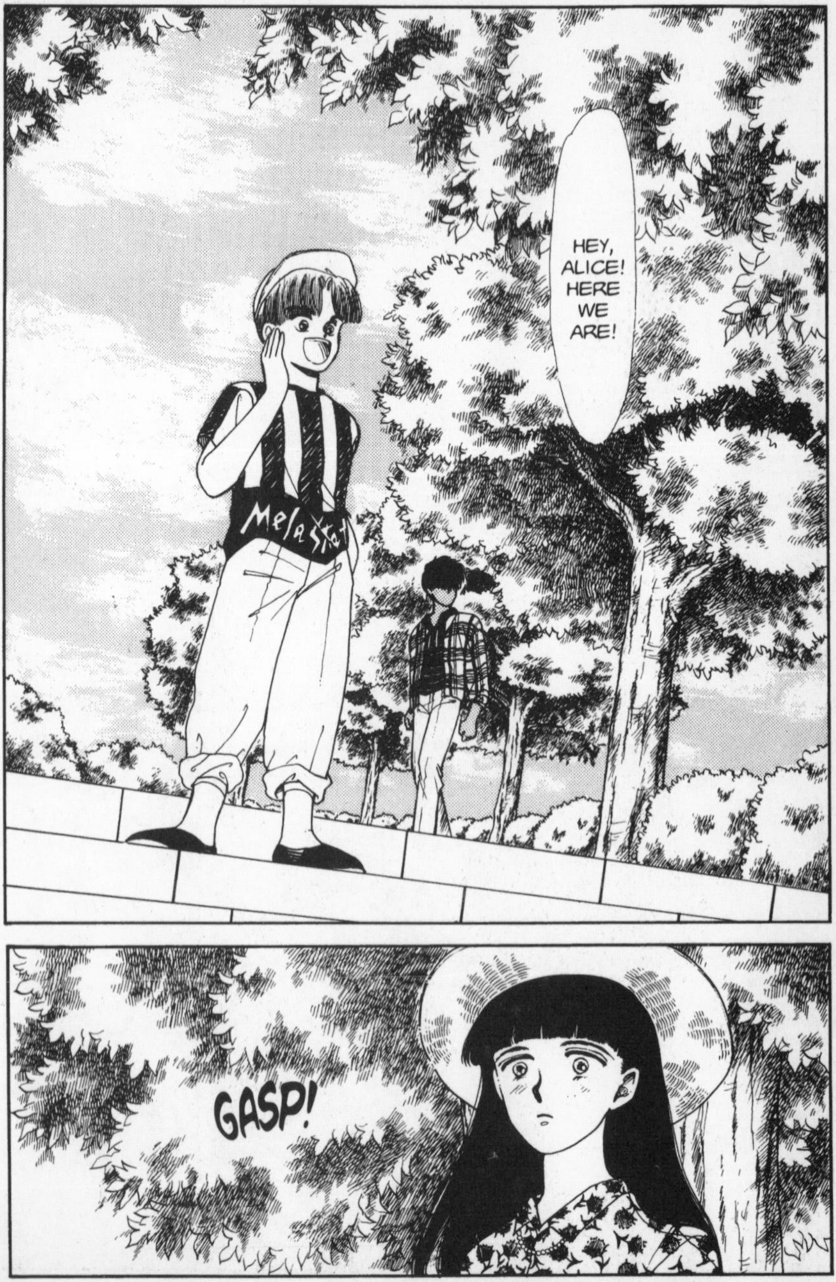
HEY, ALICE! HERE WE ARE!
Mela stet
GASP!

S-SO HE'S THE ONE, HUH?

WOW...

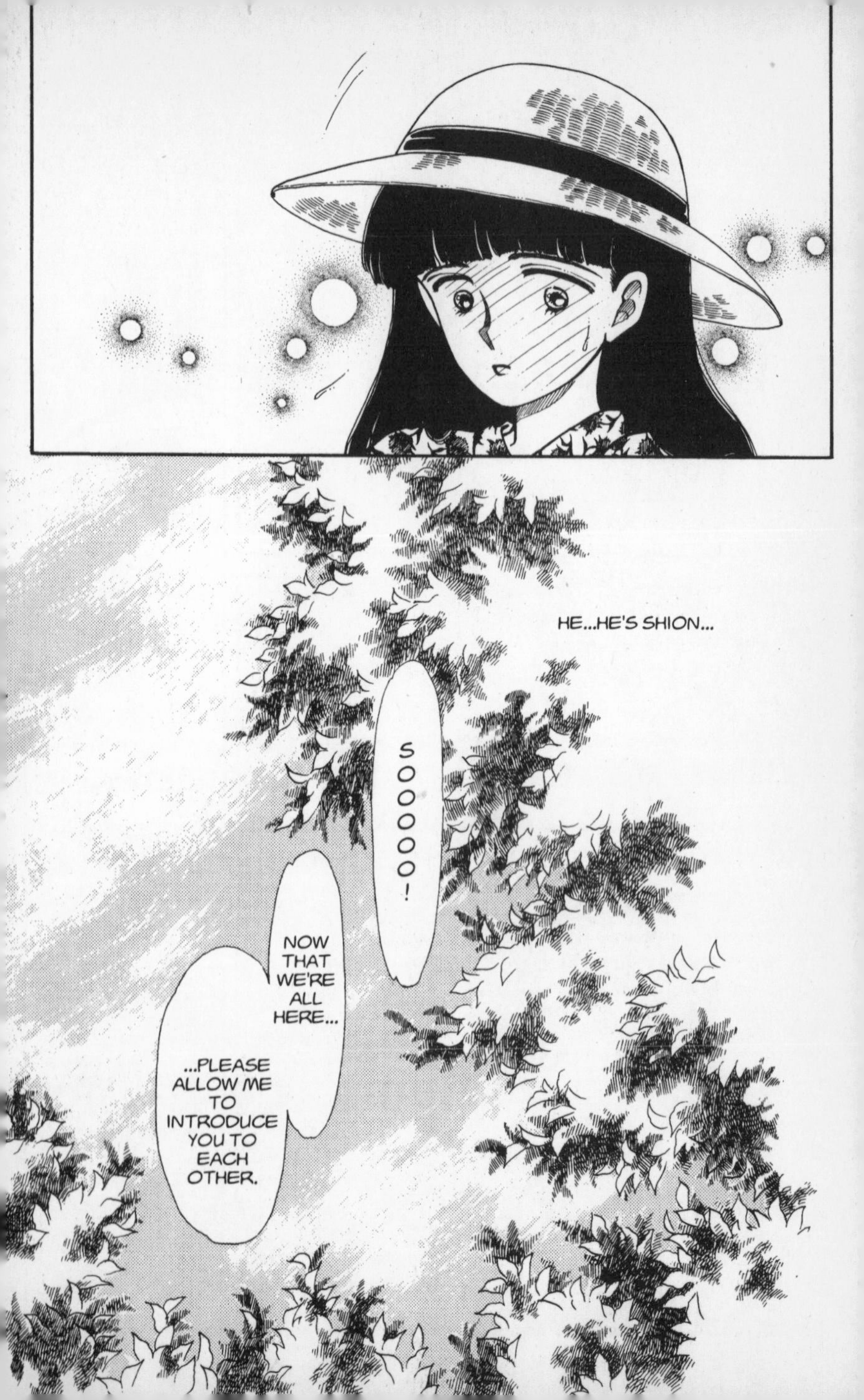
HE...HE'S SHION...
SOOOOOO!
NOW THAT WE'RE ALL HERE...
...PLEASE ALLOW ME TO INTRODUCE YOU TO EACH OTHER.

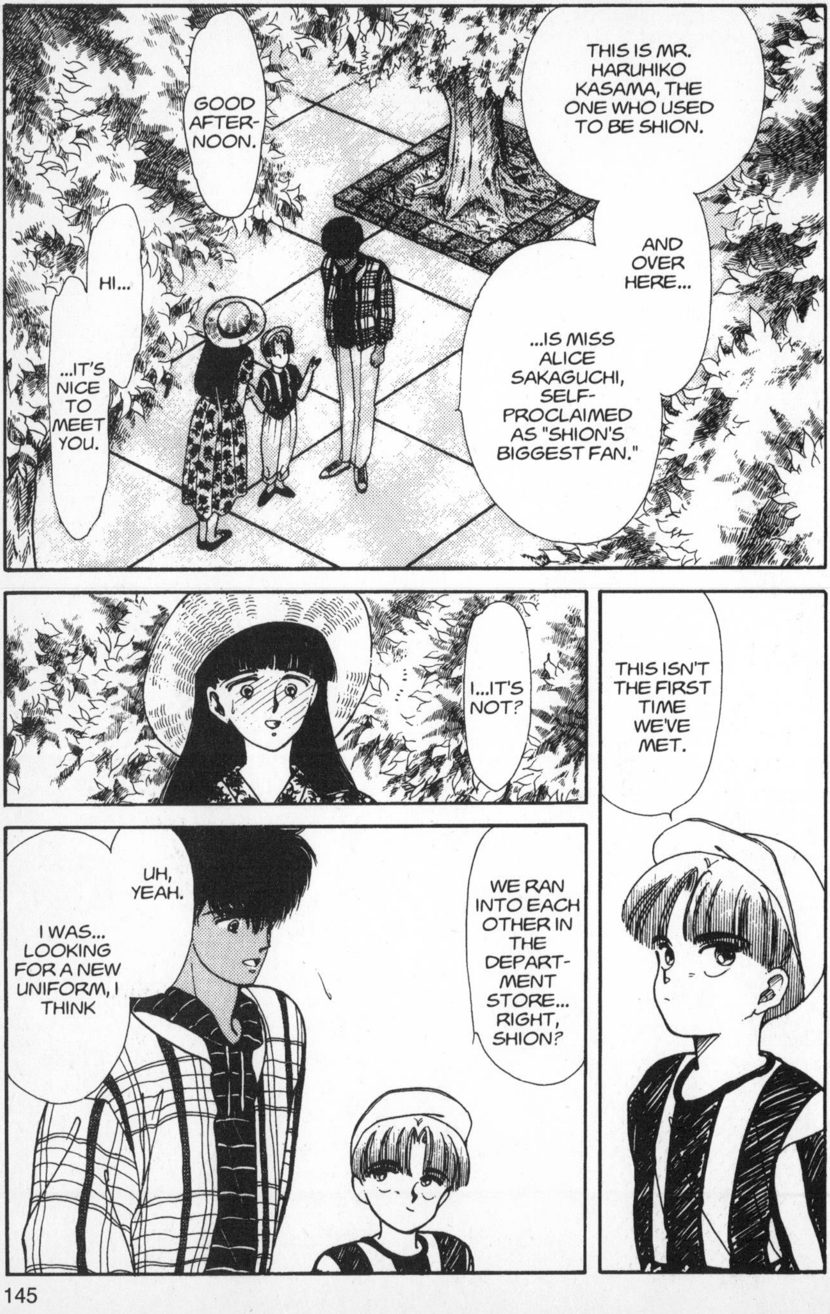
THIS IS MR. HARUHIKO KASAMA, THE ONE WHO USED TO BE SHION.
GOOD AFTERNOON.
AND OVER HERE...
...IS MISS ALICE SAKAGUCHI, SELF-PROCLAIMED AS "SHION'S BIGGEST FAN."
HI...
...IT'S NICE TO MEET YOU.
THIS ISN'T THE FIRST TIME WE'VE MET.
I...IT'S NOT?
WE RAN INTO EACH OTHER IN THE DEPARTMENT STORE... RIGHT, SHION?
UH, YEAH.
I WAS... LOOKING FOR A NEW UNIFORM, I THINK

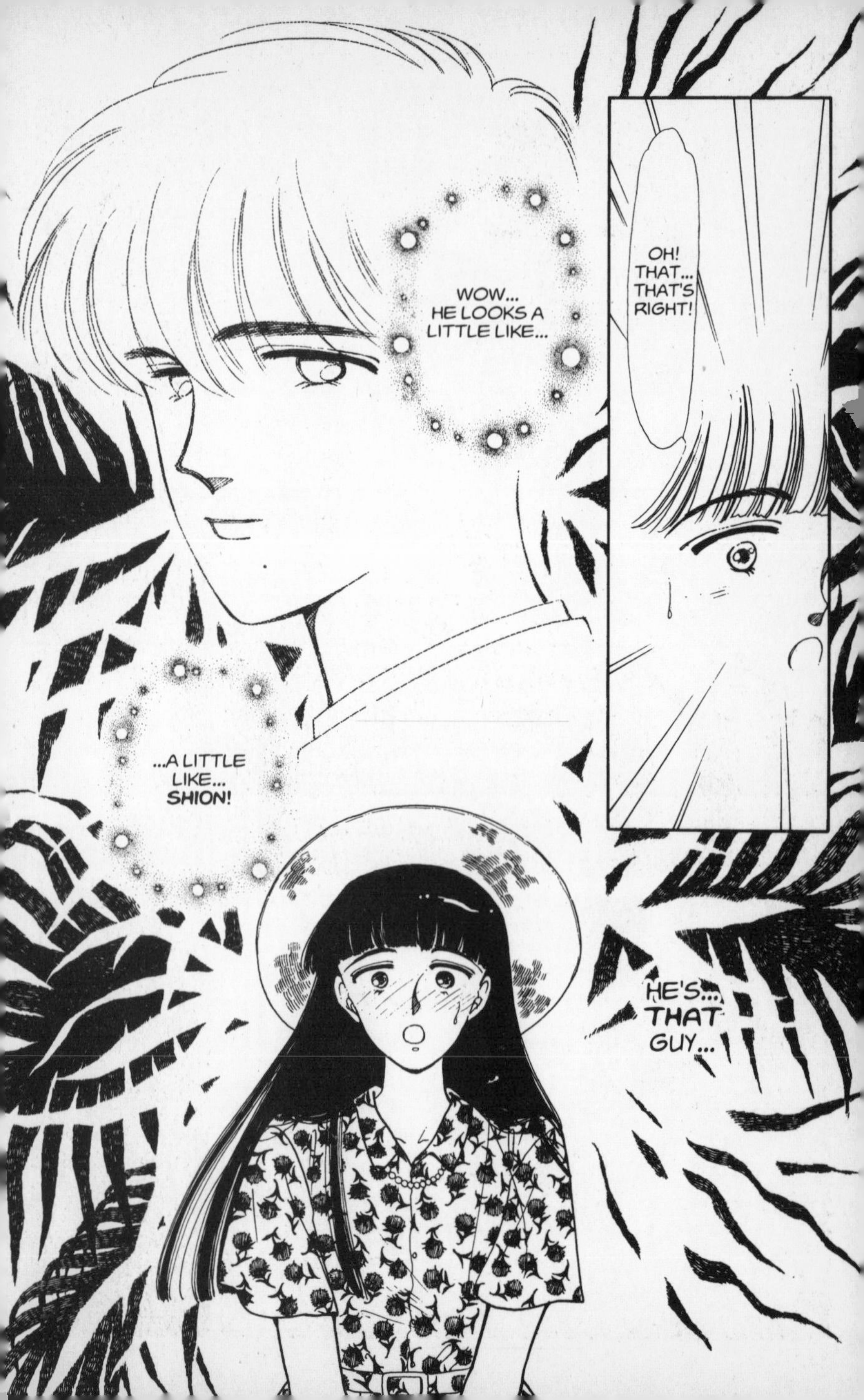
OH! THAT... THAT'S RIGHT!
WOW... HE LOOKS A LITTLE LIKE...
...A LITTLE LIKE... SHION!
HE'S... THAT GUY...

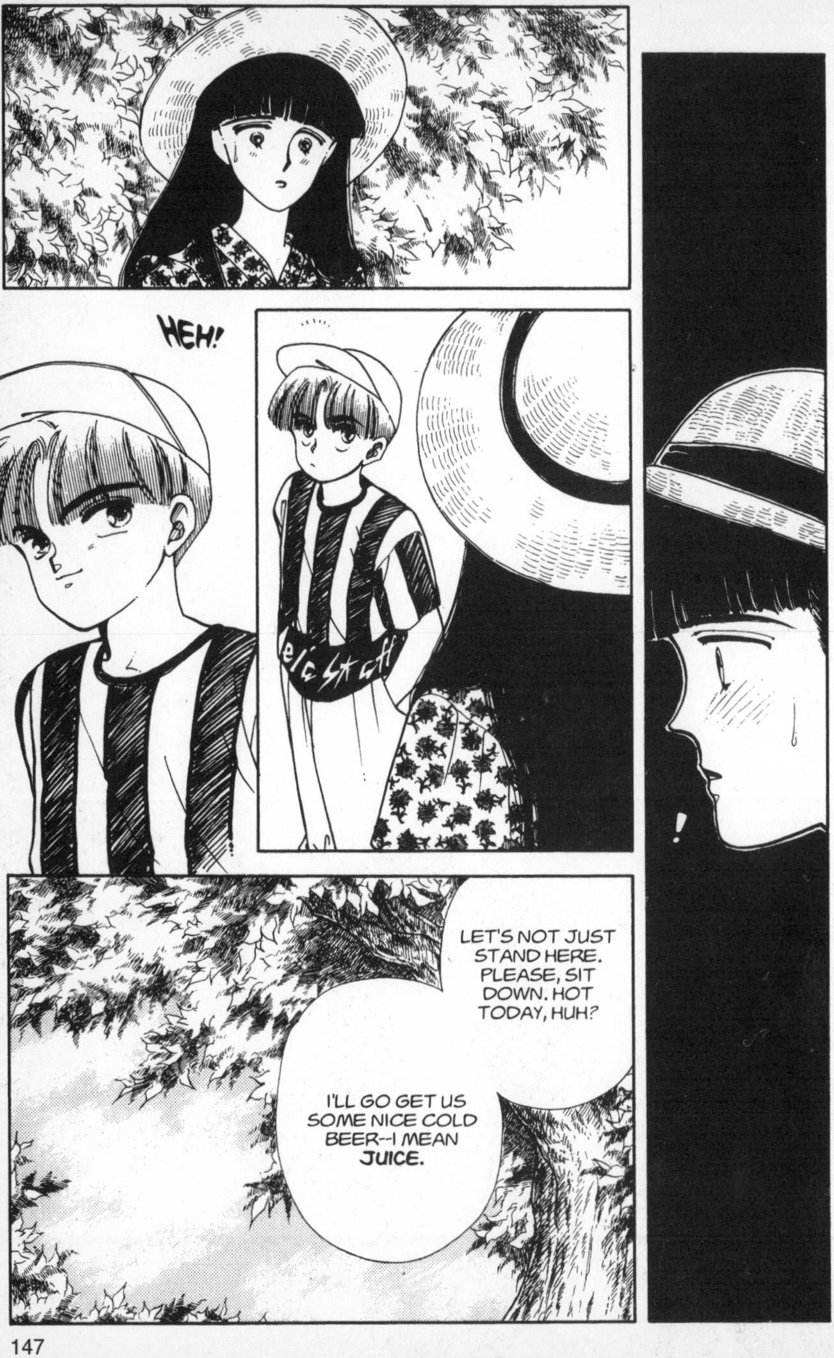
HEH!
LET'S NOT JUST STAND HERE. PLEASE, SIT DOWN. HOT TODAY, HUH?
I'LL GO GET US SOME NICE COLD BEER--I MEAN **JUICE.**

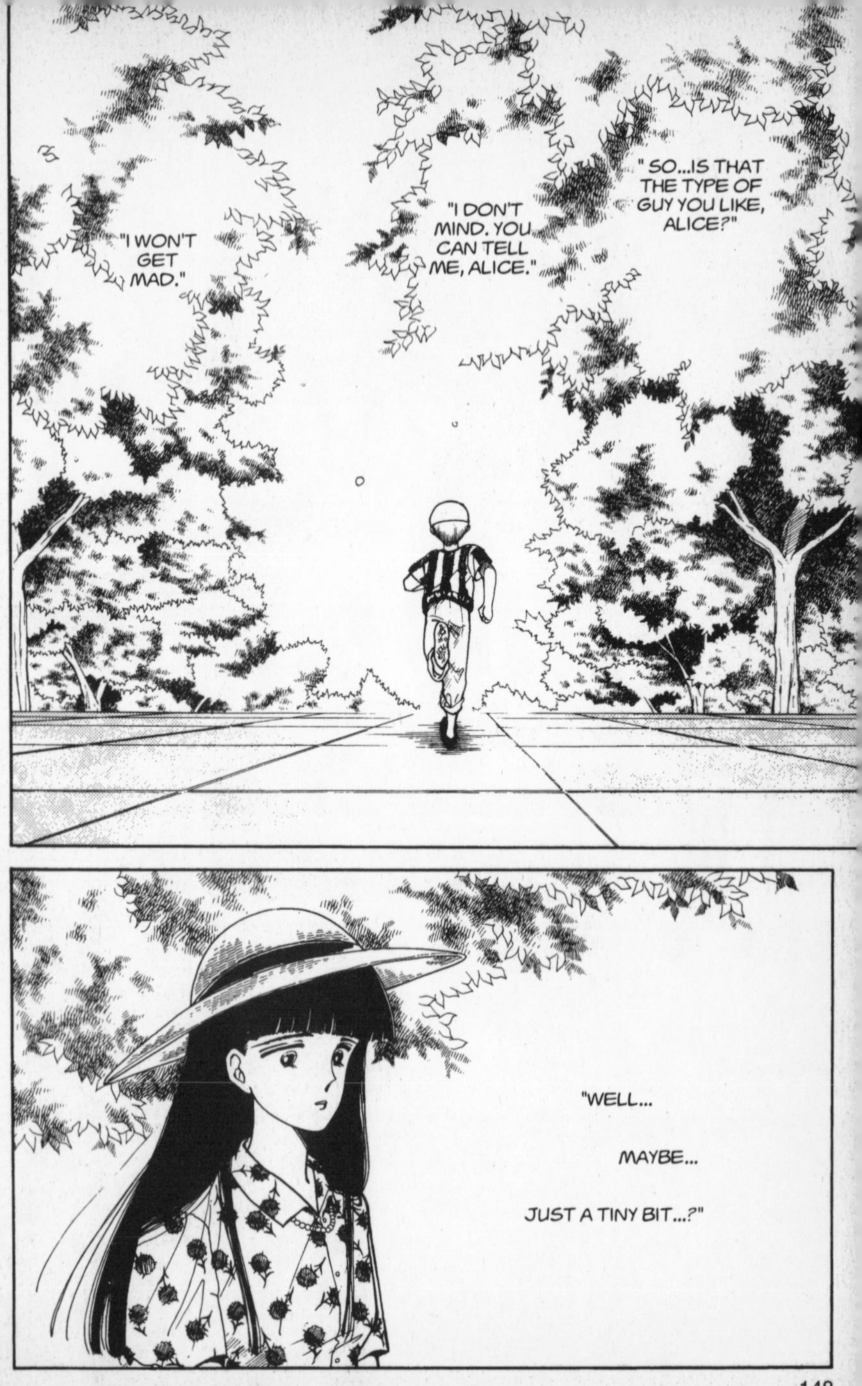
"SO...IS THAT THE TYPE OF GUY YOU LIKE, ALICE?"
"I DON'T MIND. YOU CAN TELL ME, ALICE."
"I WON'T GET MAD."
"WELL...
MAYBE...
JUST A TINY BIT...?"

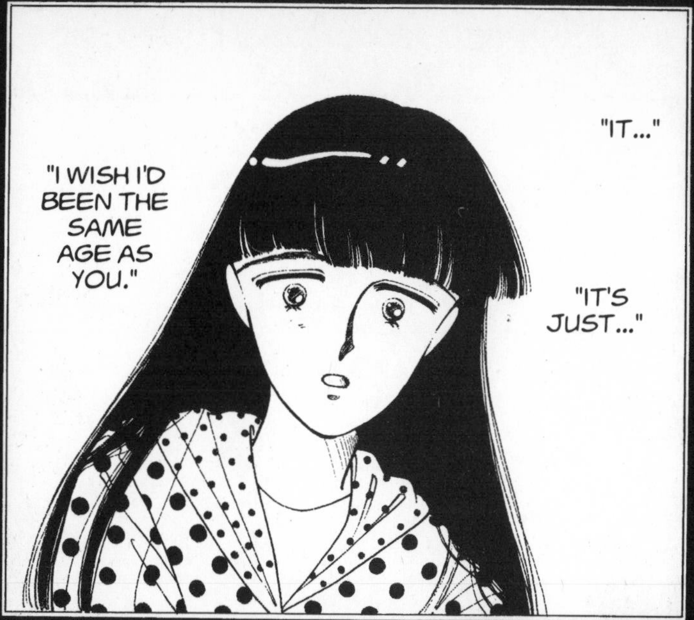
"IT..."
"IT'S JUST..."
"I WISH I'D BEEN THE SAME AGE AS YOU."
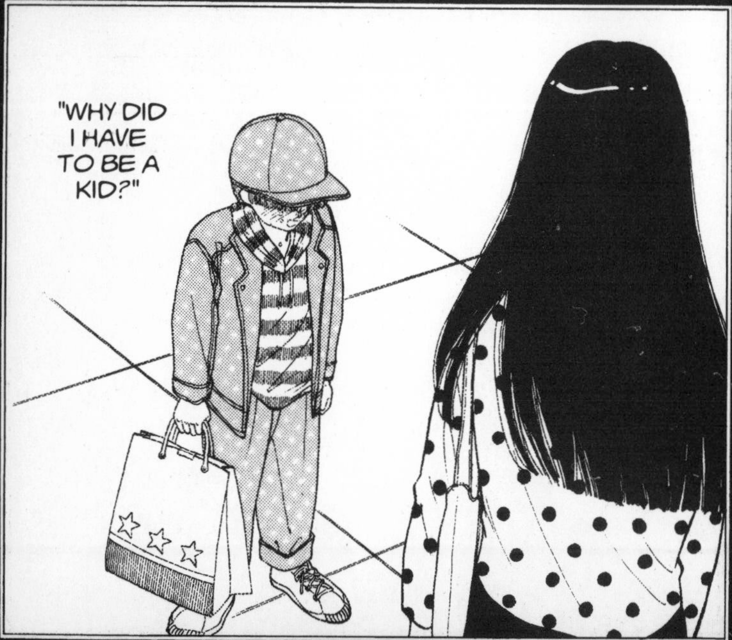
"WHY DID I HAVE TO BE A KID?"

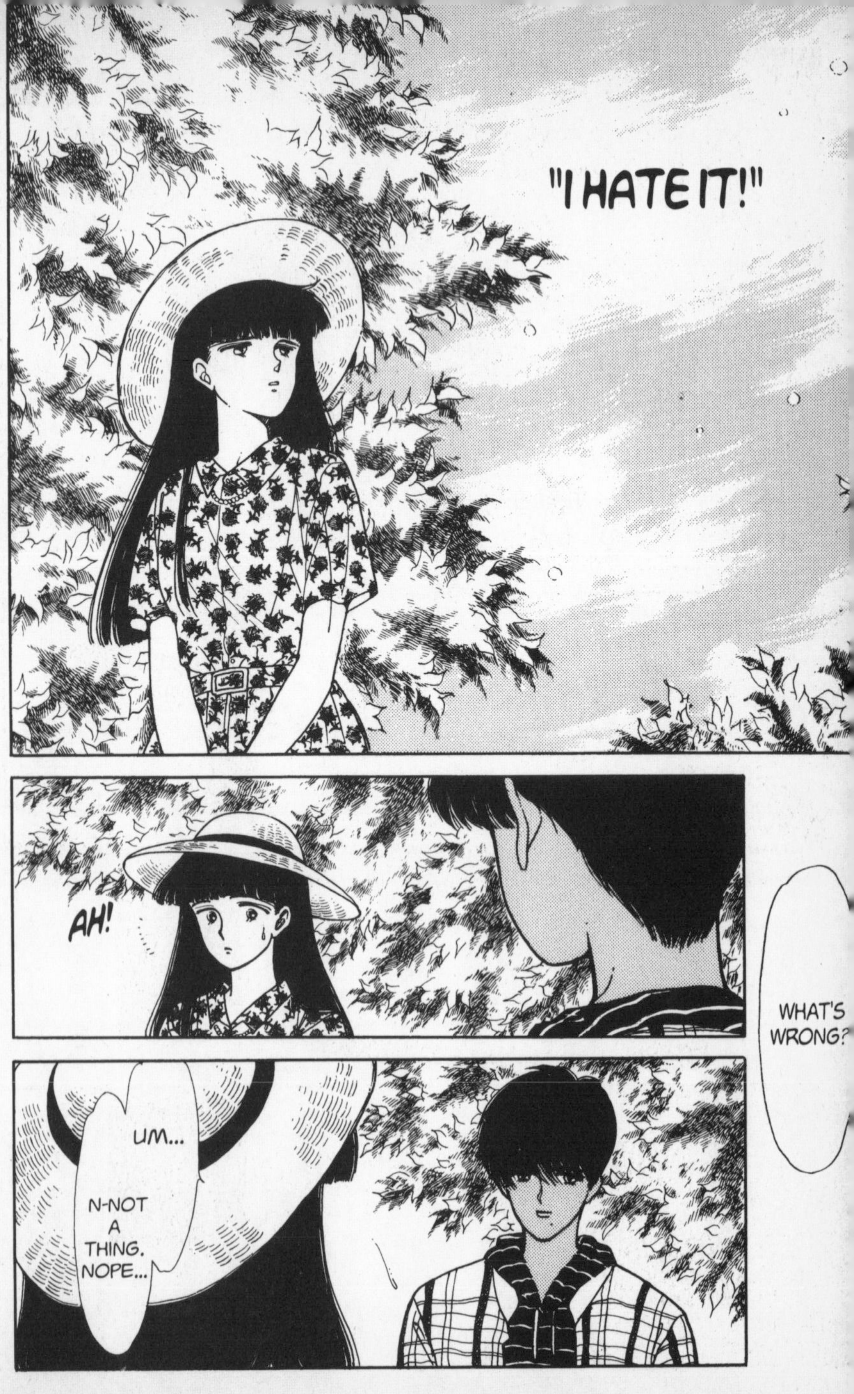
"I HATE IT!"
WHAT'S WRONG?
AH!
UM...
N-NOT A THING. NOPE...

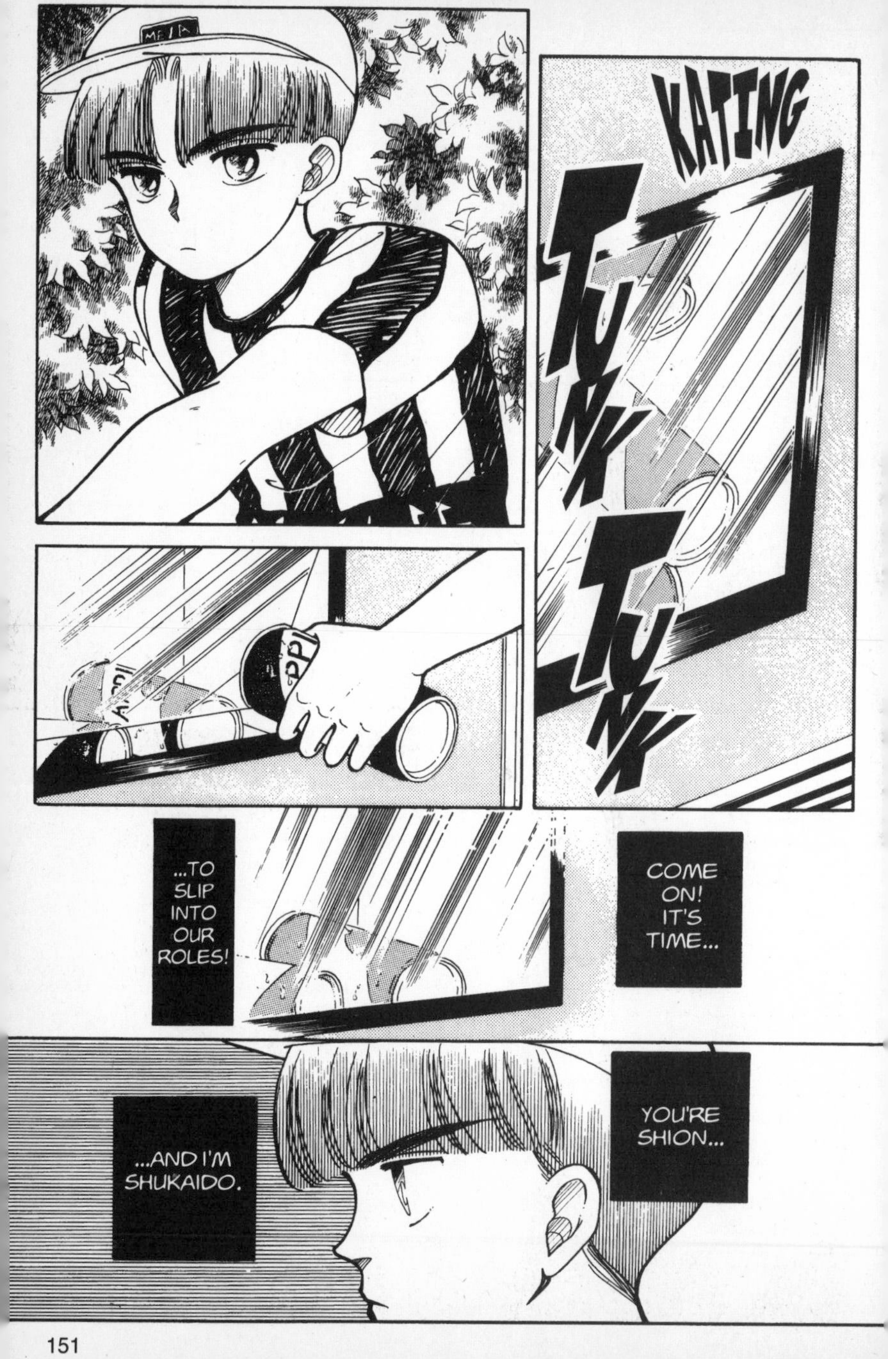
KATING
TUNK
TUNK
COME ON! IT'S TIME...
...TO SLIP INTO OUR ROLES!
YOU'RE SHION...
...AND I'M SHUKAIDO.

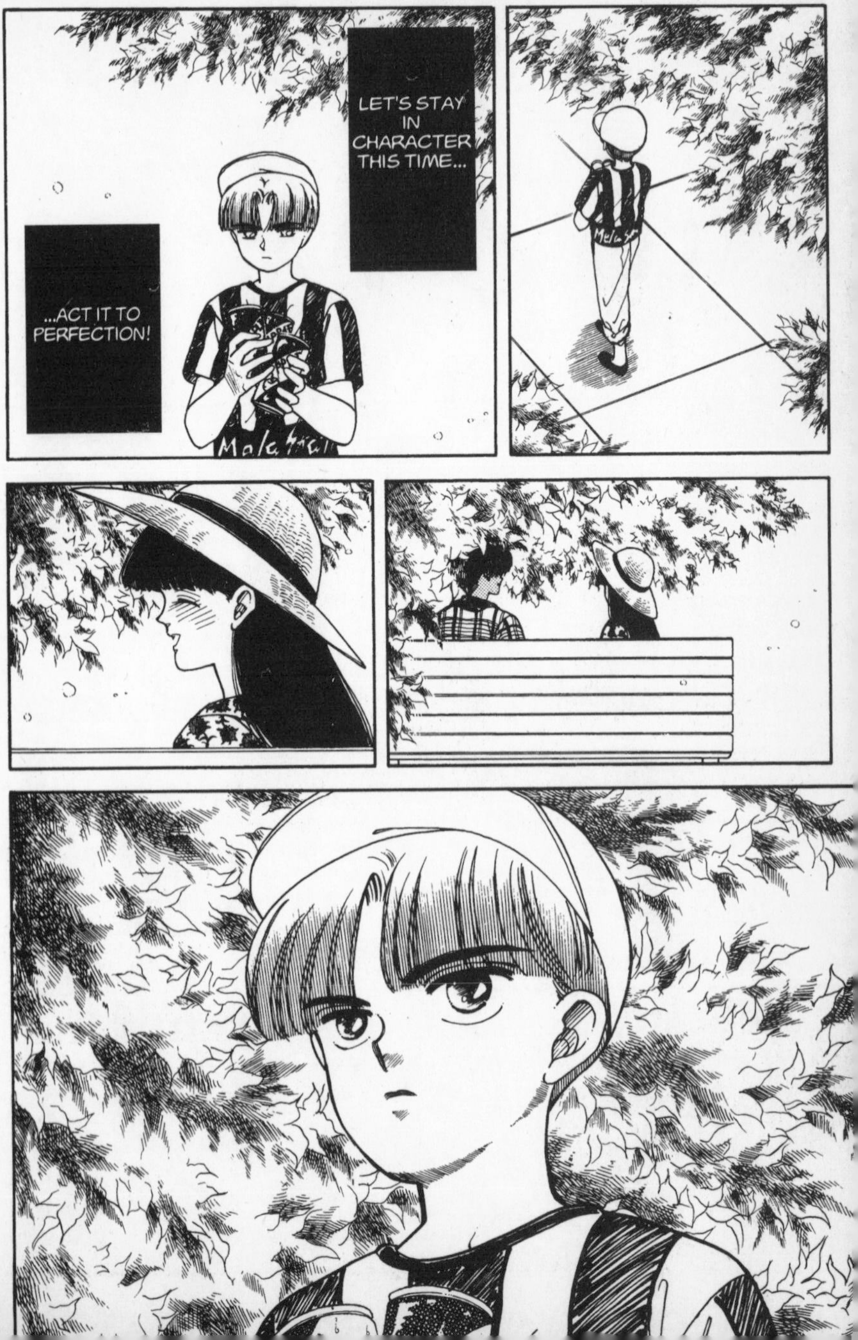
LET'S STAY IN CHARACTER THIS TIME...
...ACT IT TO PERFECTION!

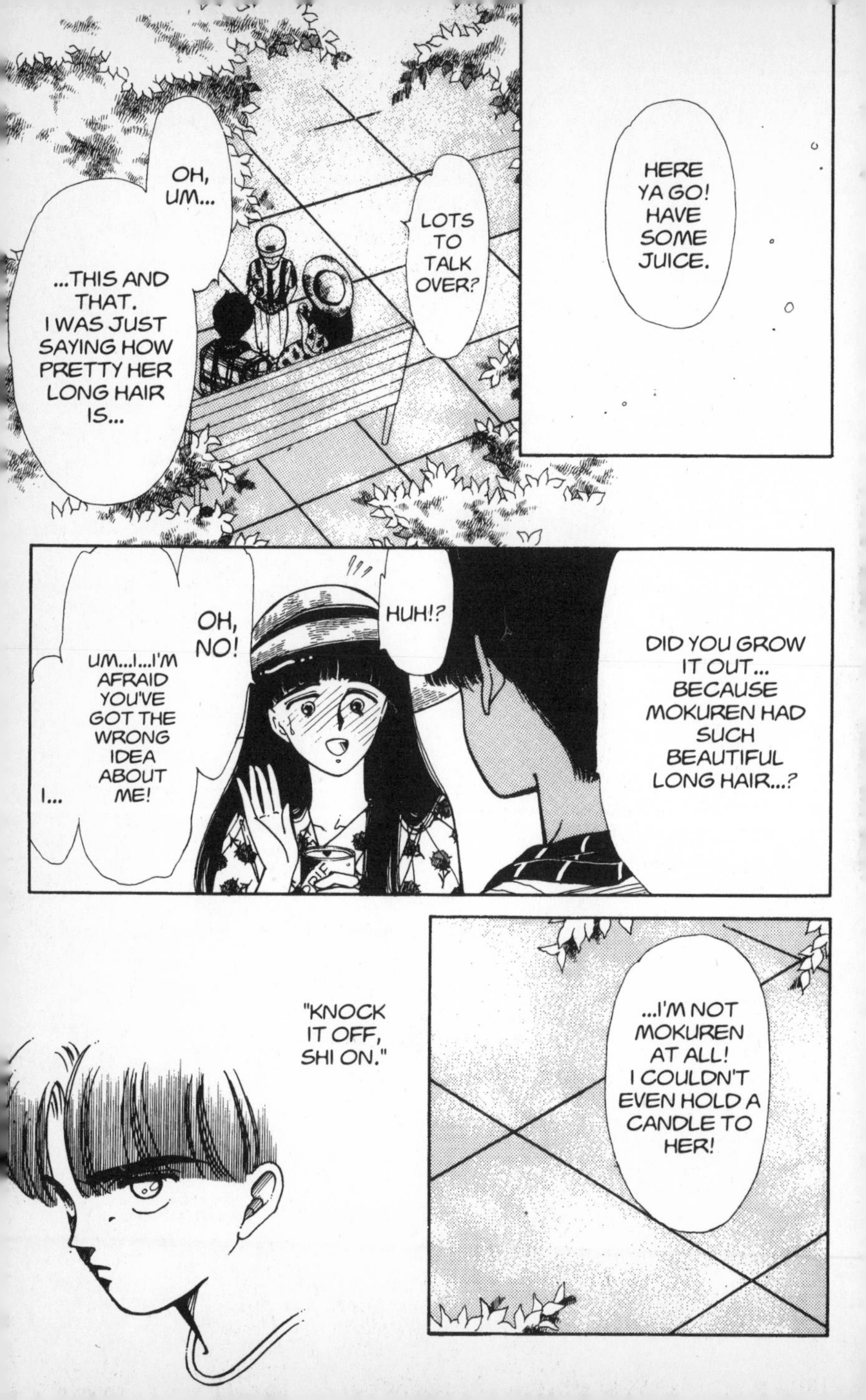
HERE YA GO! HAVE SOME JUICE.
LOTS TO TALK OVER?
OH, UM...
...THIS AND THAT. I WAS JUST SAYING HOW PRETTY HER LONG HAIR IS...
DID YOU GROW IT OUT... BECAUSE MOKUREN HAD SUCH BEAUTIFUL LONG HAIR...?
HUH!?
OH, NO!
UM...I...I'M AFRAID YOU'VE GOT THE WRONG IDEA ABOUT ME!
I...
...I'M NOT MOKUREN AT ALL! I COULDN'T EVEN HOLD A CANDLE TO HER!
"KNOCK IT OFF, SHI ON."

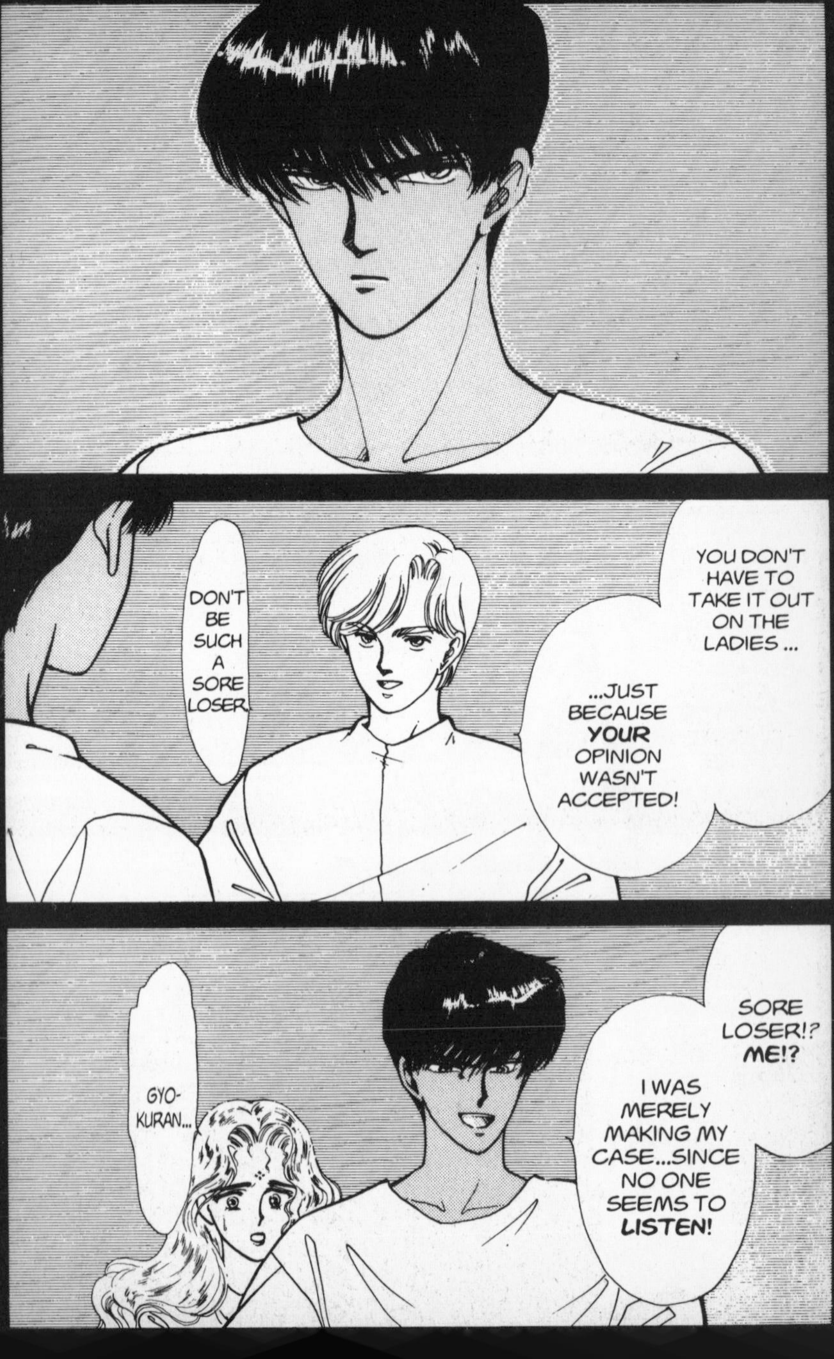
YOU DON'T HAVE TO TAKE IT OUT ON THE LADIES ...
...JUST BECAUSE **YOUR** OPINION WASN'T ACCEPTED!
DON'T BE SUCH A SORE LOSER.
SORE LOSER!? **ME!?**
I WAS MERELY MAKING MY CASE...SINCE NO ONE SEEMS TO **LISTEN!**
GYO-KURAN...

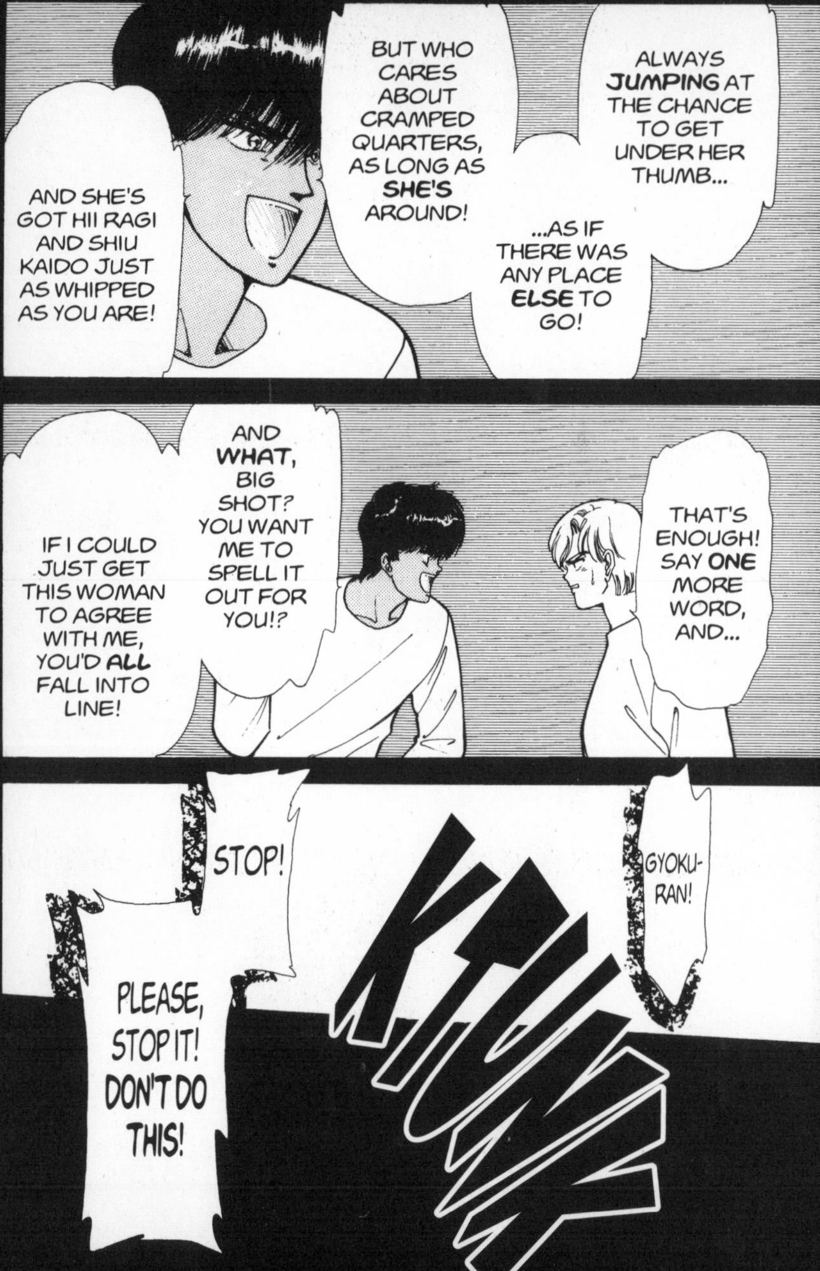
ALWAYS JUMPING AT THE CHANCE TO GET UNDER HER THUMB...
...AS IF THERE WAS ANY PLACE ELSE TO GO!
BUT WHO CARES ABOUT CRAMPED QUARTERS, AS LONG AS SHE'S AROUND!
AND SHE'S GOT HII RAGI AND SHIU KAIDO JUST AS WHIPPED AS YOU ARE!
THAT'S ENOUGH! SAY ONE MORE WORD, AND...
AND WHAT, BIG SHOT? YOU WANT ME TO SPELL IT OUT FOR YOU!?
IF I COULD JUST GET THIS WOMAN TO AGREE WITH ME, YOU'D ALL FALL INTO LINE!
GYOKU-RAN!
KTHUNK
STOP!
PLEASE, STOP IT! DON'T DO THIS!

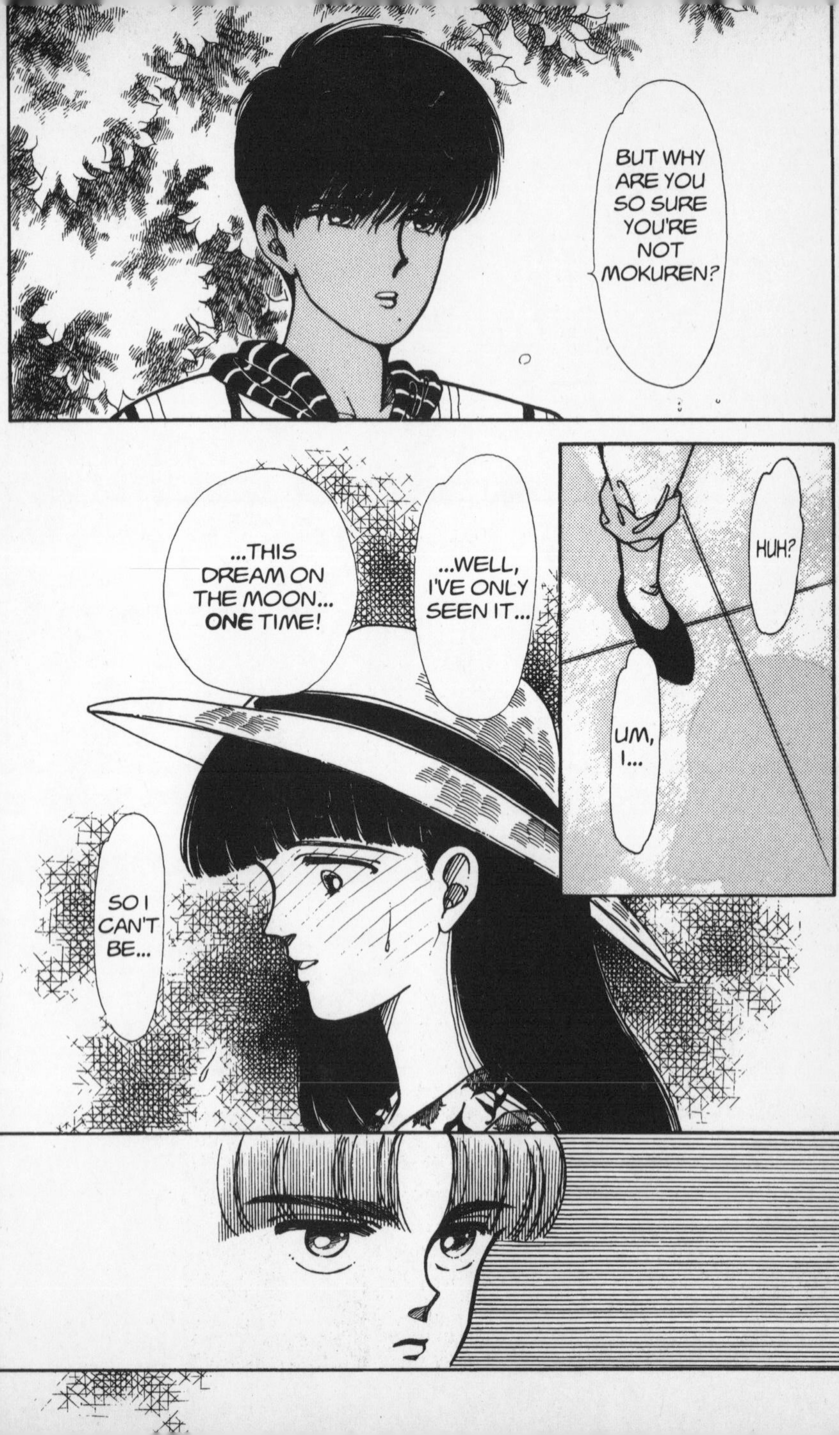
BUT WHY ARE YOU SO SURE YOU'RE NOT MOKUREN?
HUH?
UM, I...
...WELL, I'VE ONLY SEEN IT...
...THIS DREAM ON THE MOON... ONE TIME!
SO I CAN'T BE...

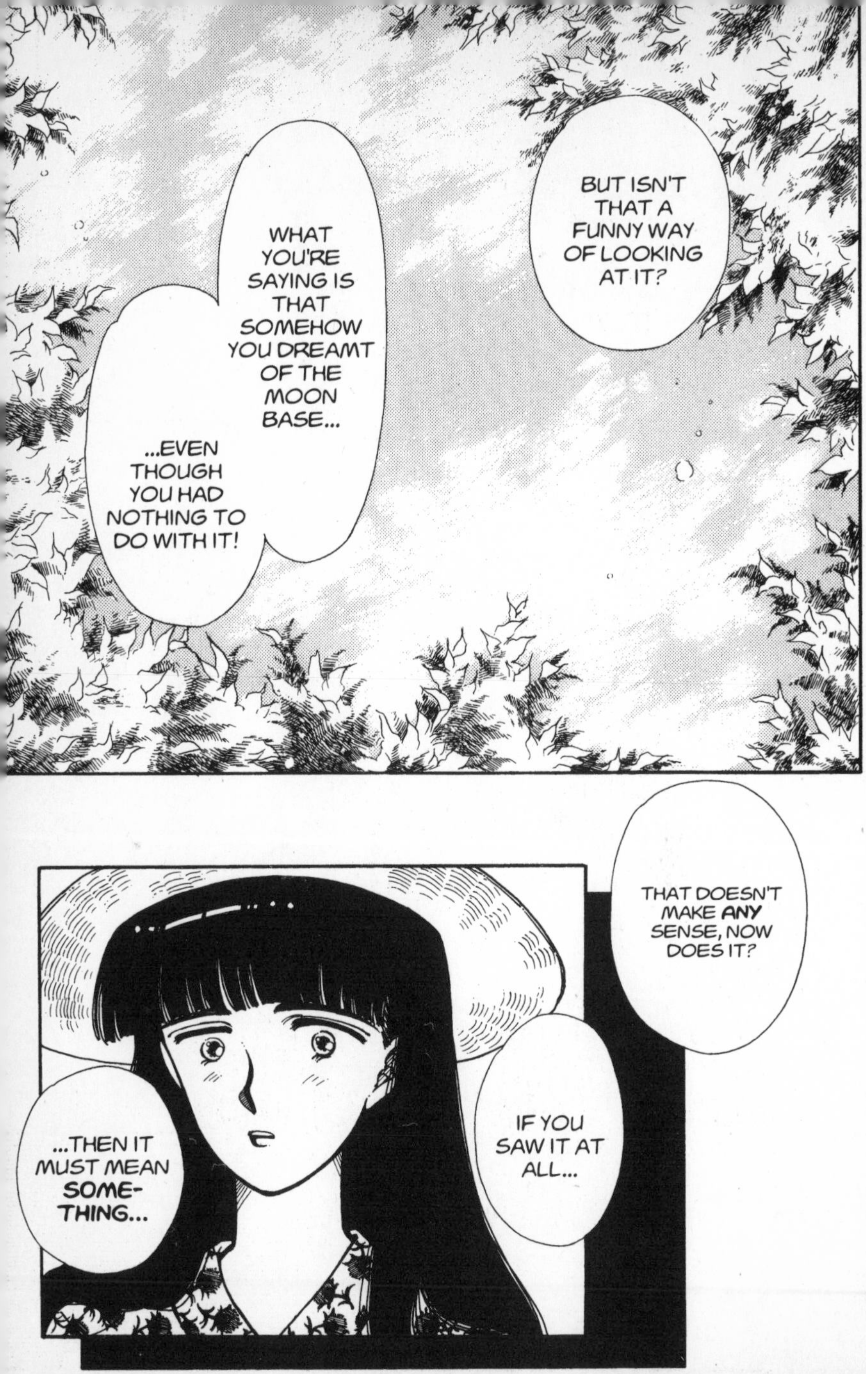
BUT ISN'T THAT A FUNNY WAY OF LOOKING AT IT?
WHAT YOU'RE SAYING IS THAT SOMEHOW YOU DREAMT OF THE MOON BASE...
...EVEN THOUGH YOU HAD NOTHING TO DO WITH IT!
THAT DOESN'T MAKE **ANY** SENSE, NOW DOES IT?
IF YOU SAW IT AT ALL...
...THEN IT MUST MEAN **SOME-THING...**

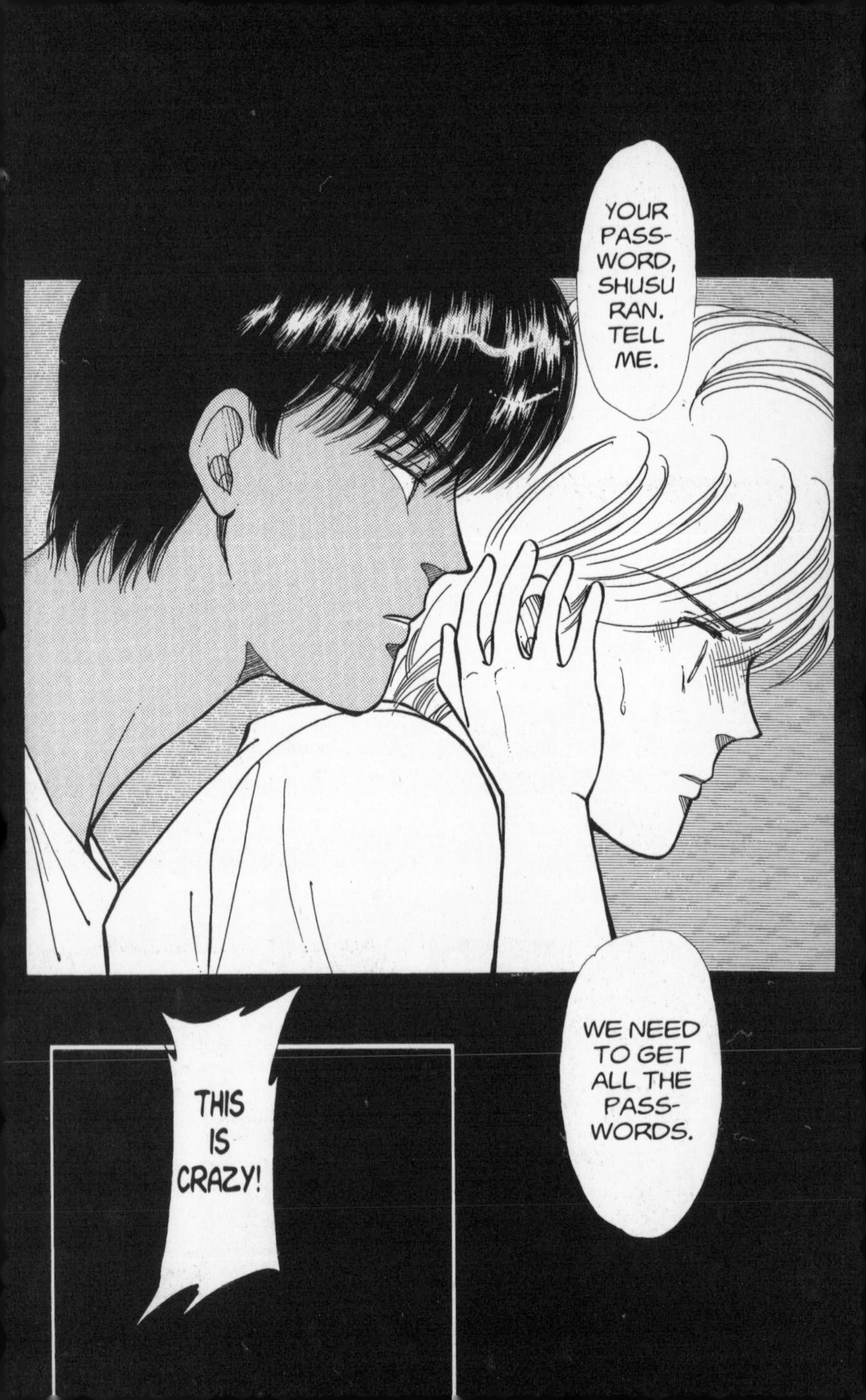
YOUR PASS-WORD, SHUSU RAN. TELL ME.
WE NEED TO GET ALL THE PASS-WORDS.
THIS IS CRAZY!

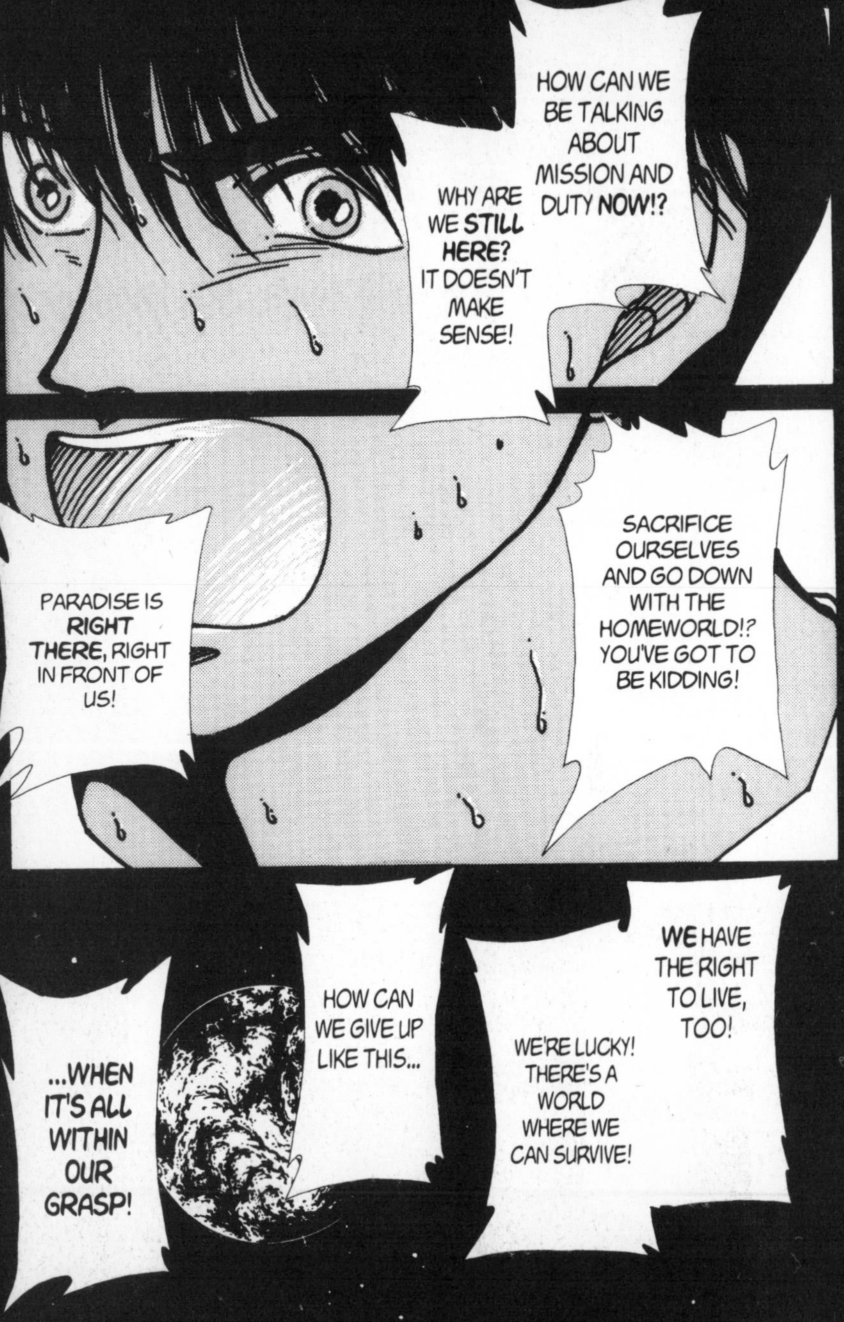
HOW CAN WE BE TALKING ABOUT MISSION AND DUTY NOW!?
WHY ARE WE STILL HERE? IT DOESN'T MAKE SENSE!
SACRIFICE OURSELVES AND GO DOWN WITH THE HOMEWORLD!? YOU'VE GOT TO BE KIDDING!
PARADISE IS RIGHT THERE, RIGHT IN FRONT OF US!
WE HAVE THE RIGHT TO LIVE, TOO!
WE'RE LUCKY! THERE'S A WORLD WHERE WE CAN SURVIVE!
HOW CAN WE GIVE UP LIKE THIS...
...WHEN IT'S ALL WITHIN OUR GRASP!

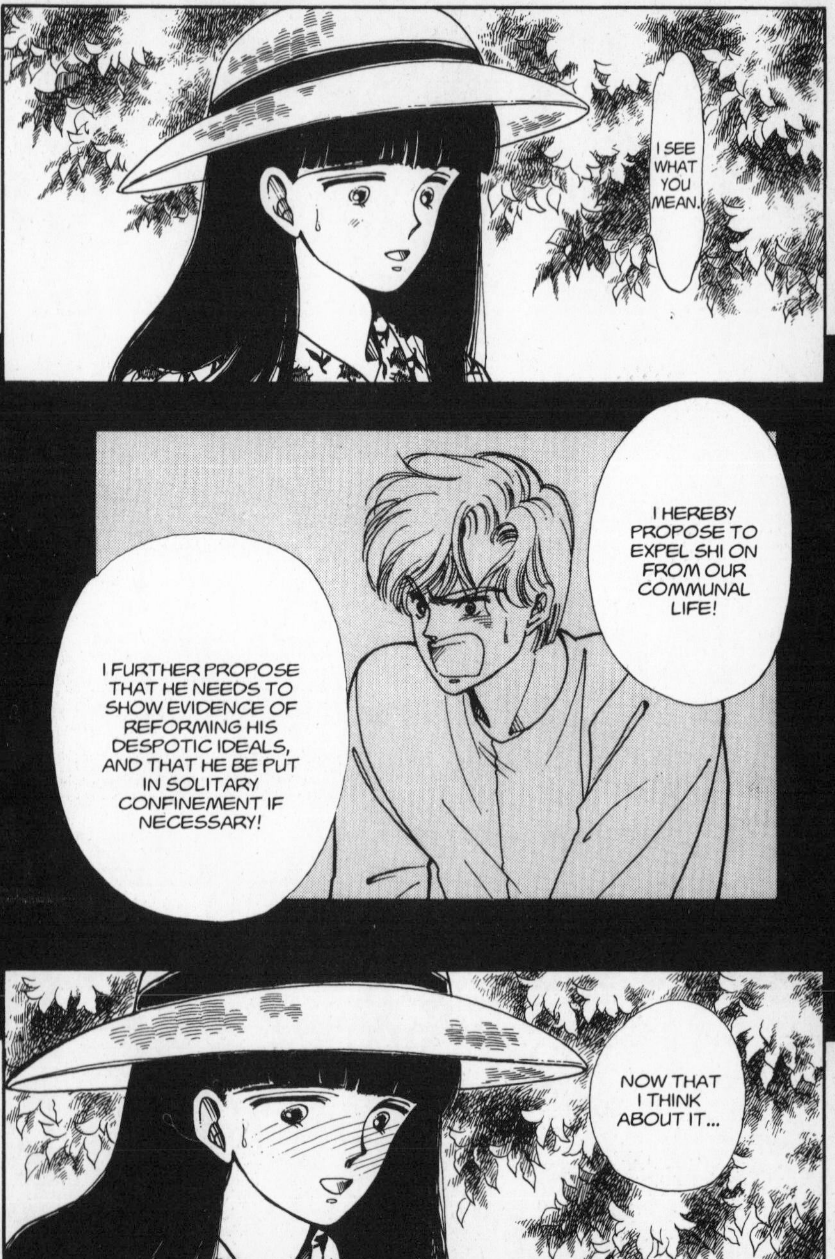
I SEE WHAT YOU MEAN.
I HEREBY PROPOSE TO EXPEL SHI ON FROM OUR COMMUNAL LIFE!
I FURTHER PROPOSE THAT HE NEEDS TO SHOW EVIDENCE OF REFORMING HIS DESPOTIC IDEALS, AND THAT HE BE PUT IN SOLITARY CONFINEMENT IF NECESSARY!
NOW THAT I THINK ABOUT IT...

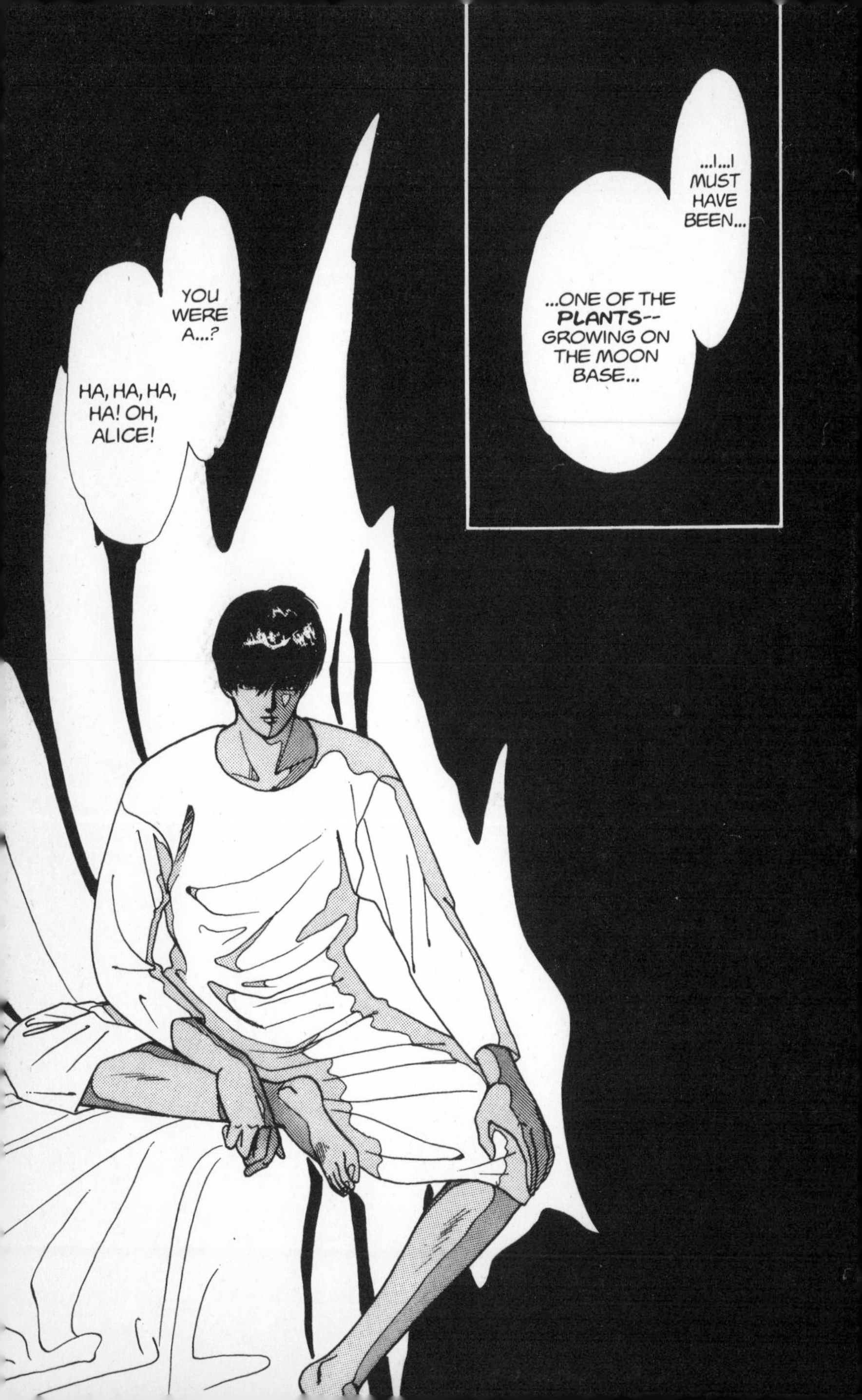
...I...I MUST HAVE BEEN...
...ONE OF THE **PLANTS**-- GROWING ON THE MOON BASE...
YOU WERE A...?
HA, HA, HA, HA! OH, ALICE!

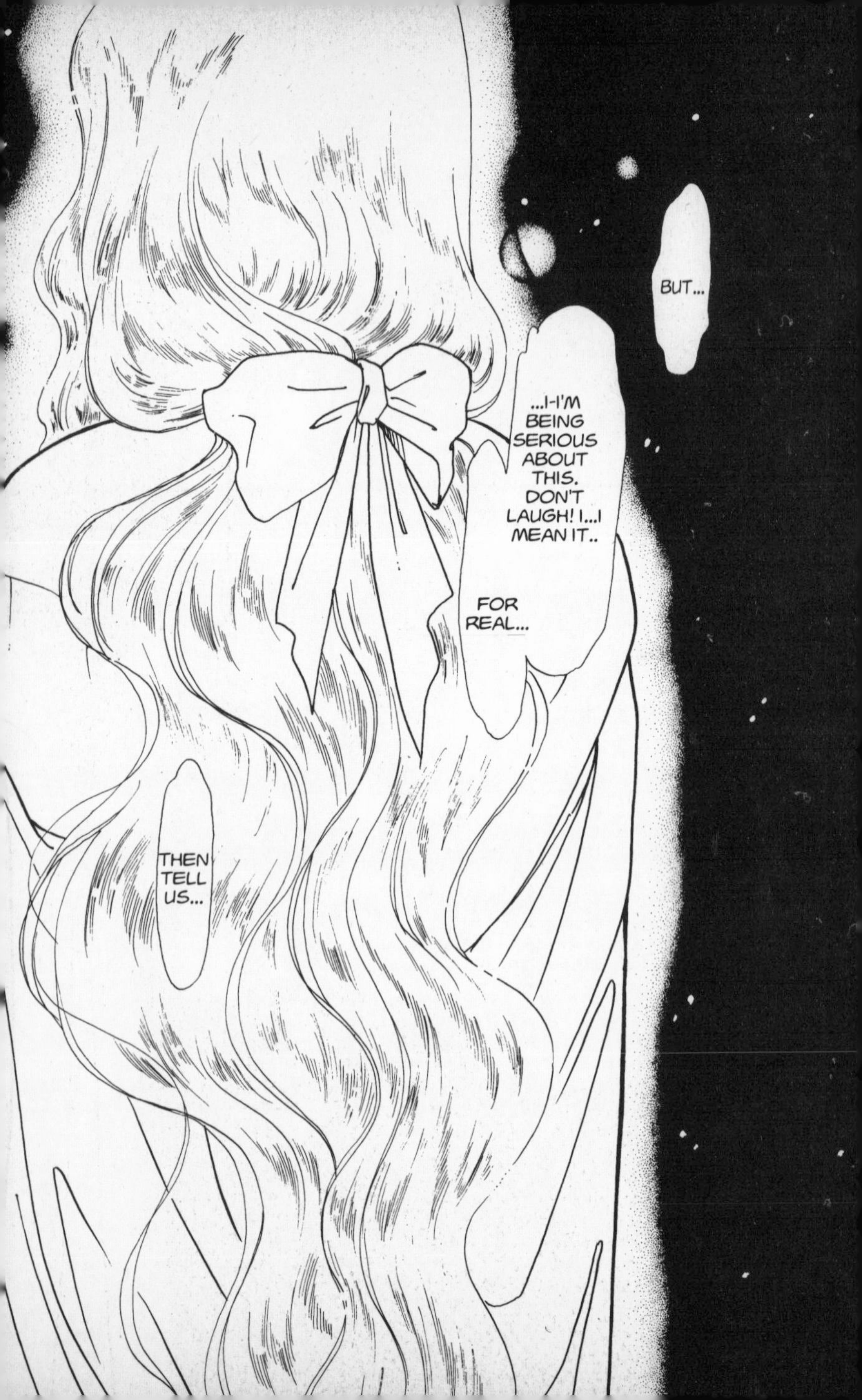
BUT...
...I-I'M BEING SERIOUS ABOUT THIS. DON'T LAUGH! I...I MEAN IT..
FOR REAL...
THEN TELL US...

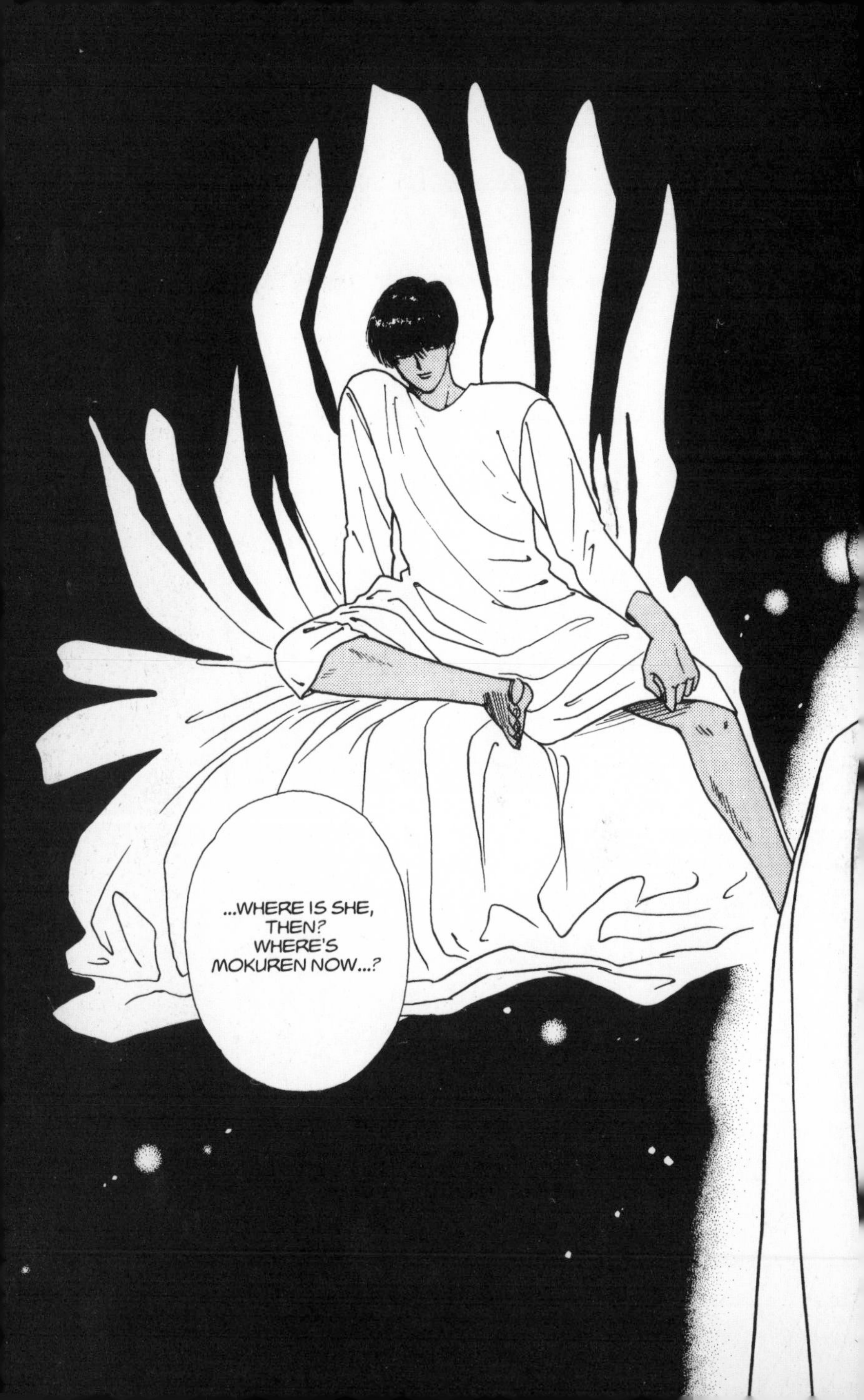
...WHERE IS SHE, THEN? WHERE'S MOKUREN NOW...?

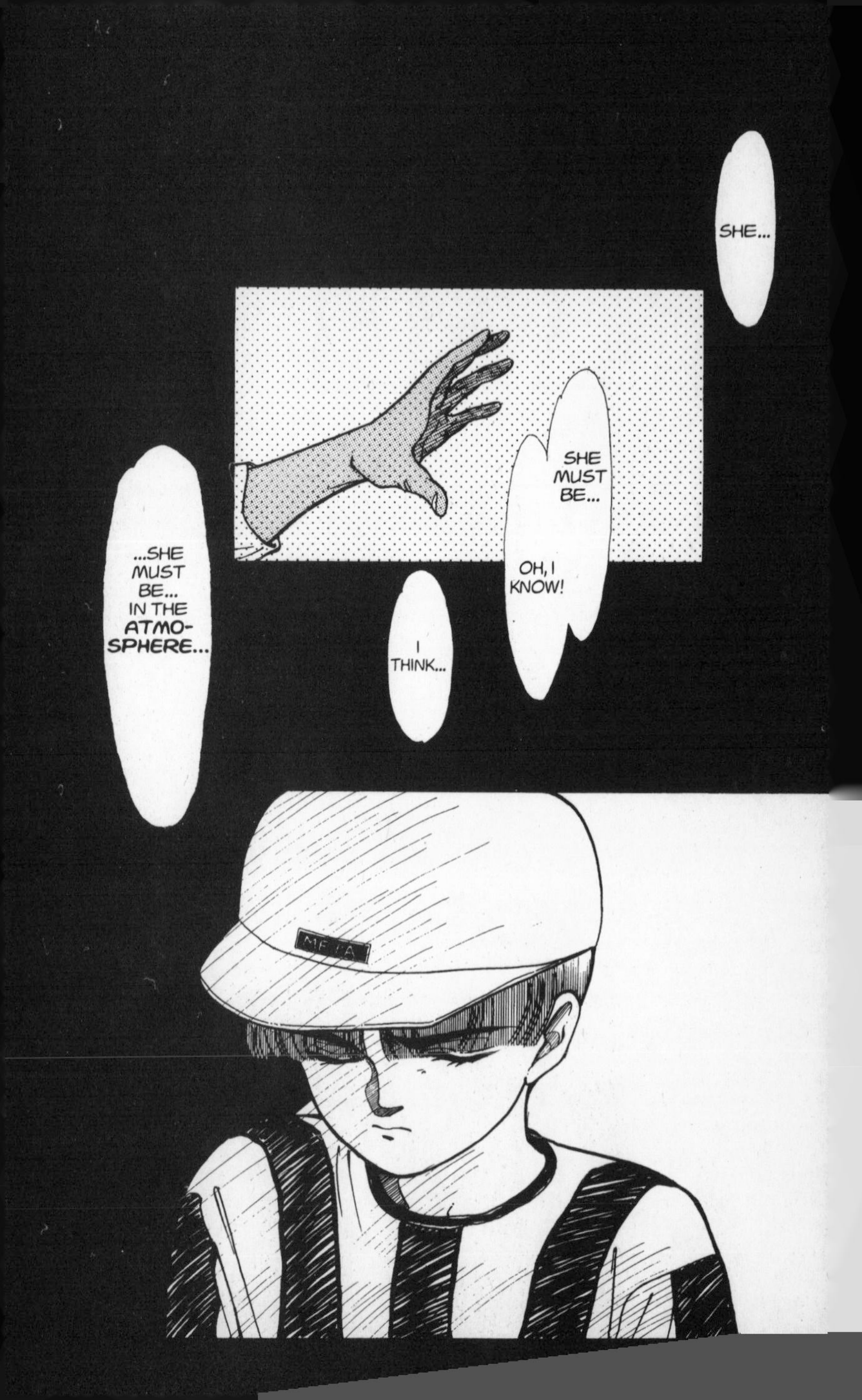
SHE...
SHE MUST BE...
OH, I KNOW!
I THINK...
...SHE MUST BE... IN THE ATMOSPHERE...

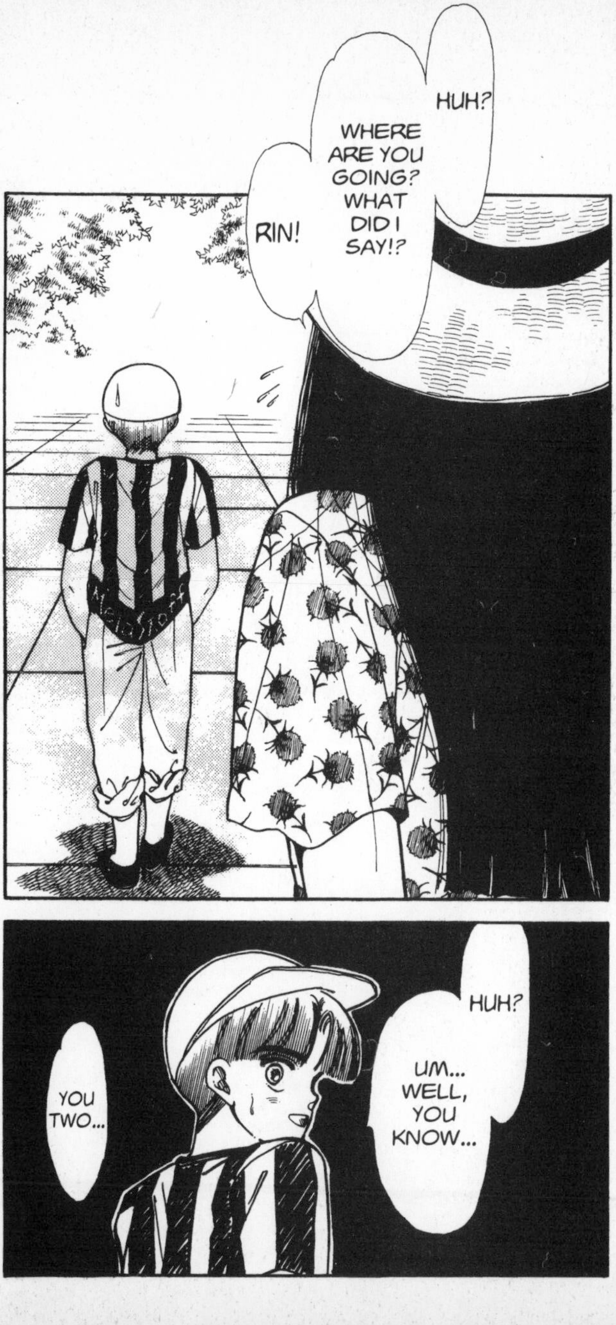
HUH?
WHERE ARE YOU GOING? WHAT DID I SAY!?
RIN!
HUH?
UM... WELL, YOU KNOW...
YOU TWO...

1/4 COLUMN NONSENSE
— PART 6 —

I also discovered that when an event like this happens, a past scene will stick out in your mind--almost like foreshadowing. For example, I remember leaving the front door of my workplace open, and that same boy--in the middle of a game of hide and seek--ran in and hid behind it. I chuckled at the time, it was such a heartwarming bit of neighborhood life.

Before I adopted my cat, Tomonori, I remember Tomo (still a healthy, nameless stray, at the time) perched on top of the wall. A friend of mine laughingly said, "That cat is cuter than the one who usually comes by."

It's not something serious like precognition, and it's not quite like déjà-vu, or a feeling in your bones... Okay, now it's just getting weird. It's "Vivid Memories, Hiwatari Arc"! Just kidding.

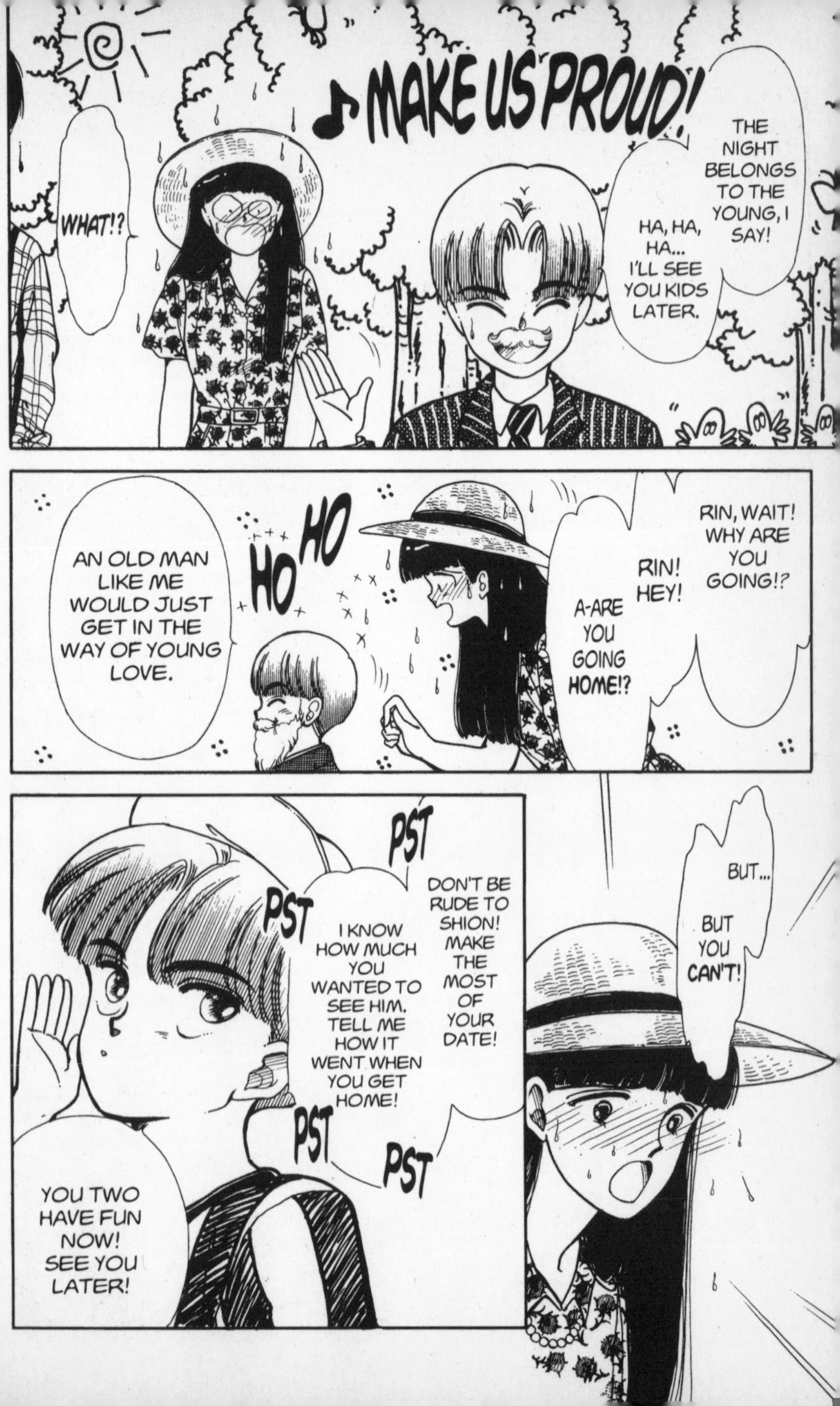
THE NIGHT BELONGS TO THE YOUNG, I SAY!
HA, HA, HA... I'LL SEE YOU KIDS LATER.
♪ MAKE US PROUD!
WHAT!?
RIN, WAIT! WHY ARE YOU GOING!?
RIN! HEY!
A-ARE YOU GOING HOME!?
HO HO
AN OLD MAN LIKE ME WOULD JUST GET IN THE WAY OF YOUNG LOVE.
BUT...
BUT YOU CAN'T!
PST
DON'T BE RUDE TO SHION! MAKE THE MOST OF YOUR DATE!
PST
I KNOW HOW MUCH YOU WANTED TO SEE HIM. TELL ME HOW IT WENT WHEN YOU GET HOME!
PST
PST
YOU TWO HAVE FUN NOW! SEE YOU LATER!

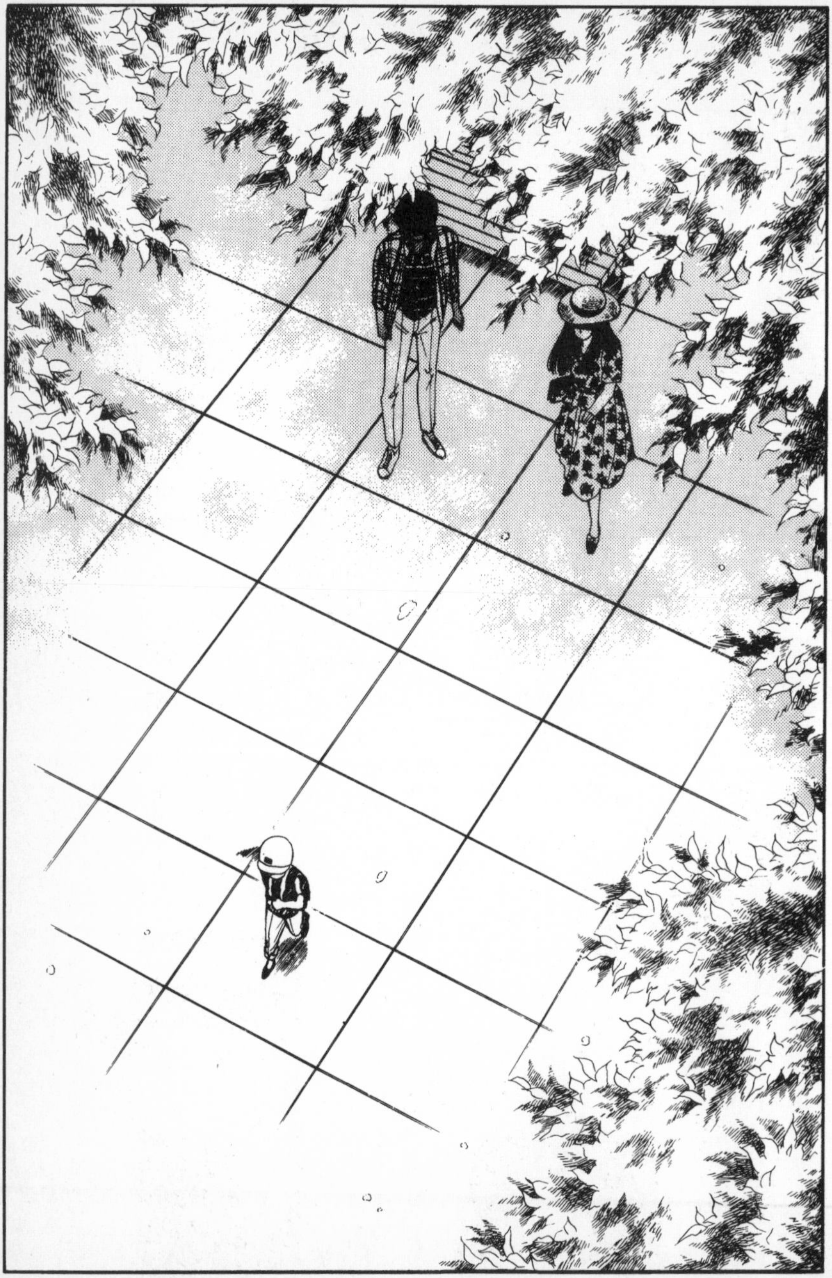

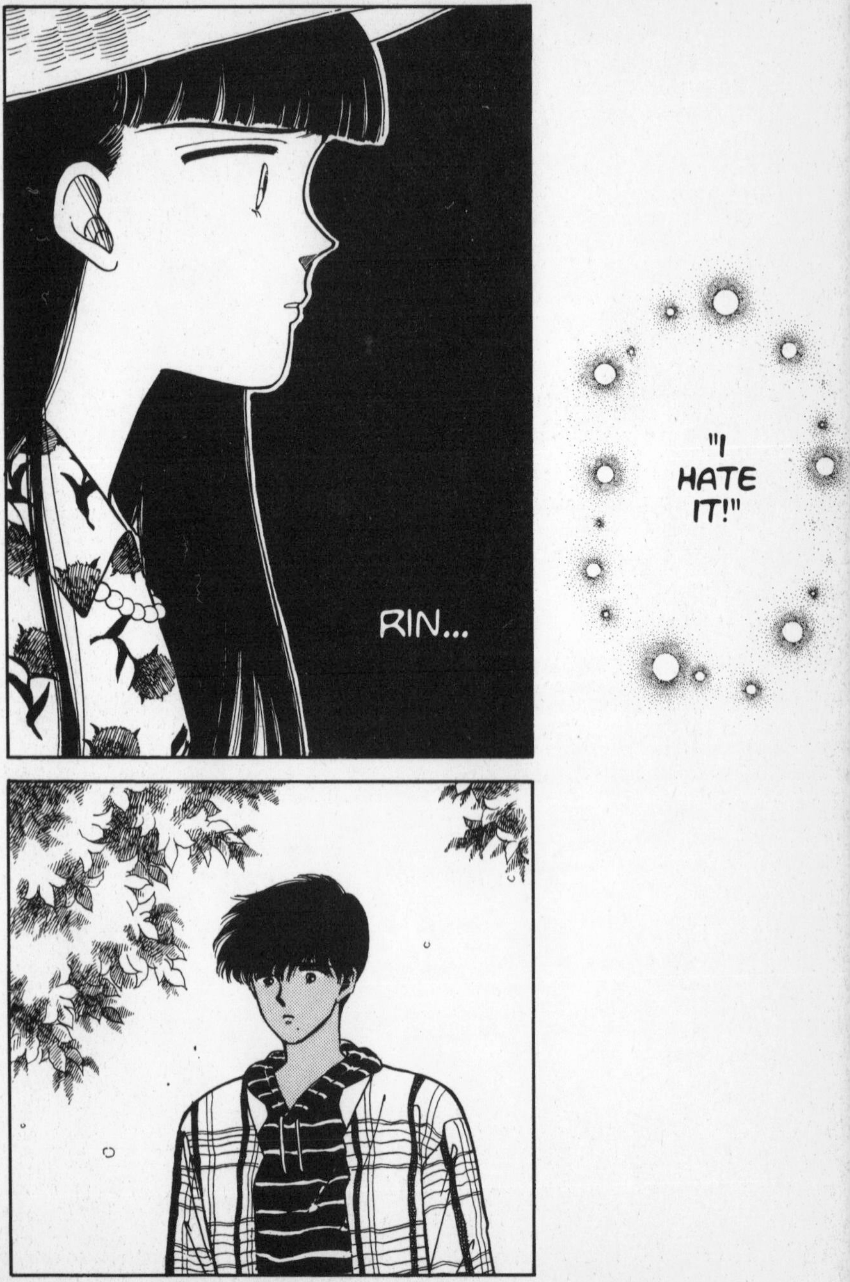
"I HATE IT!"
RIN...

WHY ON
EARTH...!?

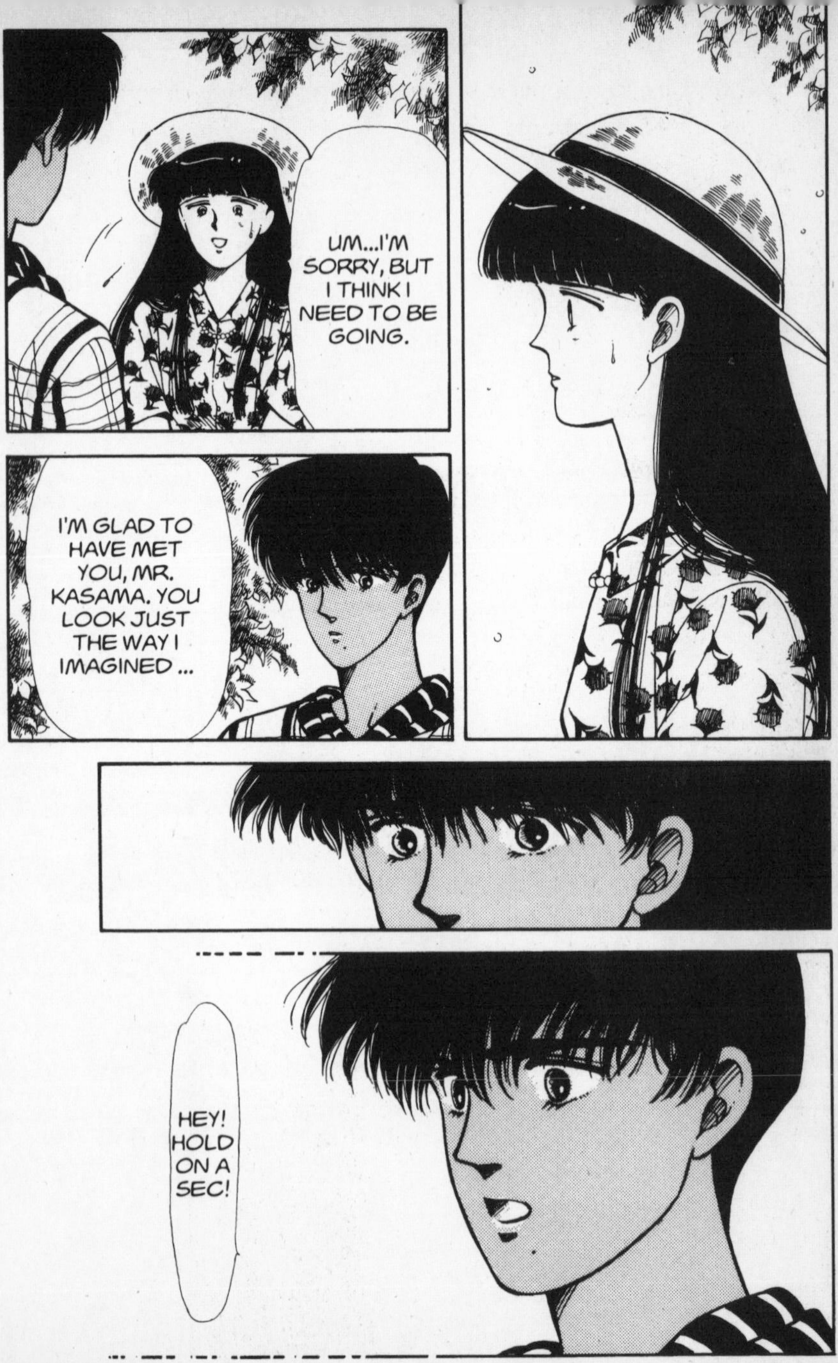
UM...I'M SORRY, BUT I THINK I NEED TO BE GOING.
I'M GLAD TO HAVE MET YOU, MR. KASAMA. YOU LOOK JUST THE WAY I IMAGINED ...
HEY! HOLD ON A SEC!

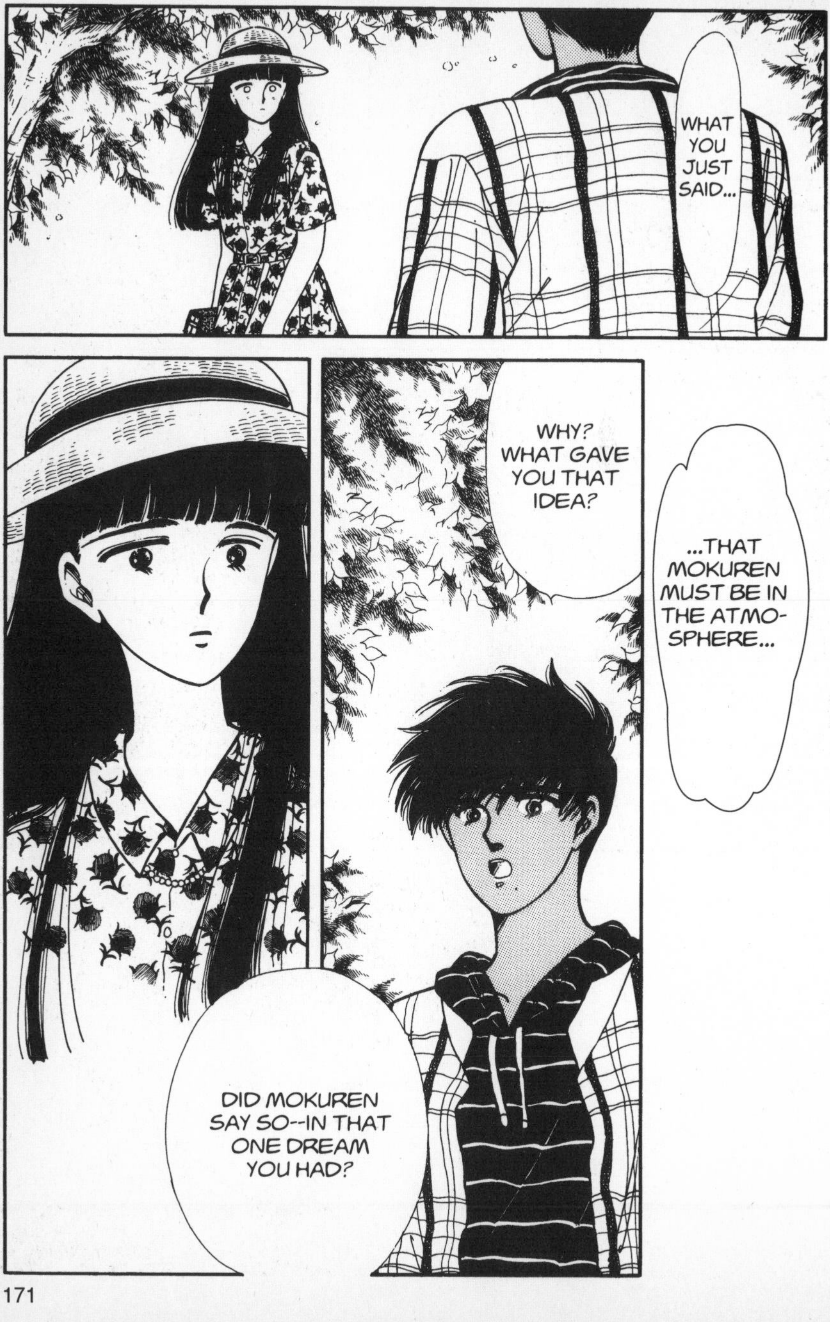
WHAT YOU JUST SAID...
...THAT MOKUREN MUST BE IN THE ATMOSPHERE...
WHY? WHAT GAVE YOU THAT IDEA?
DID MOKUREN SAY SO--IN THAT ONE DREAM YOU HAD?

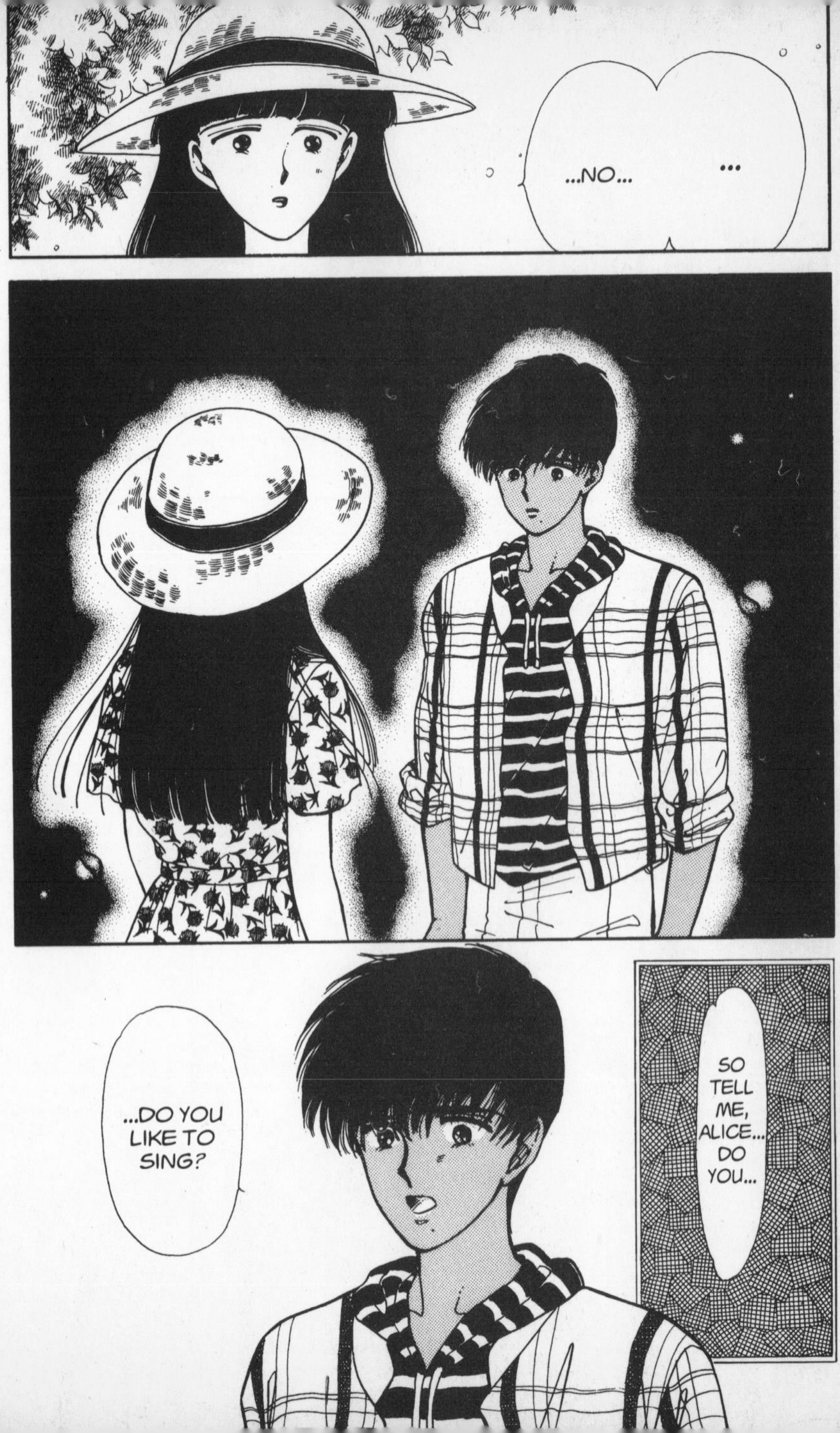
...NO... ...
SO TELL ME, ALICE... DO YOU...
...DO YOU LIKE TO SING?

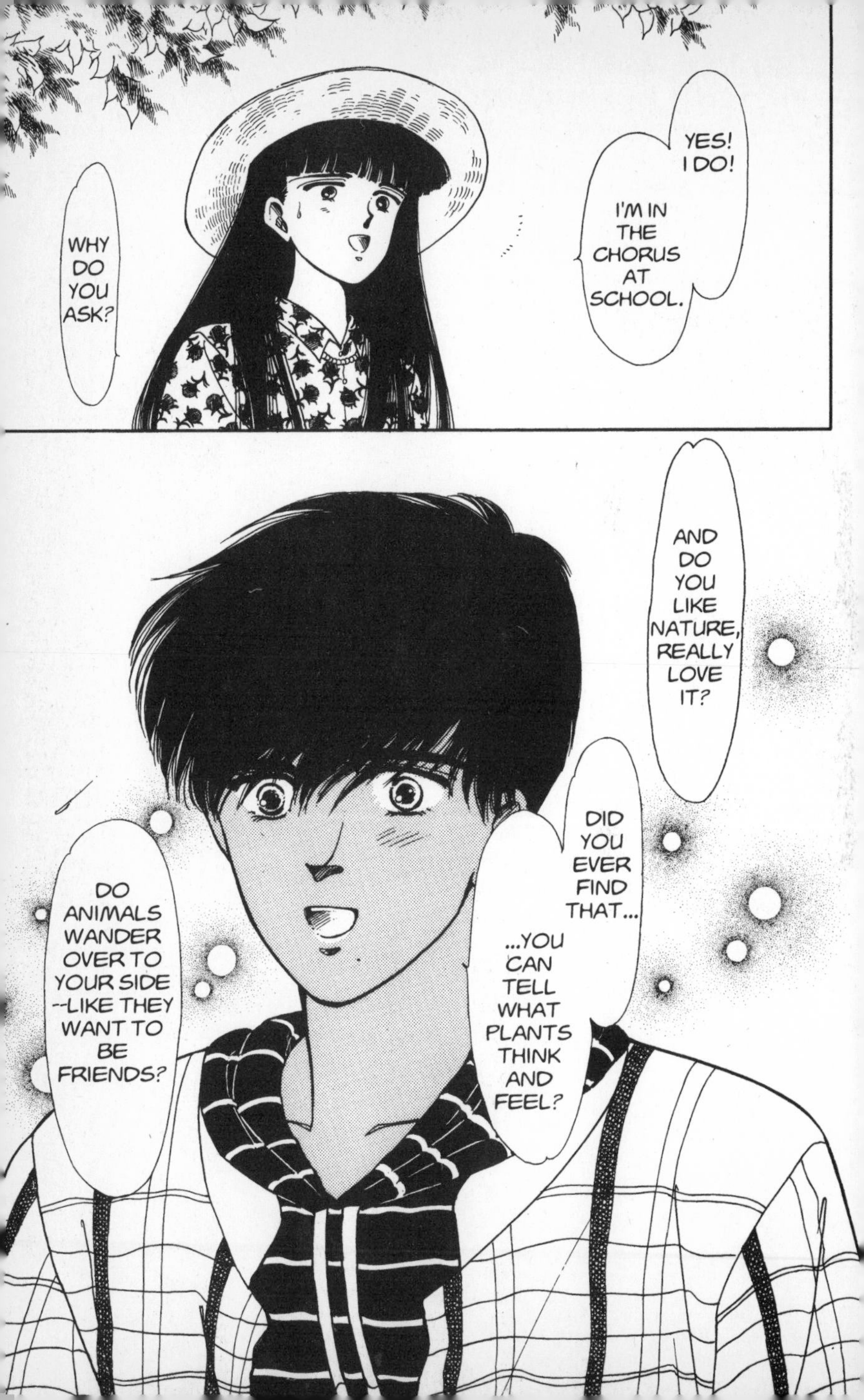
YES! I DO!
I'M IN THE CHORUS AT SCHOOL.
WHY DO YOU ASK?
AND DO YOU LIKE NATURE, REALLY LOVE IT?
DID YOU EVER FIND THAT...
...YOU CAN TELL WHAT PLANTS THINK AND FEEL?
DO ANIMALS WANDER OVER TO YOUR SIDE --LIKE THEY WANT TO BE FRIENDS?

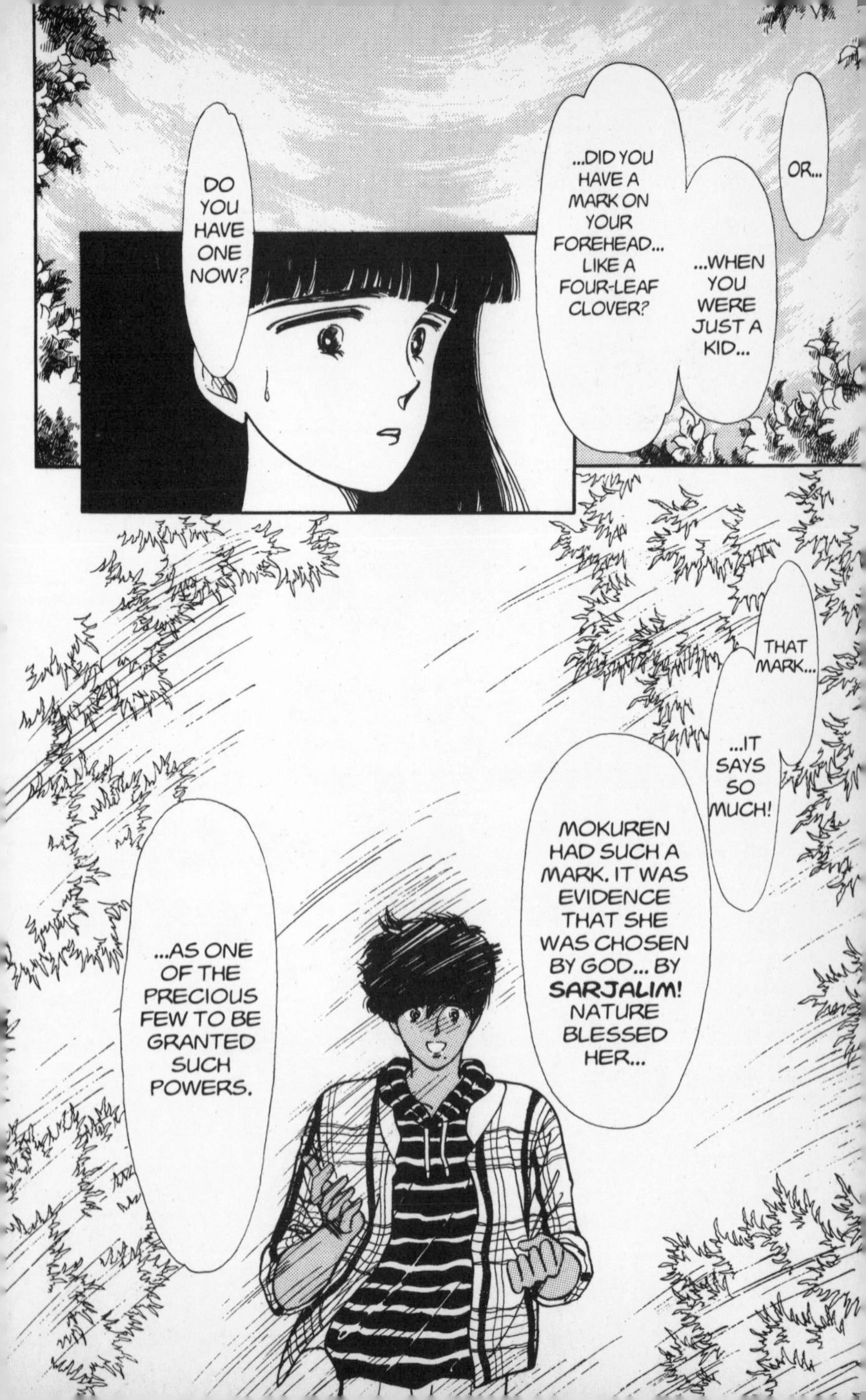
OR...
...WHEN YOU WERE JUST A KID...
...DID YOU HAVE A MARK ON YOUR FOREHEAD... LIKE A FOUR-LEAF CLOVER?
DO YOU HAVE ONE NOW?
THAT MARK...
...IT SAYS SO MUCH!
MOKUREN HAD SUCH A MARK. IT WAS EVIDENCE THAT SHE WAS CHOSEN BY GOD... BY **SARJALIM!** NATURE BLESSED HER...
...AS ONE OF THE PRECIOUS FEW TO BE GRANTED SUCH POWERS.

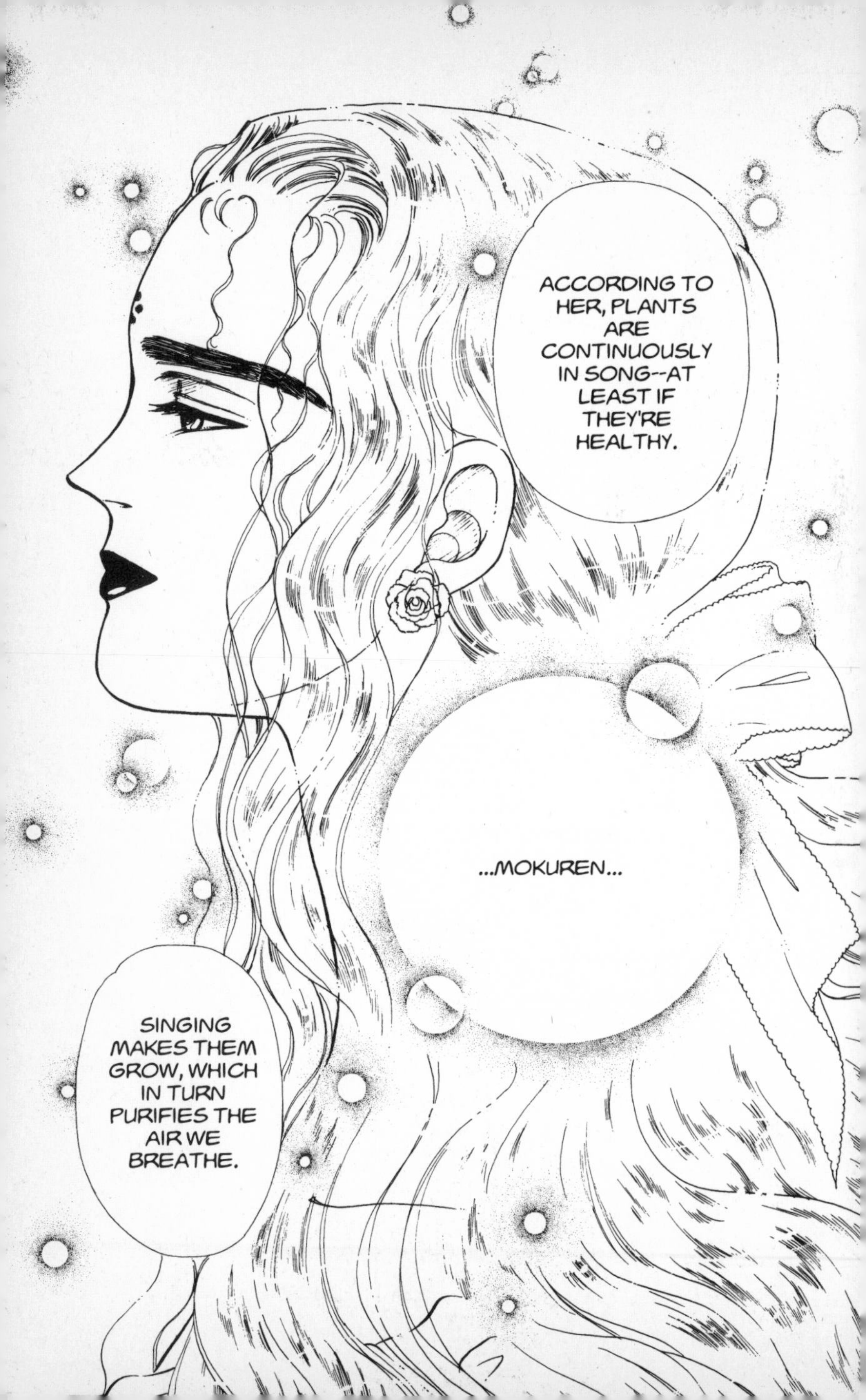
ACCORDING TO HER, PLANTS ARE CONTINUOUSLY IN SONG--AT LEAST IF THEY'RE HEALTHY.
...MOKUREN...
SINGING MAKES THEM GROW, WHICH IN TURN PURIFIES THE AIR WE BREATHE.

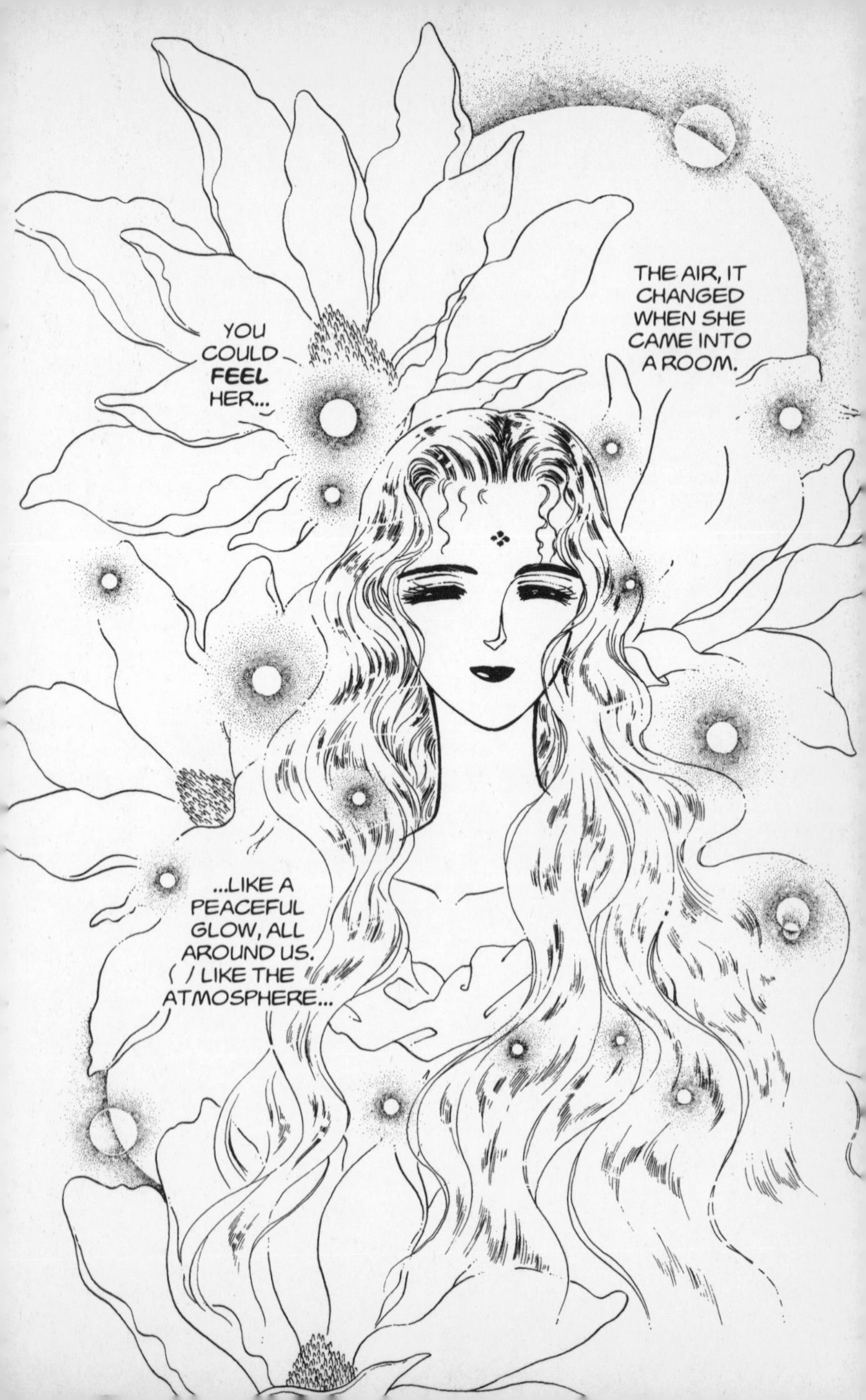
THE AIR, IT CHANGED WHEN SHE CAME INTO A ROOM.
YOU COULD **FEEL** HER...
...LIKE A PEACEFUL GLOW, ALL AROUND US. / LIKE THE ATMOSPHERE...

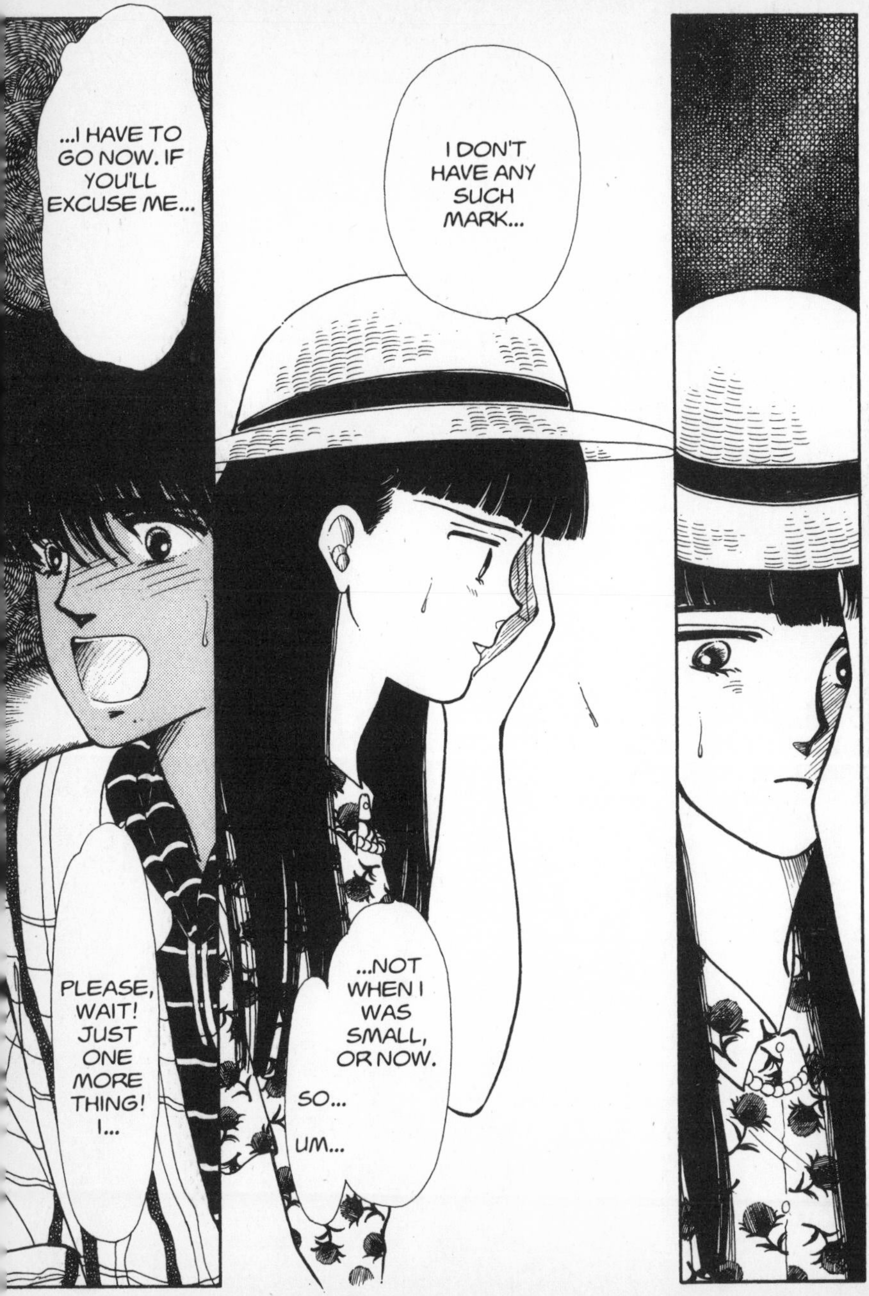
I DON'T HAVE ANY SUCH MARK...
...NOT WHEN I WAS SMALL, OR NOW.
SO... UM...
...I HAVE TO GO NOW. IF YOU'LL EXCUSE ME...
PLEASE, WAIT! JUST ONE MORE THING! I...

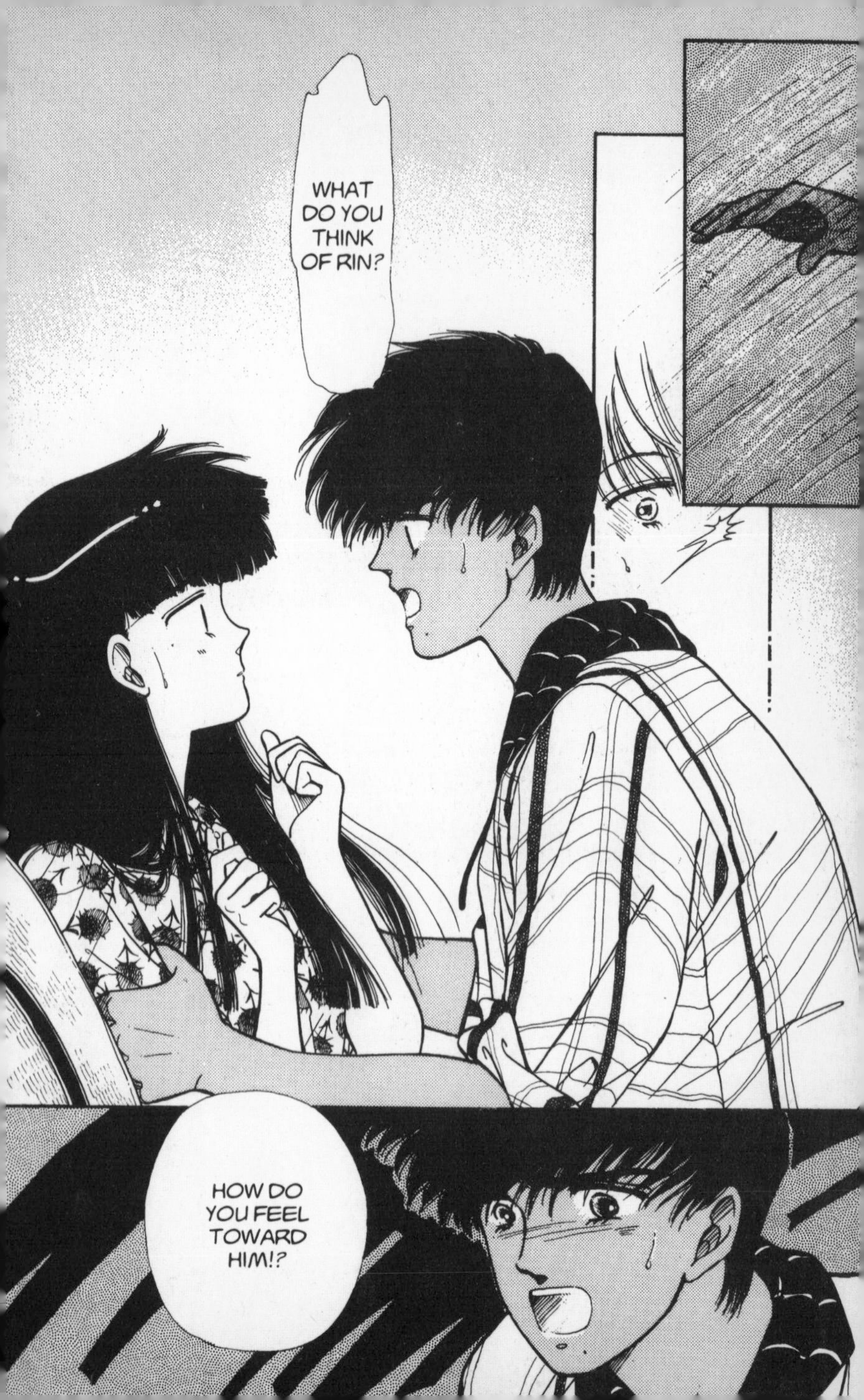
WHAT DO YOU THINK OF RIN?
HOW DO YOU FEEL TOWARD HIM!?

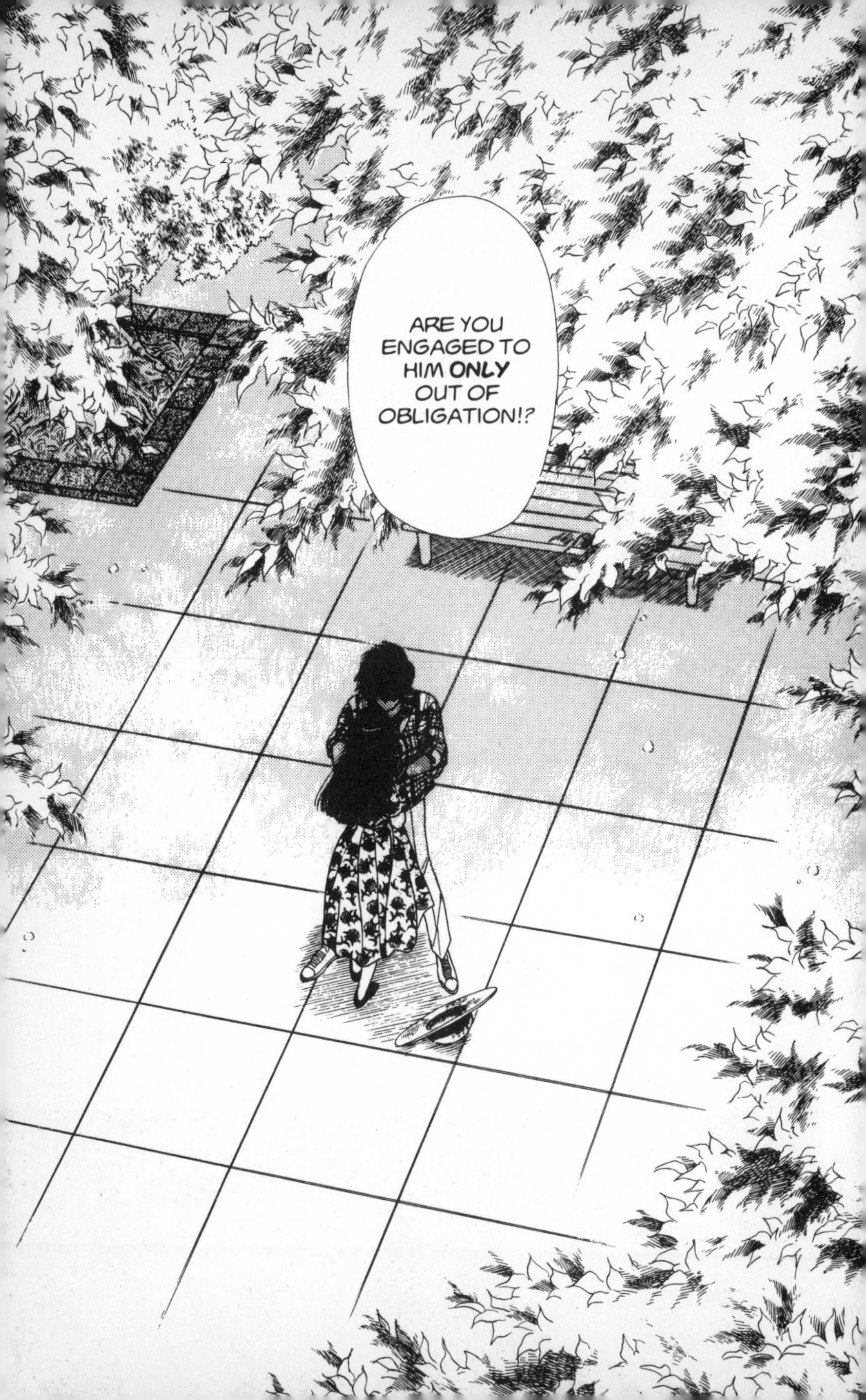
ARE YOU ENGAGED TO HIM **ONLY** OUT OF OBLIGATION!?

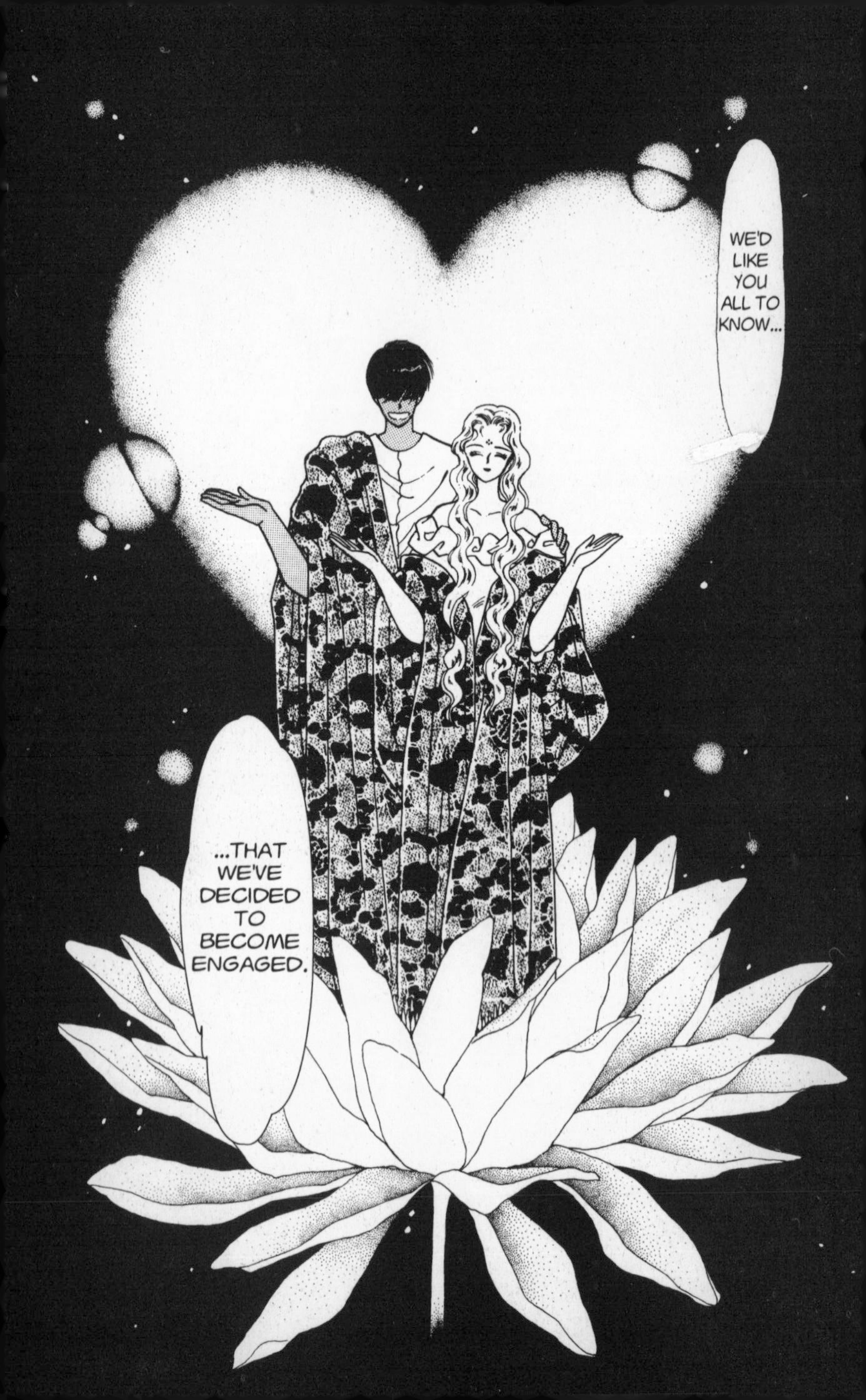
WE'D LIKE YOU ALL TO KNOW...
...THAT WE'VE DECIDED TO BECOME ENGAGED.

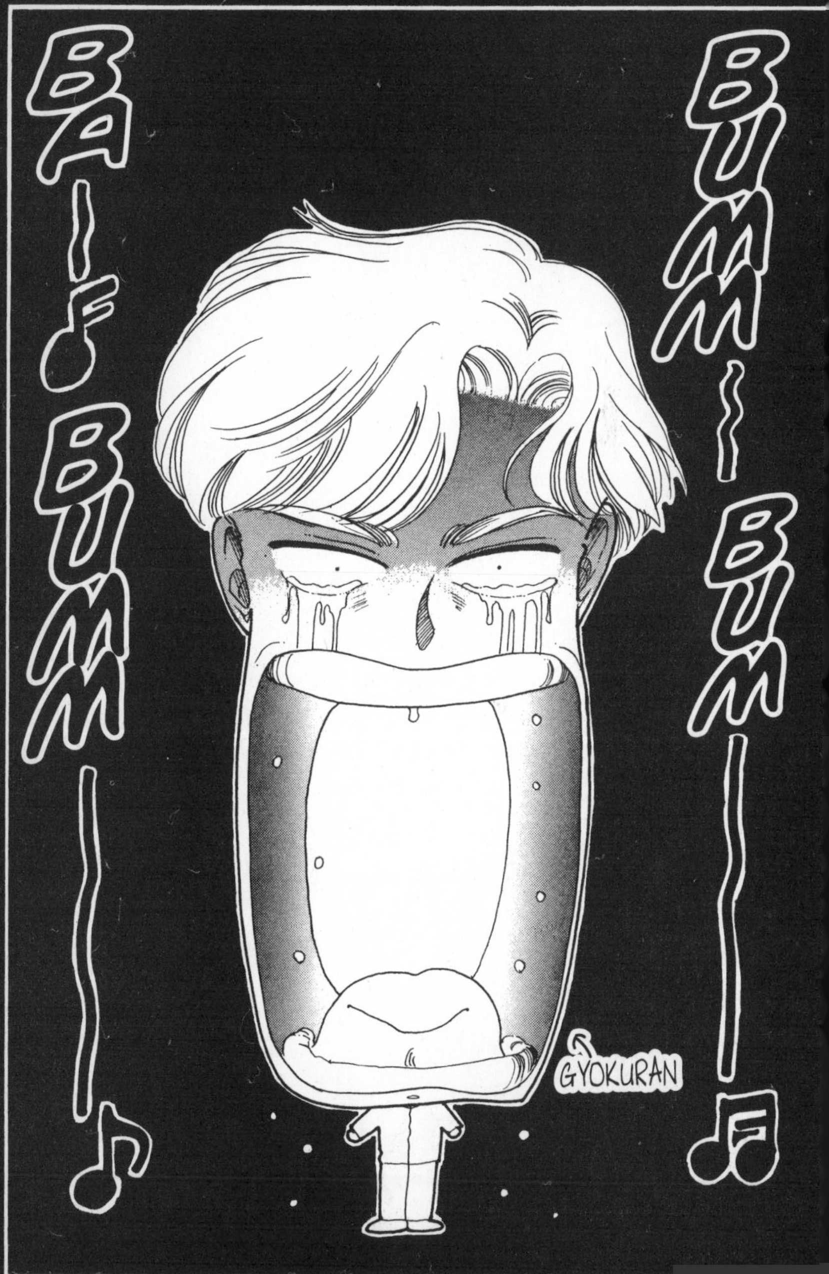
BUM~BUM~♬
BA-BUM~♪
GYOKURAN

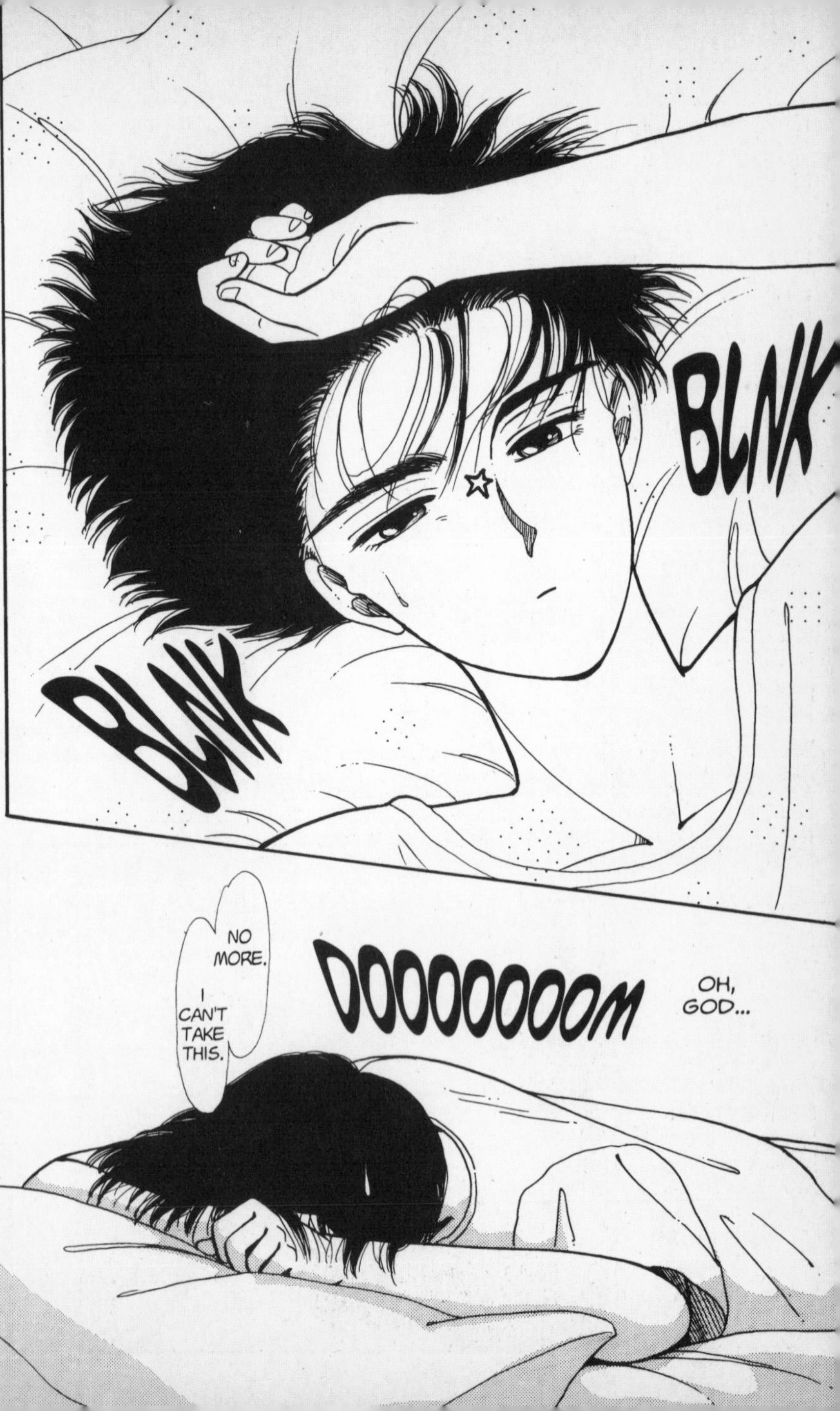
BLNK
BLNK
OH, GOD...
DOOOOOOOM
NO MORE. I CAN'T TAKE THIS.

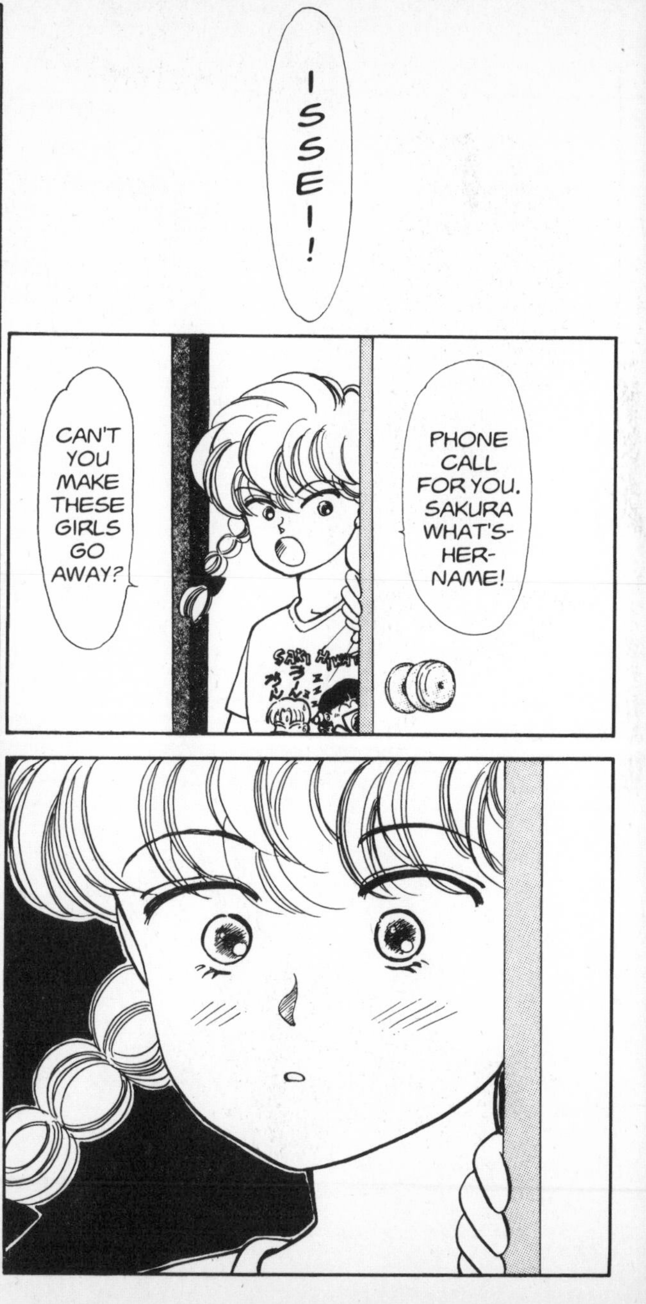
ISSE!!
PHONE CALL FOR YOU. SAKURA WHAT'S-HER-NAME!
CAN'T YOU MAKE THESE GIRLS GO AWAY?

1/4 COLUMN NONSENSE

— FINAL —

I get a lot of mail these days from people who want to be shojo manga artists in the future. I was planning to go over my own history as a manga artist here, but I ran out of space. Maybe next time!

The title of the very first manga I drew was a horror story called "The Dreaded Room No. 13." I drew it at the tender age (I think) of eight.

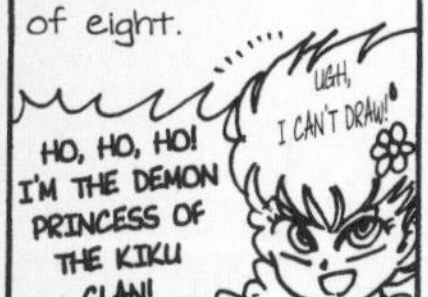
UGH, I CAN'T DRAW!
HO, HO, HO! I'M THE DEMON PRINCESS OF THE KIKU CLAN!
FROM THE 1968 ANIME SASUKE

Back then, I passed the time by scribbling and copying art like this. Tee hee! Aren't I funny? (silence...)

I'll write more next time!

Everyone, keep your feet on the ground and keep reaching for the stars! Take care! See you later!

Soundtrack for this 1/4 Column Nonsense: Crayon Factory and Yasuaki Shimizu. They're awesome

10/16/1988

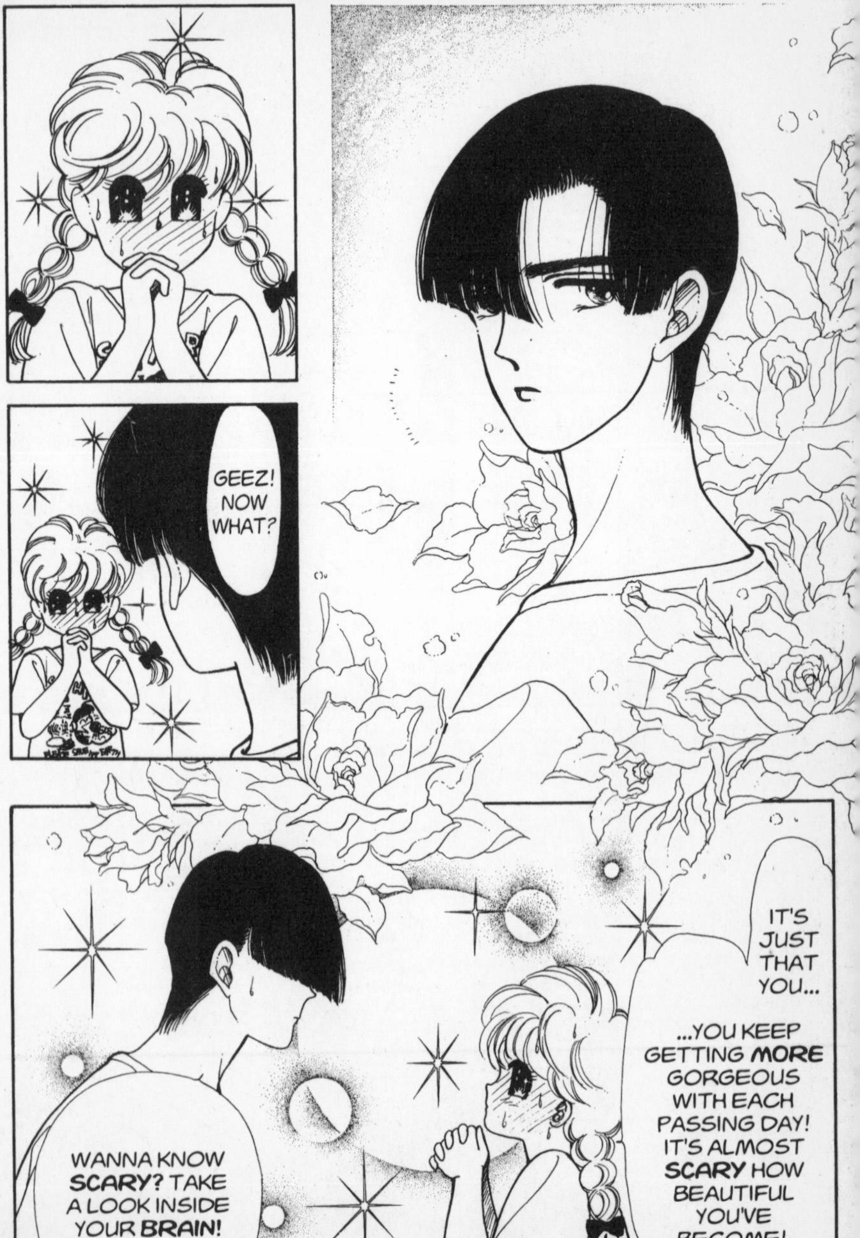
GEEZ! NOW WHAT?
IT'S JUST THAT YOU...
...YOU KEEP GETTING MORE GORGEOUS WITH EACH PASSING DAY! IT'S ALMOST SCARY HOW BEAUTIFUL YOU'VE BECOME!
WANNA KNOW SCARY? TAKE A LOOK INSIDE YOUR BRAIN!

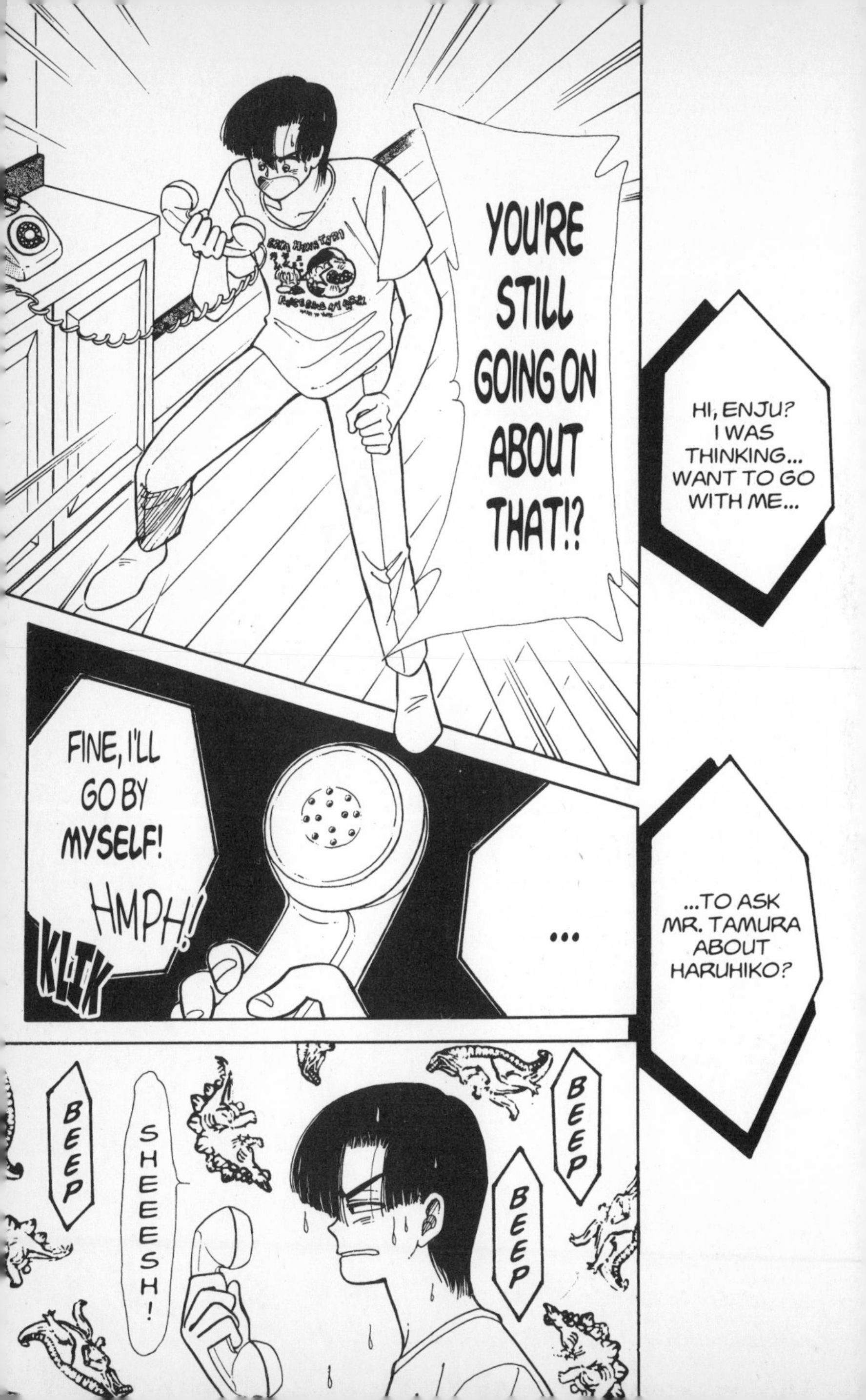
HI, ENJU? I WAS THINKING... WANT TO GO WITH ME...
YOU'RE STILL GOING ON ABOUT THAT!?
...TO ASK MR. TAMURA ABOUT HARUHIKO?
...
FINE, I'LL GO BY MYSELF!
HMPH!
KLIK
BEEP
BEEP
SHEEEESH!
BEEP

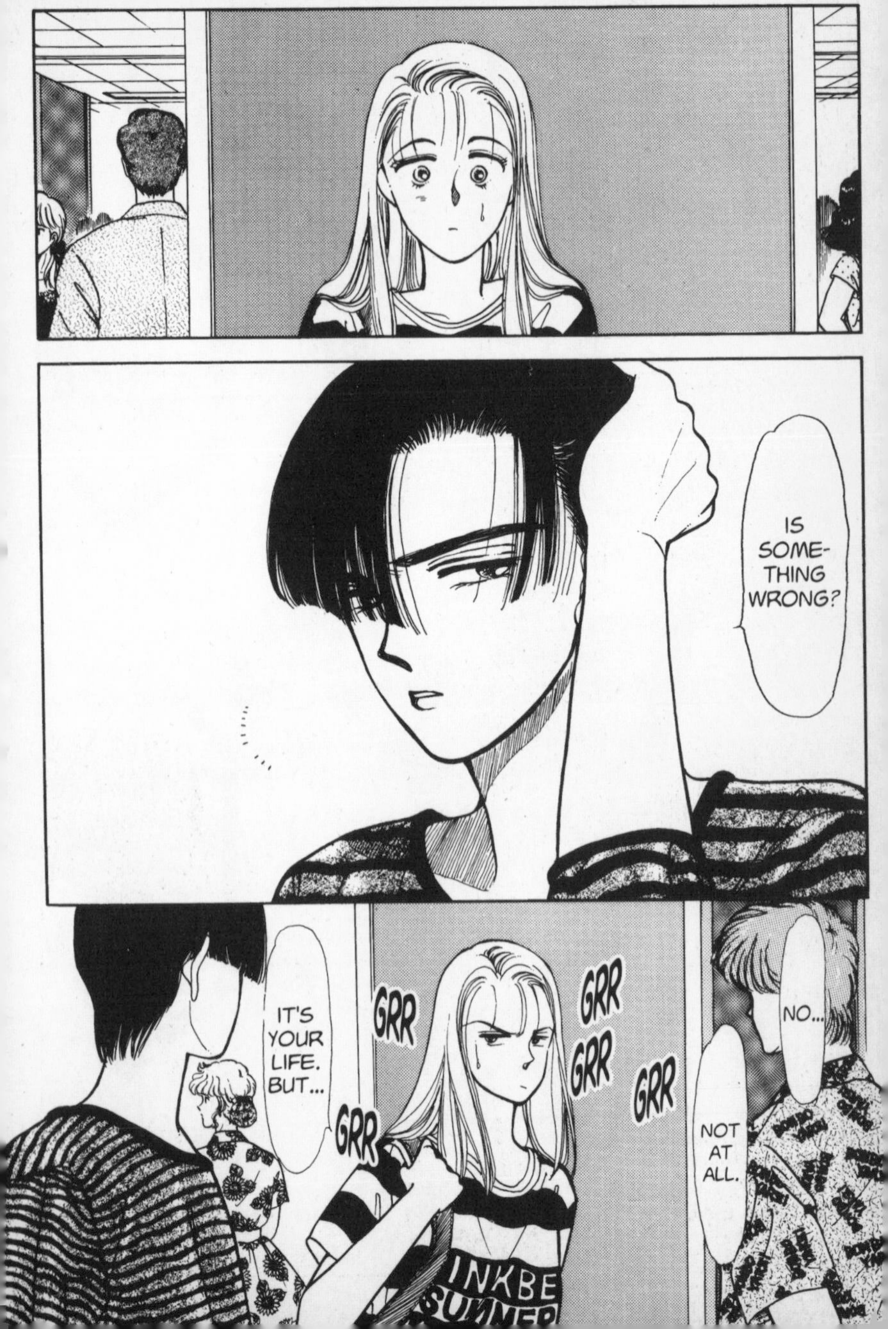
IS SOMETHING WRONG?
NO...
NOT AT ALL.
GRR
GRR
GRR
GRR
GRR
IT'S YOUR LIFE. BUT...

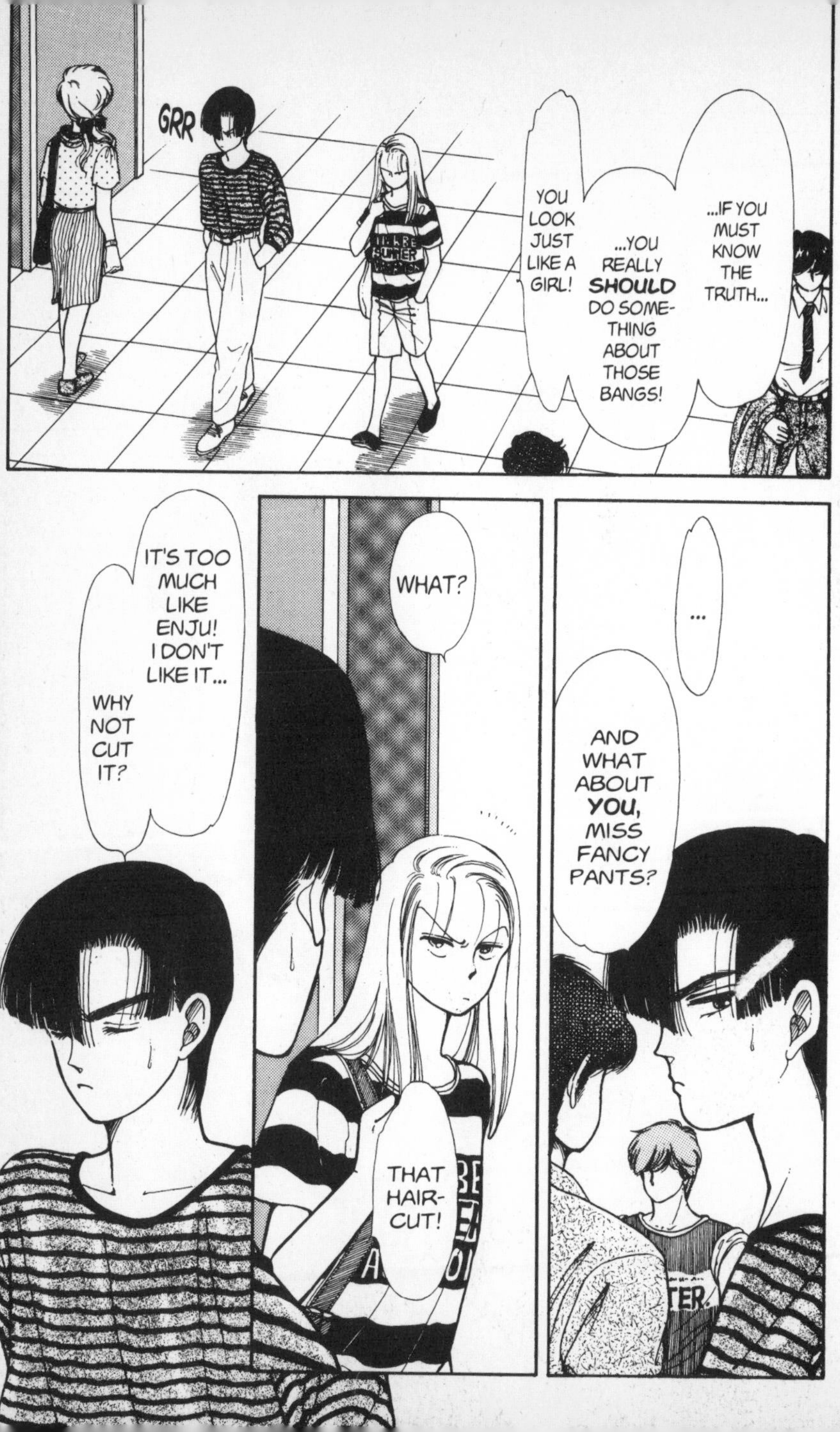
...IF YOU MUST KNOW THE TRUTH...
...YOU REALLY SHOULD DO SOMETHING ABOUT THOSE BANGS!
YOU LOOK JUST LIKE A GIRL!
GRR
...
AND WHAT ABOUT YOU, MISS FANCY PANTS?
WHAT?
THAT HAIR-CUT!
IT'S TOO MUCH LIKE ENJU! I DON'T LIKE IT...
WHY NOT CUT IT?

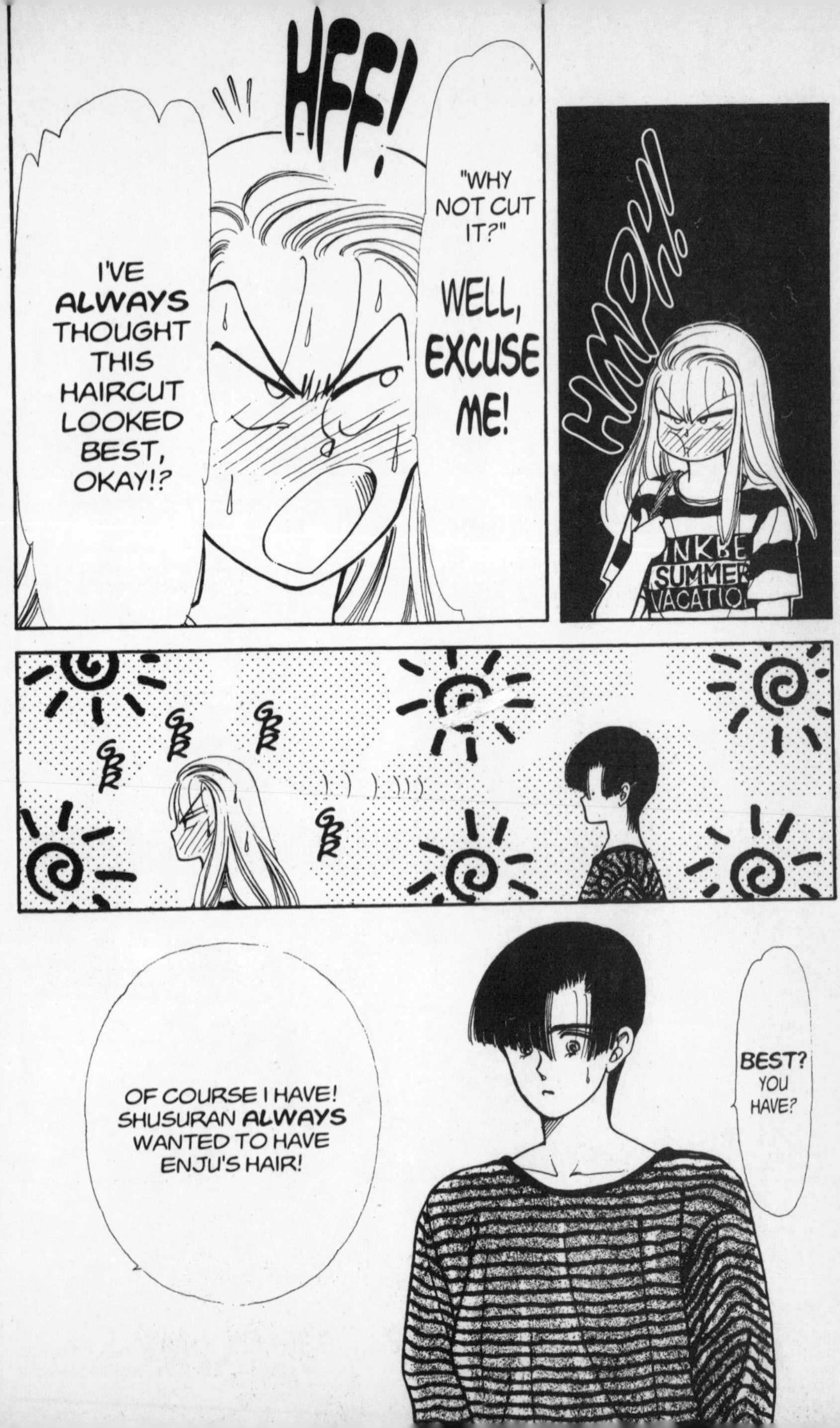
HMPH!!
INKBE
SUMMER
VACATIO
"WHY NOT CUT IT?"
WELL, EXCUSE ME!
HFF!
I'VE ALWAYS THOUGHT THIS HAIRCUT LOOKED BEST, OKAY!?
GRR
GRR
GRR
GRR
BEST? YOU HAVE?
OF COURSE I HAVE! SHUSURAN ALWAYS WANTED TO HAVE ENJU'S HAIR!

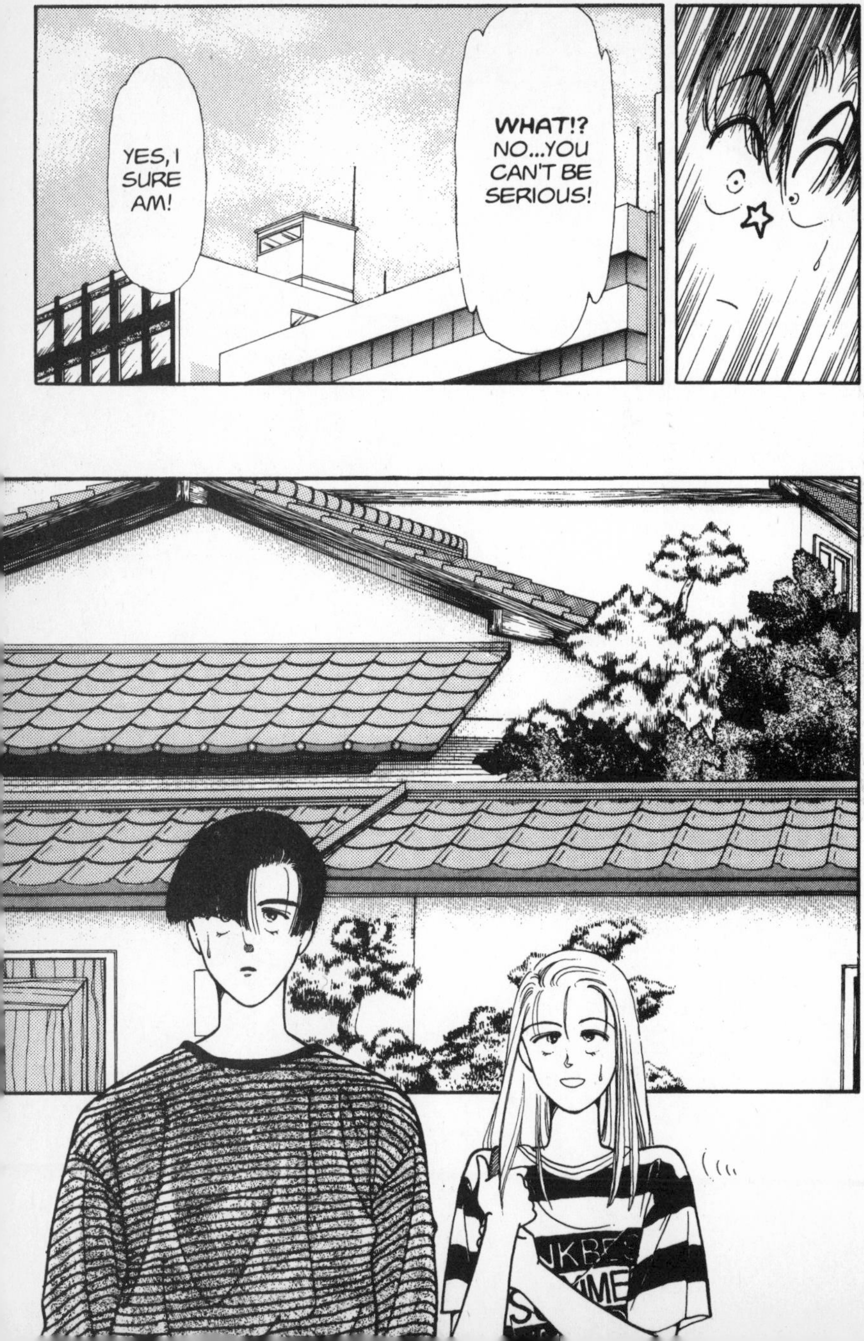
WHAT!? NO...YOU CAN'T BE SERIOUS!
YES, I SURE AM!

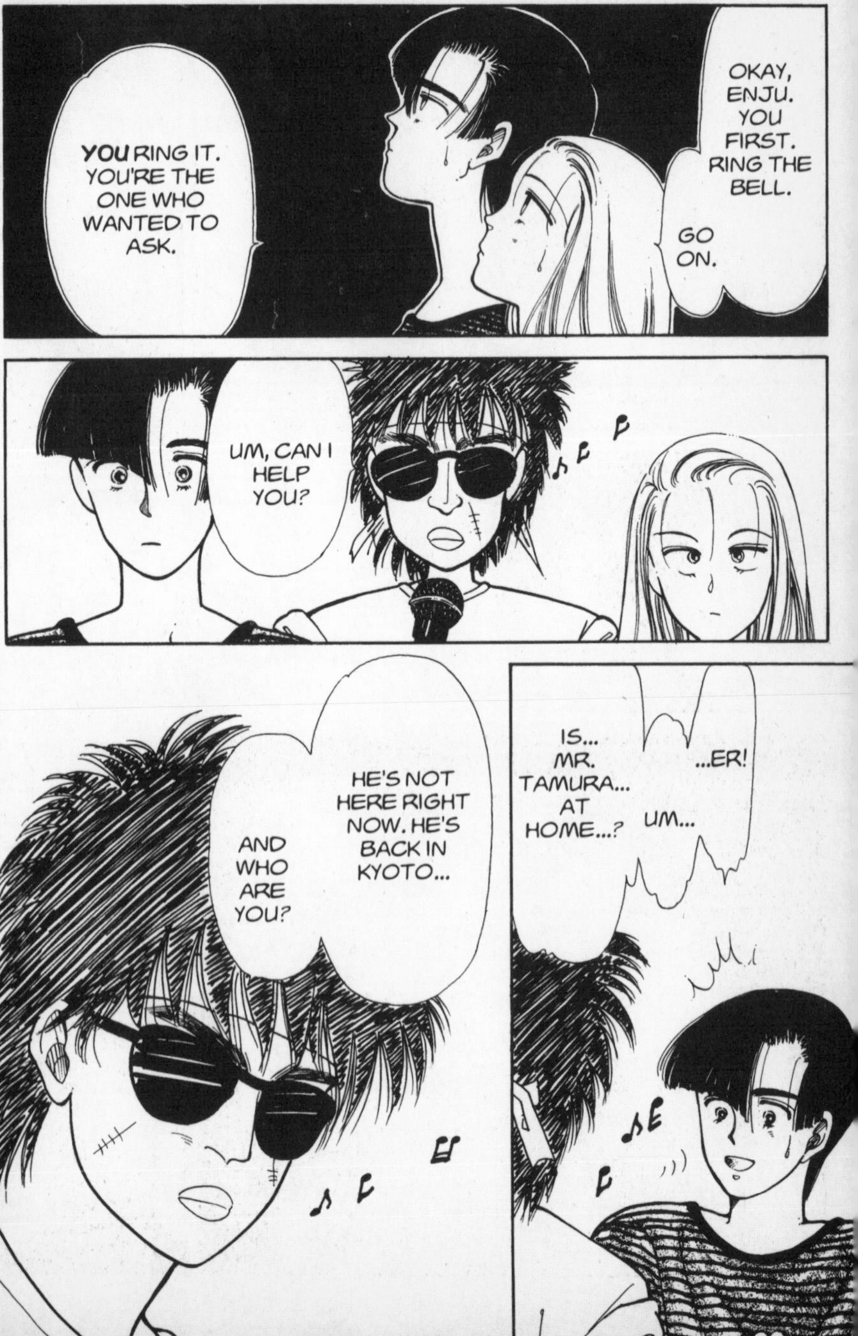
OKAY, ENJU. YOU FIRST. RING THE BELL.
GO ON.
YOU RING IT. YOU'RE THE ONE WHO WANTED TO ASK.
UM, CAN I HELP YOU?
...ER!
UM...
IS... MR. TAMURA... AT HOME...?
HE'S NOT HERE RIGHT NOW. HE'S BACK IN KYOTO...
AND WHO ARE YOU?

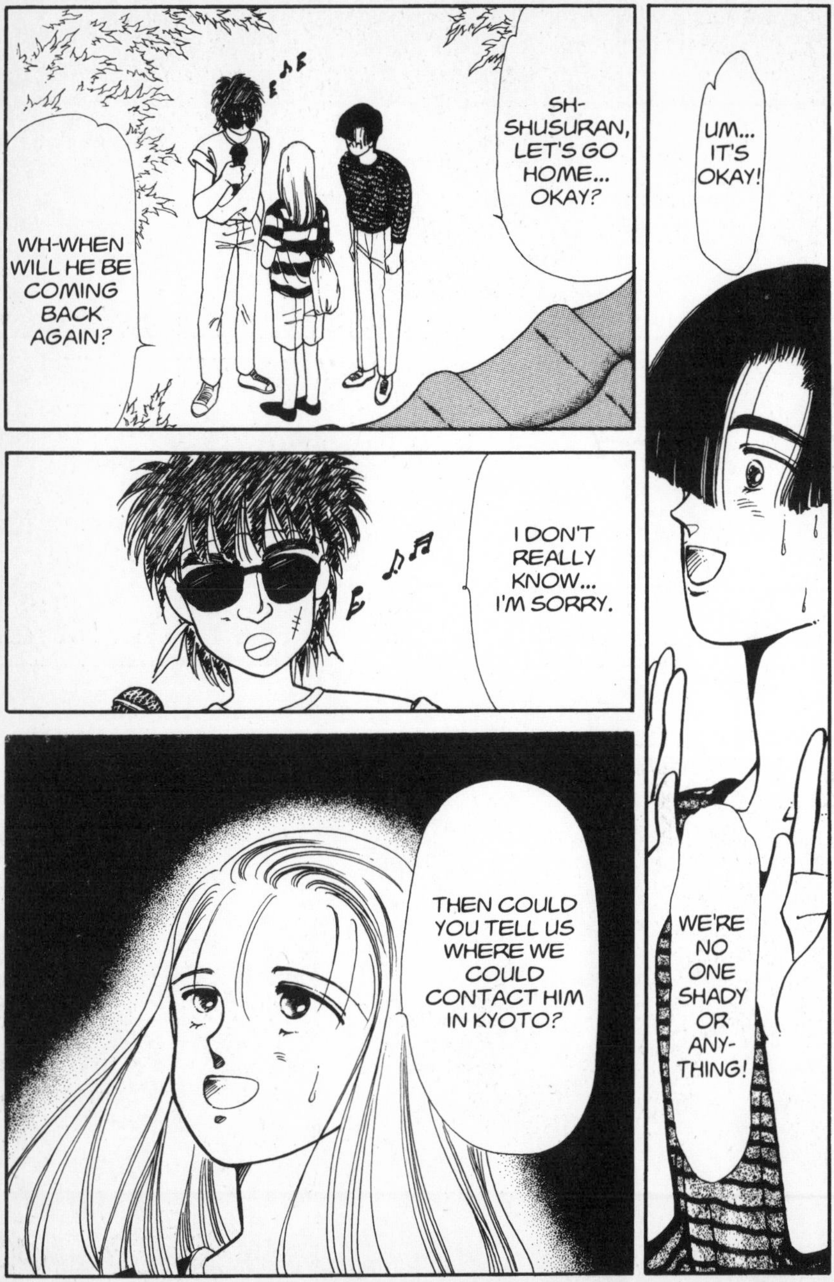
UM... IT'S OKAY!
WE'RE NO ONE SHADY OR ANY-THING!
SH-SHUSURAN, LET'S GO HOME... OKAY?
WH-WHEN WILL HE BE COMING BACK AGAIN?
I DON'T REALLY KNOW... I'M SORRY.
THEN COULD YOU TELL US WHERE WE COULD CONTACT HIM IN KYOTO?

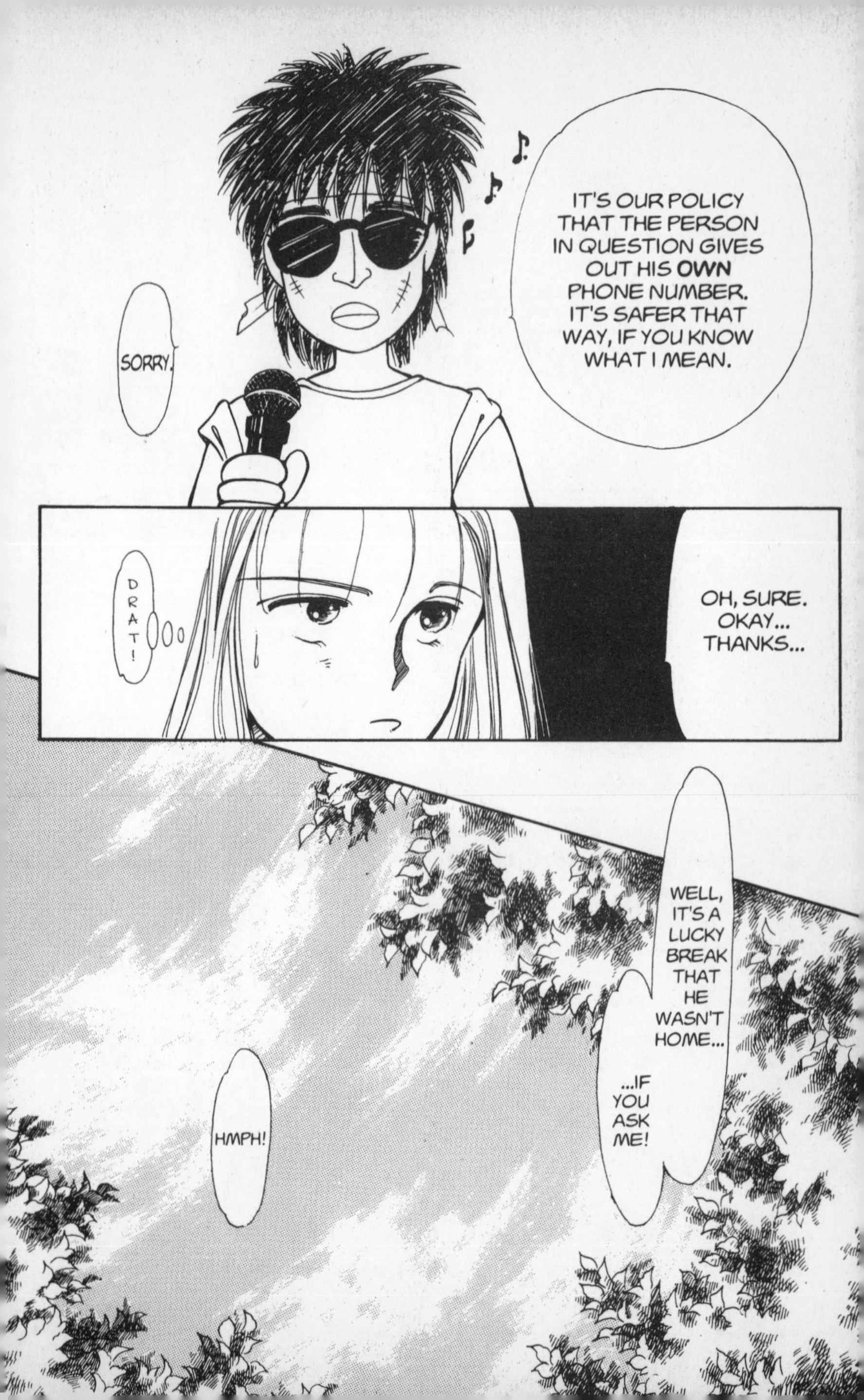
IT'S OUR POLICY THAT THE PERSON IN QUESTION GIVES OUT HIS OWN PHONE NUMBER. IT'S SAFER THAT WAY, IF YOU KNOW WHAT I MEAN.
SORRY.
OH, SURE. OKAY... THANKS...
DRAT!
WELL, IT'S A LUCKY BREAK THAT HE WASN'T HOME...
...IF YOU ASK ME!
HMPH!

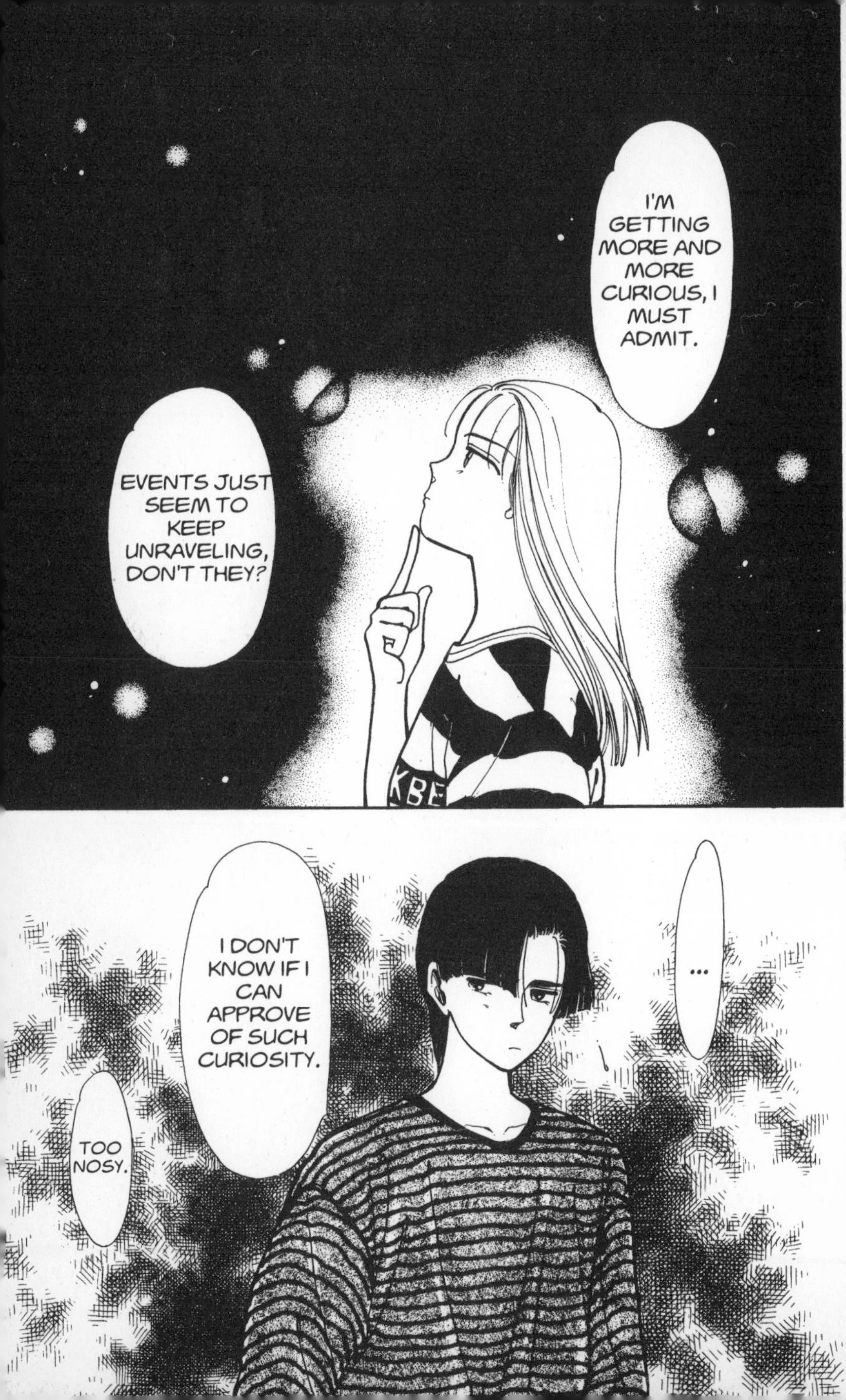
I'M GETTING MORE AND MORE CURIOUS, I MUST ADMIT.
EVENTS JUST SEEM TO KEEP UNRAVELING, DON'T THEY?
...
I DON'T KNOW IF I CAN APPROVE OF SUCH CURIOSITY.
TOO NOSY.

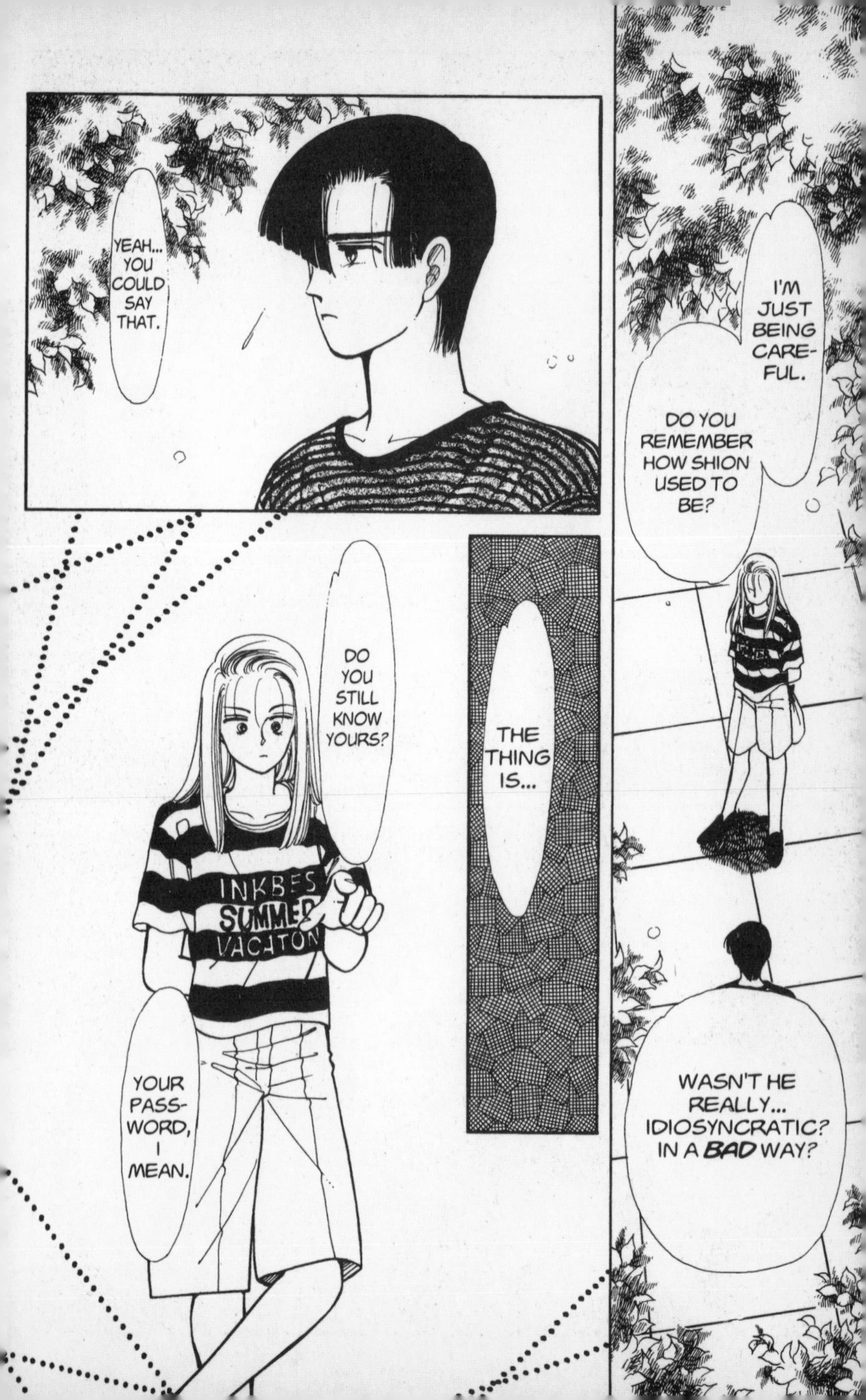
I'M JUST BEING CARE-FUL.
DO YOU REMEMBER HOW SHION USED TO BE?
WASN'T HE REALLY... IDIOSYNCRATIC? IN A **BAD** WAY?
YEAH... YOU COULD SAY THAT.
THE THING IS...
DO YOU STILL KNOW YOURS?
YOUR PASS-WORD, I MEAN.

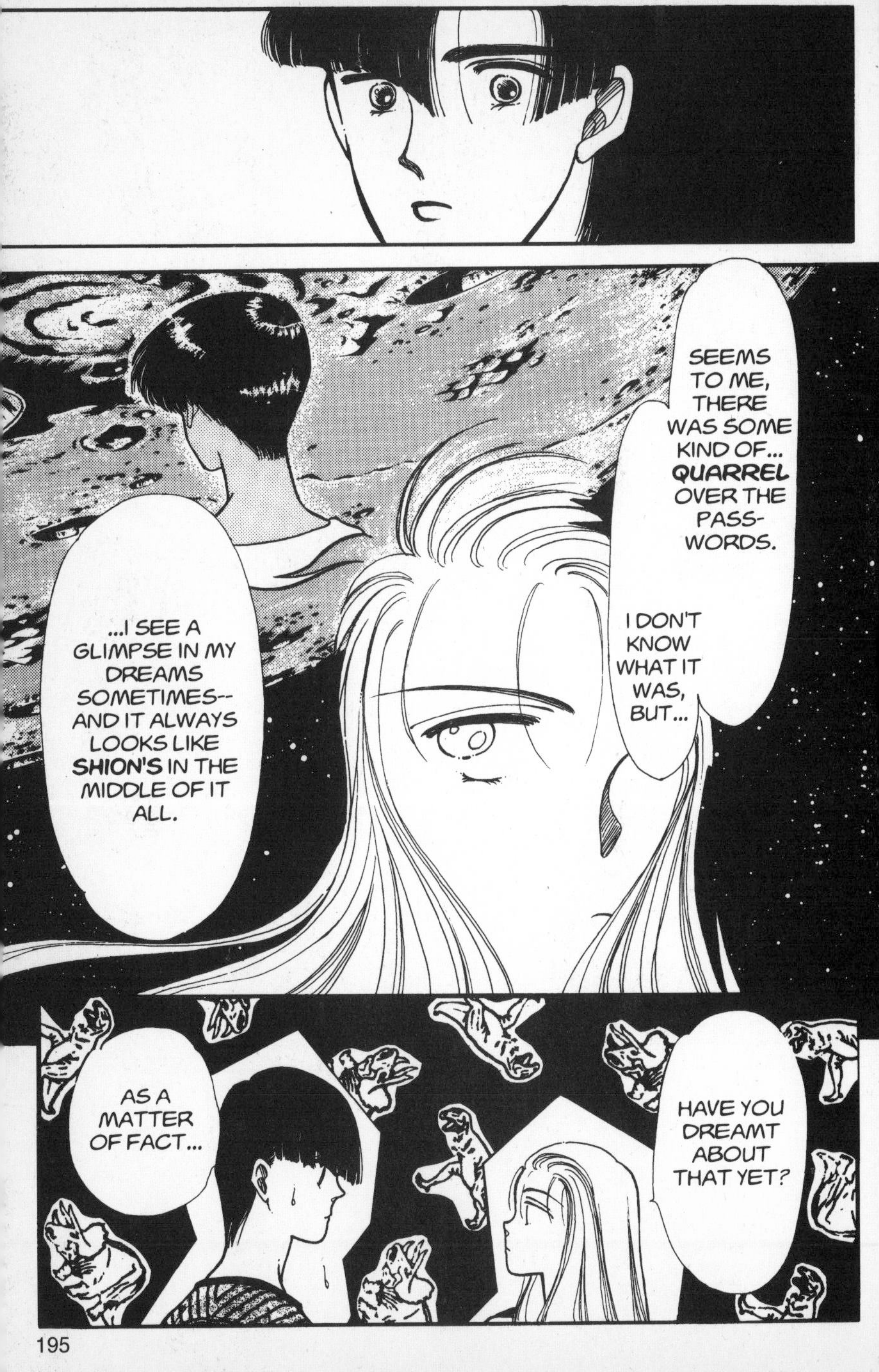
SEEMS TO ME, THERE WAS SOME KIND OF... QUARREL OVER THE PASS-WORDS.
I DON'T KNOW WHAT IT WAS, BUT...
...I SEE A GLIMPSE IN MY DREAMS SOMETIMES--AND IT ALWAYS LOOKS LIKE SHION'S IN THE MIDDLE OF IT ALL.
HAVE YOU DREAMT ABOUT THAT YET?
AS A MATTER OF FACT...

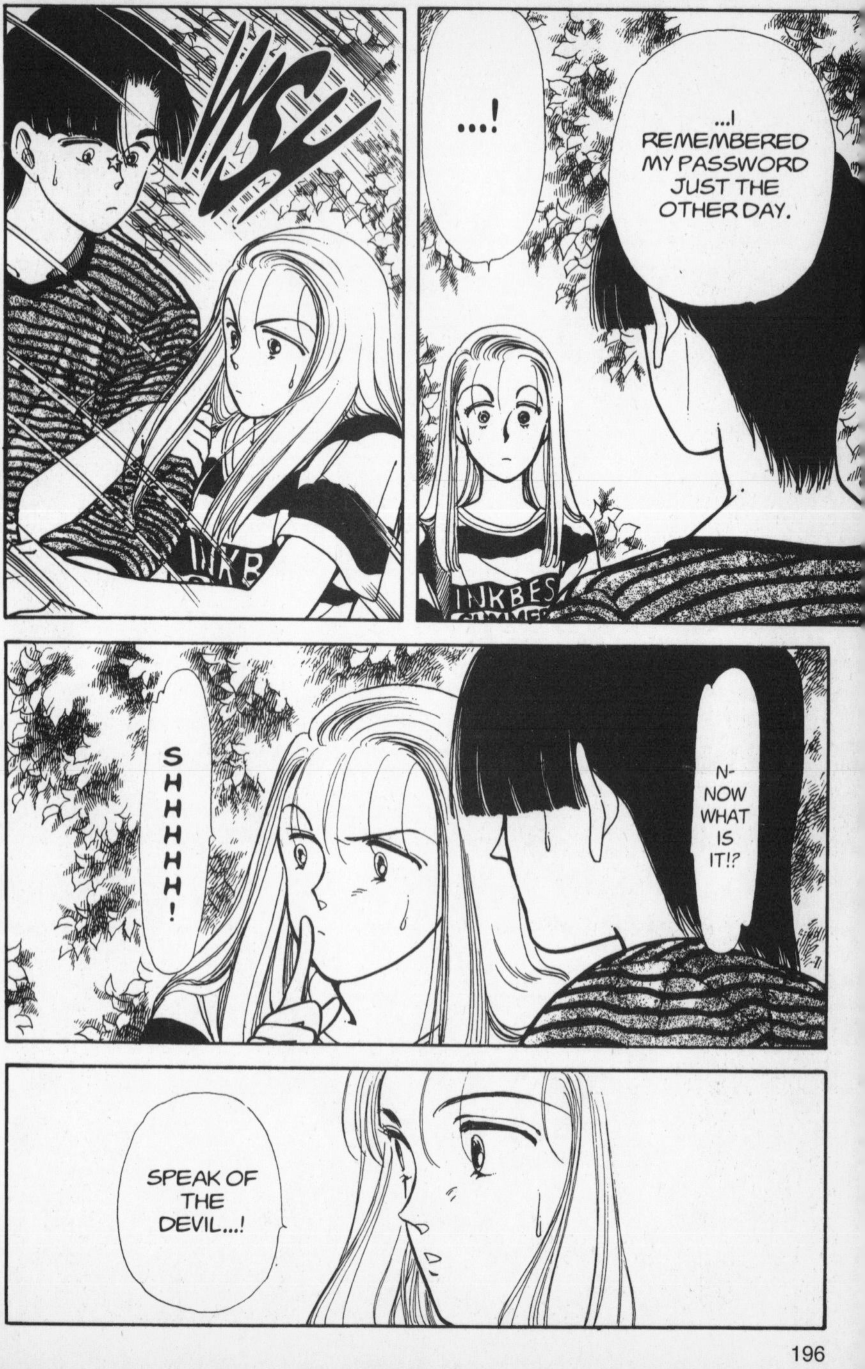
...I REMEMBERED MY PASSWORD JUST THE OTHER DAY.
...!
N- NOW WHAT IS IT!?
SHHHHHH!
SPEAK OF THE DEVIL...!

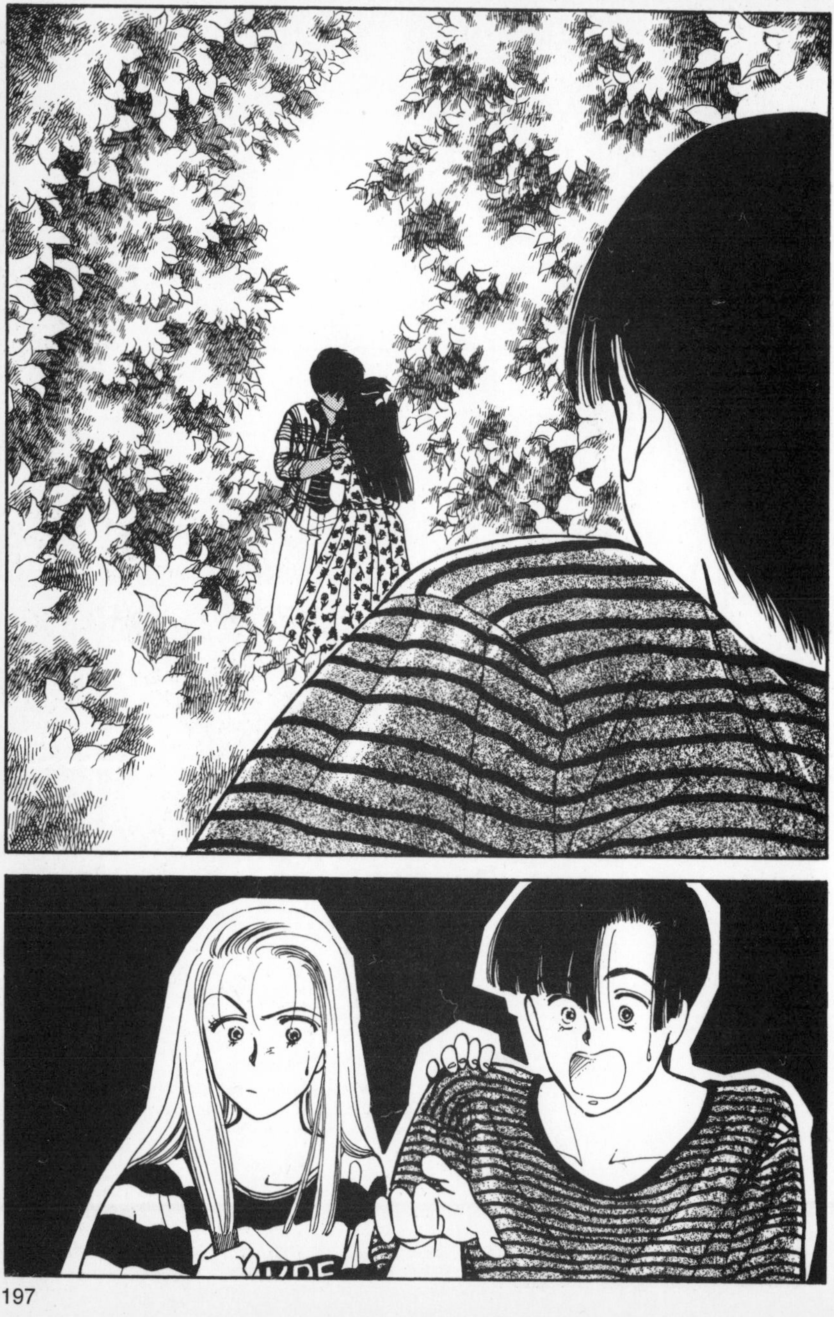

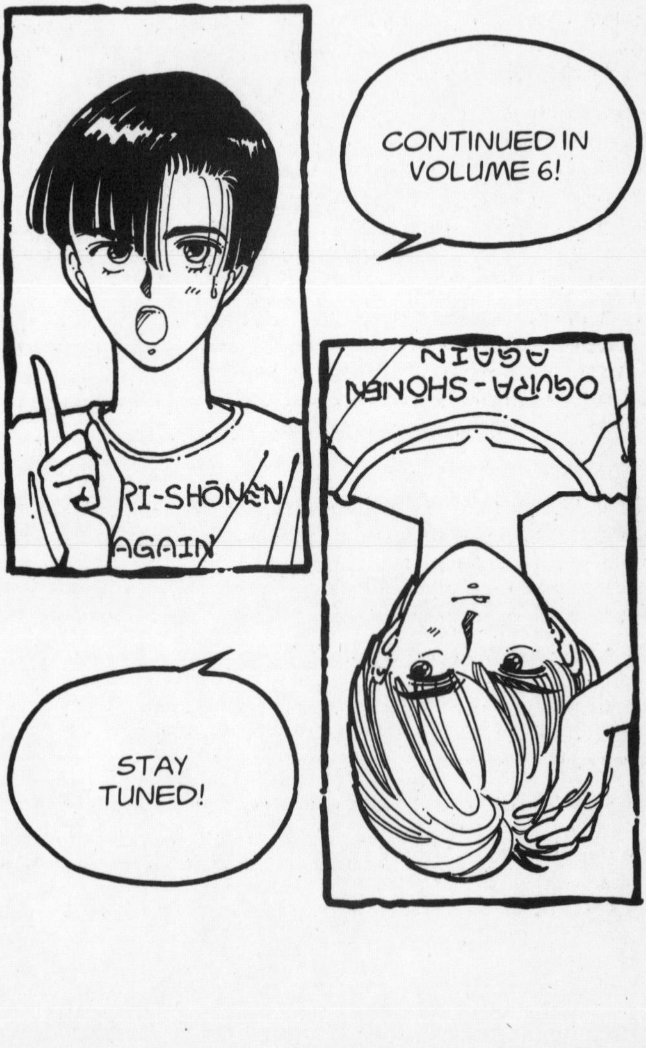
CONTINUED IN VOLUME 6!
RI-SHŌNEN AGAIN
OGURA-SHŌNEN AGAIN
STAY TUNED!

Editor's comments

An advantage to reading a manga over watching the anime it inspires is that you get the whole story. In manga, there's no need to cut scenes or characters for the sake of time limits. One character who didn't make it into the animated PSME was one of the funniest—Kyoko, Issei's little sister. Talk about a fangirl! Well, the girly-girl gaze that's meant to make her adoration of Issei amusingly mushy (see page 184) is more than just silly; it's a representation of a dated, stereotypical shôjo manga look. Influenced by the God of Manga Osamu Tezuka's big-eyed characters, all but white-less eyes were made famous by early shôjo manga artists such as Miyako Maki, Makoto Takahashi, Hideko Mizuno and Shotaro Ishimori (a guy).

With the important role Haruhiko's letter plays in this volume, I felt Japanese addresses deserved some mention. In Japan, addresses are written backwards from the way we write addresses. The postal code and prefecture (state, if you will) come first, followed by the town, district, block (many Japanese roads have no names), building and person's name. While we felt the story's flow necessitated us to translate the addresses on Haruhiko's letter, we left the others as-is. For those of you who think you might want to visit Haruhiko's house someday, don't bother. Like most addresses in entertainment, Haruhiko's is fake. Saiwai-ku is in Kanagawa, not Tokyo!

Also worth attention is the energy efficiency of Japanese water heating, as hinted at in Hiwatari's burning bathtub tale. Instead of wastefully heating a bunch of water and keeping it hot until it's used, as is most common in the U.S., in Japan, you usually heat water as you need it. Some bath designs have you fill the tub then turn on the heat. It takes a while, and apparently, it's something you can absent-mindedly forget about. Never heat an empty tub! –PD

If you enjoyed *Please Save My Earth*, you might enjoy these:

A, A' Unicorns are a low-emotion species genetically engineered for space travel. They're also the thread used to string together the science fiction stories of *A, A'* (a.k.a. A, A Prime) by legendary shôjo artist Moto Hagio. There are no hostile aliens or epic battles in this collection. Instead, Hagio explores the possible impact of such futuristic technologies as cloning and genetic manipulation through the touching stories of her characters.

Short Program This collection of modern-day stories is filled with the quiet drama of everyday people. What happens at a reunion when Kazuhiko hasn't seen his close friends in years? Will Takechi ever have the nerve to ask out that cute girl he passes every day? Has Naomi finally found a decent boyfriend in the guy next door? Mitsuru Adachi's masterful storytelling creates tales that are thoroughly engaging and full of interesting twists.

Ceres: Celestial Legend By Yû Watase, creator of *Fushigi Yugi*, *Ceres* is the gripping saga of a girl whose past life returns to tear her present life apart. On her 16th birthday, Aya receives a foul gift–a mummified hand. It awakens Ceres, the powerful celestial being residing within Aya. As the body for Ceres, Aya's family wants her dead. Even with the help of unexpected allies, Aya might not survive to uncover the mystical mysteries behind her family's twisted past.

Flower Talk

In Japan, flowers have a lot of meaning, and Please Save My Earth uses a lot of flowers, including the names of the moon dream characters. Although Saki Hiwatari claims any significance is coincidental, we thought we should give our readers a little insight into the story's many beautiful blossoms. Alice knows her flowers–now you can, too!

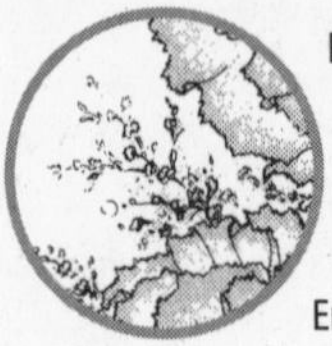

BABY'S BREATH [PP86.1, PP87.1,2,5 PP92.5]
Delicate and white, these tiny flowers compliment almost every plant. That they also maintain their appearance in both cut and dried arrangement makes them ideal filler for bouquets. An imported flower, baby's breath has no Japanese meaning, but it connotes innocence in English.

BEGONIA [pp24.2, pp120.2]
The Japanese word for begonia is "shukaido," so it's no wonder it appears when Haruhiko remembers his past-life. Originally from Brazil, this hardy flowering shrub can now be found all over the world. Most common in shades of red, the begonia blooms in many colors and prefers moist, shady, well-fertilized spots in a garden. Appropriately enough, this flower is a symbol of unrequited love. Although Shukaido's medical betrayal of Shion is a telling character flaw, he was a mild-mannered physician. So having begonias suggest kindness, politeness and care is also fitting. Interestingly, in English, begonias imply dark thoughts.

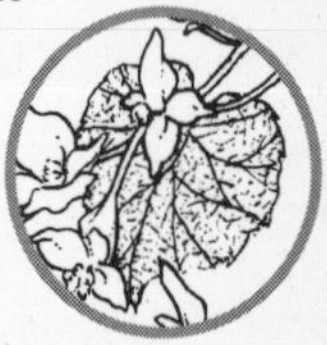

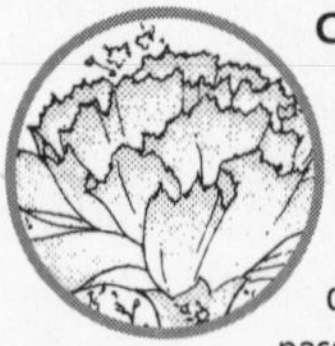

CARNATION [PP86.1, PP87.1,2,5 PP92.5]
This cheerful, sun-loving flower comes in an endless variety of colors and lasts a long time after being cut. This makes carnations a favorite for bouquets such as the one Rin gave to Alice. Representing unabashed affection and a woman's love, some individual colors have distinct meanings: white stands for fidelity and chastity; red stands for passion and heartbreak; variegated stand for rejection.

CHRYSANTHEMUM [pp98.4]
Conveying purity and nobility, these regal flowers have been an artistic component of Japanese culture for centuries. This makes them perfect for the background of a refined and imperious Kyotoite such as Mrs. Yakushimaru, especially as she dismisses Tamura with icy politeness.

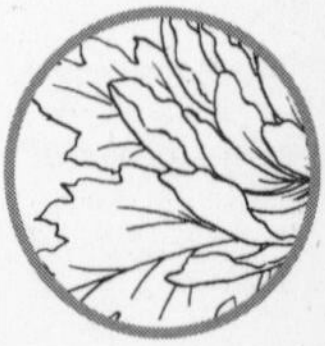

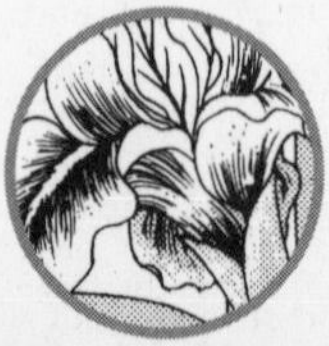

IRIS [pp95.5]
This elegant spring flower comes in a number of bold colors, though purple seems to be the most common in Japan. Representing mysterious people and expectant news, it is a suitable choice for the elegant Mrs. Yakushimaru greeting her unexpected guest.

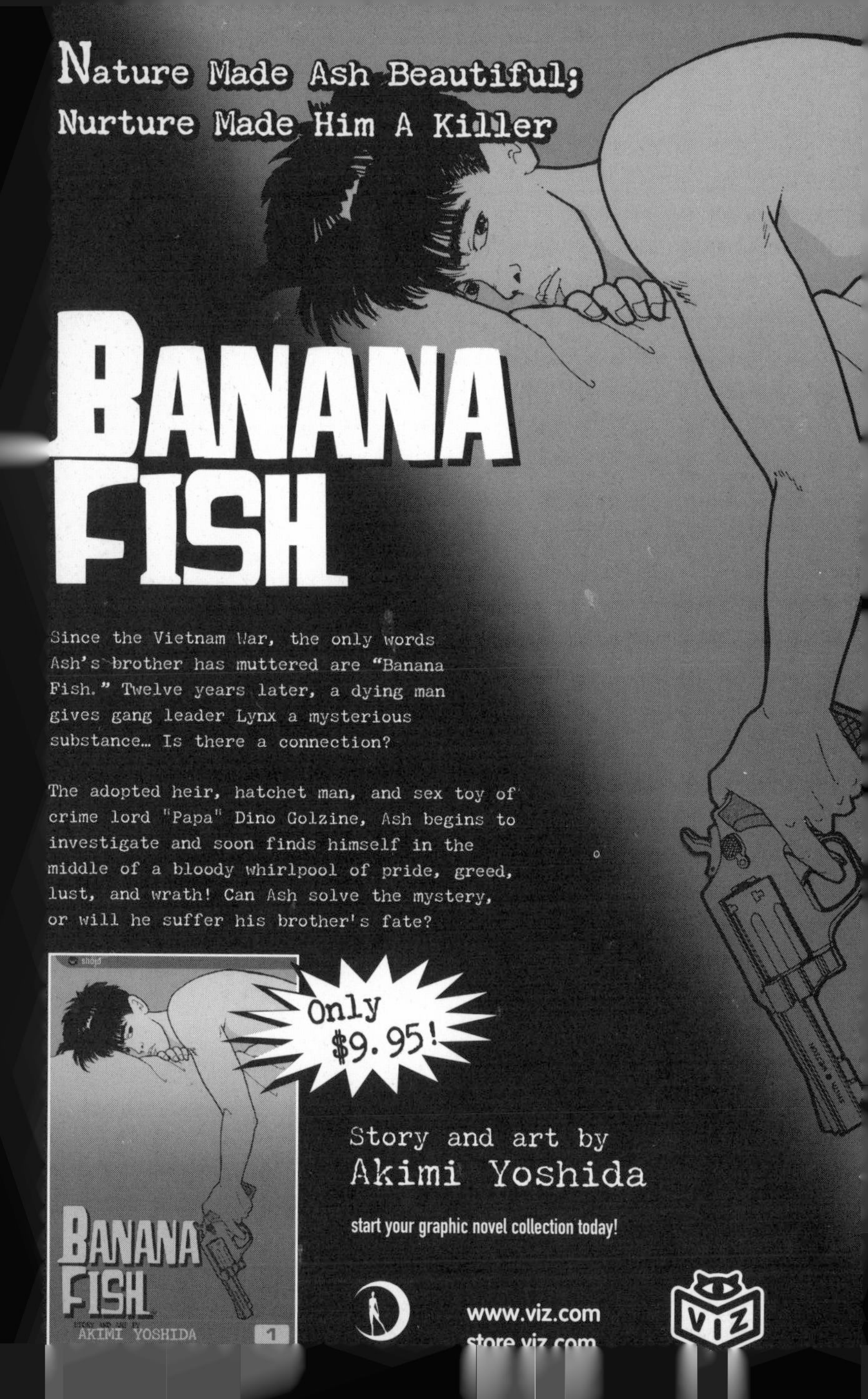
Nature Made Ash Beautiful;
Nurture Made Him A Killer
BANANA FISH
Since the Vietnam War, the only words Ash's brother has muttered are "Banana Fish." Twelve years later, a dying man gives gang leader Lynx a mysterious substance... Is there a connection?
The adopted heir, hatchet man, and sex toy of crime lord "Papa" Dino Golzine, Ash begins to investigate and soon finds himself in the middle of a bloody whirlpool of pride, greed, lust, and wrath! Can Ash solve the mystery, or will he suffer his brother's fate?
Only $9.95!
BANANA FISH
AKIMI YOSHIDA
1
Story and art by
Akimi Yoshida
start your graphic novel collection today!
www.viz.com
store.viz.com
VIZ

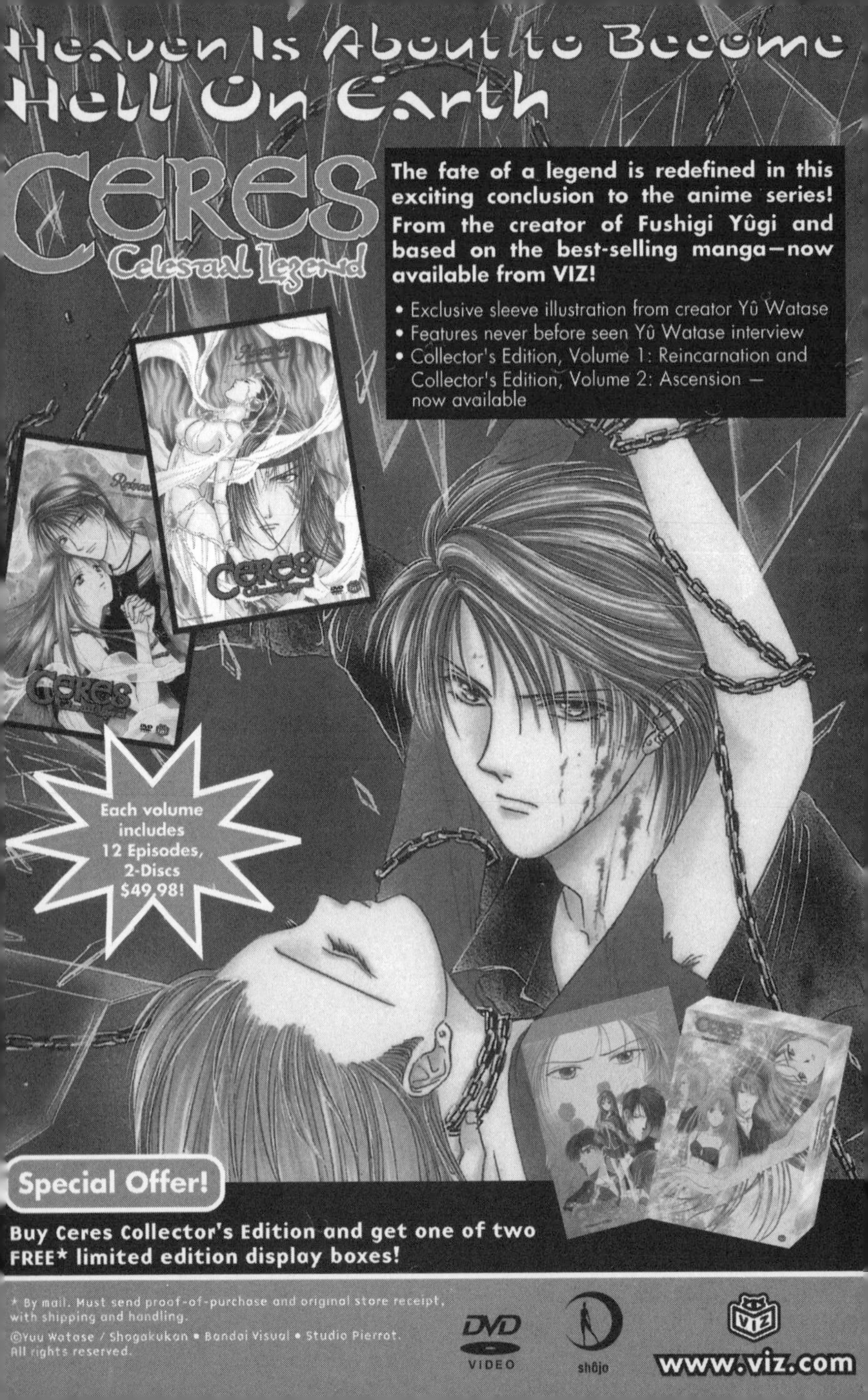
Heaven Is About to Become
Hell On Earth
Ceres
Celestial Legend
The fate of a legend is redefined in this exciting conclusion to the anime series! From the creator of Fushigi Yûgi and based on the best-selling manga—now available from VIZ!
• Exclusive sleeve illustration from creator Yû Watase
• Features never before seen Yû Watase interview
• Collector's Edition, Volume 1: Reincarnation and Collector's Edition, Volume 2: Ascension — now available
Each volume includes 12 Episodes, 2-Discs $49.98!
Special Offer!
Buy Ceres Collector's Edition and get one of two FREE* limited edition display boxes!
* By mail. Must send proof-of-purchase and original store receipt, with shipping and handling.
©Yuu Watase / Shogakukan • Bandai Visual • Studio Pierrot. All rights reserved.
DVD VIDEO
shôjo
VIZ
www.viz.com

shôjo

AT THE HEART OF THE MATTER

- Alice 19th
- Angel Sanctuary
- Banana Fish
- Basara
- B.B. Explosion
- Boys Over Flowers *
- Ceres, Celestial Legend *
- Fushigi Yûgi
- Hana-Kimi
- Hot Gimmick
- Imadoki
- Please Save My Earth *
- Red River
- Revolutionary Girl Utena
- Sensual Phrase
- Wedding Peach
- X/1999

Start Your Shôjo Graphic Novel Collection Today!

STARTING @ **$9.95!**

*Also available on DVD from VIZ

www.viz.com

COMPLETE OUR SURVEY AND LET US KNOW WHAT YOU THINK!

☐ Please do NOT send me information about VIZ products, news and events, special offers, or other information.

☐ Please do NOT send me information from VIZ's trusted business partners.

Name: _____

Address: _____

City: _____ **State:** _____ **Zip:** _____

E-mail: _____

☐ Male   ☐ Female   **Date of Birth** (mm/dd/yyyy): ___/___/___   (Under 13? Parental consent required)

What race/ethnicity do you consider yourself? (please check one)

☐ Asian/Pacific Islander   ☐ Black/African American   ☐ Hispanic/Latino

☐ Native American/Alaskan Native   ☐ White/Caucasian   ☐ Other: _____

What VIZ product did you purchase? (check all that apply and indicate title purchased)

☐ DVD/VHS _____

☐ Graphic Novel _____

☐ Magazines _____

☐ Merchandise _____

Reason for purchase: (check all that apply)

☐ Special offer   ☐ Favorite title   ☐ Gift

☐ Recommendation   ☐ Other _____

Where did you make your purchase? (please check one)

☐ Comic store   ☐ Bookstore   ☐ Mass/Grocery Store

☐ Newsstand   ☐ Video/Video Game Store ☐ Other: _____

☐ Online (site: _____)

What other VIZ properties have you purchased/own? _____

_____

How many anime and/or manga titles have you purchased in the last year? How many were VIZ titles? **(please check one from each column)**

ANIME	MANGA	VIZ
☐ None	☐ None	☐ None
☐ 1-4	☐ 1-4	☐ 1-4
☐ 5-10	☐ 5-10	☐ 5-10
☐ 11+	☐ 11+	☐ 11+

I find the pricing of VIZ products to be: **(please check one)**

☐ Cheap ☐ Reasonable ☐ Expensive

What genre of manga and anime would you like to see from VIZ? **(please check two)**

☐ Adventure ☐ Comic Strip ☐ Science Fiction ☐ Fighting

☐ Horror ☐ Romance ☐ Fantasy ☐ Sports

What do you think of VIZ's new look?

☐ Love It ☐ It's OK ☐ Hate It ☐ Didn't Notice ☐ No Opinion

Which do you prefer? **(please check one)**

☐ Reading right-to-left

☐ Reading left-to-right

Which do you prefer? **(please check one)**

☐ Sound effects in English

☐ Sound effects in Japanese with English captions

☐ Sound effects in Japanese only with a glossary at the back

THANK YOU! Please send the completed form to:

NJW Research
42 Catharine St.
Poughkeepsie, NY 12601

All information provided will be used for internal purposes only. We promise not to sell or otherwise divulge your information.